DIPSEA

The Greatest Race

Barry Spitz

Potrero Meadow

Maps: Dewey Livingston
Design: Dewey Livingston
Typesetting: Wordsworth, San Geronimo, CA
Back cover photographs:
    Jack Kirk, 1950 (courtesy Charles Richesin)
    Megan McGowan nears the end of the trail, 1992 (Gene Cohn)

ISBN: 0-9620715-4-4 (cloth)
ISBN: 0-9620715-5-2 (paper)

Library of Congress Catalog Number: 93-085457

Published by: Potrero Meadow Publishing Company
                P.O. Box 3007
                San Anselmo, CA 94979

First Edition

Printed in the United States of America

This book is dedicated to
Timothy Fitzpatrick, Mason Hartwell,
John Hassard, Oliver Millard, Emma Reiman
and all the other departed "Dipsea gods."
May they live forever.

ACKNOWLEDGMENTS

I cannot overstate the importance of Mark Reese and his pioneering book, *The Dipsea Race*, in paving the way for this work. Reese was the first to systematically gather Dipsea archival materials, saving much that would otherwise have been lost forever. His unhesitating willingness to share these treasures helped spawn this project. Reese's vigor and thoroughness cut hundreds of hours off my own research efforts. I am forever indebted to him.

Three other individuals were also there from the start and played indispensable roles throughout. Jerry Hauke, chief guardian of the Dipsea over the last three decades, offered his invaluable knowledge and support. Dewey Livingston, a true craftsman, prepared the map of the Dipsea Trail and also designed the book. And Ken Wilson, a lover of the Dipsea, was of great assistance with the photographs.

Hundreds of other people contributed information, photographs, anecdotes, research leads and more to this book. I sincerely thank all of them. High on the list are: Fred Sandrock, who was always ready to talk history; Jim Stephenson, who opened doors at the Olympic Club; Frank Maher, who provided some of the oldest files; Jay Silverberg and Scott Henry, for access to the *Marin Independent Journal* photo archives; Michael Hoy, master of all trades; Stan Rosenfeld, who cheerfully converted disks at a moment's notice; Len Wallach, whose book *The Human Race* was an invaluable resource; and Bob Knez, Merv Regan and Susan Hoagland for the support of the Dipsea Committee.

The collections of the Lucretia Little History Room in the Mill Valley Public Library, the Anne Kent California History Room in the Marin County Free Library (San Rafael), and the State of California's Sutro Library (San Francisco) and California Room (Sacramento) were also of immense help.

Errors that remain are my own. Names were particularly vexing. It was common to find a runner's name spelled three or four different ways in old newspaper accounts and programs. Also, I suspect that not all the many charming anecdotes told to me are completely true. But these legends are an integral part of the Dipsea's appeal. What really did happen that day in 1904 when Al Coney and Ben Boas raced over the Mountain to Willow Camp? We'll probably never know, and that is just fine.

I welcome reader's corrections, additions and comments.

And a special thank you to my wife, Pamela, for assisting and tolerating throughout and to Sally and Lily, my dear and lovely daughters, for putting up with my closed office door. It hurt me more than you will ever know.

Protruding roots in the Rainforest, 1993. (Brad Rippe)

THE SONG OF THE DIPSEA TRAIL

by W.O. "Bill" McGeehan, 1908

There's a patter of feet on the Lone Pine Ridge,
And the whir of the frightened quail;
Now the white forms flash in the shimmering green,
And they're off on the Dipsea Trail.

Now they press through the open and clear the madrones,
With the sun beating fierce at the back,
And their temples are burning, their nostrils are caked,
But they speed like the deerhound pack.

Oh, it's far to the top of the Hog's Back Rise,
And the breathing is labored and fast;
But it's then for the cool of the ocean breeze
When the worst of the ridge is past.

Then it strikes the hot temples, the laggards are roused;
Now they've done it and quicken the pace,
Have a care for the boulders—a loose rolling stone
And you're downed in the stretch of the race.

Now the spurt for the finish—the heart beats come fast,
And the weary heads, dust-caked and bowed;
There's a gasp and a struggle, a rush to the tape—
And the winner falls limp in the crowd.

Oh, the eyes that are bloodshot, the lips that are white,
And the stiff limbs that falter and fail!
For it's no place for weaklings—the grueling course
Of the men of the Dipsea Trail.

TABLE OF CONTENTS

PREFACE

To all who know it, the Dipsea is the greatest race in the world. There is much to love, and respect.

The Dipsea course is unsurpassed in beauty. The seven miles between Mill Valley and Stinson Beach, just north of San Francisco's Golden Gate, cross salmon-filled creeks, virgin redwood forests, meadows high on Mount Tamalpais, the haunting Steep Ravine and ocean side grasslands. Its unspoiled terrain has changed little; a runner from the first Dipsea in 1905 could find his way today.

There is danger. The race starts with the infamous 676 steps. Much of the way is root-covered, rocky and steep. Passing must be done on narrow stretches barely wide enough for one. Injuries are commonplace. Suicide, Dynamite, Cardiac, Swoop and Slash are aptly named course sections.

The Dipsea's unique handicapping system has made champions of pre-teen boys and girls, men in their 60's, women in their 50's and "ordinary" runners who had extraordinary days.

Unlike at other races, runners are free to choose any route between the start and finish. Course knowledge has often meant the difference between champion and also-ran.

The Dipsea is so popular that all 1,500 places are filled the first day applications are accepted— with no advertising. There is even a waiting list to volunteer.

There are the legends: Jack Kirk, the "Dipsea Demon," running every Dipsea since 1930; Norman Bright, eyesight failing, winning 35 years after his first attempt; Emma Reiman setting records a half century before women were allowed into any other American distance race; and countless more.

Above all, the Dipsea inspires reverence. Prayers are recited on the "opening day" of practice. Runners have willed their ashes to be scattered over the Dipsea Trail. The greatest champions are known as "gods of the Dipsea."

The history of the Dipsea survived only in yellowing newspapers and the memories and tales of its old-timers until Mark Reese, one of those who loves the Race, chronicled it in his splendid book, *The Dipsea Race*. Published in 1980, it sold out quickly and has now long been out of print.

In early 1991, I took a proposal to update the book to Reese. Busy with a growing family and his work as an attorney, he gave me his wholehearted support to undertake the project. He also lent me his meticulously researched files.

The book evolved into more than an update of the 14 Dipseas since Reese's compilation. All the yearly accounts have been completely rewritten. I've tracked down virtually every champion and talked to perhaps all still alive. Additional archival information has been uncovered. Statistical tables have been revamped and many added. Errors in Reese have been corrected (though new ones undoubtedly introduced!). Many photographs appear for the first time. Dewey Livingston's large-scale map is new.

Working nearly three years on this book has elevated my love of the Dipsea. I've come to realize that the Dipsea is more than a race. The story of the Dipsea illustrates some of the best qualities of the human spirit—tenacity, desire for excellence, friendship, ability to endure and overcome adversity, quest for challenge, competition, love of sport and the outdoors, our sense of history.

Here is the story of the Dipsea Race, and of the men and women who have run it.

MAPS

Included with this book is the new, official, four-color map of the Dipsea course. For easy reference, an "unadorned" version of the same map is printed within the book.

THE HANDICAPS

Many new to the Dipsea find its handicap system confusing; it is actually quite simple. All entrants are assigned a headstart in relation to a group of men who start last. The number of minutes of headstart is the handicap. The first to the finish line wins.

Starters in the last, zero-handicap group are known as "scratch" runners. A runner's actual running time less his or her handicap is the "clock time"—it matches what the official clocks turned on with the scratch group read. For scratch runners, actual and clock times are always identical.

A more complete review of the handicaps is presented later in the book (see "Handicaps").

STYLE

❑ Times are, unless specified, actual running times. In most cases, the runner's handicap (hc) immediately follows in parenthesis, e.g. 59:12 (5hc), 1:01:40 (8), or 30th place (1:03:06, 10hc). "Scr," or "0," is used for scratch, or no handicap.

❑ "Reese" refers to Mark Reese and his book, *The Dipsea Race*.

❑ When place names are given without a state, they are in California (unless obviously elsewhere, e.g., Boston).

❑ The three primary newspaper sources—the *San Francisco Chronicle*, *San Francisco Examiner* and *Marin Independent Journal*—are shortened to *Chronicle*, *Examiner* and *Independent Journal*.

❑ The word "race" is capitalized when referring to the Dipsea.

❑ "AAU" is the Amateur Athletic Union, the former name of the governing body for running.

❑ In the yearly accounts, selected anecdotes are distinguished at the end.

❑ Several conventions are used in the top finishers list that follows each year's account. Places are given ten deep through 1964, 20 deep through 1974 to reflect the increased entries, then 36 deep from 1975, the year shirts were first awarded.

Boldfaced notations identify the runners with the "best time" and "2nd best time" (men with the two fastest actual times), "fastest woman" (actual time), "1st HS" (winner of the high school trophy, when awarded), and, from 1971, either "first woman" or "first man." The time in brackets following the winner only is the margin of victory over second place. Below the place listings (beginning in 1919) is the winning team with its five scoring members. The final line contains the total number of finishers and a brief description of the weather during the Race.

❑ In tables, unverified figures are followed by a question mark.

APOLOGIA

The Boston Marathon has clearly long been the nation's most influential and most prestigious race. I've known and dreamed of it since I was a youngster. As a 10-year-old I wrote a short story about a runner who pushes himself beyond his limits, wins Boston, then dies! Finishing Boston in 1987 was the happiest and most emotional moment in my decades of running.

But I love the Dipsea even more. So I propose a tie; the Boston Marathon is the greatest road race and the Dipsea is the greatest cross country race. Treasure them both.

First Annual Championship
Cross Country Run

Under the Auspices of the

DIPSEA INDIANS
OF THE
OLYMPIC CLUB

SUNDAY, NOVEMBER 19th, 1905

Mill Valley to Dipsea by the Sea

OFFICERS OF THE DIPSEA INDIANS

Grand Chief - - -	T. I. FITZPATRICK
Chief - - - -	ROBERT McARTHUR
Grand Sachem - -	W. M. HERRINGTON
Grand Scribe - - -	MATT. HARRIS
Medicine Man - - -	STEVE HERRICK

Sachems and Warriors

Program of the first Dipsea. (Courtesy Frank Maher)

The precise origins of the Dipsea Race are obscure and shrouded in legend. Even the root of the name "Dipsea" remains uncertain despite exhaustive research by Reese and others. The name first appears attached to the Dipsea Inn, a hotel that opened north of Willow Camp (today's Stinson Beach) in 1904. Did the name arise from the beckoning "dip in the sea" for hotel visitors? Or from another hostelry elsewhere? From a poetic reference? From a corruption of the words "deep sea"? Or from the seeming dip into the ocean of the trail to the Inn? No one is certain.

Marin, the county just north of the Golden Gate from San Francisco, was a bucolic land in 1904, the year the seed for the Dipsea Race was planted. The last wild bear had been killed less than two decades earlier. Dairy farms covered the landscape. The population was only 15,000 in 521 square miles—the first significant influxes would follow the San Francisco earthquake and fire of two years later. The huge Spanish and Mexican land grants were just breaking up. The parcels that were to become central Mill Valley had only been laid out and sold in 1892, the city itself incorporated in 1900. The first subdivision map for Willow Camp would not be drawn until 1906. Outside of a few town commons, none of Marin's land was in public hands. Indeed, the canyon that was to become the first public park—today's Muir Woods, through which the Dipsea Trail passes—had been saved from a proposed dam only the year before.

Four separate elements converged to create the Dipsea Race. First was a nascent distance running boom on the West Coast, spurred by marathons at the first Olympic Games (1896) and Boston (1897).

Second was the rise in popularity of hiking, which, in the San Francisco Bay Area, was then (and still largely is) centered on Marin's crown jewel, 2,600 foot Mt. Tamalpais. A favorite hikers route on Tam was the Lone Tree Trail, today known as the Dipsea Trail.

Third was the opening in 1903 of an electric rail line connecting the San Francisco-Sausalito ferry to Mill Valley. That made the depot in Mill Valley the principal starting point for most Mt. Tamalpais hikes.

Fourth, in 1904, the Dipsea Inn opened on an isolated sand spit north of the tiny Pacific Ocean resort hamlet of Willow Camp. The Inn was built in anticipation of a proposed rail line, to connect with existing tracks of the Mt. Tamalpais & Muir Woods Railway at West Point and the Northwestern Pacific Railroad in Point Reyes Station. The Inn would serve the trainloads of tourists, but the line was never built.

Immediately after the Dipsea Inn opened, it was visited by a hearty band from San Francisco's Olympic Club. The group regularly hiked long distances on Mt. Tamalpais out of member Alfons Coney's weekend cabin. Someone, perhaps under the influence of spirits at the new hotel itself, got the idea of racing from Mill Valley to the Inn. Coney and another Olympic Club hiking stalwart, Charles Boas, took up the challenge. On an unknown day in 1904 the two set off on their epic race, with bets placed by Club members and pride on the line. Boas won, his time and margin of victory unknown. (In later years, after Boas had died, Coney would claim there was a dispute over just who won!)

The success of the match race led the celebrating Olympians to consider making an annual competition of it, open to all. The influential, all-men's Olympic Club had been founded in 1860, the oldest athletic club in the United States. In the early years of the century, the club was fielding teams that were competitive with the finest professional and collegiate squads in most every sport. A race sounded appealing.

A week later, the hiking group organized itself as the Dipsea Indians, after the Dipsea Inn. A Grand Chief (Judge Timothy Fitzpatrick) was chosen and race committees established. The new run would be called the Dipsea Race.

The Dipsea Indians deserve lasting praise for the thoroughness of their preparations. Putting on a large, point-to-point, cross country race is a daunting task at any time. To stage an inaugural edition, using part-time volunteers in an era before automobiles and modern communications, was truly a feat of organization. If the 1905 race came off as anything less than a complete success, the Dipsea would likely have been only a brief footnote in the annals of regional running.

Prior to the first race, the Indians settled on two of the enduring foundations that were to forever make the Dipsea special. One was that, although a suggested route was well-marked, runners were free to choose their own way. Thus, perhaps out of necessity (monitoring the full course was all but impossible), was born the idea of an open course. The course remains technically "open" to this day, though several areas have recently been declared off limits.

The second was headstarts, or handicaps. They were based on a runner's ability, so as to theoretically give every competitor a chance to win. This handicap system, which was one day to make Dipsea champions of 9-year-old girls and 60-year-old men, also continues today, though now based strictly on age and sex.

The stage was set for the first Dipsea. The considerable prestige of the Olympic Club ensured that the best runners in Northern California, and all the major newspapers, were on hand. And so, on a rainy November 19, 1905, 84 men gathered in downtown Mill Valley to run to the Pacific Ocean.

The Dipsea Race was born.

(Right) Timothy Fitzpatrick, co-founder of the Dipsea and long-time Race director, 1924. (Courtesy Frank Maher)

(Below) Olympic Club members Charles Boas and Alfons Coney, whose 1904 match race spawned the Dipsea, circa 1914. (Kennard Wilson, courtesy Olympic Club)

Charles Boas,
test race winner.

Al Coney,
test race loser.

THE DIPSEA COURSE

THE DIPSEA TRAIL by Waldeman Young

Oh, the wind is in the canyon, and the redwood sirens wail
In their massive lamentations as we swing along the trail,
While the purple shadows muster like ambassadors of night
Where the glooming mountain lingers like a phantom on the right.

Oh, we pull across the ridges and salute the lone pine-tree
Where it watches like a sentinel above the western sea,
And Bolinas waits below us at the finish of the run,
And we see the water glaring as it fuses with the sun.

Oh, we see the boasting breakers come a-sprawling on the sand,
Like some endless game of ten-pins played by Neptune's mighty hand,
And the sky is like a vision as the evening star ascends,
Like a Phoenix from the sunset where the ash of evening blends.

Oh, there's nothing like the tonic of the rolling Dipsea Trail,
For we breathe its boundless spirit and the world's distortions pale
While we feel the red blood pulsing as it hits a swifter pace
Like a wild thing loosed to the circle in the rapture of the race.

The Dipsea course may be unsurpassed among the world's footraces for its combination of stunning scenery, physical challenge and colorful history. That said, it must be noted that the Dipsea actually has no "course"! From the first race in 1905, runners have been free to go from Mill Valley to Stinson Beach by any route they choose. (Although, beginning in 1977, some sensitive areas have been placed off-limits.) The route generally follows the Dipsea Trail, which may have been blazed by the Miwok Indians before the arrival of European settlers. It was certainly in use as a cross-Marin route when California was part of Mexico and appears on the first published County trail map of 1854.

Described below is the route presently followed by most runners. It is marked by blue and white ribbons on Race day. (In the 1960's, red ribbons marked hazardous areas, such as barbed wire.) Some earlier paths, and some of today's shortcuts, are cited as well.

The start of the Dipsea Race has always been beside the depot in downtown Mill Valley. This was the terminus station of a spur, connecting with the Sausalito ferry dock, on the Northwestern Pacific electric rail line. This ferry-rail connection brought most of Mill Valley's visitors during the line's operation, from 1903 to 1940. The depot was also the start of the Mt. Tamalpais & Muir Woods Railway, which ran up the Mountain from 1896 to 1930. After train service ended, the depot served as a bus stop. Today, the building is a popular cafe and bookstore.

The starting line has varied by a few feet over the years. For decades now it has been fixed at the flagpole on Lytton Square. This precise spot was chosen simply because it was the best place to tie a start rope. Lytton Plummer Barber was the first Mill Valley resident killed in World War I. For many earlier Dipseas the start was at the historic clock (dedicated to Mill Valley's volunteer fire fighters) on the square's corner. In the crowded years of the 1970's, runners backed up around the block to the movie theater.

The course begins west up Throckmorton Avenue, named for Samuel Throckmorton, who once owned much of southernmost Marin, including what became Mill Valley. After around one-quarter mile, runners veer left through redwood-lined Old Mill Park. The runners go left or right around the bathroom. (This is the only public bathroom on the route, and the adjacent fountain is likewise the only one between the start and finish). The "old mill," built by John Reed in 1834, that would give the town its name has been rebuilt and is visible to the left. To the right is restored gravity car #9 from the Mt. Tamalpais & Muir Woods Railway. Runners cross the wood bridge over Old Mill Creek.

The bridge meets the intersection of Cascade Drive and Molino Avenue; runners go straight between the two streets onto the steep path of Cascade Way. Within 75 yards, and .40 miles from the start, begin the infamous Dipsea steps (don't take the first private stairway on the left). This is the most talked-about part of the course, challenging everyone. From the late 1960's, when a major step rebuilding project was completed, there were 671 steps in the three flights (307, 221, then 143). This number became the basis for Jack Kirk's famous line, "Old Dipsea runners never die. They just reach the 672nd step." Subsequent repairs have raised the number to 676 in 1993.

The first flight, to Millside Lane, is the longest, presently with 313 steps. The topmost 33 rock steps are the steepest. The runners then go right on Millside Lane a few yards, then left onto Marion Avenue. Several unrelated old trail signs are nailed to the redwood at the Millside-Marion junction.

Immediately up Marion is the second flight (222 steps). It has a short non-step section near the top that tempts running. Runners then go left 20 yards on Hazel Avenue to the third flight (141 steps, 142 counting the curb). This last set was the most recently built. It empties onto Sequoia Valley Road at Edgewood Avenue. Victorino's refreshment stand once stood here, serving the hikers turning off for the Pipeline Trail (today largely covered by Edgewood) to Mountain Home and other Tam destinations.

Runners proceed right up the narrow shoulder of busy Sequoia Valley Road. (A safer hiking path was recently carved above the road on the right, beneath the Belvedere Reservoir water tank.)

In 150 yards, runners enter the stone gateway of Walsh Drive; the climbing resumes in earnest. Until the late 1980's, this was the site of the Flying Y Ranch, where horses and dogs would be companions along the dirt path. Now million-dollar homes flank both sides of the road. There is a dedicated trail easement on the right.

The pavement gives way, past a gate, to a dirt connector to Bay View Drive. Halfway through this French broom-lined section is the one mile mark. When an overhanging branch on an adjacent Monterey cypress was removed some 20 years ago, the words "One Mile Tree" were written on the cut. The tree is slowly healing the wound and the words are now almost covered.

Bay View is then paved to its junction with Panoramic Highway at the ridge aptly named Windy Gap. For the first 60 years of the Dipsea, runners would proceed straight across and plunge down the very steep hillside. In 1969, the first of a pair of houses across Panoramic was built. Years of increasingly nasty confrontations over through access ensued; one homeowner came to be known as "the barbed wire lady" for her fencing. All attempts to secure an easement failed. So, in the mid-1970's, Jerry Hauke led the construction of a longer alternate trail that begins 50 yards to the right on State Park property. Don Pickett later dubbed this section, which marks the entry of the Dipsea onto public lands (where it remains to Stinson Beach), as "Hauke Hollow." The steep shortcuts runners once blazed through it are now off-limits.

The Trail bends sharply left after crossing planks over a rivulet. Two paths to the right are then passed; the first, unmarked, connects to Ridge Road and the second is Sun Trail to the Tourist Club.

The trail empties, after some steep steps, onto Muir Woods Road, principal auto access to Muir Woods National Monument. Here stood the old Redwood Roost refreshment stand, which served early Muir Woods travelers. Across the road is a new (built in 1981) section of the Dipsea Trail. It is quite attractive, passing through lush foliage, but all racers choose the roadway, where they can stretch their legs for the first time.

After .44 miles of fast downhill, runners veer left off the pavement at a stand of mailboxes atop private Camino del Canyon Road. (In the earliest Dipseas, runners would proceed a few yards beyond Camino del Canyon, then drop left down a path through deep woods to Joe's Place, a long-gone restaurant on the valley floor.)

This next downhill has been the scene of much controversy in recent years. In the 1960's and '70's, runners went onto Camino del Canyon until the first bend, then plunged directly down an open hillside (now covered with broom) over several dusty, slippery, dangerous paths that collectively came to be known as "Suicide." In 1978, the State Park restored a more gradual, longer trail (dubbed "The Rangers Trail," though now a part of the Dipsea Trail) directly to the right of the mailboxes.

State Park and Muir Woods officials have increasingly insisted on keeping all runners on the "Ranger's Trail" while Dipsea officials have fought to keep Suicide open. By 1991 the conflict had gotten so serious that the permit for the Race was threatened. A compromise was finally reached, with the top and lower sections of Suicide closed and improvements made to the Dipsea Trail. In 1992, nine runners were cited at the base of Suicide by Muir Woods officials for alleged violations of Monument rules and came within a day of going to court. In 1993, the State widened and cleared a steep alternate path for Race use to the left of the "Rangers Trail." It is joined behind a wooden barrier, with a removable middle section, and is presently lined with mesh fencing.

The Ranger's Trail, sections of which are lined with poison-oak not usually cut back until near Race day, and the new alternate path meet in an open, paved area (mile 2). A children's day care center stood here in the 1960's. The former direct Suicide route emptied onto Muir Woods Road, after a steep final jump, about 100 yards to the left.

All runners then cross Muir Woods Road (also known as Frank Valley Road) and enter the parking lot. They proceed down a short flight of steps to Redwood Creek, which runs through the heart of Muir Woods National Monument and still supports a salmon run. Today's footbridge was built in 1974 after a campaign led by famed Marin nature instructor Elizabeth Terwilliger. When erected, it bore a sign, "No Running On Bridge," so some

runners continued to splash through the creek as before. (Ironically, because it is relatively low, the bridge is removed during the rainy winter season, when it is most needed. This forces hikers and runners to take a half-mile detour left on Muir Woods Road to the base of the Dipsea Fire Road.)

(Before World War II, runners crossed Redwood Creek on a different bridge about 100 yards upstream. It led to a very steep uphill known as "Butler's Pride," apparently for a San Francisco nautical instruments dealer who had a cabin in the area. During World War II, Butler's Pride—the area little used and the bridge to it washed away during a flood in the winter of 1938—became overgrown and the crossing shifted downstream.)

In the 1960's there were two options uphill; a steeper, more direct one named "Dynamite" and a more gradual (and more runnable) alternative dubbed "Switchback." Although the direct line is now off-limits, the whole half-mile ascent is still called Dynamite. A carpet of sword ferns adds to the sylvan beauty but beware of the equally abundant poison-oak.

The Trail leaves Muir Woods National Monument at the junction with the Dipsea Fire Road (also called Deer Park Fire Road). Here too the alternate "high water" route (when the Redwood Creek bridge is out) rejoins. The Dipsea Fire Road was widened from an historic trail in the 1930's. It snakes across the Dipsea Trail until the base of Cardiac. In 1989, the fire road was designated as part of the unfinished 400-mile Bay Area Ridge Trail.

This next 1.06 mile section is called the Hogsback (or, less commonly, "The Meadows"). It is open grassland, the grasses now almost entirely non-native species. Bracken fern, baccharis (coyote-bush) shrubs and a few young Douglas-fir trees are now colonizing this formerly fenced, grazing land.

The Hogsback was once part of the huge Brazil Brothers ranch. In the 1960's, a 2,150 acre parcel was purchased by John Fell Stevenson (presidential candidate Adlai's son) then sold to

(Left) The stone steps atop the first flight are the steepest of the 676. (Brad Rippe)

(Above) An overhanging limb on this Monterey cypress between Flying Y and Bayview was removed in the 1970's and the words "ONE MILE TREE" written in the cut; in 1993, the lettering is all but covered. (Photo by author)

(Left) Part of the old Flying Y Ranch, now site of million-dollar homes, just before mile 1, 1979. (Courtesy Mark Reese)

the First Christian Church of America. After the "church" was discovered to be only a front for a real estate development firm, the land was acquired by the State in 1968 for $3 million.

The Dipsea Trail stays just to the right of the fire road. It climbs first under trees, then through the open terrain. The Trail unites with the fire road for about 100 yards, then separates by going straight (actually slightly left). Some runners stay on the broader fire road right for better passing. Views open, to the ocean and to the three summits of Mt. Tam. Dipsea veterans feel that it is on the Hogsback, slightly uphill but much less so than the climbs before, that fast times are made or lost; it must be raced, not walked or jogged.

The Trail and fire road again recombine for some 100 yards (mile 3). This time the Trail leaves to the right, into a steeper section wooded with oaks. The Trail then crosses the fire road.

The prominent lichen-covered rock outcropping on the left past the first telephone pole is called "Halfway Rock." It is less than half the distance (44% in 1979 per Reese) but, because so much of the route to it is uphill, roughly marks half the time it takes most runners to finish the full course. Soon after is a formerly muddy seep, fairly dry recently, known as Hogsback Spring. The Trail enters another wooded stretch, then re-emerges back into grassland.

The Dipsea leaves the grassland, the Hogsback and Mt. Tamalpais State Park to re-enter Muir Woods National Monument and what runners call "The Rainforest." Summer fog often drips like rain off the Douglas-firs, redwoods, tanbark oaks, madrones and laurels here to turn the ground muddy. Another common name for this deep woodland is Deer Park, and in early Dipseas it was called Deer Forest.

Just in is a good spot for sharp-eyed runners to spot, in spring, orchids such as spotted coralroot. What was long known as "The Log," a huge, downed Douglas-fir which forced runners to clamber over, is now cut in two. Protruding roots must be heeded.

At a prominent signpost, marking the upper end of the Ben Johnson Trail (which descends to the main Muir Woods canyon), the Dipsea Trail bends left. It then unites, .33 miles into the Rainforest, with the Dipsea Fire Road for the last time (mile 4). After 150 yards, the Trail departs right at the base of the infamous one-fifth-mile long Cardiac Hill. (A humorous "no u-turn" sign once stood here.)

The uphill markedly steepens. Most all runners, weary from the climbing, walk-run, or just walk. A signed intersection with TCC Trail marks the start of the final push. The Dipsea Trail leaves Muir Woods for the last time as it emerges from the tree canopy.

The Trail enters grassland, then tops at the glorious, open, 1,360+' summit of Cardiac, highest point on the course. The term "Cardiac" was, according to Reese, coined by Dr. Alfred Duff in 1954 and quickly gained in popularity. It had long been called "The Sugar Lump." A water station provides refreshment here Dipsea day. The unsurpassed views, and knowledge that the serious climbing is over, give added relief.

(There has been a lively debate over the years as to the true highest point on the Dipsea Trail, Cardiac or Lone Tree just ahead. To settle the affair, Race director Jerry Hauke took sophisticated surveying equipment to the area in August, 1993. I served as "rod man," meaning I held the measuring pole. After several measurements, it was determined that the trail was a mere FIVE INCHES higher at Cardiac than at Lone Tree. It is possible that the trail was once higher by Lone Tree before today's fire road was bulldozed.)

The Trail crosses the Coastal (or Old Mine) Fire Road and descends gradually. This .19-mile stretch from Cardiac to the junction with Lone Tree Fire Road is known as Farren's Rest. James Farren, Jr. was a devoted Mt. Tam runner and Dipsea lover who died of cancer in 1981 at the age of 39. A group of his friends gathered at Cardiac, then spread his ashes along the trail (a practice now outlawed by the State Park). A trophy for "Sportsmanship, leadership and dedication to the Dipsea" is named for him.

There is then a short climb to the fire road, beside the historic Lone Tree. The Lone Tree was long the most famous landmark on the whole route; the Dipsea Trail itself was originally known as Lone Tree Trail until around 1916. Photographs show that, in the early 1900's, the only tree on the hill to the right (which was even known as Bald Hill) was a lone redwood. But the hillside, free from fires and grazing for decades, is now covered with Douglas-firs. That redwood, the Lone Tree (or, wrongly, Lone Pine), still stands; it is plainly evident from Cardiac and closer as the large tree on the lower left, of a different profile than the Douglas-firs above.

A few feet past the fire road junction, a small path right leads up to Lone Tree Spring. A fountain tapping it, built by the Tamalpais Conservation Club in 1917, has long been the only reliable source of water for Dipsea runners practicing in summer. (The current policy of Tam land managers is to discourage drinking from non-filtered sources.)

In 100 yards, the Trail departs left from the fire road (some racers stay on the fire road all or part of the next sections). After 250 yards, the Trail and fire road meet again for an up-and-down stretch, also 250 yards, after which the Trail departs left. In another 100 yards, the Trail crosses the fire road.

At a marked signpost, the Dipsea Trail goes right, though many racers stay on the fire road another 150 yards before making their cut. The continuation of the fire road, as it seemingly "dips into the sea," is a possible source of the name "Dipsea". (Until the late 1920's, when Steep Ravine became part of Mt. Tamalpais State Park, runners remained on the fire road contour even longer. They then veered right and ran down the ridgeline above Swoop Hollow. That now-overgrown route, referred to as "the Hog's Back" in old accounts, emptied into Webb Creek, via a steep pitch called "Devil's Slide," just west of, and below, the base of Insult.)

After a short section of shrubs and trees with low, overhanging branches, the Dipsea Trail meets (mile 5) a new fence. This is the top of "The Swoop," so named by Jack Kirk, and another area of recent controversy. State Park officials are seeking to close the direct route down the grassy ravine. In 1977, a new .36-mile section of the Dipsea Trail (dubbed "The Gail Scott Trail" for the 1986 champion who mistakenly took it in '87, possibly costing her a repeat victory) was carved through the haunting redwood, Douglas-fir and laurel forest to the right. But Dipsea officials have been adamant in keeping the Swoop part of the Race. So, in 1991, as a compromise, a fence was erected with a section that is removed Dipsea day.

At the base of the Swoop is the old "Slash" or "Trench," off-limits since 1981 and now overgrown but once a direct entry into Steep Ravine. The modern route bends right and joins the base of the "Gail Scott" section.

Just past an old survey marker, the Dipsea enters Steep Ravine, frequently cited as one of the most beautiful parts of the Bay Area. William Kent donated it to the new Mt. Tamalpais State Park the day before he died in 1928.

Racers rarely notice Steep Ravine's charm because the extreme drop, rocks and roots demand undivided attention. Passing in this .22-mile section, often critical because some runners are flying (the best downhillers leap four steps at a time) while others are moving cautiously, produces the most dangerous situations in the race and the most serious injuries. The steps, scary enough, are themselves considered an improvement by some from earlier years; 1946 champion Charlie Richesin vividly describes descending much of Steep Ravine sliding on his rear end. Several other old-timers maintain that Steep Ravine is markedly less runnable now than it was decades ago. An old alternate route, overgrown though still evident, ran just to the left of and above today's trail. It too emptied by the old "Devil's Slide."

The Trail crosses Webb Creek on a sturdy bridge (which replaced a rail-less earlier one) and bends left. It is briefly joined with Steep Ravine

Trail, which, to the right, ascends the same canyon on the other bank of Webb Creek.

The lands from the base of Steep Ravine to Stinson Beach were the last major section of the Dipsea to remain in private hands. In 1968, George Leonard, the principal landowner, presented a permanent public easement for the Dipsea Trail to the County. Then, in 1971, Leonard sold 1,311 acres (including the Dipsea Trail) to the new Golden Gate National Recreation Area. (Leonard ran the 1970 race with his daughter, Barbara Robben, and grandson, Michael. Leonard's widow Wilma recalls that each year Dipsea officials were granted permission to cut through their ranch fence stiles on condition they would promptly repair them; they would invariably be left open and cows would escape!)

The briefly combined Dipsea-Steep Ravine trails pass a small reservoir, built in the 1960's to augment the community of Stinson Beach's water supply. Next is Insult Hill. It was named by Don Pickett; the course's final "Insult" to the racers who thought they had conquered all the uphills. It's short but stiff, and many winners have walked it. Halfway up, Steep Ravine Trail veers off left.

A white barn stood for decades in a clearing on the left near the top of Insult. The barn, part of the old White Gate Ranch, was torn down around 1970 soon after the ranch became part of the Golden Gate National Recreation Area. This area is still alternately called White Barn and White Gate. The broad path coming in from the left was actually once a section of the original Highway 1.

Runners then face a fork; the marked Dipsea Trail veers left uphill onto the Moors (also named by Pickett), the fork right rises to a gate and Panoramic Highway. Most of the top runners take, as they have for decades, this latter option. They run downhill on the Panoramic Highway road shoulder (mile 6). After .2 miles, at a spot usually marked with white paint, they cut left and descend a narrow path, dubbed "Leonard's Lane" because it was part of the trail easement George Leonard donated to Marin County. At the path's base, runners veer

right, duck under a limb, cross a seep, then clamber up a few steep yards to rejoin Panoramic at a wide bend.

This second stretch on Panoramic is some 250 yards. At the highway milepost marker 8.48, just before a signed bend right, the speeding runners cut left again.

They immediately face a short but extremely steep and root-covered plunge to the southern fork of Easkoot's Creek. This drop is among the two or three most dangerous spots in the whole Dipsea. It has also been the scene of some of the Race's highest dramas; for example, the collapses of Ralph Perry in 1956, Alan Beardall in 1957 and Joe Ryan in 1981, the shortcut of Carl Jensen in 1967 and the blunder of Russ Kiernan in 1979. It was that latter incident that gave the fording its name today, "Kiernan's Crossing." (Until around 1970, runners crossed the creek farther downstream; that option ended when a house was built downhill.)

The alternate Moors route was opened in 1975 after long being fenced for grazing. It has better footing, room to pass and great views, but one additional uphill. It was even clearly quicker than Panoramic until its final downhill (called "Moose Hill" or "MacDouche") into Stinson Beach was closed off for the 1977 Race. The Moors option, which is the official Dipsea Trail, rises to meet and cross Fire Road 640. This was the access to a World War II enemy ship spotting installation still visible to the left. The route then descends (passing mile 6 near the top) through grassland. A half-mile down, before the barbed wire fence that closes off Moose Hill, the Trail bends right into woodland.

The Moors and "shortcut" routes merge in a lovely coastal forest. Runners can sense the nearby ocean. The Trail crosses a boggy area below over a wood bridge; a single plank sufficed in earlier years.

Decades ago, runners exited the Trail just beyond this bog and crossed Panoramic Highway. They then entered, via a stile, a fenced-in area called "The Horse Pasture" and descended to Shoreline Highway. Later, the crossing was lower

Runners ascend last hill on the Moors; the beach and surf at Stinson in sight, 1988.
(Robert Tong, Independent Journal)

on Panoramic, over a diagonal shortcut still used in the Double and Practice Dipseas.

The "hiker's" Dipsea Trail ends with a bend right and exit onto Panoramic Highway at a large sign. From 1977, as a concession to Stinson Beach officials trying to improve traffic flow, Dipsea runners were barred from crossing Panoramic and directed left to Highway 1. This adds extra yards through tall grass and final challenges, the leap over the stile and the short but very sharp drop to Highway 1. This infamous stile, scene of many falls, has become perhaps the Dipsea's most photographed locale.

Highway 1 was originally Bolinas Highway when it was built as a stage road in 1870; today it is also called Shoreline Highway. Those with energy remaining begin a 150-yard downhill sprint on the pavement.

For almost all Dipseas through 1963, the finish was straight ahead, at Calle del Mar in front of Airey's Hotel, the still-standing building that now houses the town grocery store (renamed Becker's By The Beach in 1993). From 1964 through 1973, racers were directed left on Arenal Avenue to finish in front of the Parkside Cafe. Now runners are directed left onto the 200-yard long park maintenance driveway—called Lawrence by some for the long-time Stinson Beach family of that name—just before Arenal. A fence blocks through access on non-Race days.

At the Stinson Beach parking lot, the route now goes left for the final, crowd-lined 490' straightaway. The very welcome finish line is at the entrance to the south, dirt parking lot. This lot covered a brackish pond long known locally as "Poison Pond."

(Note: For descriptions of the intersecting trails, and all other Mt. Tamalpais trails, readers may wish to refer to my book, *Tamalpais Trails*.)

OFFICIAL COURSE CHANGES

Here is a summary of significant, official changes to the Dipsea course. Distances through 1979 are from Mark Reese's "The Dipsea Race." Post-1979 changes have added approximately .1 mile to the course; the current Dipsea entry form gives the distance as 7.1 miles.

1905 The Race started on the Miller Avenue side of the train depot. The finish was in front of the Dipsea Inn (today's 198 Seadrift Road). This meant running some 1.3 miles on the sand at the end. It also made the total distance much the longest ever. (8.16 miles per Reese)

1906 The finish remained on the beach, but with only the final 300 yards on sand. (6.99 miles)

1907 The finish line was established at the intersection of Bolinas Highway (today's Shoreline Highway) and Calle del Mar, in front of Airey's store, the building that is today's Becker's By The Beach grocery. (6.83 miles)

1954 The finish line for this year only—which celebrated the 50th anniversary of the original Boas-Coney bet and the birth of the Dipsea Indians—was on the Stinson Beach State Park (now Golden Gate National Recreation Area) maintenance yard driveway that the runners traverse today. (6.84 miles)

1964 The runners turned left on Arenal Avenue and finished at its intersection with Calle del Mar. This finish, in front of the Parkside Cafe, is still used in the Practice Dipsea. (6.81 miles)

1974 The finish was again moved to the park maintenance driveway, 150 yards down from Highway 1. (6.75 miles)

1975 Runners were permitted on "The Moors" from the top of Insult Hill to near the Panoramic Highway/Shoreline Highway junction. (6.84 miles)

1976 Because runners were backing up to Highway 1, the finish line was moved another 130 feet down the maintenance yard. (6.87 miles)

1977 The finish line was set on the Stinson Beach parking driveway at the near edge of the south lot. Also, the first three course restrictions ever in the Dipsea were imposed. Runners had to go right when crossing Panoramic Highway at Windy Gap onto the newly constructed trail; the old downhill route directly across, which had been blocked by new homes for years, was officially declared off-limits. Second, the final downhill (nicknamed "Moose Hill" and "MacDouche") into Stinson Beach was closed. This had the unintended effect of returning the top runners to the two sections on Panoramic Highway. Third, to improve auto traffic flow, runners were directed left in the final yards of the Dipsea Trail and made to cross Highway 1 just south of Panoramic. (6.87-6.96 miles)

1979 Beginning in the late 1970's, a series of restrictions, not all immediately recognized by the Dipsea Committee, have been placed by State and Muir Woods officials on the most direct routes down Suicide. The first was banning the lower section below the pump house.

1980 Running on private was banned.

1981 The "Trench" or "Slash," the direct connection between Swoop and Steep Ravine, was closed.

1984 To prevent runners from repeating a new route (which avoided the Steps, Muir Woods and Cardiac) pioneered the year before by Ron Rahmer, runners were barred from Panoramic Highway between Mountain Home and Insult.

1991 Runners were required to stay on marked trails while in Muir Woods National Monument. Also, old shortcuts in Hauke Hollow were closed.

SPLIT TIMES

Russ Kiernan, one of the most respected of Dipsea competitors with 14 top-10 finishes, has calculated split times at key landmarks for runners aiming for 60 and 70 minute finishes. These intermediate times are (60 minute pace first): first step (3:00, 3:30); top of steps (7:15, 8:30); One-mile Tree (10:30, 12:30); bottom of Hauke Hollow (13:45, 16:30); Redwood Creek (18:30, 22:00); Halfway Rock (30:00, 35:00); top of Cardiac (41:30, 48:00); and bottom of Insult (51:30, 1:02:00).

THE STILES

For decades, significant portions of the Dipsea passed through privately held lands, much of it fenced for livestock grazing. Stiles permitted access for Dipsea racers through the fence lines. Some stiles were two-posted (with 2x4's nailed across the barbed wire for safety) and were hurdled, others were three-posted to be "zig-zagged" through. These latter caused delays as the Race became more crowded.

In a letter written to me in 1993, Jack Kirk describes 15 stiles that had to be negotiated by Dipsea racers during the 1930's and after. Here is his list, by order on the course. All are "two-posters" unless noted.

#1 Just beyond Redwood Creek at base of Butler's Pride. Some runners avoided it by staying right of the fence line.

#2 Early in the Hogsback, just before the trail joins the fire road for the first time (three-poster). It was called stile #1 in the 1960's, when it was a ham radio checkpoint. (See photograph of William Mazzini squeezing through.)

#3 Just up from the dip at the start of the Rainforest (three-poster, still evident).

#4 Top of "Sugar Lump" (Cardiac).

#5, #6 Entering and leaving a small enclosure that kept cattle from polluting the spring at Lone Tree.

#7 At the bottom of the Trench, at the entry into Steep Ravine (three-poster, still evident).

#8 At White Barn (the gate on the other side onto Panoramic was left open Race day).

#9 At the first shortcut left off Panoramic.

#10 At the end of the first shortcut, just before the muddy ditch and the return to Panoramic. Called by Kirk, "always the most difficult to get over."

#11, #12 Just down from the second trail shortcut off Panoramic (both still evident).

#13 Where runners used to approach and cross Panoramic for the last time.

#14, #15 Where runners entered and exited the horse pasture (no longer part of the course) northeast of the Highway 1-Panoramic junction. Kirk avoided the last stile by sliding under the barbed wire.

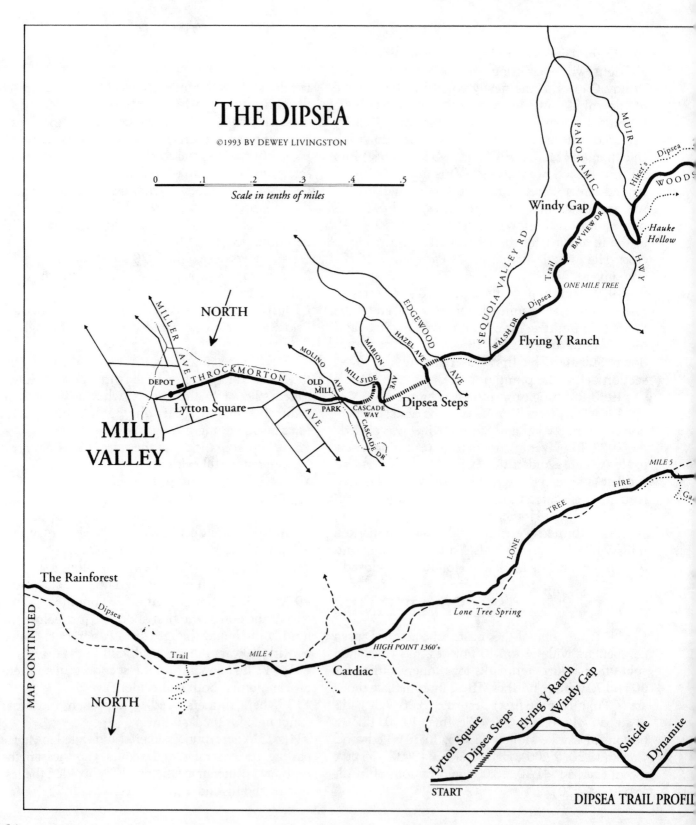

THE DIPSEA

©1993 BY DEWEY LIVINGSTON

0   .1   .2   .3   .4   .5

Scale in tenths of miles

NORTH

Windy Gap

Hauke Hollow

WOODS

MUIR

PANORAMIC

BAY VIEW DR

SEQUOIA VALLEY RD

ONE MILE TREE

Hiker's   Dipsea

Trail

Dipsea

Flying Y Ranch

WALSH DR

MILLER AVE

EDGEWOOD

HAZEL AVE

MARION AVE

MOLINO AVE

MILL SIDE

DEPOT

THROCKMORTON

OLD MILL

Lytton Square

PARK AVE

CASCADE WAY

CASCADE DR

Dipsea Steps

MILL VALLEY

The Rainforest

MILE 5

FIRE

Ga...

TREE

LONE

Lone Tree Spring

MAP CONTINUED

Dipsea

Trail

MILE 4

HIGH POINT 1360'±

Cardiac

NORTH

Lytton Square

Dipsea Steps

Flying Y Ranch

Windy Gap

Suicide

Dynamite

START

DIPSEA TRAIL PROFIL...

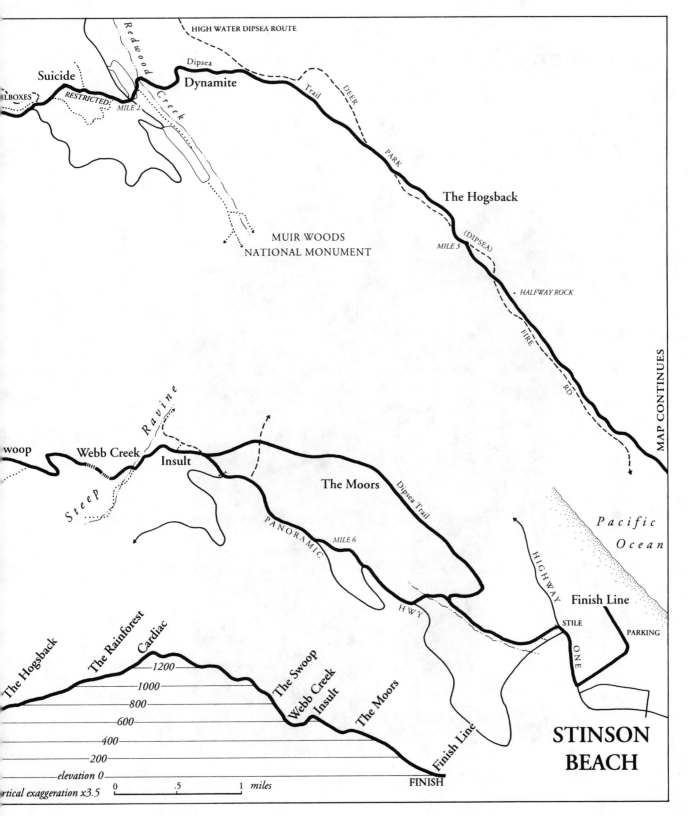

HIGH WATER DIPSEA ROUTE

Suicide

Dynamite

Dipsea

RESTRICTED:

ILBOXES

MILE 2

Redwood Creek

Trail

DEER

PARK

The Hogsback

(DIPSEA)

MILE 3

MUIR WOODS
NATIONAL MONUMENT

• HALFWAY ROCK

FIRE

RD

MAP CONTINUES

Ravine

woop

Webb Creek

Insult

The Moors

Dipsea Trail

Steep

PANORAMIC

MILE 6

Pacific
Ocean

HIGHWAY

Finish Line

ONE

HWY

STILE

PARKING

The Hogsback

The Rainforest

Cardiac

1200

1000

800

600

400

200

elevation 0

rtical exaggeration x3.5

The Swoop

Webb Creek

Insult

The Moors

Finish Line

STINSON
BEACH

0   .5   1   miles

FINISH

THE DIPSEA RACES

1905-1993

A crowded, dusty, descent of Suicide, 1969. (Roger Bockrath, Independent Journal)

1st Dipsea
November 19, 1905

The first Dipsea captured the imagination of the San Francisco sporting public as perhaps no other footrace before or since. All the major San Francisco newspapers gave the Race feature coverage (and would continue to do so for decades). The *Chronicle*, for example, splashed a bold headline across the entire width of its front sports page proclaiming, "Great Cross-Country Run From Mill Valley to Dipsea." Below a picture of the contestants was the caption, "The contest proved to be the greatest athletic event ever held in the history of the Olympic Club." The *Morning Call* said, "The success of the contest, both in its record entry [111 runners—double the estimates and high by standards of the era] and in its outcome, is expected to have a strong influence on athletics on this coast." The *Examiner* proclaimed the Race, "The greatest cross-country run that was ever held in this or any other country."

Besides being first, 1905 stands apart because of its substantially longer course. Once they reached the coast, the runners had to run a considerable distance (1.3 miles per Reese, longer in other accounts) north on the beach to reach the finish in front of the Dipsea Inn. This was to duplicate the terms of the original Boas-Coney bet, and to promote the new Inn.

Here, in full, is the *San Francisco Chronicle's* next day story.

Youth won out in the great cross-country run of the Dipsea Indians and of the Olympic Club yesterday. Age and experience came second.

[John Geoffrey] Hassard, a seventeen-year-old [actually 18] stripling of the Oakland High School, took the handicap prize, while [Cornelius] Connelly, 28 years old, of the Emerald Gaelic Athletic Association, took the time prize, coming in second from scratch. Hassard had a time allowance of ten minutes.

It was the most wonderful contest of the kind ever seen in California. Never in the history of athletics in the State has such an event ever before taken place. It is a question if such a grueling event has ever been pulled off in any part of the world. The athletes went a little over nine miles, but in that distance they had to climb to an altitude of 1680 feet [overstated], and then come down to the water's edge.

Not only was it a course of one mountain, but in the distance there some three or four; none, however, was as high as the last, where the runners had to pass the Lone Tree.

From that point it was all down hill to the sea, and when that was reached there were two miles of a stretch through soft sand.

The course under favorable circumstances is hard enough, but yesterday 'it was the limit,' for, as the men started off, rain began, and they had hardly reached the top of the first hill before the trail became thoroughly wet, and those who had smooth-soled shoes began to slip and fall. In some cases there were those who took the down grade in a tumble. Those who came after the first lot found the trail in a fearful condition. It was full of mud, and, with the rain, it was hard work to keep on the course.

The work of the high school boy, Hassard, was the finest exhibition seen in many a day, for it was pure grit that won out for him. He had ten minutes' time allowance, and those ahead of him had only a start of two minutes [the maximum handicap was 12 minutes]. By the pace he was travelling it was but a short distance before he overtook them and was in the lead.

He had no one before him to cut out the pace; there was none to overtake. He practically set the pace for them all. In speaking of Hassard, Connelly said on the way home:

"When they sent me away I went at it on a run, and one by one I had them behind me until I left what I thought was the last near the Lone Tree. I went down to the ocean at a fast gait, always thinking that I had the prize to win. When I got straightened out on the beach I saw some one running ahead of me, and I could not understand it, but tried to get him. But 'nix,'

he was going like a cyclone. I don't know where that kid got his speed."

Hassard finished about the freshest of any of the eighty-four that went over the course. He finished with an easy stride and looked as if he was good for many miles more.

This was in contrast to many of the others, for over twenty of them dropped when they had crossed the tape, and had to be carried to the house, where they were brought around by Bob Cornell, the Olympic Club trainer. It showed what fine condition the boys were in, for when it was time to eat not one of them was missing at the table.

Connelly, who took the time prize, was a wonder. He went the course in 1h. 4m. 22s. This burned up a lot of money for the talent, for many wagers had been made that the course would not be covered in less than 1h 20m 5s.

The second time prize goes to [Lester] Thompson, another high school boy hailing from Lick, who made the distance in 1h. 12m. flat.

G. Evans of the Wai Kai Kais took the second handicap prize; G. Burgers, unattached, the third handicap prize; M. McCourtney of Lick the fourth, and Guy Ransom of the Dipsea the fifth.

Every one that took part in the contest will receive a silver bar from the Olympic Club. Of the eighty-four that started seventy-one came well within the time limit of 1h. 50m.

There was the best of sportsmanlike spirit shown by the contestants. When a man would catch up with those ahead and show signs that he wanted to go by, those in the lead would give him room to pass. There was no holding the trail to keep the lead.

When Connolly came up with a number near Lone Tree they realized that he was going at a killing pace, and they stopped and gave him a great cheer as he went by.

Van Fleet's [Van Vliet's] cottage at Willow Camp had a sign painted on the roof, showing four Indians hitting up the trails and over it read, 'Go to it, you Indians.'

After all the contestants had arrived there was a hot lunch served by the Olympic Club. There were over 500 athletes and guests who sat down to the feast.

After the sharp edge of the appetites had been taken off, [Olympic Club] President William Greer Harrison called for silence, and told the boys that the race was the greatest event ever held by the members of the Olympic Club, and that what the Dipsea Indians had started was going to be an annual event. He finished by calling for three cheers for Al Coney, who, he said, was responsible for the Dipsea race.

Saturday night there was a pleasant surprise for Al Coney at the potlatch. The Dipsea Indians presented him with the first of the club medals struck off after the adopted design. Instead of being bronze, this one was made of gold.

Hassard was quoted in Douglas Erskine's Examiner story:

This is the first time I have ever been over the trail. At Lone Pine I asked the judge which way I had to go, but I had no trouble finding the flags and the confetti which marked the course. I felt good the whole way over, and at no time did I feel distressed. I am glad I won, of course, and I shall always prize the cup on account of the big field of good runners which I was lucky enough to beat to-day.

❏ Cornelius Connelly's silver best time trophy, with three stag horns for handles, turned up 80 years later at a Morgan Hill flea market. It was purchased by Frank Silva of Sausalito.
❏ Connelly and Andrew Glarner were the only racers who started from scratch, dubbed "the place of honor." Only two others had fewer than four minutes handicap.
❏ The starting line was on the Miller Avenue (west) side of the train depot; in all future years it would be on the north side.
❏ Eleven men, those with the maximum handicap, shared the distinction of being the first runners ever to set off in the Dipsea Race, at 10:20 a.m.
❏ The previous year, 1904, the West Point Inn was built on the westernmost point of the Mt. Tamalpais

Railway. The first Dipsea saw the start of a tradition for spectators to take a special early train from Mill Valley to West Point, then hike downhill four miles to the finish or to other places on the course. Jack Kirk recalls taking the train back to Mill Valley in his first Dipsea in 1930.

❑ Another nascent tradition was the Dipsea Indians' big "pow-wow" the night before the Race. Club members would hike over to the coast the day before, to prepare the trail and finish line area. They would then hold a raucous party, lit by bonfire, on the beach at night.

❑ The Olympic Club, along with supplying most of the Race workers, also had the most finishers, 15. San Francisco's St. Ignatius High School (alma mater of Dipsea Race co-founder Timothy Fitzpatrick) was next with 10.

❑ Reese calls fourth-place finisher Thompson "the unsung hero of the first Dipsea race." In what may have been an unintended handicapping quirk, the Lick junior received five fewer handicap minutes than Hassard though both were high schoolers. So while Thompson ran 45 seconds faster than Hassard, it is Hassard's name that heads, for all-time, every compilation of Dipsea champions.

❑ Harold Atkinson, who became one of the most important trail builders on Mt. Tamalpais (a bridge is dedicated to him at Barth's Retreat) finished 35th.

1. John Hassard, 1:12:45 (10) [1:37]
2. Cornelius Connelly, 1:04:22 (0) **best time**
3. G. Evans, 1:15:40 (9)
4. Lester Thompson, 1:12:00 (5) **2nd best time**
5. George Burgers, 1:18:45 (11)
6. L.J. Brown, 1:13:15 (4)
7. M. McCourtney, 1:21:40 (12)
8. Guy Ransom, 1:16:50 (7)
9. Joseph Valentine, 1:19:20 (9)
10. D.A. Cushing, 1:15:55 (5)
71 finishers; rain began after the start

2nd Dipsea
October 7, 1906

The finish of the 1906 Race remains among the most thrilling in the Dipsea's long history. Certainly it is unsurpassed for late lead changes—three different front runners collapsed within sight of the finish.

The finish had been moved from the Dipsea Inn, mercifully eliminating most of the long run through the sand. But the new finish line, which not all the runners were aware of, still required 300 grueling yards on the beach. Here are the somewhat differing San Francisco newspaper accounts of the dramatic conclusion.

The second annual open race of the Dipsea Indians from Mill Valley to Willow Camp yesterday was the greatest cross-country event ever held in the United States. The finish was so close that it was impossible to tell the winner until the tape was reached. J.G. Hassard, the winner of last year, came back and won again, but the reduction of his handicap [from 10 to five minutes] gave him a much harder contest.

Hassard won the handicap from John Little of the California School of Mechanical Arts by three seconds. If Little had not been all in when he struck the sandy beach and dropped for a few seconds, thinking that he had reached the finishing line, he undoubtedly would have carried off the prize. Little [12hc] and Julian Wagnet [or Waggenet or Wagenet, 13hc] were leading to the sand, and as they reached the tidewater they dropped from exhaustion. Those who were patrolling that part of the course shouted to them to get on their feet and go down the beach to the finishing line. Little managed to get up and go on, but he was in a dazed condition and hardly knew where he was running. Wagnet made two or three attempts to resume the race, but kept falling and the last time went out and was never able to cross the line, having to be carried to the tent, where he came to later. —Daily Mail-Call

Waggenet, a youthful runner from the same club [Century] as Hassard, had the race won when he got to the beach at Willow Camp, but his exertions in the hot sun over the heart-breaking course had been too much for him, and within 150 yards of the finish, when no other competitor was within a hundred yards of him, he dropped to the sand and was unable to go on.

Hassard in the meantime had come up on the leader, and having plenty of speed left was able to nose out Little for the honors. He was in splendid condition and finished almost as strong as he did last year. In fact, he did not show any signs of distress. —Examiner

Hassard won the race and the trophy that goes with it on the last stretch of sand. He was fourth when the first bunch of contestants dashed across the stile that pointed to the beach.

Wilkins [James Wilkins, owner of Wilkins Ranch at the head of the lagoon north of Willow Camp and uncle of future best-time winner Bill McCurdy], a Bolinas man, who with a liberal allowance of 15 minutes, the outside mark, had kept well in front, had the lead at that point. He dropped back and Julian Wagenet . . . took the vantage position. Wagenet collapsed as he struck the sand and dropped. Hassard had one man to pass, Little from Lick. Little dropped to the sand within 200 yards of the finish, understanding that he had already finished. Friends urged him on but Hassard was quick to note the advantage and could not be overtaken, although the Lick man was a close second. —Chronicle

McCurdy, long-time track coach at Harvard, recalls yet a different version from his uncle Wilkins: "Jim [Wilkins] was leading when he hit the soft sand and was told that was the finish. By the time he regrouped the winner was out on the harder wet sand near the water and he couldn't catch up."

Hassard's finish in 49:55 astonished onlookers and the timing was even called to question. It took Mason Hartwell's 47:56 six years later, breaking Hassard's mark, to remove any doubt. Given the added yards on the sand that no future Dipsea runner would ever have to face, Hassard's was indeed an exceptional effort; sub-50 minute times remain rare today. One account noted the harder than usual preparations that Hassard and his Century Athletic Club teammates had undergone: "[They] have been for thirty days going out three nights a week training for the event." Century runners took four of the first 10 places, Lick High runners two more.

The sizable crowd then awaited the expected imminent arrival of Cornelius Connolly, best time winner the previous year and the star runner in the field. Connolly alone started from scratch; only one other finisher had as few as three handicap minutes. But Connolly ran an extra half-mile because of a wrong turn. When he finally appeared (he finished 12th) on the sand, it became a battle to see if he could beat Hassard's actual running time. He missed by four seconds, Hassard becoming the first of 11 men who would both win the Race and record the fastest time.

❑ Murray Van Vliet, of the prominent Willow Camp family and a Dipsea Indian, donated a trophy for the first high school runner. A high school trophy is still awarded today.

❑ Legendary Cal track coach Walter Christie was the starter and the *Chronicle* noted, "he gave the different runners a talk concerning good sportsmanship."

   1. John Hassard, 49:55 (5) [:03] **best time**
   2. John Little, 56:58 (12) **1st HS**
   3. James Wilkins, 1:00:18 (15)
   4. S. Estrella, 55:40 (10)
   5. M. Moore, 59:30 (13)
   6. R. Frederickson, 58:50 (12)
   7. William Moir, 54:55 (8)
   8. Otto Boeddiker, 54:05 (7)
   9. J.E. Raber, 1:00:54 (13)
10. George Maundrell, 59:51 (11)
12. Cornelius Connolly, 49:59 (0) **2nd best time**
95 finishers; hot

3rd Dipsea
October 13, 1907

Few could fault the handicapping in the first two Dipseas. The 1905 Race was an experiment while 1906 produced an extremely tight finish with even the lone scratch runner in contention. The 1907 Race, however, was clearly oddly handicapped, rivaled only by 1962 in this regard. The maximum handicap had been raised from 12 to 15 minutes, and it was awarded to 31 of the slim field of 44 finishers. Of the top 10 finishers, nine set off with the lead group, the other one minute behind.

Two related handicapping problems that haunt the Dipsea to this day surfaced. One was giving too great a handicap to a talented but little known runner; William Joyner, who just 16 months later would beat outright all the best Northern California distance men in the West Coast's first marathon, started with the maximum handicap group. The other was that the winning "clock" time of 40:35 (Joyner's actual running time less handicap) was too low to give a scratch runner any chance of winning. The clock times of the first two finishers from 1907 remain 1-2 on the all-time Dipsea list.

The 17-year-old Joyner, a San Francisco native and son of Irish immigrants, was a recent graduate of Lick High School. The slightly built (5'6") Joyner had trained hard for the Dipsea. He ran over Twin Peaks every day, and on the Dipsea Trail on Sundays. Joyner and 18 other finishers were members of a new club, the Siaplamat (Tamalpais spelled backwards) Indians. The club would produce three consecutive titleists. Runner-up Frank Bartosh, who closed to within 25 seconds of Joyner at the tape after starting a minute behind him, was a teammate.

John Hassard, the two-time defending champion, was the only scratch runner. He started a hopeless 4 1/2 minutes after the next closest runner, Otto Boeddiker, who would win the best time award. Indeed, only five other runners set off within ten minutes of Hassard.

The *Examiner* described Hassard's fate: "[Hassard had] to make his own pace, with no one in sight until the hardest part of the trip had been covered. He had reached the Lone Pine before he passed any of the handicap men, and the long journey had its effect. Coming down the 'hog's back,' [the Steep Ravine bypass no longer used today] Hassard slipped, and being unable to regain his feet on the steep, slippery slope he slid over a hundred yards, severely bruising his leg. He was able to continue, however, and finished in good shape." Hassard came in 31st, 6:19 behind the winner.

Joyner was the third teenager to win in the Race's three editions. Ironically, an outcry over the difficulty of the previous year's Dipsea almost prompted a ban on runners under 18. (Such bans on younger runners would appear on and off, both loosely and strictly enforced, over the next six decades.) In the *Chronicle's* account: "After the race last year considerable criticism was thrust upon members of the Dipsea Indians for encouraging athletes of tender years to enter this severe trial and thus subject themselves to overtaxation and probable permanent injury. It was figured that although the course was not too long the grades encountered were too steep and called for an amount of endurance that is not generally found in the youngsters."

On the other side of the age spectrum, newspaper accounts gloried over the effort of Ed Hartley, who finished 5th at age 49. Indeed, the *Examiner* (which mistakenly had Hartley as 54) said, "The performance of Hartley is one of the most remarkable feats ever accomplished by a man of his age." Hartley, a one-time champion swimmer from San Francisco, ran 57:35, a time surpassed by only five other runners.

There was an unusual nearly five minute gap behind Hartley before the next bunched pack came in. They were headed by A. Codington, from now gone Cogswell High School (San Francisco), claiming the high school trophy.

The finish line was moved to the intersection of Bolinas Highway (today's Shoreline Highway) and Calle del Mar, in front of Airey's Hotel and Store. This would remain the finish for every Dipsea (except 1954) until 1964. The still-standing building is today occupied by the Becker's By The Beach grocery store (known as Ed's Superette until 1993). Elimination of the final debilitating run on the beach was welcomed by all the racers then and for ever more. The *Chronicle* reported, "All of the runners finished perfectly free from any evident distress . . . This was no doubt due to the elimination of the finish on the sandy beach."

1. William Joyner, 55:35 (15) [:25]
2. Frank Bartosh, 55:00 (14) **2nd best time**
3. Robert Howden, 56:20 (15)
4. Frank Kispert, 56:20 (15)
5. Ed Hartley, 57:35 (15)
6. A. Codington, 1:02:17 (15) **1st HS**
7. S.V. Connolly, 1:02:32 (15)
8. F. Coffey, 1:02:35 (15)
9. C. Fisk, 1:02:55 (15)
10. M. Hartman, 1:01:33 (13)
12. Otto Boeddiker, 53:35 (4:30) **best time**
44 finishers; fog lifted during Race, cool

4th Dipsea
September 13, 1908

George Behrmann, previously little known in the running community, won after a battle with William Howden. Behrmann was given a nine minute handicap, one less than the newly reduced maximum of 10. Upon learning this, his Siaplamat Indians teammates immediately predicted him to win.

Howden, beginning a distinguished Dipsea career that would climax with a best time award in 1918, started two minutes later. He caught Behrmann but was repassed. Behrmann won by 80 seconds.

Third in was George Hartwell, older brother of a man soon to become one of the greatest of all Dipsea runners, Mason Hartwell. (Another brother, Ben, is over 100 years old and still living in Mill Valley. There is also a surviving sister, Florence.)

Much interest centered on the three scratch runners. Two-time champion John Hassard fared poorly, running 1:01:25 and finishing 63rd. J.B. "Soldier" King was 32nd. The *Examiner* reported, "[King] was not at his best, his duties in the army requiring him to fire sixty rounds in target practice on Saturday, which did not improve his chances." Cornelius "Con" Connelly showed up at the last minute, too late to enter. He was allowed to run, solely to try for the course record. But his 53:05 failed to even win the best time award. That went, for the second of three successive years, to Otto Boeddiker, a San Francisco plumber.

William Joyner ran 15 seconds faster than in his winning effort effort of the year before but, with seven fewer handicap minutes, came in 20th.

The finish line crowd was estimated at 1,000.
❑ Earlier in the year, Redwood Canyon was donated by William Kent to a somewhat reluctant United States government and became Muir Woods National Monument. Kent had purchased

Siaplamat Indians, strongest team of the earliest Dipseas, celebrating on beach after 1908 Race. Winner George Behrmann is kneeling and Con Connelly, 1905 best time winner, is at left. (Courtesy Linda Chirone estate)

the canyon and its tract of virgin redwoods in 1905 to thwart a plan to dam Redwood Creek for a reservoir. If the dam had been built, it would have inundated Muir Woods and likely ended the Dipsea Race.

❑ *Chronicle* sportswriter William O. McGeehan's poem, *The Song of the Dipsea Trail*, which is reproduced at the front of this book, first appeared at Race time.

1. George Behrmann, 54:20 (9) [1:20]
2. William Howden, 53:40 (7) **2nd best time**
3. George Hartwell, 57:00 (10)
4. Elliot Craig, 54:55 (7:30)
5. Angus McMillan, 57:15 (9)
6. Arthur Mauerhan, 58:11 (9)
7. Nelson Schou, 59:35 (10)
8. Otto Boeddiker, 51:45 (2) **best time**
9. J.J. McShane, 1:00:15 (10)
10. Loyed Logan, 59:00 (8:30)
12. William Maghetti, 1:00:45 **1st HS**
77 finishers; sunny, fog at Lone Tree

5th Dipsea
September 5, 1909

The 112 finishers were a high for the Dipsea, not surpassed until 1963. Various newspaper accounts said: "At no time in the history of athletics on the Coast have so many contestants been entered in one race"; "[The Dipsea] is now recognized as the biggest event of the year in California's out-of-door sports"; and "[The Dipsea is] the greatest race in the West."

As in the previous year, an unknown Siaplamat Indian—one headline labeled him "Winner Unknown to Athletic World"—was awarded what his teammates knew to be too generous a handicap and won the race. This time it was Basil Spurr. He received eight minutes, "the safety handicap" for runners without a known cross country racing record, then ran 55:00 to win by 30 seconds.

The finish was actually tighter. Spurr was locked in a duel with Cloverdale's Charles Wallbridge as both came down the last hill (which was visible to finish line spectators). But Wallbridge suddenly gave up the fight, later citing painful blisters.

Third was the colorful Isaac Day of Bolinas. A 51-year-old veteran of every Dipsea, Day ran in full street dress, including a hat. He had led the race until Lone Tree.

There was a thrilling battle for the high school trophy, in an era when many San Francisco area schools sent competitors. Will Henderson of the City's Humboldt School just outsprinted, by one second, William Maghetti of San Rafael High, winner of the title the previous year.

Two men started scratch; two-time champion John Hassard and two-time fastest-time winner Otto Boeddiker. Boeddiker prevailed, and again won the time award, but his 51:46 got him only 21st. Only in 1929 would a best time winner finish farther back. Hassard was well behind (66th) with his 58:02, but seven seconds in front of defending champion George Behrmann (59:39, 1:30hc). Just ahead of both of them was 1907 winner William Joyner (58:10, 1hc). It would be the last time every champion was in the same Dipsea. Future (1911) winner Albert Gorse was 7th.

Over half the field (60 runners) came in within 10 minutes of the first finisher. This was common in early Dipseas, unheard of in recent years.

1. Basil Spurr, 55:00 (8) [:30]
2. Charles Wallbridge, 56:30 (9)
3. Isaac Day, 58:40 (10)
4. John Salmi, 54:05 (5)
5. Charles Walters, 57:40 (8)
6. William Rehberg, 54:42 (5)
7. Albert Gorse, 57:43 (8)
8. John Johnson, 52:55 (3)
9. Floyd Van Tassell, 1:00:03 (10)
10. Wayne Russell, 55:11 (5)
13. Will Henderson, 1:00:30 (10) **1st HS**
18. William Howden, 52:12 (1) **2nd best time**
21. Otto Boeddiker, 51:46 (0) **best time**
112 finishers; cool and windy, fog at higher elevations

6th Dipsea
September 18, 1910

Two of the greatest Northern California runners of all-time, Oliver Millard and Mason Hartwell, made their Dipsea debuts. Millard would later win three Cross-City (Bay to Breakers) races and finish second twice. Hartwell would win seven Dipsea best-time awards. Their great 1910 confrontation ushered in an era of even higher level competition to the Dipsea.

This year it was Millard, a San Francisco draftsman, first to the tape. He was described in the *Chronicle's* story as "unknown in the world of athletics and claiming no affiliation with a club or asociation," and as a "figure in black running upper and white knickers presenting a mysterious appearance to the many enthusiasts along the route who endeavored to establish his identity." Hartwell, competing for the Olympic Club, was already known in running circles; in 1907, at Oakland High School, he had run a sensational 4:35 mile.

Millard had been assigned a six minute handicap—the maximum had been reduced to eight. He needed just about all of it to hold off Hartwell. Hartwell, with a 3 1/2 minute handicap, had passed everyone but Millard by Lone Tree. There then ensued a splendid two-man race, as "cheers from those who welcomed [Hartwell's Olympic Club] Winged 'O' were opposed by the shouts of unbiased spectators who were inspired at the sight of the unknown showing the way to the tape." The bespectacled Millard ran strongly to secure a 13-second victory. Millard would himself then join the Olympic Club and was later bestowed an honorary life membership.

Hartwell had to content himself with second place and the first of his fastest-time trophies. That trophy, nearly as shiny as the day it was awarded, still resides in the home of Mason's son Thomas.

The *Chronicle* also noted that Hartwell ran back "over the trail shortly after" finishing.

Walter Andres of the Tamalpais Athletic Club, successor to the disbanded Siaplamat Indians, was 3rd. Mason Hartwell's older brother George was 4th and another brother, William, was 42nd. Basil Spurr, the defending champion, finished 13th (56:22, 3hc). Otto Boeddiker, who had won the three previous best-time titles, was the only scratch runner. On an off-day (the *Chronicle* says he had "met with an accident," and this would be his last Dipsea), he was 26th (56:43). John Hassard, champion the first two years, missed his first Dipsea. He never ran another, though returned to watch the race as late as 1965.

1. Oliver Millard, 55:00 (6) [:13]
2. Mason Hartwell, 52:43 (3:30) **best time**
3. Walter Andres, 57:00 (7)
4. George Hartwell, 56:30 (5:30)
5. Harold Young, 58:30 (7) **1st HS**
6. A. Gustafson, 58:01 (6:30)
7. James McGee, 53:33 (1:30)
8. William Howden, 53:00 (:30) **2nd best time**
9. Al Jung, 58:01 (5:30)
10. F. Refford, 58:33 (6)
80 finishers; pleasant, mild

7th Dipsea
September 18, 1911

Once more it was an obscure but fast-improving club runner (the *Chronicle* said he was "practically unknown in local athletics"), who broke the tape. Albert Gorse was assigned a six minute handicap—eight was again the maximum—after an up-and-down Dipsea career of 7th place (57:43, 8hc) in 1909 and then 49th (1:04:45, 5hc) in 1910.

Twelve runners started ahead of Gorse, a butcher who ran for San Francisco's Visitacion Valley Athletic Club. Starting a minute after him was a huge group, 73 of the 112 entrants. The South San Francisco resident took the lead early. Gorse then toughed it out in the heat—it was the hottest Dipsea to date—to hold off all pursuers for a 30-second win.

Next was Paul Westerlund, described as a "former Swedish-American star [who] has been competing in long distance races for some time past." Third was Mason Hartwell. His 52:01, 42 seconds faster than in 1910, earned him fastest-time award #2.

Next was Robert Howden, Jr. His cousin William Howden, one of the four scratch runners, was 7th (and had the Race's second fastest time for the fourth year in a row). However, Robert's brother Watson collapsed, unable to finish, 100 yards from the end. Mason Hartwell's older brother George was 5th after suffering a fall of his own early in the race.

Two Navy runners from the *U.S.S. Colorado*, W.D. Blumenthal and J.S. Richards, were 9th and 14th, respectively. Defending champion Oliver Millard came in 11th (57:14, 2hc). Basil Spurr, the '09 king, was well behind (1:06:40, 3hc). Gorse's teammate William Rehberg, a scratch runner, was 13th (55:30). The final scratch contestant, who had requested to start with the last group, was Randolph Munro of Berkeley; he failed to finish.

The *Daily Mail-Call* reported, "the whole population of Bolinas had turned out to root for [Isaac] "Pop" Day, the youth of 53 summers and a hero of every Dipsea race since their inception." He finished 18th.

The first high schooler, H.L. Morton of Mountain View High School, was 23rd after receiving an exceptionally low handicap of one minute. He was noted as a "champion of the Academic League."

The extreme heat, which slowed the runners, proved a boon to the post-race festivities. The *Examiner* wrote, "Willow Camp had seldom seen such a crowd as gathered to enjoy the day and watch the runners finish the race. When the eighty runners who had completed the course and the large gathering of Dipsea Indians and other enthusiasts were ready for a dip in the ocean, the supply of bathing suits ran out and many of the boys went into the surf in the running costumes which they wore on the mountain trail. The beach looked like the [San Francisco] Cliff House beach on a busy Sunday afternoon."

1. Albert Gorse, 57:00 (6) [:30]
2. Paul Westerlund, 55:30 (4)
3. Mason Hartwell, 52:01 (0) **best time**
4. Robert Howden, Jr., 58:35 (6)
5. George Hartwell, 57:15 (4)
6. William Johnson, 58:30 (5)
7. William Howden, 53:34 (0) **2nd best time**
8. John Salmi, 57:30 (3:30)
9. W.D. Blumenthal, 1:00:11 (6)
10. Charles Craig, 59:47 (5)
23. H.L. Morton, 58:47 (1) **1st HS**
80 finishers; extremely hot

8th Dipsea
September 16, 1912

In one of the Dipsea's landmark efforts, Mason Hartwell ran a course record 47:56, a time that would be bettered just once (by Norman Bright in 1937) over the next 48 years. But even such an extraordinary run did not secure a win; Hartwell finished 3rd. It was a theme that would be repeated; no course record effort after Hassard's in 1906 would produce a win.

First in was Berkeley High School's Donald Dunn. Like all previous champions, Dunn was relatively unknown in the "elite" running circles of the day. So he received a six-minute handicap, two short of the maximum, yet ran a time, 52:36, that was bettered by only three other runners.

Dunn knew the course. His parents had a summer house in Willow Camp (family members still live in Stinson Beach) and he practiced diligently on the trail for at least the six previous weeks. He had also run in the 1911 Dipsea, but had dropped out halfway through, in 5th place, when "his shoes burst."

Dunn took the lead from Fremont High's Edison Lloyd at "Echo Point, near the half-way mark" (a one-time landmark now unknown). The defending champion, Albert Gorse, who had started two minutes behind Dunn, closed to within 50 yards at Lone Tree. Dunn widened his lead going down Steep Ravine, only to be exhausted at Insult, where he began to walk. A spectator reminded him the uphill was short and the remaining distance to the finish was downhill. That, or the sight of the ocean that soon greets the runners, was enough to renew him and Dunn strided to a 70 second victory over Gorse. First to congratulate him was his sister, who had been telling the other onlookers he would win.

Four years later, Dunn would become the first Dipsea champion to die. He was killed, at age 23, fighting in France during World War I.

Hartwell's effort astonished all; no one thought the course could be covered so fast. Hartwell was the lone scratch starter. He quickly caught William Howden, who had started 30 seconds earlier and who recorded the second-best time four years in a row. Howden related, "I just reached the bottom of [the] steps when Hartwell came along with a handkerchief in one hand and a watch in the other. He went up the stairs like a deer leaping from crag to crag, and disappeared from the top step while I was busy about the middle of the flight."

According to the *Chronicle* report, Hartwell sped up Butler's Pride (beyond Redwood Creek), "As if he cared not for the laws of gravity. Men who had big handicaps were astonished to see the scratch man overtake them so early in the race, and most of them willingly gave way so that the Olympic [Club member] might have the best opportunity to break the record for the course." Hartwell passed all but four runners by Lone Tree, then two more on the following downhill. He got to within ten seconds of Gorse, whose 51:46 would have won the best-time award the three previous Dipseas, but that was it. Hartwell had knocked 1:59 off John Hassard's 1906 mark, itself a time that had been considered remarkable.

Lloyd hung on for fifth and, because the Dipsea then awarded only one trophy to a runner (and Dunn naturally received the first place prize), ended up with the high school trophy. A Stanford runner, George Branner, came in 6th. Right behind was 1910 champ Millard.

Again some of the loudest applause was reserved for Isaac Day, the colorful Bolinas character who had run every previous Dipsea in street clothes. This year, described in one account as 59 years old (but probably 54), "he actually discarded his heavy boots, his corduroy trousers, his heavy woolen shirt and his wide-brimmed felt hat" for running attire and ended up 9th.

❑ All 81 starters finished, a first for the race. The first 50 received coveted Dipsea bars.

❑ The runners raced without bib numbers; an official forgot to bring them. This error had a lasting impact; both a photograph of all starters and the Race program survive but, without bib numbers, the names and faces cannot be matched.

❑ On January 1, 1912, another point-to-point race of roughly similar distance was inaugurated in San Francisco. It was called the Cross-City; today it is known as Bay to Breakers. Because it never missed a year (the Dipsea has missed six), Bay to Breakers is now only one edition behind the Dipsea.

Cross-City also had strong Olympic Club ties; the race mirrored a long-time practice of Club members to run to Ocean Beach each New Year's Day, then dip in the frigid Pacific. The Olympic Club also captured the team title in 19 of the Cross-City's first 22 years.

The 1912 race was won by a St. Mary's College student, Robert Vlught ("va-loo"). Just two seconds behind was Oliver Millard, the 1910 Dipsea champion. The first race had 121 finishers, slightly higher than the biggest Dipsea (112 in 1909). There were 126 finishers in 1913. Then, like the Dipsea, numbers fell below 100 for decades, not to rise above again until 1964 (the Dipsea went over 100 in 1963). While the Dipsea routinely outdrew it (for example, every year from 1946 though 1968), Bay to Breakers is now often the world's largest footrace, usually with over 60,000 official entrants plus many thousands more unregistered.

Over the decades, only three men have proved fast and versatile enough to win both races, and none in the same year. They are Oliver Millard (two Dipseas and three Cross-Cities), Norman Bright (Cross-City in 1937, Dipsea in 1970) and Jim Shettler (Dipsea in 1950, Cross-City in 1952 and '62). Mary Etta Boitano, who won the 1973 Dipsea, was first woman in three Bay to Breakers (1974-76).

❑ 1912 was a key year elsewhere on Mt. Tamalpais. The Marin Municipal Water District, which now manages most of the Mountain's land (but no part of the Dipsea Trail), was formed. The original Mountain Home Inn opened. And the Tamalpais Conservation Club, which would play a key role in the creation of Mt. Tamalpais State Park, was founded.

❏ The careful medical preparations were noted in newspaper accounts. The *Chronicle* reported, "Trainer Al Lean of the Olympic Club had established a little tent hospital at the end of the course ... Every man that crossed the line was placed in Lean's hands, but his ministrations this year were confined to brief rubdowns and a few bandages for blistered feet."

1. Donald Dunn, 52:36 (6) [1:10]
2. Albert Gorse, 51:46 (4)
3. Mason Hartwell, 47:56 (0) **best time**
4. Harold Beatty, 53:06 (5)
5. Edison Lloyd, 55:22 (7) **1st HS**
6. George Branner, 57:28 (8)
7. Oliver Millard, 50:46 (1) **2nd best time**
8. J. Reading, 55:47 (6)
9. Isaac Day, 57:51 (8)
10. Charles Molinari, 55:44 (5)
81 finishers; mild

9th Dipsea
September 21, 1913

Oliver Millard matched two of John Hassard's achievements; winning the Dipsea with the fastest actual time and becoming a two-time champion. The latter feat would not be achieved again for 54 years.

Millard dominated the Race. He won by two minutes, 20 seconds. And his 51:18 was an extraordinary four minutes, 50 seconds swifter than the second best time, a margin to be topped only once (by Joe Kragel in 1950). Immediately after, Millard said, "I feel as if I could go over the course again right now in just as good a time ... I didn't have an anxious moment from start to finish."

Millard, now 29 and representing the Olympic Club, started last with a 1:30 handicap; there were no scratch runners. (Mason Hartwell, assigned scratch, did not compete.) But, because the maximum handicap was only six minutes, the lowest ever, Millard set off just 4:30 after the first group. Only two other runners, past champions Albert Gorse and Basil Spurr, had handicaps under four minutes. The other 95% of the field (56 of the 59 finishers) set off within two minutes of one another, making for a nearly "open" race.

Millard was in fifth place by Lone Tree, then descended "the almost perpendicular path that leads from the Hog's Back [the former route to the base of Steep Ravine] ... so fast that several of his competitors lost their footing trying to keep up with him." Spurr was one, hitting a rock and ending up 11th.

Millard took the lead up Insult from Charles Craig, who finished second. In only two other years, 1917 and 1966, were the first two finishers also 1-2 in actual running times.

Wint Blackwell, twin brother of Lee Blackwell, who would win in 1915, took 3rd. Gorse came in 7th. Charles Hunter, who would go on to compete

(Left) Early Dipsea aid station; woman pours water into runner's cupped hands, circa 1912. (Courtesy Mark Reese)

(Below) Finish line crowd, 1913. (Courtesy Frank Maher)

in the 1920 Olympics, win Cross-City in 1921, then become very closely associated with the Dipsea as both the Olympic Club and Race trainer, was 36th. Fred Robbins and William Higgins, two San Francisco newspapermen who wrote a popular series on Bay Area hiking trails, came in together just behind Hunter. A trail through Kent Canyon, just west of the Dipsea, was named for them. Harry Ludwig, who would win Cross-City in 1919, only managed 54th.

Approximately 75% of the runners, including finishers two through five, were listed as unattached.

❑ In 1913, another enduring Mt. Tamalpais tradition, the Mountain Play was born. The play is presented in a natural amphitheater (the stone seats were installed in the 1930's) 2,000 feet high on Tam. Music from performances (currently on six Sunday afternoons in May and June) can be heard along the Dipsea Trail near Lone Tree. Since there is now a play scheduled on Dipsea day, some runners head up after the Race to see it, making for a tradition-filled day on Tam.

❑ A few months later (January 1, 1914) Millard set a course record of 40:46.6 at the Cross-City Race. It stood until 1937, when broken by another Dipsea great, Norman Bright.

1. Oliver Millard, 51:18 (1:30) [2:20] **best time**
2. Charles Craig, 56:08 (4) **2nd best time**
3. Wint Blackwell, 58:31 (6)
4. Will Spanton, 58:51 (6)
5. James Nehar, 57:57 (5)
6. Clarence Fugua, 59:05 (6) **1st HS**
7. Albert Gorse, 56:24 (2:30)
8. George Branner, 57:36 (3:30)
9. Charles Bocchio, 58:34 (4)
10. Hy Abarinate, 60:37 (6)
59 finishers; sunny

10th Dipsea
October 11, 1914

The previous year, Dipsea organizers had cut the maximum handicap to six minutes. In 1914 they went to the opposite extreme, raising the maximum to 15 "so that lads who can only go over the course in 70 to 85 minutes should be given a chance to place well up." Two runners were awarded this unprecedented start and one, Andrew Ahern, ended up winning. His 1:01:00 was the slowest actual time to win (other than the long-course year of 1905) until 1955. It was the first time (again excluding long course years 1905 and '06) anyone running over an hour had even finished among the Race's top five.

The tall Ahern, in his first Dipsea, was unknown in the running world. Competing unattached, he led comfortably from start to finish. One newspaper account said Ahern "simply loped in front all the way." He went on to a long running and coaching career with the Olympic Club and finished third in the 1922 Cross-City.

William Johnson, starting seven minutes behind, got closest, two minutes at the finish. Johnson would continue racing the Dipsea through 1949. Basil Spurr, the '09 winner, was next. Cogswell High School's Ray Glennon took 4th, claiming the high school trophy. Wint Blackwell, whose brother Lee would win the next year, was 5th. Albert Gorse, the 1911 champ, placed 6th.

Defending champion Oliver Millard ran an excellent 49:30, the second fastest time ever recorded. But, starting as the lone scratch runner, 3 1/2 minutes after anyone else, could do no better than 7th. Including Ahern, there were thus four Dipsea champions in the top seven.

❑ The number of finishers fell to a low of 42. But an impressive seventy-four percent of them broke 65 minutes.

1. Andrew Ahern, 1:01:00 (15) [2:00]
2. William Johnson, 56:00 (8)
3. Basil Spurr, 53:10 (4:30)
4. Ray Glennon, 1:00:50 (12) **1st HS**
5. Wint Blackwell, 53:35 (4:30)
6. Albert Gorse, 52:50 (3:30) **2nd best time**
7. Oliver Millard, 49:30 (0) **best time**
8. Ray Locke, 58:00 (8)
9. Oliver Jones, 1:05:16 (15)
10. Hugh Foley, 59:25 (9)
42 finishers; sunny

11th Dipsea
October 3, 1915

Though Lee Blackwell won the Dipsea, to many observers it was Mason Hartwell who won the real race.

The 27-year-old Blackwell had trained hard for the Dipsea. He and his twin brother Wint rented a cabin at Willow Camp and made numerous practice runs, learning the trail well. Wint, who was fifth the year before, was sick Race day and did not start, leaving the family's fortunes with Lee. He started with a sizable 7 1/2 minute handicap, then turned in the day's fourth fastest actual time. The only ones to run faster were the great open runners Hartwell, two-time Dipsea and three-time Cross-City champ Oliver Millard and future (1918) Cross-City winner Edgar Stout.

Lee took the lead in Deer Park and came into Willow Camp with a comfortable one minute, 42 second margin over Stout. Indeed, the victory appeared so easy that some skeptics claimed the identical twins each only ran half the distance, Lee running to Lone Tree and Wint finishing. But Wint was confirmed as having been at Willow Camp cheering his brother to the line.

Meanwhile, Hartwell and Oliver Millard who, between them, had won the previous five best time awards, were going head to head from scratch for the first time. Indeed, the Olympic Club teammates were the only scratch runners. No one else started within three minutes.

Hartwell built a lead on the uphills, Millard would gain on the downslopes. The October 1915 *Olympian* magazine said Millard was, "long and rangy, with great driving power on the flat, and not too little on the grade, but just a little less than his rival [Hartwell]." The pair caught everyone but Blackwell and Stout. Millard got closest to Hartwell at the base of Steep Ravine, but Mason pulled away on Insult. Hartwell then continued to pad his lead and finished 3rd overall, 45 seconds ahead of Millard. It was his fourth of seven best time titles.

❏ Runner-up Stout had also been second, to Millard, in that year's Cross-City.

❏ Albert Gorse, the 1911 champion who finished 6th, had a handicap of three minutes, 15 seconds. This was the first time quarter-minute handicaps were used; the practice was discontinued after 1918. It was also Gorse's sixth top 10 finish, then a record.

❏ Isaac Day, the only runner to do all the first ten Dipseas, missed the Race.

❏ Reese was told by Carroll Locke that Hannes Kolehmainen, the Finn who had won three gold medals at the 1912 Olympics (5,000 and 10,000 meters and cross country) and would win another (marathon) in 1920, ran the Dipsea Trail in 1915. Kolehmainen was in the area for a road race, which he won, marking San Francisco's Pan-Pacific Exposition and was invited to Marin by local runners. He then declined to return for the Dipsea, starting the fanciful legend that it was too tough for him.

1. Lee Blackwell, 56:00 (7:30) [1:42]
2. Edgar Stout, 54:12 (4)
3. Mason Hartwell, 50:40 (0) **best time**
4. Oliver Millard, 51:25 (0) **2nd best time**
5. R.B. Gelding, 1:01:32 (10)
6. Albert Gorse, 55:19 (3:15)
7. N.E. Dundas, 1:00:17 (7:30)
8. A.M. Portost, 57:19 (4:30)
9. Lloyd Perkins, 1:00:08 (7)
10. Frank Woodside, 57:50 (4)
15. E. Schwarz, 1:05:43 (10) **1st HS**
63 finishers; sunny and warm

12th Dipsea
September 17, 1916

Once more the winner, Henry A. Anderes, was labeled as "unknown," both to the press, which printed absolutely no details on him, and to the Dipsea handicappers, who gave him the maximum handicap. He was apparently a Swiss-born, 23-year-old.

The Race was among the closest ever. Thirteen men started with the new, reduced maximum of 12 minutes and three of them finished 1-2-3, just fifteen seconds apart. The trio—Anderes and high schoolers Maurice Roach (Fremont H.S.) and J. Fredericks (Mission H.S.)—ran fairly closely the whole way. They had no one to catch, and no one threatened them from behind. Anderes pulled away late from Roach for a narrow win.

In 4th was Alfred Pinther. Pinther became the second head of the Mountain Play Association and his name is memorialized on a plaque at the theater.

Fifth was another high schooler, E. Schwarz (Oakland Evening H.S.). Since Roach and Fredericks received place trophies, Schwarz was given the Van Vliet high school award for the second year in a row.

Sixth was Ray Locke, 58. The San Francisco letter carrier ran in 12 of the first 20 Dipseas. Ray's son Carroll, who saw the '08 race, was interviewed by Reese in 1979.

Two more high schoolers—Hood of Humboldt Evening and Morrison of Lick—made for a record total of five in the top 10.

Newspaper accounts gloried over the effort of Walter "Grizzly" Jones, who recorded the day's fastest time. The Stockton runner had won a race up Mt. Tamalpais in June, so was known locally. Yet he had never been in the Dipsea, or even run the course. To make matters worse, he made the long journey from Stockton on Race morning and "had practically no sleep." Jones' stride was described as "that grizzly gallop eating up great distances out of the dusty road." (The grizzly bear is now a symbol of the Dipsea, depicted on the winner's trophy.) Jones ran 51:18 and finished 12th with his 30 second handicap; everyone ahead had at least a 10 minute handicap.

Oliver Millard, one of the two scratch runners (with William Howden), was 24th with the second best time.

Defending champion Lee Blackwell ran the third fastest time but, with his handicap cut by five minutes, only managed 29th. William O'Callaghan, a future winner (1920), made his Dipsea debut, coming in seven seconds in front of Millard.

❑ The traditional post-race lunch for the runners was held in Willow Camp's new Sea Beach Hotel.

❑ The "Al Coney Trophy" for the overall winner, awarded since the first Dipsea, was replaced by a new "perpetual trophy . . . that must be won in three consecutive races before finally awarded." No one would achieve that feat until Sal Vasquez in 1984, when the trophy had long been replaced. Each winner did, however, receive "an individual cup."

❑ There was a mention, for the first time, of runners' clothing being transported to the finish by automobile, the debut of the "sweats" van.

❑ News of the death in combat in France of Donald Dunn, the 1912 champion, had just reached the local running community and added a somber note to the morning.

1. Henry Anderes, 58:50 (12) [:12]
2. Maurice Roach, 59:02 (12) **1st HS**
3. J. Fredericks, 59:05 (12)
4. Alfred Pinther, 58:23 (10)
5. E. Schwarz, 58:46 (10)
6. Ray Locke, 1:01:00 (12)
7. F. Hood, 59:33 (10)
8. W. Haaviland, 1:02:17 (12)
9. F. Kappelmann, 1:00:24 (10)
10. J. Morrison, 1:00:35 (10)
12. Walter Jones, 51:18 (:30) **best time**
24. Oliver Millard, 52:24 (0) **2nd best time**
74 finishers; apparently foggy and wet

13th Dipsea
September 17, 1917

Reese, writing in 1979, called Mason Hartwell "the greatest all time Dipsea runner." He set a course record in 1912 that stood for 25 years, and was then not beaten again for another 33 years. He captured a record seven best-time awards; no one garnered more than three until Mike McManus over six decades later. But it was only in 1917 that Hartwell won.

An epic battle was foreseen as three great runners were pitted from scratch: Hartwell; Oliver Millard, who had already won two Dipseas; and Walter Jones, fastest time winner the year before. All three wore the "Winged O" of the Olympic Club. With the maximum handicap cut back to a more catchable 10 minutes, the duel among the scratch men took on even more significance.

But it proved no contest. Hartwell pulled away from Millard early and then Jones dropped out, the victim of a faulty pair of untested, custom-made shoes that fell apart during the run. Millard had the day's second fastest time and was runner-up. But Hartwell ran 2:48 faster to score a huge victory, the Race's biggest winning margin until 1952. There was another full two minute gap to third place. And newspaper accounts said Hartwell looked "fresh as a daisy."

Hartwell became the first winner from scratch. No one duplicated the feat until Walter Deike in 1952. And just three other runners have done it since; Fernando Leon ('58), Peter McArdle ('62) and Carl Jensen ('66). In only one other year, 1966, would scratch runners finish 1-2.

Two more minutes passed before the third-place runner, Victor Hay Chapman, arrived. Chapman, representing Commercial Evening, took the high school trophy. Two years later he would win the Dipsea outright.

Hartwell's time of 51:39 was almost four minutes off his record; Millard's three minutes from his best. An all-time low of only three runners broke an hour (23 had just the year before). The falloff was apparently due to exceptionally hot weather. Hartwell reported, "Some of [the runners were] hanging to fences to rest. They didn't start up even when I went by."

❑ The crowd of spectators, over 2,000, was called "the biggest on record."

❑ Awards were presented the following Wednesday at the Olympic Club.

❑ The press made much of their ride to and from the finish in "Al Mills' . . . Kissel car."

1. Mason Hartwell, 51:39 (0) [2:48] **best time**
2. Oliver Millard, 54:27 (0) **2nd best time**
3. Victor Chapman, 1:03:27 (7) **1st HS**
4. William Howden, 58:51 (2)
5. James Woodside, 1:02:03 (5)
6. Philip Lopez, 1:06:15 (8)
7. Richard Denton, 1:06:39 (8)
8. Edgar Jacobson, 1:09:08 (9)
9. John Mauras, 1:07:45 (7:30)
10. Martin Kemmerle, 1:08:54 (8)
68 finishers; exceptionally hot

14th Dipsea
September 29, 1918

Yet another runner labeled as "unknown" and "a dark horse" came in first. This time it was San Francisco native Percy Gilbert, 20, representing the Oakland YMCA.

Gilbert had been inspired to train for the Dipsea after seeing Oliver Millard training on the course—Gilbert was a long-time hiker on Mt. Tam—some years before. Awarded a handicap of 8:30, close to the maximum of ten, Gilbert was left with only one runner to catch out of Steep Ravine. Here is his own account, as related to Reese in 1979, six years before his death:

Leaving the Lone Tree area and down to the creek below, there were a couple of fellows just up from the creek and they had a pitcher of water and splashed my face with some and gave me a drink. They pointed up the trail to another runner [the Olympic Club's Clifford Carroll, who had started a minute ahead] and said he was all in and to go after him . . . I passed him on the ranch trail [beyond White Gate] and soon dropped down to the road below . . . I called on my second wind and let out to the finish and wasn't pressed by Carroll at this point . . . It was a nice feeling to finish through a crowd of spectators who cheered me on to the finish line.

Gilbert's victory margin over Carroll was 31 seconds. Carroll, in turn, finished just one second ahead of Lane McMillan.

Ray Locke, at 60 probably the oldest finisher yet, came in 6th and was roundly applauded. Locke's 58:57 meant he "ran under his age" (time in minutes below age in years), a feat to be matched only by Norman Bright (in 1970 and '71) and Sal Vasquez (1993) in Dipsea history.

American involvement in The Great War was at its peak—the headline on a pre-Race story read, "Kaiser Can't Stop Dipsea Indians"—and at least three past champions were now in the military. They were William Joyner, Henry Anderes and Basil Spurr (who ran anyhow). Donald Dunn had already been killed in France. Much attention was given to a donation wired from the European front by Olympic Clubber Lt. Frank Marisch to finance a special trophy for the first enlisted man to finish. The trophy was captured by the Army's Martin Kemmerle, 18th overall, of Fort McDowell (Angel Island). A separate Navy prize proved a bit sticky as there was debate over "whether a marine is a sailor." The issue was resolved with trophies to both Al Pinther (Marines) and "Sailor" Fred Murphy.

The Olympic Club's Pete Gerhardt finished 59th. Gerhardt had been the oldest sprinter (36) ever to represent the United States in the Olympic Games, in Stockholm in 1912.

William Howden, who had achieved the second fastest time in four of his previous nine Dipseas, finally won the coveted best time trophy. But his 54:38 would prove to be the slowest time to win the award (outside of the long-course year of 1905) until 1940. Howden finished 14th.

❑ There were no starters with handicaps of under two minutes after scratch man Oliver Millard withdrew.

❑ The Race started late, almost 30 minutes beyond the scheduled 10 a.m.

❑ The *Chronicle* reported, "The committee of Winged-O [Olympic Club] men in charge of arrangements for the [Dipsea] will exercise every possible precaution against allowing men unfitted for the struggle to participate." The newspaper also carried a map of the route which showed the distance as 6.7 miles.

❑ Earlier in the year, on April 21, the first Women's Dipsea Hike—a pioneering event in the history of women's sports in the United States—was held. One hundred seventy-seven women participated, more than in the men's Dipsea. Winner Edith Hickman's time was 1:18:48, faster than that recorded by five men in the 1918 Dipsea.

1. Percy Gilbert, 55:56 (8:30) [:31]
2. Clifford Carroll, 57:27 (9:30)
3. Lane McMillan, 56:58 (9)
4. Hugh O'Neill, 55:46 (7:30)
5. Bruno Saredio, 57:48 (9)
6. Ray Locke, 58:57 (10)
7. Al Washauer, 55:58 (5:15)
8. John Mauras, 57:47 (7)
9. Al Perfoss, 55:59 (5)
10. Ralph Ebner, 1:00:04 (9)
14. William Howden, 54:38 (2:30) **best time**
17. Harry Ludwig, 55:01 (2:00) **2nd best time**
23. William Crockett, 1:00:45 (7) **1st HS**
80 finishers; sunny, mild

15th Dipsea
September 21, 1919

California Senator James Phelan donated a handsome trophy for the winning team and that started decades of lively club competition in the Dipsea. Scoring was, and remains, by place (not time) with the positions of a team's first five finishers added together. (In modern cross country scoring, the places of finishers who are not on any team, or are on incomplete teams, are not counted; the Dipsea has followed this rule some years and not in others.)

Immediately several of San Francisco's strong Italian athletic clubs entered teams, swelling the finisher list to a then all-time high of 117. And one, the Unione Sportiva Italiano (USI), just organized a few months earlier, scored an epic upset. They bested the Olympic Club, not only long the West's most prominent athletic club but the founders and organizers of the Dipsea and with the largest team (18 finishers). But the Italians—they would later recruit non-Italians—placed all their top five men in the first 20 (including 2nd and 3rd) and triumphed handily, 57 points to the Olympic Club's 126.

The Race was won by Victor Hay Chapman. Though he had finished 3rd in 1917 and was called "the Stanford distance champion" in the *Examiner's* preview for 1918 (when he had a 4:30 handicap but did not run), he was now somehow awarded a 6:30 handicap. The maximum was ten. Chapman proceeded to turn in the day's second fastest time.

Chapman was the 23-year-old son of the *Chronicle's* golf editor Hay Chapman. He had "trained faithfully, when he hasn't been working at his wartime trade as an aviator" (*Examiner*). Chapman set off together with USI runners Primo Caredio and Gaetano Capaletti, who would finish 2-3. The trio would turn in three of the day's four fastest times. But it was Chapman, who had run the Dipsea before

while the Italians had not, pulling well away to win by 69 seconds. Chapman received, along with his trophy, a special medal brought back by Olympic Clubber Dr. Henry Abraham from the just-ended war in Europe.

Fourth was Alameda High School's Clifford Vis, one place ahead of schoolmate Robert Rutherford. The defending champion Percy Gilbert ran 2:10 faster than in 1918 but, losing four handicap minutes, was 7th.

The day's best time was turned in by one of Northern California's greatest distance runners ever, William Churchill. He would run for the United States in both the 1920 and 1924 Olympic marathons and win Cross-City four times. Starting as the lone scratch runner, Churchill came in 11th, the first Olympic Club member to finish.

❑ Ed Hartley and Ray Locke, both said to be 61, set new records as oldest finishers. Hartley was 35th and Locke 71st.

❑ In June of 1919 a new race was added to the regional calendar, the Statutos, celebrating Italy's national "Statute Day." It too survives (held a week before the Dipsea), never having missed a year. It is still organized by the San Francisco Athletic Club, an Italian club in North Beach. The original eight-mile route has recently been replaced by an eight kilometer one.

1. Victor Chapman, 52:46 (6:30) [1:09]
2nd best time
2. Primo Caredio, 53:55 (6:30)
3. Gaetano Capeletti, 54:06 (6:30)
4. Clifford Vis, 55:22 (7:30) **1st HS**
5. Robert Rutherford, 54:59 (6)
6. Oliver Albright, 57:31 (8:30)
7. Percy Gilbert, 53:46 (4:30)
8. Jose Sequeria, 56:09 (6:30)
9. Marchant Buttery, 1:00:10 (10)
10. Amadeo Tomasini, 54:13 (4)
11. William Churchill, 50:14 (0) **best time**
117 finishers; foggy
Team Unione Sportiva Italiano: Caredio, Capeletti, Ottorino Scribante (14th), Natale Fiora (18th) and N. Emenegildo (20th)

Third flight of steps, 1920. (California Alpine Club)

16th Dipsea
September 26, 1920

The 1920 Race marked a high water mark in participation. Buoyed by dozens of runners from San Francisco-based Italian running clubs, records were set for entries (167), starters (124) and finishers (121). These totals would not be surpassed for another 44 years. Indeed, there were not again even 100 finishers until 1963. There also had been a high of 305 starters in the Women's Dipsea Hike four months earlier.

For the second successive year, a runner who started with a sizable handicap turned in the day's second fastest time and scored an easy victory. Now it was 24-year-old William O'Callaghan, running for the Unione Sportiva Italiano (USI) club.

O'Callaghan, whose parents had both been born in Ireland (although the 1920 *Chronicle* account called him "Irish-Italian"), was raised in an orphanage in Watsonville, CA. He began running by accident. A close friend was scheduled to participate in a race but fell ill. O'Callaghan tried on his friend's shoes, found they fit, ran and enjoyed himself.

His talent emerged quickly. While still a teenager, he was recruited as an athletic member of the Olympic Club and was part of their winning team in the 1916 Cross-City. He then went off to Europe with the military in World War I, where he was injured. He stayed in Europe an extra year, running for an Army team. When O'Callaghan finally returned to San Francisco in 1920, he was literally barred, apparently by mistake, from reentering the Olympic Club. So he shifted his loyalties to the predominantly Italian USI club.

O'Callaghan, out of local competition for several years, received a five-minute handicap; 10 was the maximum. He proceeded to run a 51:30, which would have captured the best time prize at all but four previous Dipseas. And O'Callaghan appeared comfortable in his effort. He got particularly sweet revenge by leading USI to the team trophy in a very close competition over the Olympic Club, both having four men in the top 15. The Olympians then tried to lure O'Callaghan back but he would not forgive the earlier slight.

Watson Howden, cousin of perennial contender William Howden, started a minute after O'Callaghan and finished 2nd, 1:14 behind at the tape. Several historic Dipsea Trail photographs taken by Watson Howden appear in Reese's book. Third-placer William Maghetti, who had won the high school trophy in 1908, was another 49 seconds back.

Mason Hartwell won his sixth best-time award in six tries. Starting once again as the lone scratch runner, the Olympic Club star turned in a 49:57, the fourth best time yet recorded. Hartwell finished 8th.

The defending champion, Victor Chapman, turned a spike on his shoe while still on Throckmorton. He stopped to try to repair it, then gamely limped in 39th. Other former champions also fared poorly—Percy Gilbert (29th), Henry Anderes (43rd) and Andrew Ahern (45th).

Paul Nieman, who would finish 2nd in the 1921 Cross-City on January 1, was 17th and part of the winning USI team. O'Callaghan would end up fourth in that same Cross-City after injuring his leg in the interim.

Isaac Day, the colorful veteran of the earliest Dipseas, returned to race for the last time at age 62. He finished 105th (1:11:41, 5:30hc).

1. William O'Callaghan, 51:30 (5) [1:14]
2nd best time
2. Watson Howden, 51:44 (4)
3. William Maghetti, 55:03 (6:30)
4. Giovanni Cariani, 55:48 (7)
5. Michele Mulas, 55:53 (7)
6. Granville Edmonds, 59:12 (9:30)
7. C.C. Frost, 55:20 (5:30)
8. Mason Hartwell, 49:57 (0) **best time**
9. Lane McMillan, 54:44 (4:30)
10. Charles Ludekins, 53:56 (3:30)
37. Bert Hooper, 1:01:59 (7) **1st HS**
121 finishers; "perfect" weather
Team Unione Sportiva Italiano: O'Callaghan, Cariani, Mulas, Natale Fiora (13th) and Paul Nieman (17th)

17th Dipsea
September 18, 1921

Dan Quinlan won in his first Dipsea. It remains unclear, however, what his time or margin of victory was, as newspaper accounts list a certainly wrong running time.

Quinlan was described as "unknown" in the racing world and as "only a youngster" in Race stories. He was therefore awarded a handicap of nine minutes, one less than the maximum.

Quinlan took the lead for good early, just beyond the top of the steps, after passing the ten runners who had started ahead of him. Quinlan was then apparently unpressed to the end, running solo in the rain over a muddy course.

But his actual time as listed in all the newspapers and in subsequent Dipsea programs, 59:25, has to be in error; it would have earned him only 5th place. (All accounts, and the program, agree his handicap was indeed nine minutes.) If Quinlan's time was 58:25, his victory margin would have been only five seconds yet no account talked of a tight finish. Also, since the *Chronicle* account said, "the race run by [Quinlan] yesterday proved he is one of the best Dipsea runners developed in several years," and that he would be noted by local clubs—he was indeed recruited into the Olympic Club for the following Dipsea—his time was likely among the faster ones in the Race. So Quinlan's running time may have been anywhere from 53:25 to 57:25. I'll use the conservative latter figure. (Also, although Quinlan was called "Dan" in next-day news stories, he was listed as "Douglas" in several future Dipsea programs.)

After Quinlan, the top finishers were tightly bunched, closer even than in modern races when many times the number of runners compete. Only one minute, 47 seconds separated places two through 11.

Second was Robert Rutherford, who recorded the day's second fastest time. He ran unattached and was also described as a "youngster" and a "boy"; two years earlier he had finished fifth running for Alameda Evening High School. Next was Burton Hooper, who had won the high school trophy the year before and was still a student at San Francisco's Humboldt High. Since Hooper claimed the third place prize (the AAU rule of awarding only one trophy per runner was still in force), the high school trophy went to C. Green, who finished 20th.

But "the real honors of the great race," in the words of the *Chronicle*, went to William Churchill. Churchill, now 33, had run the Olympic marathon in Antwerp the year before. "The Olympic Club Wonder," as he was dubbed, ran 50:40 over a course that was "slime and mud covered the entire seven miles." It was 2:20 faster than anyone else and, given the conditions, considered one of the Dipsea's greatest efforts ever. As one of three scratch runners, he finished 6th. The other scratch men were Paul Neiman, Cross-City runner-up that year, 27th (53:50), and defending champion William O'Callaghan, slowing over two-and-a-half minutes to finish 29th (54:08).

Ray Locke became, at age 63, the oldest finisher yet (26th in 1:03:43 with a 10-minute handicap). The 1918 champion Percy Gilbert was 14th (53:48, 1:30hc) and 1916 winner Henry Anderes was 46th (1:02:48, 5hc).

William Magner finished 42nd (1:03:45, 6:30hc). Magner would win in 1930. He would also finish the Dipsea as late as 1984, making for a record span of 63 years (matched by Jack Kirk in 1993).

❏ The majority of the field, including the first five finishers, ran unattached. That left only two complete teams, the Olympic Club and Unione Sportiva Italiano. After a close finish, both initially claimed the team trophy. There was a delay of several days before the award went to the Olympians.

1. Dan Quinlan, 57:25? (9) [1:05?]
2. Robert Rutherford, 53:00 (3:30)
2nd best time (tie)
3. Bert Hooper, 54:15 (4:30) **1st HS**
4. Charles Ludekins, 53:32 (3:30)
5. Joseph Mancuso, 59:30 (9)
6. William Churchill, 50:40 (0) **best time**
7. Cam Caldera, 56:47 (6)
8. Fred Kienzle, 57:55 (7)
9. Watson Howden, 53:00 (2) **2nd best time (tie)**
10. Amadeo Tomasini, 54:06 (3)
Team Olympic Club: Churchill, Kienzle, William Maghetti (18th), Hugh O'Neil (34th) and John Lobig (50th)
77 finishers; rain, muddy

18th Dipsea
September 17, 1922

The 1922 Race produced one of the more exciting of all Dipsea finishes. And again it was a young, first-year Dipsea runner drawing a substantial handicap who won. This time it was Earl A. Fuller, an 18-year-old candy store employee from San Francisco's Richmond district.

C.W. Miles had started in the first 10-minute-handicap group with two other men; Humboldt Club teammate Edwin Richards (who would finish last) and 64-year-old Ray Locke (19th). Fuller set off two minutes later. Miles led all the way, until 200 yards from the finish. Then, spent, and in full sight of the spectators lining the road, he was passed by the sprinting, fresh-looking Fuller. Meanwhile Miles "was wobbling and just did stagger across the finish line." He was in the medical area for an hour before recovering.

Fuller had been trained for the Dipsea by the Olympic Club's Lane McMillan, who had finished third in 1918. Because of his job, Fuller did most of his many Dipsea runs "at night and on Sundays." He had moved into second place shortly beyond Lone Tree, after passing Victor Yamakawa.

Yamakawa, described as "a little Japanese boy, about as big as a pint of cider," held 3rd. He too was part of the winning Humboldt team, which had five men in the top ten. Reese also notes that the Dipsea's first black runner, Fred McWilliams, running for Humboldt as well, finished 36th.

The 8th place finisher was Pietro Giordanengo, who would go on to win the 1928 and '29 Cross-City races. He received the Arata trophy as first Italian.

William Churchill won his third fastest-time award in his last of three Dipseas. No one else who ran more than once would ever be undefeated in best time competition. Churchill, the lone scratch man, clocked a relatively off 53:55 and came in

Exceptional panorama taken during Women's Dipsea Hike, circa 1920. Runners visible for nearly two miles from Suicide (foreground), past Joe's Place on Muir Woods Road, through the Hogsback. (Ted Wurm collection)

18th. Indeed, times were exceptionally slow throughout—only two runners broke 55 minutes.

Percy Gilbert, the 1918 winner, had the third best actual time (55:24) and came in 22nd. Defending champion Dan Quinlan struggled, running 1:03:00 and finishing 38th.

No mention is made of high schoolers in the results or awards list. The trophy for first high schooler would not be reinstated until 1954. There is a note of a 15-year-old, H.S. Hooper, running; the lower age limit was supposedly 16.

❏ The last Women's Dipsea Hike was held three months earlier (June 11). Emma Reiman won in a course record of 1:12:06, swifter than 10 of the 71 men in the 1922 Dipsea. There would be no documented faster woman's crossing until 1969.

1. Earl Fuller, 58:10 (8) [:18]
2. C.W. Miles, 1:00:28 (10)
3. Victor Yamakawa, 59:11 (8:30)
4. Tom McNamara, 54:21 (3:30) **2nd best time**
5. Carl Newkirk, 56:00 (5)
6. Frank Sutcliffe, 56:07 (5)
7. Earl Carroll, 59:57 (8)
8. Pietro Giordanengo, 1:01:09 (9)
9. William Maghetti, 55:58 (3:30)
10. John Shearn, 59:30 (7)
18. William Churchill, 53:55 (0) **best time**
Team Humboldt: Miles, Yamakawa, McNamara, Carroll, Shearn
71 finishers; warm in the first half, light fog near the coast

19th Dipsea
September 23, 1923

The Dipsea had been a young man's race, with all previous winners ranging in age from 17 to 29. Indeed, Oliver Millard had been labeled "old" in newspaper accounts when he won at 29. So it was banner news, and a precursor of Dipseas far to the future, when a 43-year-old captured the 1923 Race.

Dr. Illtred William Letcher was a dentist going "against the advice of his brothers in the profession who scoffed at the idea of a man of 43 attempting to beat younger entrants in such a grind." But the native Minnesotan and one-time amateur featherweight boxing champion trained hard for 18 months. He ran the course once a week; three times weekly the final month.

Letcher started in the small, first, 10 minute handicap group, which including an even older runner, Ray Locke, 65. Letcher was unpressed in leading the whole way, winning by a huge margin. Ernest Bohm was runner-up, a distant 1:54 behind. Since Letcher had boxed for the Olympic Club, he was claimed by them as a member, but he ran unattached. No older runner would win until Jack Kirk, 44, in 1951.

The best time award went to Paul Nieman, the only scratch runner after William Churchill withdrew because of illness. Nieman, a banker who once worked for the *Chronicle*, was second, third and fourth in four Cross-City races between 1921 and 1924.

Earl Fuller, the defending champion, ran almost four minutes faster than the previous year but, with his handicap also cut four minutes, finished 6th.

The Olympic Club just edged out the Humboldt Club, which had been so dominant the year before, for team honors.

❏ "Big Chief" Judge Timothy Fitzpatrick announced that the Dipsea Indians would stage just one more Dipsea, their 20th, then turn the Race over to "a younger group." He was "unanimously voted down" but this was indeed the Indians' penultimate Dipsea. During the Saturday night pre-race party, the traditional fireworks were replaced by "an unknown aviator who inscribed the word 'Dipsea' in letters of fire in the heavens."

1. William Letcher, 56:32 (10) [1:54]
2. Ernest Bohm, 54:26 (6)
3. Frank Sutcliffe, 51:22 (2:30) **2nd best time**
4. Bert Hooper, 52:33 (3:30)
5. Joseph Mancuso, 57:17 (7:30)
6. Earl Fuller, 54:22 (4)
7. Leland Stanford, 58:23 (8)
8. Louis Belmour, 56:30 (5:30)
9. Paul Nieman, 51:01 (0) **best time**
10. Carl Newkirk, 54:24 (3)
Team Olympic Club: Hooper, Mancuso, Stanford, W. Whitman (11th) and Emil Heino (20th)
55 finishers; weather "best in years"

20th Dipsea
September 14, 1924

William Westergard became the fourth Dipsea runner to both win and record the fastest time; no one else would do it for 28 years. Westergard, 23, was born in Denmark—he changed the spelling of his name from the original Westergaard. He lived in San Francisco and worked for the old Russell Creamery there. He ran for the Olympic Club, as did his brother Andrew.

Westergard set off with a four-minute handicap; 10 was again the maximum. He proceeded to run a 51:39, almost a minute faster than anyone else. Only Homer Latimer (in 1977 & '78) would win the best-time award with a larger handicap.

Little-known Clarence Hazeleur, the leader until Westergard passed, followed 36 seconds later. William Magner, a future champion (1930), was 3rd. Frank Eames, who would win the Cross-City Race in 1926 and '27, was 5th. The 1916 Dipsea victor Henry Anderes took 8th. Next was Vincenzo Goso, a recent immigrant from Italy. A few months later (January 1, 1925), he would win the Cross-City Race, with Westergard runner-up, 19 seconds behind.

Dominic Stratta, a prominent name in Northern California running for the next several decades, made his first Dipsea appearance, finishing 11th. With his son Tony, who still runs the Dipsea, he would win the first father-son trophy when that award was inaugurated in 1947. Dominic's wife, Laura (née Vezzani), had finished 13th in the 1921 Women's Dipsea Hike. In 1993, she attended the Hike's 75th anniversary celebration.

Ray Locke, 66, competed in his 12th and last Dipsea, though he would continue to run until he was 70. He died in 1932. His son Carroll then carried out Ray's last request, to have his ashes scattered on the stretch of Dipsea down Suicide Hill to Redwood Creek.

William Churchill, winner of three best time awards, was delayed in his journey back from the 1924 Olympic Games in Paris (where he ran the marathon) and missed the Dipsea. Frank Sutcliffe was therefore the only scratch runner.

The 20th Dipsea was the last sponsored by the founding Dipsea Indians. The next seven Dipseas were managed directly by the parent Olympic Club, although many of the original Indians continued to play key roles. Indeed, surviving Indians periodically stepped forward to aid the Dipsea in times of crisis into the 1950's.

1. William Westergard, 51:39 (4) [:36] **best time**
2. Clarence Hazeleur, 56:15 (8)
3. William Magner, 54:45 (6)
4. Clifford Carroll, 55:45 (7)
5. Frank Eames, 53:15 (4)
6. Jules Lindner, 55:20 (6)
7. Ernest Bohm, 52:56 (2)
8. Henry Anderes, 57:00 (6)
9. Vincenzo Goso, 55:01 (4)
10. Albert Tiensu, 58:30 (7)
12. John Shearn, 52:33 (1:30) **2nd best time**
Team Humboldt Club: Hazeleur, Anderes, Tiensu, Shearn, Jacob Nathan (14th)
63 finishers; weather "fine"

21st Dipsea
September 20, 1925

As had become almost standard fare, San Francisco newspapers used the terms "dark horse" (*Examiner*) and "unknown" (*Chronicle*) to describe the winner.

Johnny Cassidy was a newcomer to the Dipsea, to the racing world, and to the country, having arrived from Scotland in 1921. The 20-year-old was awarded a nine-minute handicap, one short of the maximum. He needed all of it, finishing 20 seconds in front of William Schwartz, who had started a minute ahead. It was truly a two-runner race; there was a huge three-minute gap behind Schwartz.

The *Examiner* account relates, "[Cassidy] finished fresh as a daisy ... and his condition was a marvel to all ... At the end this merry young Scotch-Irishman had plenty of air left in his lungs to delight an appreciative audience with several quips with a brogue which could almost be cut with a knife."

Defending champion William Westergard, one of the two scratch runners (with Vincenzo Goso, the current Cross-City champion), had the fastest time for the second year in a row. He had apparently boasted at the start line that he would. Westergard, 12th, was the first of nine Olympic Club men home. His brother, and teammate, Andrew was 24th. Goso wound up 32nd; he would run several other Dipseas in mediocre times, seemingly proving the local axiom that great open speed does not necessarily translate to fast Dipseas.

Three other former Dipsea champions finished tightly bunched in the second half of the field. Most prominent was Mason Hartwell, whose course record from 1912 had still not been approached within 90 seconds. Though he had been in retirement, Hartwell was still granted only one handicap minute. He ran 57:12, finishing 31st, but holding off Goso by two seconds. It would prove to be the only one of his eight Dipseas in which he did not win the best time award. Earl Fuller, the '22 winner, was 17 more seconds back. William Letcher, the '23 champion, was 37th.

The Humboldt Club achieved a dominance of the team competition that was not surpassed until 1961. The club placed the top three finishers and five of the first seven.

❏ The *Chronicle* account relates, "The trail was in excellent condition, due not only to the recent rains, but also due to grading and filling in."

❏ I had the pleasure of talking to runner-up William Schwartz's widow Mary shortly after his death, at age 90 in 1991. She related that the German-born Schwartz lived his last 83 years in the same Visitacion Valley (San Francisco) house, that he was inspired by the Dipsea exploits of another Visitacion Valley runner, 1911 champ Albert Gorse, and that the couple, although from the same neighborhood, had not met until hiking on Mt. Tamalpais early in the 1920's. Schwartz, only half-jokingly, had always claimed that he could have won in '25 had he not been saving his energy to do a post-finish handstand on the beach, which he performed.

❏ For the first time the familiar Dipsea Indian chief logo was gone from the program and other Race materials, though veteran Dipsea Indians still worked prominent roles. The Olympic Club staged the event entirely under its own name.

1. John Cassidy, 55:26 (9) [:20]
2. William Schwartz, 56:46 (10)
3. John Cameron, 58:41 (9)
4. Edward Ardoin, 59:51 (10)
5. William Magner, 54:00 (4)
6. John Shearn, 53:19 (2) **2nd best time**
7. Uno Tiensu, 1:00:23 (9)
8. Jules Lindner, 55:24 (4)
9. Joseph Mancuso, 1:01:33 (10)
10. Dominic Stratta, 56:36 (5)
12. William Westergard, 52:00 (0) **best time**
Team Humboldt Club: Cassidy, Schwartz, Cameron, Shearn, Tiensu
56 finishers

22nd Dipsea
September 26, 1926

Though the official times don't reflect it, the 1926 race may have had the closest finish of any Dipsea. The two leaders, Andy Myrra and Lloyd Newman, were locked in a duel as far as the crowds lining the road in Stinson Beach could see. Myrra held a slight edge with Newman "creeping up." The pair were shoulder to shoulder with just fifty yards left. The *Chronicle* said, "Newman staged a mighty sprint and succeeded in overtaking [Myrra] and won out in the last few yards." By the *Examiner's* account, "They battled shoulder to shoulder down the home stretch . . . They remained even until near the tape; until Newman put forward a tremendous effort and won . . . by three yards, Myrra almost falling the last few feet in a attempt to catch [Newman]." If three yards is correct, it would be the tightest Dipsea finish ever. The six-second difference that appears in the printed results seems in error.

Once more, the winner was labeled as "dark horse" and "unknown." Newman, in his first and only Dipsea, ran unattached with an eight minute handicap. Myrra had the maximum ten, though he was a good enough runner to win the best time award the following year. Myrra was the younger brother of Jonni Myrra, who won Olympic gold medals for Finland in 1920 and 1924 in the javelin and was the world record holder in the event. The next three finishers also had handicaps at, or just one under, the maximum.

Equally stirring as the battle for first to the "thousand spectators" was the arrival in 6th place of Mason Hartwell, now known as "the grand old man" of the race at age 37. Hartwell's 52:43 (4:30hc) was well off his course record 47:56 but good enough to win his 7th best time award, in eight Dipseas. That total of seven remains the all-time Dipsea high. Also impressive, and unmatched, is the 16-year span between his first best time award (in 1910) and this, his last.

Chronicle sports writer Howard Smith described Hartwell's 1926 effort for that November's *Olympian* magazine. In part, it reads:

Their faces tell the story of the hard Dipsea Trail as the runners come down the road between the double bank of spectators at the Willow Camp finish. Their glistening, sweaty bodies speak of the heat encountered on the hilltop, their tied-up leg muscles show the effects of unaccustomed strain. But their faces usually tell the old-timers at the finish that the youngsters have taken it faster than they were trained for.

But there comes one that must have ducked in from the side a short stretch back. He's coasting along like a miler on a good track. There's a half smile on his face as he comes down the stretch. His legs work with an easy, loose-muscled action.

It's Mason Hartwell, an Olympian and greatest of Dipsea runners. But he didn't duck in from the side. He started behind most of the pack, a low handicap man, and passed many of these hard-sweating youths on the way over hard mountain trails that separate Mill Valley from the Pacific Ocean.

No trainer reaches to catch Hartwell as he crosses the finish line. Leave the cots and the rubbing for the youngsters. The veteran has just come over in [the] fastest time of the day, but he's fresh as a daisy, and without resting, goes to join his family, for he has another race on his day's schedule. He has promised to swim out beyond the breakers with his 11-year-old daughter, and Mason Hartwell will tell you that the daughter is a hard one to beat when she swims out beyond the breakers.

One place behind Hartwell was Charles Helganz. The previous year, while in fourth place, Helganz fell in Steep Ravine, twisted his ankle and had to be taken to Stinson by car.

John Cassidy, who had a nine-minute handicap when he won the previous year, was given two minutes but insisted on starting scratch. Cassidy's request was granted and he ended up the lone scratch runner, setting off 90 seconds after anyone else. Cassidy improved his running time 36 seconds but finished 29th. The 1925 runner-up, William Schwartz, his handicap halved to five minutes, was 38th. Vincenzo Goso, winner of the previous year's Cross-City race, was 41st.

The team title was as tight as the open race; the top three teams were within two points. Unione Sportiva Italiana won with a score of 39 (the places of unattached finishers were not figured in the team scoring), followed by the Olympic Club with 40 and the Humboldt Club with 41.

1. Lloyd Newman, 53:01 (8) [:06]
2. Andy Myrra, 55:07 (10)
3. John Cunningham, 54:54 (9)
4. T. DeMartini, 56:48 (10)
5. Otto Mackoto, 56:45 (9)
6. Mason Hartwell, 52:53 (4:30) **best time**
7. Charles Helganz, 55:36 (6)
8. Milton Maata, 56:48 (7)
9. Uno Tiensuu, 58:39 (8:30)
10. Angelo Pampa, 58:35 (8)
14. Frank Sutcliffe, 53:19 (1:30) **2nd best time**
Team Unione Sportiva Italiana: Cunningham, De-Martini, Magner (16th), John Ardizzone (22nd) and B. Carrara (25th)
49 finishers; warm

23rd Dipsea
October 2, 1927

For the sixth time, the winner (William Fraser) came from the maximum handicap group. Like the first to pull off the wire-to-wire leading feat, John Hassard, Fraser would prove his 10-minute handicap seemingly excessive by capturing, just two years later, the best time award. Ironically, the man Fraser beat to the tape by a scant 15 seconds, Andy Myrra, had had the maximum handicap the year before and now turned in the day's best time.

Of the 1927 Race's 39 finishers, 15 had the limit handicap of 10 minutes. One was Fraser, apparently considered a novice because he was a high schooler (Mission, San Francisco), but already a seasoned runner as a member of the Humboldt Club, which was dominating Dipsea team competitions. Fraser soon after became a standout for the Olympic Club and finished second in the 1929 Cross-City Race.

Myrra was tantalizingly close for the second successive year. The Finn improved his running time by two minutes from 1926, when he was nipped at the tape, but had lost six handicap minutes. Now the pursuer, Myrra came up just short. He got some consolation in capturing the time trophy by an even narrower margin, five seconds, over 1925 Dipsea champ John Cassidy.

For the fourth year in a row, the number of finishers declined, hitting a new low. Of the 39 (some accounts say 41), 23 were from just two clubs, Humboldt and Olympic.

Mason Hartwell was entered and given a five-minute handicap but did not run. The Dipsea racing career of one of the event's greatest figures was over, although he served as a volunteer for years and jogged until in his 70's.

Newspaper reports emphasized the day's "unprecedented heat." Onlookers offered cups of water.

1. William Fraser, 58:48 (10) [:15]
2. Andy Myrra, 53:03 (4) **best time**
3. Al Tiensuu, 59:33 (10)
4. John Cassidy, 53:08 (3) **2nd best time**
5. E. Tamlander, 57:11 (7)
6. Frank Sutcliffe, 54:01 (3:30)
7. Uno Tiensuu, 59:21 (8:30)
8. Roland Eisman, 1:00:53 (10)
9. John Shearn, 54:12 (2:30)
10. Steve Ehret, 1:01:45 (10)

Team Humboldt: Fraser, A. Tiensuu, Cassidy, U. Tiensuu, Eisman and Shearn
39 finishers; "unprecedented heat"

(Right) The Lone Tree (redwood, lower left) and Dipsea Trail, 1923. Compare with photograph below, showing the later fire road and invasion of Douglas-fir trees. (Watson Howden, courtesy Mark Reese)

(Below) Farren's Rest section of Dipsea Trail by Lone Tree, 1993. (Brad Rippe)

24th Dipsea
September 30, 1928

Generous handicaps, and good running, produced fast clock times. Wayne Morefield, an unattached runner in his first Dipsea, covered the course in 52:00. With his 8:30 handicap, awarded despite a good effort in the city's Examiner Marathon earlier in the year, he came in with a clock time of 43:30. No swifter clock time was recorded in the Dipsea between 1907 and 1961. Runner-up Ray Cocking, 20 seconds behind, also notched one of the Race's rare sub-44 clock times. Cocking would go on to win Cross-City in 1932.

Twenty-five of the 52 finishers, a very high 48%, had actual running times of under one hour.

Entries rebounded from several years of decline, partly due to the entry of seven members from an all-Japanese team, Showa Athletic Club. ("Showa" was a name applied to the new Emperor Hirohito's reign.) Victor Yamakawa, who had finished as high as third (1922) was the club's top man, taking 18th. The Humboldt Club, however, was again the team winner, placing five men in the first 12.

John Cassidy and William Fraser, the only two former champions in the field, had a spirited battle. They both set off with four minute handicaps and produced the top two actual times. Cassidy won the duel, finishing 12 seconds and one place ahead in 9th.

Pietro Giordanengo, winner of the 1928 and '29 Cross-City races, was 22nd.

Ed Fratini, who would captain the Petaluma Spartans in their Dipsea glory years of the 1930's, debuted and finished 40th. Now in his 90's, he still lives in Petaluma. Fratini holds an outstanding collections of Dipsea team trophies along with other running memorabilia.

❑ Mt. Tamalpais State Park, one of the first in the California system, was established earlier in the year. Its creation was the result of years of grass-roots volunteer effort, legal battles, and legislative wrangling. The park would be enlarged over the years to cover most of the route of the Dipsea Trail.

The section of the Dipsea through Steep Ravine was added to the State Park as a deathbed bequest of William Kent later in the year. The Kent family had been the largest landowners on Mt. Tamalpais, and it was once possible to walk from the Bay in today's Kentfield to the Pacific entirely on their property. William Kent served as an independent United States congressman from Marin. He was also the Dipsea's Honorary Referee, listed first in the program, for years. Kent had previously made another important donation of Dipsea Trail to the public; Muir Woods in 1908.

❑ Panoramic Highway, now the main auto route between Mill Valley and Stinson Beach, also opened in 1928. Actually, it was fears of residential development on Mt. Tamalpais to follow the road's construction that helped spur creation of the State Park. Dipsea racers used to cross Panoramic Highway twice, at Windy Gap and east of the Highway 1 junction in Stinson Beach. The latter crossing was eliminated in 1977. Panoramic Highway also cut across the historic direct route down from the top of Insult to Stinson. Many still follow this old line by running two stretches on the roadway.

❑ The Examiner reported, "The start [was] witnessed by a large crowd of hikers and distance running fans. Like crowds lined the course through its length over the Marin Hills to Stinson Beach."

1. Wayne Morefield, 52:00 (8:30) [:20]
2. Ray Cocking, 52:50 (9)
3. Carlos Murillo, 53:30 (9:30)
4. Joe Pappas, 54:04 (10)
5. Joseph Mancuso, 55:06 (10)
6. Ernest DeLisle, 54:38 (9)
7. S. Whittock, 54:43 (9)
8. Richard Davis, 52:46 (6)
9. John Cassidy, 50:54 (4) **best time**
10. William Fraser, 51:06 (4) **2nd best time**
Team Humboldt Club: Cocking, Mancuso, Cassidy, Fraser, Edward Ardoin (12th)
52 finishers; weather "good"

25th Dipsea
October 3, 1929

The top four finishers, and 14 of the first 16, had the maximum handicap (10 minutes). That moved one newspaper writer to state, "[This] tends to prove handicapping was not as strict as it could have been."

Among this large group of Dipsea "limit" men—just over half the field—was Angelo Frediani. Frediani was a 26-year-old who had been born in Italy. He lived in the City's Italian North Beach section and worked as a cement mason. His brother-in-law was Attilio Maggiora, long associated with the Dipsea and head of the handicap committee! The *Chronicle* account said Frediani had "been running with fair success since 1922. Until yesterday, however, he had never won a major race."

Frediani ran with the front runners from his sizable pack of fellow starters to the top of the stairs, then "quickened his pace and was not headed the rest of the way." Fellow scratch men Wilbert Annis, Otto Mackoto and Donald Arndt apparently "threatened . . . at times" but Frediani won by a comfortable 1:38. The next four finishers were then bunched within 21 seconds.

Frediani ran for Unione Sportiva Italiana Virtus, one of the powerful North Beach clubs of the era. Frediani led his club to the team title as well; all their five scorers were in the top ten.

The Race's three scratch runners, Bert Hooper and past champions William Fraser and John Cassidy, finished in a row in places 27-29. Fraser won this race within a race, taking the best time award as well. Confirming the handicap criticism, this was the worst place ever for a best-time winner.

Well back were two runners of note. William Magner, who would win the Dipsea the following year, was 47th of the 51 timed finishers, running 1:07:29 (3hc). And Vincenzo Goso, who had a quar-tet of top four Cross-City finishes including a win in the years 1925-29, was next-to-last (1:08:22; 2hc).

❏ Reversing a trend, only eight of the finishers ran "unattached."

❏ The program makes no note of any special 25th anniversary celebration.

1. Angelo Frediani, 56:32 (10) [1:38]
2. Wilbert Annis, 58:10 (10)
3. Otto Mackoto, 58:14 (10)
4. Donald Arndt, 58:20 (10)
5. Edward Ardoin, 56:31 (8)
6. Albert Tiensu, 59:20 (10)
7. Irving Leonard, 59:34 (10)
8. Carl Newkirk, 55:28 (5:30)
9. Harvey Mielenz, 1:00:12 (10)
10. John Ardizzone, 1:00:51 (10)
23. Ray Cocking, 53:33 (1:30) **2nd best time**
27. William Fraser, 52:29 (0) **best time**
Team Unione Sportiva Italiana Virtus: Frediani, Arndt, Tiensu, Newkirk, Ardizzone
51 finishers

26th Dipsea
August 3, 1930

This was an historic Race as the paths of the two men with the longest Dipsea careers, William Magner and Jack Kirk, each with a span from first to last Dipsea of 63 years, first crossed. The pair finished 1-2.

Magner ran his first Dipsea in 1921 and his last in 1984. This was Kirk's first Dipsea and he has not missed one since—58 total through 1993, and still going—the longest streak in American running. (Johnny Kelley recorded 61 consecutive Boston Marathon finishes, ending in 1992. But Kelley started his streak two years after Kirk, in 1932. The difference arises from the six years of missed Dipseas since 1930.) Kirk would become intertwined with the Dipsea more closely than any other runner and achieve an unsurpassed status in Race annals. Because Kirk vividly remembers and shares details going back to his first Dipsea, 1930 is a watershed year for historians. (Although there remain many survivors from the 1920's; one, a spry Victor Sagues, who ran in 1927, attended the 1993 Dipsea Dinner.)

Adding to the day's drama was the presence, as spectators, of the two great figures of the Dipsea's first quarter-century, the Olympic Club's John Mason Hartwell and Oliver Millard. Magner too wore the Club's "Winged O"; he had run unattached in all his previous nine Dipseas.

Perhaps reacting to criticism from the previous year, when over half the field had the maximum ten-minute headstart, just eight men set off in the first group. Magner started a minute later. He had been awarded a whopping nine-minute handicap, six more than in 1929 when he finished 47th of 51 (1:07:29, 3hc). But in 1924, Magner had run 54:45 and been 3rd and in 1925 ran 54:00 and taken 5th.

Did Magner deliberately run poorly in 1929 to earn a larger handicap in 1930, a strategy that surely tempted Dipsea runners in the pre-handicap formula days? Magner's 1929 time was his slowest, by over six minutes, of his prior eight Dipseas and more than 13 minutes off his best mark. But given Magner's character and lifelong devotion to the sport (he coached others for almost 60 years), it seems unlikely. In 1930, the *Chronicle* described him as "a plodding type of runner who was conceded little chance of winning."

Magner went by some of the "limit" starters before the steps and soon after all but two (brothers Richard and Joe Estep) of the rest. After Joe Estep was overtaken on Butler's Pride three miles into the Race, Magner ran solo to the finish. Magner's wife Georgette, who had participated in the 1922 Dipsea Women's Hike, was on hand to greet him.

The ten efforts it took Magner to win was a Dipsea record until surpassed by Kirk himself, who won in 1951 on his 16th try. William Mazzini, 4th place in 1930, would finally win the Dipsea after 25 years (1955).

Kirk mounted a challenge—passing 1928 winner Wayne Morefield late to move into second place—but was a distant 1:55 behind Magner at the tape. Kirk also just missed, by three seconds, winning the best time award in his maiden race.

That honor went to 1927 champion William Fraser. Fraser and Bert Hooper, Olympic Club teammates, were the only two scratch men and they waged a great see-saw battle all the way. Hooper led coming into Stinson Beach (Dipsea programs still called the finish "Willow Camp Beach" until 1939). Then, according to the *Chronicle*, "With the finish almost in view, Hooper slipped on the rough ground, tearing the skin from both knees. This mishap probably cost him the honor of finishing in the fastest time." Hooper's 51:43 was eight seconds off Fraser's time and five slower than Kirk's. Fraser finished 24th; Hooper, passed by 1927 best time winner Andy Myrra while on the ground, 26th. Of the 43 finishers, a record low of five ran unattached.

❏ Within a couple of years, Kirk had earned his

immortal title of "The Dipsea Demon." Neil Decker, 9th in 1930, affixed the nickname on Kirk after a trail run together, saying "The way Kirk runs down those hills, he must be a 'Demon'".

❑ The train that ran up the slopes of Mt. Tamalpais since 1896 suspended operations days after the Race. Many spectators and officials, and some of the competitors returning to the start (Kirk was one), rode what was known as "the world's crookedest railroad" between Mill Valley and West Point. The route between West Point and the finish was negotiated either by foot, stage coach, or, later, automobile.

1. William Magner, 54:13 (9) [1:55]
2. Jack Kirk, 51:38 (4:30) **2nd best time**
3. Wayne Morefield, 55:20 (8)
4. William Mazzini, 52:55 (5:30)
5. Merio Cavalini, 55:35 (8)
6. Louis Larson, 54:30 (6)
7. Warren Dixon, 59:20 (10)
8. Ettore Fozzi, 54:58 (5:30)
9. Neal Decker, 57:32 (8)
10. Peter Lucia, 57:13 (7:30)
24. William Fraser, 51:35 (0) **best time**
Team Olympic Club: Magner, Morefield, Dixon, Bill Pappas (11th) and Jack Keegan (12th)
43 finishers; weather "perfect for running, although early morning conditions probably kept several … entries from appearing at the start"

27th Dipsea
August 2, 1931

"Another startling upset" was the *Chronicle's* lead in describing Francis O'Donnell's 1931 victory.

O'Donnell was born in Ireland in 1904, then emigrated to Canada. He joined the Canadian Grenadier Guards in Montreal in 1919. There he became an excellent boxer in the bantamweight (118 pound) class and also began running. He moved to the United States' east coast and began racing competitively. He ran four Boston Marathons, finishing 12th in 1929. In 1927 O'Donnell ran an impressive 2:33:35 at the Port Chester Marathon (the Olympic record was then 2:32:36), finishing one place ahead of the great Clarence DeMar, 1924 Olympic bronze medalist in the event. O'Donnell came to California in 1929 after serving in a support crew for a run/walk across the United States. He lived first in Watsonville, was recruited by Olympic Club coach Charles Hunter and moved to San Francisco.

Since most all of O'Donnell's fine running record had been made elsewhere, and because he had only placed 17th in that year's Cross-City (with a time more than 3 1/2 minutes slower than Jack Kirk's), O'Donnell received a generous six minute handicap for his 1931 Dipsea debut. O'Donnell trained hard for the Dipsea with his Olympic Club teammates and did step repeats by himself up Telegraph Hill. Still, the newspapers again used the label "dark horse" in describing him, as well as "little Irish lad" and "fighting little Irishman."

Reese talked to O'Donnell after the 1979 Dipsea and recorded his story.
Race day, felt fine, liked my handicap of six minutes, but no thought that I would be the winner. Started passing runner after runner on the stairs. Soon as I was able to see the front runner, knew I would likely be the front runner, as I was moving ahead of the ones in front of me. On the Hogsback, I was in the lead. Had

a stitch, shortened my stride and rubbed my side. It went away fast. Just flew down the gully like a young deer. Would say now that it was dangerous, never thought about it at the time. Coming out into the farm land, saw someone behind me, did not know who, just tried to run strongly, saving some for a final sprint, if necessary. Felt at rate I was going it would not be easy for them to pick up on me. My thoughts when ahead were, "Would the scratch runners reach me?" . . . The papers said I was tired; anyone that competes the course has got to be, yet it was my thought if I had to go farther, I could have done so at the same rate for a few more miles. It just seemed to me that I was running within myself, a lucky day and felt great. Happy to win it, but would have been happier to have the best time.

The pursuing runner that O'Donnell saw was Ariadono (Ave) Motioni. Motioni stirred the crowd by closing some of O'Donnell's big lead over the last quarter-mile, but O'Donnell responded with a final sprint of his own. The results show a final victory margin of 30 seconds but most accounts (The *Olympian* magazine said O'Donnell's closing burst "proved enough to nose out his rival") indicate a tighter finish. O'Donnell's 52:00 was the third fastest of the day.

Jack Kirk ran what would remain his personal Dipsea record, a 50:54 that won best time honors but brought him only 17th. Directly before the start, Kirk declined the 30 second handicap he was awarded. Instead he set off scratch with two runners from the rival Olympic Club; William Fraser, the 1927 champion who had won the previous two best time awards, and Ronald Davis. Kirk's time was 30 seconds faster than Fraser's, reversing his three second "defeat" from the year before. (To this day, Kirk claims his 1931 time was faster and his margin over Fraser greater, the printed results reflecting chicanery on the part of the Olympic Club.)

The oldest participant, 51-year-old Charles Ludekins, ended up sixth. Ray Cocking, who would win the '32 Cross-City, was 24th (54:34, 2:30hc).

O'Donnell's win marked the end of an era. It would be another 37 years before a runner wearing the "Winged O" of the Olympic Club, the organization which founded the Dipsea and was so closely associated with it, would be first to Stinson.

The Olympic Club also withdrew its sponsorship after the 1931 Dipsea. With the nation in the midst of the Great Depression, no other organization stepped forward and the Dipsea was discontinued for two years. (In 1932, Kirk brought $100 of his own money, a good percentage of the Dipsea's total budget then, to the local AAU office in an unsuccessful effort to try to save the Race.) The Dipsea re-emerged in 1934.

1. Frances O'Donnell, 52:00 (6) [:30]
2. Ariadono Motioni, 55:30 (9)
3. George Wilson, 56:21 (8)
4. Steve Ehret, 56:30 (8)
5. Neil Decker, 54:09 (5:30)
6. Charles Ludekins, 58:49 (10)
7. Alberto Buselli, 55:20 (6:30)
8. Walter Sarlin, 52:51 (4)
9. Amerigo Mericone, 56:39 (7:30)
10. Bill Pappas, 56:40 (7:30)
17. Jack Kirk, 50:54 (0) **best time**
21. William Fraser, 51:24 (0) **2nd best time**
Team Olympic Club: O'Donnell, Ehret, Decker, Pappas and Wayne Morefield (11th)
50 finishers; "clear" weather

28th Dipsea
September 23, 1934

The Dipsea returned after a two-year hiatus. The Olympic Club, which founded the Race and sponsored it ever since, had withdrawn. Jack Kirk bitterly blames the Club's long-time trainer, Charlie Hunter. Even Kirk's request to help finance the Race himself was turned down. Finally coming to the rescue was San Francisco's Sunrise Breakfast Club. It was headed by Pete Maloney, listed as president of the Northern California Baseball Managers. Maloney was well-connected to the City's mayor Angelo Rossi, who was named Honorary Referee, and to Alfred Cleary, the City's Chief Administrator, who would later be named Honorary Marshall of the Course.

Much of the veteran organizing staff stayed the same. Original Dipsea Indian Timothy Fitzpatrick was again the referee. Walter Christie remained the starter and on the handicap committee (to which Hunter was added as a fourth member). Hunter continued to be the Race's trainer. George Dixon was still the announcer. Dipsea legends Oliver Millard and Mason Hartwell served as finish line judges. Another past winner, William Joyner ('07), was a timer. And the Olympic Club itself would once more take team honors.

Continuing another tradition, winner Torrey Lyons was described as a "dark horse" in newspaper accounts. Lyons was a 19-year-old University of California sophomore out of Stockton. Lyons, who ran for Cal but who had never even been on the Dipsea course, was assigned a five minute handicap (along with another future winner, Paul Chirone); the maximum handicap had been cut to eight.

Lyons passed all but one of the runners starting ahead of him by Lone Tree, including Walter Bertram, fast enough to finish third in the next Cross-City Race. The last was William Pappas, a 46-year-old barber. Pappas vainly tried to stay with Lyons but the younger man pulled away to a 62-second-margin at the tape. Lyons' running time of 53:02 was surpassed by only three men.

Tommy Laughran, a 1-minute-handicap man who was considered the pre-Race favorite, got lost in Steep Ravine after running strongly. He ended up 24th. Laughran would later serve for many years as an official with the AAU and the Dipsea.

Best time honors went to Leo Karlhofer, an Austrian pastry baker just embarking on his outstanding Dipsea career. Karlhofer would win Cross-City five months later.

❑ In 1932, Archie Upton, stepson of Nathan Stinson, had donated 3,600 feet of Stinson Beach shoreline to Marin as a county park. This was the genesis of today's larger park, now part of the Golden Gate National Recreation Area, in which the Dipsea now finishes.

1. Torrey Lyons, 53:02 (5) [1:02]
2. William Pappas, 57:04 (8)
3. Walter Bertram, 55:02* (6)
4. Walter Sarlin, 52:43 (3)
5. William Robinson, 56:16 (6:30)
6. Vernon Linn, 57:50 (8)
7. Leo Karlhofer, 51:39 (1) **best time**
8. Joe Ortega, 56:15 (5:30)
9. George Wilson, 54:53 (4)
10. George Clough, 58:42 (6:30)
11. Neil Decker, 52:13 (0) **2nd best time**

*Bertram's correct time has to be at least three seconds slower

Team Olympic Club: Pappas, Sarlin, Linn, Wilson and Decker

44 finishers; rain

29th Dipsea
September 15, 1935

Norman Bright, among the fastest runners the Dipsea has ever seen and destined to become one of the Race's most legendary figures, made his debut. Bright was already an international class runner and was just returning from a European track tour.

But in 1935 Bright could only manage 2nd; it would take him 35 years to win the Dipsea.

Bright started scratch, together with Jack Kirk and defending best time winner Leo Karlhofer. Bright won this personal duel by recording the fastest time of the day, 52:53, over a muddy course described as a "veritable morass" from the previous night's rain. That was 25 seconds quicker than Karlhofer.

But Bright could get no closer than 200 yards to winner John Hansen. According to an anecdote related decades later by Hansen's Petaluma Spartan teammate Arnold Scott, Hansen deliberately slammed shut a gate in the late stages of the Race, forcing Bright to stop and open the latch. The delay may have been critical. Bright would soon enough himself learn every Dipsea trick and shortcut, and invent many new ones.

Hansen, then 32, operated a poultry business in his native Petaluma. He was born hunchbacked but still became one of the region's better runners. Hansen had been awarded four handicap minutes for his Dipsea debut in 1934. But he only ran 58:22, placing 18th of 44 finishers. So, for 1935, he was given an extra minute, to five.

Hansen quickly distanced himself from the four other starters in his group; the last to fall behind was his teammate and business partner Pete Christensen. He then passed the 11 runners who started ahead of him and comfortably held off the 16 challengers from behind.

Andy Myrra, the 1927 best time winner, ended up 3rd after being passed by teammate Bright 300 yards from the finish. Karlhofer was 4th. Christensen, who had earlier participated in a cross-United States race, took 5th. Defending champion Torrey Lyons ran 1:29 slower than in '34, and, having lost all but 30 seconds of his five minute handicap, was 7th. William O'Connor, noted as the oldest entrant at age 53, was third from last but "breathing only slightly in comparison to his younger opponents."

The team competition was tight, with the Olympic Club edging Hansen's up-and-coming Spartans by a single point. Even that was in doubt because Bright, the leading OC finisher, had discarded his mud-splattered singlet and finished bare-chested, a technical violation of Amateur Athletic Union rules. Bright was not, however, disqualified. The Spartans, which had begun as a soccer squad known as the Petaluma Roosters, would go on to take seven Dipsea team titles.

There were 61 entrants but, likely due to the heavy rains the previous night, only 32 started and 31 finished ("the other one was found roaming around on the beach looking for the finish line" according to the *Chronicle*). Both the number of starters and finishers were, and remain, all-time lows. The finish line crowd was estimated at only 200, also quite low.

There was actually one more starter. Jimmy McClymonds happened upon the Race while preparing to hike. He then set off, unofficial, with the scratch men. McClymonds would win the Dipsea the following year.

❏ Among the 18 prizes awarded to winning runners were cigarette cases.

1. John Hansen, 57:22 (5) [:31]
2. Norman Bright, 52:53 (0) **best time**
3. Andy Myrra, 56:33 (3:30)
4. Leo Karlhofer, 53:18 (0) **2nd best time**
5. Pete Christensen, 58:36 (5)
6. Joe Ortega, 57:15 (3:30)
7. Torrey Lyons, 54:31 (:30)
8. George Wilson, 56:50 (2)
9. Walter Bertram, 58:54 (3)
10. Earl Lockhart, 59:55 (4)

Team Olympic Club: Bright, Myrra, Wilson, Walter Sarlin (14th) and Edson Burroughs (21st)

31 finishers; weather clear but course muddy and slippery

30th Dipsea
September 27, 1936

Jimmy McClymonds had run the 1935 Dipsea unregistered, "in high boots and long trousers"; he had stumbled upon the Race when setting off to hike on Mt. Tamalpais. McClymonds started with the scratch men and passed several runners in covering the full course. Pleased with what he learned about his ability, McClymonds "devoted many months of the past year [1936] to training over the trail," according to the *Examiner*.

McClymonds was of Scotch (father)-Mexican/Indian (mother) ancestry, and was sometimes referred to as "the Indian." He was raised from age two in a City orphanage after his mother died, then later attended the City's Polytechnic High School. Now 31, he worked in San Francisco as a lithographer.

McClymonds entered just before the Tuesday night cutoff. Based on his seemingly advanced age and lack of Dipsea or other racing experience (this was first competitive race although he had been regularly "hiking over the hills of Northern California for ... years"), McClymonds was awarded an eight-minute handicap.

He proceeded to pass the only three runners (including one with a new maximum 12-minute handicap) who started ahead of him, and to hold off the later-starting pursuers. McClymonds covered the course in 55:47, the day's seventh best time, and "had something to spare." He finished 35 seconds ahead of runner-up Jack Kirk.

Kirk, in turn, was just one second ahead of Clarence Hall, who would win in 1938. The pair, starting together in the five-minute group (along with 4th placer Bob Alexander), battled the whole way to the finish line. Behind them, only six seconds separated places 4-5-6.

That 5th place finisher, George Wilson, scored an even bigger upset than McClymonds by winning the fastest time trophy (53:09, 4hc). Norman Bright was expected to assault Mason Hartwell's 24-year-old course record, and Hartwell himself was on hand to watch. But Bright had blistered his feet trying to make the Olympic 1,500 meter team and struggled to a 53:33. That was 24 seconds slower than Wilson, five slower than Kirk and four slower than Hall. As the lone scratch runner, Bright ended up 19th. Six places farther back was Paul Chirone, who would win the following year.

The defending champion, John Hansen, improved his time by 1:24 over the previous year's mudbath, and had lost only 30 seconds of handicap, but ended up 10th.

Only 40 runners registered, the Race's all-time low. Most, including the top five, ran unattached. There were actually more officials than runners.

❑ The University of California's famed coach Walter Christie, who had been the official starter for every previous Dipsea, finally had his streak broken.

❑ James Lloyd Henry made a ten-minute, 8mm color film of the '36 Race; Reese viewed it.

1. Jimmy McClymonds, 55:47 (8) [:41]
2. Jack Kirk, 53:28 (5) **2nd best time**
3. Clarence Hall, 53:29 (5)
4. Bob Alexander, 54:07 (5)
5. George Wilson, 53:09 (4) **best time**
6. Eric Juhl, 56:43 (7:30)
7. Walter Sarlin, 54:33 (5)
8. Frank Valin, 57:17 (7)
9. Pete Christensen, 57:19 (6)
10. John Hansen, 55:58 (4:30)
Team Petaluma Spartans: Juhl, Valin, Christensen, Hansen and Bruce Rich (18th)
37 finishers; sunny

31st Dipsea
October 31, 1937

The 1937 Dipsea is considered one of the most dramatic in the Race's history. It saw a battle between two friends for first, and one of the greatest runs ever over the course.

Paul Chirone, 24, had been an outstanding local runner while at Mill Valley's Tamalpais High School. He achieved notoriety for his almost daily race against the special school train which passed near his house in San Anselmo. Chirone headed over the hills while the train hugged the flatlands and Chirone was usually at Tam first. He also did repeat charges, wearing weights, up San Anselmo's steep, 600' Red Hill as amused students of the adjacent Sunny Hills School watched. And Chirone ran ultra-distances, up to the 100-mile range. Another Tam student, Bill McCurdy, himself a fine Dipsea runner who went on to become the long-time track coach at Harvard, said Chirone could have become one of the nation's outstanding marathoners. But he already was devoting most of his time to his lifelong work as a stonemason.

Though denied by a technicality the chance to compete in college when he transferred to Stanford University, Norman Bright, now 27, had compiled a brilliant career since. He beat the world's best miler, Glenn Cunningham, set American records for the two-mile both outdoors and indoors, and was part of a world record distance relay team. Earlier in 1937, Bright set a course record at the Cross-City (Bay to Breakers) that was not surpassed until 1964.

Bright had made his Dipsea debut in 1935, winning the best time award and finishing second. Now, a schoolteacher in Sunnyvale, he again resolved to break the seemingly untouchable Dipsea course record of 47:56 that Mason Hartwell set in 1912. In the quarter-century since, only Hartwell himself (a 49:57 in 1920) and Oliver Millard (49:30

in 1914) had even broken 50 minutes. Hartwell would be on hand to watch. But Chirone was equally determined to win.

Chirone and Bright began training together after they met at Stinson Beach, where the nearly broke Bright was camping. Chirone claimed he never won a race while at Tam, and had made undistinguished times in finishing behind Bright in the two previous Dipseas, so Bright figured he would not pose a challenge. Bright showed Chirone every shortcut he knew (although Chirone, as a Marin native, undoubtedly knew a few himself) and shared other training and racing tips. The two lived together before the Race both at Stinson and in Chirone's house. But they ran for the era's two great rival teams; Chirone for the Petaluma Spartans, Bright for the Olympic Club.

Bright's preparations were meticulous. According to Reese, "Bright and his friends manicured the course with rakes and hoes and removed every obstacle . . . gates were opened, wire fences taken down, rocks picked up, grass and branches chopped down." Bright had obtained a map of the course as it was in 1912 and discovered there were then only three fences to be cleared. So, just before the Race, Bright and two friends secretly cut through the several fences added since. He also placed unobtrusive markers (many not found until decades later) at obscure shortcuts.

All seemed ready until it started to rain the night before, with a drizzle continuing during the Race. The course was muddy. Bright was talked into wearing a pair of jumping spikes; the heel spikes were filed down and made ready only at the last moment. Bright continues to complain about those shoes, and their poor fit, to this day (they were recently donated to the new Dipsea Hall of Fame).

Chirone set off with a six-minute handicap, one more than he had when he finished 25th of 37 the previous year. Bright was the lone scratch runner; the nearest man set off two minutes ahead.

Chirone went out strong—it was his strategy, and one he preached to others for decades after, to

(Right) Norman Bright finishing his historic 1937 run, the only breaking of the course record from 1912 to 1970.
(Below) Paul Chirone wins the 1937 Dipsea.
(Wesley Swadley)

view the Dipsea as a race to Cardiac with the subsequent downhill taking care of itself. He quickly passed the handful of runners who had started before him to take the lead.

Bright, meanwhile, was apparently struggling. Mason Hartwell, again on hand to see if his record would hold, reported that Bright was 90 seconds off his pace at the top of the stairs. Then Bright's watch stopped at 14 minutes, making it impossible to note his carefully planned splits. That probably helped him, as he then tore into the course. (During Eve Pell's winning 1989 effort, she too had her watch accidentally stop, also likely to beneficial effect.)

Bright passed everyone, including previous best-time winners George Wilson and Leo Karlhofer (and hurdled over Eyrle Aceves, who had fallen in Steep Ravine), except Chirone. Paul got to the line 16 seconds first. Bright, his red hair flowing in a widely-reproduced photograph, followed. The *Chronicle* reported, "In another quarter mile the chances are [Bright] would have caught Chirone and passed him."

Chirone's running time was 53:06, over seven minutes faster than his two previous Dipseas. He became the first Marin resident to win the County's great race. (There have been 14 Marin winners since.)

Bright's time was 47:22. That knocked 34 seconds off Hartwell's ancient record. Bright's time would not be surpassed until 1970, ironically the year Bright would finally win. Put another way, Bright's was the only breaking of the Dipsea course record for a period of 58 years.

Still, to this day, Hartwell's son Thomas maintains that Bright's route was shorter than the one taken by his father; both because the depression-era Civilian Conservation Corps had made a number of trail improvements and because other shortcuts had been blazed over the years. Judge Timothy Fitzpatrick, the original Dipsea Race director, also never recognized Bright's mark, saying that "Official checking wasn't done in accordance with the rules laid down by the committee which

had charge ... when Olympians sponsored the run." Just about everyone else, though, recognized the record.

Karlhofer ran an excellent 50:18, which would have won the best time trophy in all but four previous Dipseas, to finish 5th.

❏ The Race was dedicated to Owen Merrick, a sportswriter credited with reviving the Dipsea after the missed years of 1932-33, who had just died. The *Chronicle* noted, "It was agreed that funds will be raised to erect a testimonial marker near the finish of the race at Stinson Beach in memory of Merrick." It is not known if the marker was ever placed.

1. Paul Chirone, 53:06 (6) [:16]
2. Norman Bright, 47:22 (0) **best time**
3. Albert Savedra, 52:04 (4)
4. Ed Thall, 54:15 (6)
5. Leo Karlhofer, 50:18 (2) **2nd best time**
6. Eyrle Aceves, 53:45 (5)
7. Bruce Rich, 52:41 (3)
8. Al Ludlum, 52:45 (3)
9. Herb Wright, 1:00:47 (10)
10. Jack Kirk, 54:19 (3:30)
Team Petaluma Spartans: Chirone, Savedra, Rich, Ludlum and William Ellison (15th)
37 finishers; drizzle after night rains

32nd Dipsea
September 25, 1938

Members of the University of California cross country team were looking for new challenges. The Dipsea, held early in cross country season, seemed appealing. In 1938, three Cal men finished in the top four with the winner the former track captain, Clarence Hall, who had graduated a few months earlier.

It was a Cal senior, Eyrle Aceves, who had the lead at Lone Tree. Moments later, however, Hall, who had started two minutes behind, pulled even and then ahead. Aceves hung on and recaptured the lead plunging down Steep Ravine. But he tired badly at Insult and Hall, now running for the San Francisco YMCA (which won team honors), again passed him. Aceves renewed the chase on the downhill and saw Hall crossing the finish line, 13 seconds ahead. Hall's 50:41 (if correct, see note below results), was the fastest time by a Dipsea winner between 1906 and 1960.

Hall had grown up on a farm in the Sacramento Valley and, to his Cal teammates' amusement, retained his penchant for drinking only milk. He finished third in that year's Cross-City, and would again in '39.

After Petaluma Spartan Bruce Rich (3rd) came another Cal runner, Bob Baker. The five runners in places 3-7 were separated by just nine seconds.

Austrian Leo Karlhofer, who had been given a place of honor at the 1936 Olympic Games, turned in a 49:15 to win best time honors. It was the third fastest Dipsea ever, behind only the record runs of Bright the previous year and Hartwell in 1912. Karlhofer finished 7th. He received a "fancy box" supposedly containing a shaving kit; when opened, it was empty.

Defending champion Paul Chirone dropped to 18th.

Andrew MacCono, representing the East Bay Club for the Deaf, debuted in 38th place. MacCono would remain an important figure in regional running for decades as head of the Walnut Festival Races (founded in 1941 and now the fourth oldest race, after the Dipsea, Bay to Breakers and the Statutos, in the Bay Area).

❏ Aceves would return to complete the 1992 and 1993 Dipseas. He thus achieved a 55-year span (1938-1993) in the Race, surpassed only by Jack Kirk and William Magner.

❏ The program noted that the 65 registered entrants was a 24-year high. Over two-thirds were members either of the YMCA, Olympic Club or Petaluma Spartan teams.

❏ The program also acknowledged that the "Loud Speaking System" was "courtesy of Harry J. McCune System," today the leading supplier to Bay Area races.

❏ A "very valuable 21 Jewel Wrist Watch" was donated by the Albert S. Samuels Jewelry Company (still in business in San Francisco) to the "boy who makes the best time."

❏ The Saturday, pre-Race banquet, a Dipsea tradition since 1905, was held in San Rafael.

1. Clarence Hall, 50:41* (2:30) [:13]
2nd fastest time
2. Eyrle Aceves, 52:54 (4:30)
3. Bruce Rich, 51:36 (2:30)
4. Bob Baker, 54:08 (5)
5. Frank Lara, 54:12 (5)
6. William Mazzini, 54:13 (5)
7. Leo Karlhofer, 49:15 (0) **fastest time**
8. William McCurdy, 54:41 (5)
9. John McNabb, 52:43 (3)
10. Jack Kirk, 55:59 (6)
*Hall's time here differs from Reese (50:08). There are other discrepancies as well. These results are corroborated by Eyrle Aceves.
Team San Francisco YMCA: Hall, Baker, Karlhofer, Walter Bertram (12th) and Edward Thall (13th)
43 finishers; weather pleasant, fog at coast

33rd Dipsea
November 26, 1939

Three men from the maximum 10-minute handicap group ended up 1-2-3.

Leading the way was a 20-year-old, blond-haired runner of Finnish descent, Allan Nelson. Nelson was a recent graduate of Cal, where he both swam the backstroke and ran track. He had made his Dipsea debut in 1938, finishing 25th (1:02:38, 7hc).

Nelson's recollection of the 1939 Race, written to Reese 40 years later, is worth reprinting:

[The 1939 Dipsea] is the only race I ever have won! I had been training for it during the summer and had gone over the course a time or two with Ernie Marinoni [a Petaluma Spartam teammate who would win in 1940]. We had observed several places where there was a choice of paths to follow and worked out which seemed to be the best from a time and energy-saving standpoint. I had also decided that I would wear shoes with short spikes to avoid slipping in the long swale that leads to the steep ravine and in the ravine itself. Somewhere farther along there was a stile and I also practiced hurdling over it rather than climbing it to save time in the race . . . And before the race I elicited a promise from my girlfriend that she would kiss me in front of everybody at the finish if I won.

Well, during the race I caught or kept ahead of everyone except Neil Decker and Herb Wright by the time we reached the swale. I saw that they were not wearing spikes and so I just let 'er go full blast down the hill past them and I knew that nobody could pass me in the ravine. As I led the way up that last hill as you leave the ravine, a Petaluma Spartan teammate . . . began running along with me shouting encouragement. I became a bit irritated at this as I didn't need the coaching and felt that it might be considered pacing and that I might be disqualified, so I told him to leave me alone. I had enough strength to sail over the stile and loped on

into Stinson Beach with a comfortable lead and finding it hard to believe that I had won. I almost forgot to collect the kiss but, sweaty as I was, I got it from my happily surprised girlfriend. The sponsors started a new perpetual trophy that year, I believe it is still in use [see below] and I am proud to have my name as the first one on it.

Allan married that girlfriend, Vergie Ludwig, the following year and they remain wed today.

The defending champion, Clarence Hall, improved his time by six seconds but had to settle for 10th. He won the best time award by just one second over Cal ace Ted Vollmer, who had started a minute behind Hall from scratch.

❏ A 15-minute handicap group, which included long-time Dipsea competitor Wilbur Taylor, was reintroduced.

❏ San Francisco's Sunrise Breakfast Club, which had "saved" the Dipsea after the 1932-33 hiatus, withdrew its sponsorship. The mantle passed to Marvelous Marin, Inc., acknowledged first in the previous year's program, and the Mill Valley Chamber of Commerce. Each had race committees, the former chaired by William Thomas, the latter by Emil Pohli (whose late brother Austin is memorialized by Pohli Rock at the Mountain Theater on Mt. Tamalpais). The Dipsea was again "under supervision [of the] Pacific Association Amateur Athletic Union" and many of the same officials continued to work the Race. Several accounts praised the new sponsors' lavishness. It included showers, an awards luncheon for all runners afterwards at the Sea Beach Hotel and 26 "handsome" trophies for 39 finishers.

❏ New was a team trophy based on combined times in addition to the traditional one based on finish places. The Petaluma Spartans won on finish order while the time trophy went "by one point" to the Olympic Club. (My tally shows the Spartans ahead under both methods; apparently only one trophy was awarded per team.)

❏ For several prior years, the overall winners were given a silver goblet; it took three triumphs to claim and "retire" the substantial victor's trophy. As no one won even twice, the rules were finally altered and a new perpetual winner's trophy inaugurated; Nelson's is the first name inscribed on it. It remained in use until 1988, when replaced by "The Bear" award.

❑ The Race date, November 26, remains the latest in Dipsea history.

1. Allan Nelson, 55:21 (10) [:20]
2. Neil Decker, 55:41 (10)
3. Herb Wright, 55:54 (10)
4. Arnold Scott, 55:50 (7:30)
5. Loren McIntyre, 51:00 (2:30)
6. Pete Zink, Jr., 56:11 (7:30)
7. Bill McCurdy, 53:15 (4:30)
8. George Wilson, 53:39 (4:30)
9. Don Torrengo, 59:34 (10)
10. Clarence Hall, 50:35 (1) **best time**
12. Ted Vollmer, 50:36 (0) **2nd best time**
Team (by place) Petaluma Spartans: Nelson, Scott, Al Ludlum (13th), Albert Handley (14th) and John Hansen (16th)
Team (by time) Olympic Club: McCurdy, Wilson, Eyrle Aceves (53:55, 3hc), Tommy Loughran (1:00:39, 7:30hc) and Bill Peters (1:07:05, 10hc)
39 finishers; bright, sunny, cool

34th Dipsea
September 29, 1940

The 1940 Race was held on an oppressively hot day, perhaps the hottest in Dipsea history, with morning temperatures rising above 90 degrees. Jack Kirk won the best time award with a 55:20, then the slowest to win that honor. And champion Ernie Marinoni's time of 1:00:04 was the second slowest winning effort to date. (Both excluding the long course year of 1905.)

Marinoni was born in North Beach, raised in Santa Rosa and had lived in Petaluma, where he hooked up with the Dipsea power Spartan team. He had been inspired in his childhood by a meeting with Dorando Pietri, who gained fame by staggering across the finish line first at the 1908 Olympic Marathon only to be disqualified for receiving help. Pietri was from the same Italian village, Vercelli, as Marinoni's father.

But it was boxing—Marinoni fought 183 fights as a lightweight under the name Johnnie Costello—that got him into running. He found himself enjoying the roadwork and continued it after he retired from the ring. He soon was doing long runs in the Berkeley hills, then became an active member of the Bay Area racing scene. He was also fit from his new second job at the Berkeley YMCA; he then worked as a trucker for Western States Grocery as well.

In his maiden Dipsea at age 34 in 1939, Marinoni had run an unimpressive 1:06:43 (7:30hc), finishing 28th of 39. He therefore saw his handicap rise to 10 minutes—the maximum was 15—for 1940. (There were no scratch runners; the last to start had a two minute handicap.)

Marinoni pushed hard from the start to Cardiac. He recalls, over 50 years later, the severe heat; "I liked the conditions. I had this ability to withstand punishment, to punish myself. The tougher it was, the better." He had his wife, two daughters and young son stationed at White Barn for support.

Then he came to a fork. "I didn't know the way," Marinoni remembers. "I shouted out, 'Which way?' and Kirk, who was not far behind, yelled out 'Go left.' I was then able to hold him off to the finish." Achieving a remarkable 6:39 improvement in time despite the heat, Marinoni ended up 16 seconds ahead of Kirk at the tape. Marinoni became the Race's second oldest winner to date (behind William Letcher, 43) and the *Chronicle* headline read "Oldster First."

Marinoni was the fourth individual winner to wear the Petaluma Spartans "Winged S" in six years and led them to their fourth team title in five years. Two other Spartans who had won Dipseas, John Hansen and defending titleist Allan Nelson, finished 6th and 28th, respectively.

The bridge over Redwood Creek in Muir Woods that the racers used had been washed away in a flood during the winter of 1938-39. For 1940, a new trail, roughly today's Dynamite, was carved downstream to replace the old Butler's Pride climb. Over the next years there would be references in the media to a new course for record purposes, but runners continued to recognize Bright's mark from 1937.

1. Ernie Marinoni, 1:00:04 (10) [:16]
2. Jack Kirk, 55:20 (5) **best time**
3. Robert Seaman, 58:56 (8)
4. Ray Dewey, 57:09 (6)
5. Ray Isle, 57:16 (6)
6. John Hansen, 1:00:03 (8)
7. Bruce Rich, 56:40 (4:30)
8. J. Carleton, 1:02:15 (10)
9. J. Montenrose, 59:32 (7)
10. Bill McCurdy, 55:29 (2:30) **2nd best time**
Team Petaluma Spartans: Marinoni, Seaman, Hansen, Rich and Arnold Scott (11th)
47 finishers; extremely hot, over 90 degrees

35th Dipsea
September 14, 1941

Willie Dreyer, winner of the 1941 Race, had tuberculosis as a child. He credited a healthy lifestyle, which included long-distance running, with his complete cure and subsequent longevity. He began running at age 14 in his hometown of Berington, Illinois. He went on to become one of the nation's best ultramarathoners, winner of three Milwaukee-to-Chicago 100 Mile Races. One, the year before his Dipsea triumph, was in an American record of 16 hours, 5 minutes, 2 seconds.

But when Dreyer moved to the Bay Area from Chicago just three months before the 1941 Race, he volunteered none of this information to Dipsea handicappers. So, as a rather unknown, seemingly aged 36-year-old, Dreyer was placed in the eight minute group, the Race's largest. Dreyer quickly pulled away from his starting group, which included '39 winner Allan Nelson. Passing the few others who started before him, and holding off two modest challenges from behind, Dreyer scored a 36-second victory. He replaced 1940 winner Ernie Marinoni as the Race's second oldest winner.

Runner-up was Dreyer's teammate on the relatively new Victory Athletic Club, John Kwartz. Kwartz, an outstanding swimmer, was just embarking on a 29-year career with the San Francisco Police Department during which he would be highly decorated for several daring ocean and bay rescues. Dreyer and Kwartz led the San Francisco-based club to the team trophy in a close battle over the Petaluma Spartans and the Olympic Club.

The Olympic Club's William McCurdy, starting with the 5-minute handicap group, won the best time award and finished 3rd. McCurdy had been a California State champion miler while at Tamalpais High School in Mill Valley, then was a standout runner for Stanford. His uncle, James Wilkins, just missed winning the 1906 Dipsea. McCurdy later became one of the nation's most respected track coaches in a decades-long career at Harvard. (One of his athletes, Dane Larsen, presented McCurdy the black shirt he won at the 1987 Dipsea). Ironically, McCurdy's lone best time award came in his slowest effort in four Dipsea tries.

❑ It was at the awards ceremony that Willie Dreyer met his future wife, Nancy. They married two months later. She would attain prominence in the Race as the first woman to run the Dipsea (unofficially) in 1950.

❑ Less than three months after the Race, the Japanese bombed Pearl Harbor and this country was drawn into World War II. There was a significant military presence on Mt. Tamalpais, including a still-evident enemy ship spotting station just west of the Dipsea route at the top of Insult. With sizable parts of the Mountain closed off to civilian use, the Dipsea was forced into a second hiatus. It missed four years, returning in 1946.

1. Willie Dreyer, 56:26 (8) [:36]
2. John Kwartz, 55:02 (6)
3. William McCurdy, 54:18 (5) **best time**
4. Robert Seaman, 57:49 (8)
5. Arnold Scott, 56:34 (6)
6. Gene Haran, 54:44 (4) **2nd best time**
7. Allan Nelson, 58:50 (8)
8. Herb Wright, 1:01:18 (10)
9. Ray Isle, 56:46 (5)
10. John Van Zant, 59:47 (8)

Team Victory Athletic Club: Dreyer, Kwartz, Haran, Armando Pelleretti (29th) and Bruno Bassini (32nd)
39 finishers

36th Dipsea
September 8, 1946

With World War II over and Mt. Tamalpais again fully open to the public, the Dipsea Race was resumed. Four consecutive races (1942-45) had been missed, making a total of six (with 1933-34) since the Dipsea's founding. The chief sponsor remained the Mill Valley Chamber of Commerce, this time with the Stinson Beach Progressive Club assisting.

Charles Richesin, 17, was a standout miler at San Rafael High School; his school record at the distance would stand for 28 years and he had placed 5th at the California State Meet three months earlier. Bill McCurdy, winner of the best time award at the last Dipsea and head of a running group called the Mill Valley Athletic Club, needed a fifth man for his team in the Dipsea. With few runners to choose from in those days, he turned to Richesin, who had never even heard of the Dipsea. McCurdy took Richesin on two practice runs over the course and they worked out on the steps.

With his 10-minute handicap, which he still labels as "a gift" decades later, Richesin took the lead early. He repeatedly asked course monitors the correct way to go. He recalls sliding down portions of Steep Ravine on his rear end. Richesin won by 25 seconds. And Richesin's new club made off with the team trophy. (Discrepancies in the results makes some of the times and names suspect. For example, the *Chronicle* account credits third place to Arner Gustafson in the text and to Bob Coughlin in the results while Ed Fratini's usually reliable hand-written notes lists Ed Siemens.)

William "Wrong Way" Steed, so named because of an error he made during a race in Antioch, was 4th and won the best time award by a huge margin. Steed had finished 3rd in Cross-City in 1945, and would do so again in 1947. Merle Knox, who would win Cross-City in 1947 and '49, was one of the two scratch starters and finished 16th.

Despite the five-year hiatus, seven former and future Dipsea champions competed. In finish order, they were: Richesin, Ernie Marinoni, Jack Kirk, Willie Dreyer, Leslie McGregor, John Hansen and Paul Chirone. Also on hand to welcome the Race's return were three of the legendary runners from the Dipsea's earliest days; John Hassard, Oliver Millard and Mason Hartwell.

❑ Because there had been no Race for five years, and the Dipsea Trail little hiked during World War II (much of Mt. Tamalpais was closed by the military), the course had become overgrown. Runners went on work parties marking turns with gypsum.

❑ The program offered a tribute to members of the Dipsea Indians, the group that founded the Race, "who are still with us and who are special guests this day." Listed are: Charles Arata, Michael Buckley, Frank Foran, Vincent Finigan, Judge Timothy Fitzpatrick (who "spoke over the loudspeaker"), Louis Ferrari, Frank Marisch, Oscar Turnblad, Tiv Kreling, William Nelson, Floyd Russell, Harry Smith, Stanislaus Riley, Otto Walfisch and Leon Pinkson.

❑ Runners were given a slip of paper at the start to write down their estimated finish time. Steed had the closest guess and won an additional trophy.

❑ The finish line crowd was kept informed of the Race in progress through "a short wave system of walkie talkie hook-ups along the route." Today, volunteers from the Marin Amateur Radio Club still report from checkpoints along the course, mainly, though, for medical emergencies.

❑ There was a post-Race luncheon for contestants and officials at Stinson's Surf Hotel at 1:30 p.m. The trophies were then handed out in the County Park (later a State Park, now part of Golden Gate National Recreation Area), as they still are. For 1947, the luncheon was also moved outdoors, as it is today (although now meals are provided only for volunteers; runners arrange their own picnics).

1. Charles Richesin, 1:00:22 (10) [:25]
2. Frank Campbell, 1:03:47 (13)
3. Ed Siemens, 59:47 (8)
4. William Steed, 52:55 (1) **best time**
5. William McCurdy, 55:27 (3:30)
6. Ernest Marinoni, 1:01:16 (9)
7. Robert Seaman, 1:01:53 (9)
8. Bruce Rich, 59:48 (6)
9. Takeo Takushi, 55:06 (1) **2nd best time**
10. Jack Kirk, 1:01:21 (7)
Team Mill Valley Athletic Club: Richesin, Siemens, McCurdy, Donald Branson (11th) and Robert Wallace (18th)
42 finishers; mostly clear, some fog on higher sections

37th Dipsea
September 7, 1947

With the former strict age requirements lifted, a 15-year-old, Allan Baffico, won in his first Dipsea. He was the youngest Dipsea champion ever, retaining that distinction until 1969, when 10-year-old Vance Eberly won.

Baffico's older brother Andrew had run the Dipsea the year before and finished 36th of 41. Allan was a miler at Balboa High School, which was across the street from the family home. Both brothers entered the 1947 Dipsea as members of the newly formed Excelsior Marathon Club (unrelated to today's Excelsior Running Club, though also with roots in the Excelsior district of San Francisco). Andrew was given 11 handicap minutes and Allan 14, one short of the maximum. They took one training run over the course.

Allan recalls (in a conversation in 1993) passing a few runners, then wondering where the others were. "I didn't see anyone. I thought they were either going very fast or I was going too slow. I thought I was far behind so I just kept going faster to catch them. I particularly didn't want my brother to beat me. I had no idea I was winning until I saw the finish line. By then I was getting sick [he was weaving, and would throw up], but I made it. It was a great day."

Allan finished with a torn jersey, the result of a brush with a fence. "I couldn't see it through the fog," he told reporters.

Fellow Excelsior member George Miller, who started with the earliest group, finished 2nd, exactly a minute behind. Andrew, running eight seconds slower than Allan, took 3rd. Joe King, who would have a long and brilliant running career (he won the 1,500 meters gold medal in the 65-69 age group at the 1991 World Veterans Games, and plans to compete again in the 1994 Dipsea), debuted in 4th.

Five of the first 14 finishers (Baffico, Jack Kirk, Ernie Marinoni, defender Charlie Richesin and Willie Dreyer) were past, present or future Dipsea champions.

The program said, "Due to the fact that the original course has been altered and lengthened approximately one-half mile, this year's race will establish a new course record to stand until broken." Newspaper accounts picked up on this and proclaimed George Cole, a Naval officer who ran for the Olympic Club, as the new course record holder after he won the best time award in 55:06. But runners considered Norman Bright's 1937 time of 47:22 as obviously superior and that remained the course record to beat. The extra distance, certainly less than a half-mile, stemmed from the closure of Butler's Pride, the historic route uphill beyond Redwood Creek in Muir Woods. With direct access to Butler's Pride cut off after the bridge to it washed away, and the area little run or hiked during World War II, the route had become overgrown. Runners now used the newer trail downstream.

❑ There were particularly strong Cross-City ties this year. Fred Kline, who had already won three Cross-City races (he would win four), was the lone scratch man. He ended up 21st with the day's second fastest time. Merle Knox, who won the '47 Cross-City (and would win it again in 1949) was 27th (59:15; 1hc). And John Holden, another future Cross-City winner (1951), was 10th.

❑ Robert Seaman, one of the era's outstanding Dipsea runners, apparently started in the wrong handicap group, one minute too early. He was later dropped from 11th to 16th in the official results, which had a bearing on the team scoring.

❑ The team title seemingly went to the Petaluma Spartans although at least one account says the Olympic Club won. Further complicating matters, the Excelsior Marathon Club, which swept places 1-2-3 and also #15, would have claimed the prize if they had one more runner. Tony Stratta, who finished 33rd in his first Dipsea (he still runs the Race), was listed as an Excelsior member in a

Runners leave Mill Valley, circa 1948. Today, redwoods obscure the Lytton Square flagpole. (Mill Valley Public Library)

(Left) Charles Richesin vainly attempts to defend his crown in 1947.
(Below) Leslie McGregor about to collapse in official Joe Tracy's arms as he breaks the tape in 1948. (Independent Journal)

different competition just one week later; here he ran for Lowell High School. Tony's father Dominic, a fireman who had begun racing in 1924, was 36th. This earned the Strattas the first father-son trophy, an award begun at Dominic's suggestion. The Strattas (sometimes the only entry) would win four consecutive years before the award was temporarily discontinued.

❏ The sponsoring Mill Valley Chamber of Commerce awarded trophies to every finisher.

1. Allan Baffico, 59:27 (14) [1:00]
2. George Miller, 1:01:27 (15)
3. Andrew Baffico, 59:35 (11)
4. Joe King, 57:00 (7)
5. Jack Kirk, 57:17 (6)
6. George Cole, 55:06 (3) **best time**
7. Ernest Marinoni, 59:17 (7)
8. Arner Gustafson, 57:30 (5)
9. Bruce Rich, 58:57 (6)
10. John Holden, 57:03 (4)
21. Fred Kline, 56:25 (0) **2nd best time**
Team Petaluma Spartans: Gustafson, Rich, Walter Bertram (14th), Robert Seaman (16th) and Kenneth Williams (18th)
49 finishers; overcast, low fog

38th Dipsea
September 12, 1948

This was a particularly exciting Dipsea. There were several late passes, the smallest gap ever (two seconds) separated the first two finishers, and the winner collapsed across the tape. Ham radio operator reports of the unfolding drama kept the finish line crowd tense.

Robert Banfield, a 15-year-old at Tamalpais High School who started one minute after the first (15 minute) group, led much of the way. A mile from the finish, Stewart Cramer and Robert Annis joined the lead pack. Annis, also 15, was a San Rafael High student who had overcome polio. Leslie McGregor and Charlie Richesin, in 4th and 5th positions, were closing.

At the end it was McGregor, overhauling the lead trio and just holding off, by ten yards, the hard charging Richesin. McGregor's official victory margin of two seconds is the smallest in Dipsea history. The effort—he lopped almost nine minutes off his time from the previous year—caused McGregor to collapse seconds after finishing. Indeed, an official was ready to hold McGregor upright at the tape.

McGregor, not well known in the running world and competing unattached, was a 30-year-old highrise construction worker living in San Francisco. He had attended high schools in Johnstown, Pennsylvania, and Phoenix, Arizona, as well as the City's Galileo High School, where he ran. McGregor spent two years at the University of Pennsylvania. From there he entered World War II as an Air Corps fighter pilot, seeing action in the Pacific theater. But most remarkable, McGregor had already experienced the first signs of Parkinson's disease. The illness, which ultimately would completely debilitate him and take his life, was in remission during 1948.

Though entered in the 1941 Dipsea, McGregor did not run. The next Dipsea held was in 1946 and

McGregor placed 21st of 41 finishers (1:06:21; 7hc). That same year, he was second in the Petaluma Marathon, though ran over 4 hours. He was 23rd of 49 in the 1947 Dipsea (1:04:54; 8hc). McGregor therefore retained his eight minute handicap for 1948. Many practice runs over the course helped to produce his improvement, and triumph.

Richesin came close to becoming the Race's first double winner since 1913; he still rues not starting his finish drive sooner. He had some consolation in handily winning the best time trophy. His 52:06 was more than eight minutes swifter than his overall winning effort two years earlier. Richesin had two brothers in the Race, Carlo (43rd) and Jimmy (54th).

In 10th place was Jesse Van Zant, one of the finest open runners ever to compete in the Dipsea. He won a host of national distance titles and four Cross-City races and was third at the 1948 Olympic Trials Marathon in Boston (but passed over for the Olympic team on a technicality).

Frank Grundisch took a serious fall, both hurting his knee and losing his shorts. He finished, in 51st and wobbly, clad in his athletic supporter.

Several prominent runners were behind even him. Fred Kline, a four-time Cross-City champion, was 52nd. Wilbur Taylor, who had first run in 1915, was 55th. Leo Karlhofer, winner of the best time award in 1934, returned and finished 56th. Jimmy McClymonds, the 1936 winner, was next to last. And the final finisher, with the slowest time yet recorded on a results sheet (1:59:40), was none other than a scratch runner who would later win Cross-City, John Holden. He presumably got lost.

The 1940 winner Ernie Marinoni finished 21st and his 10-year-old son Robert 66th. Robert was, by several years, the youngest Dipsea finisher yet. The AAU had only recently dropped the lower age limit from 17 to 15.

Both the Mill Valley Athletic Club and the Petaluma Spartans won team trophies. The Mill Valley quintet were Tam High runners assembled by Ted Wassam (8th); they went to 1937 champion Paul Chirone, a Tam grad himself, for training tips. One of their members was 14-year-old Lynn Ludlow, who lived at the base of the Dipsea steps (his mother still resides there). He would later write about the Race for the *Examiner* and *Independent Journal*. The Spartans' award was called the time prize, based on scoring without consideration of handicaps.

❑ The number of finishers, 71, was the highest since 1922.

❑ To raise money for the financially shaky Race, there was an auction of "Pacific Islands curios" donated by one of the officials.

1. Leslie McGregor, 57:04 (8) [:02]
2. Charles Richesin, 52:06 (3) **best time**
3. Stewart Cramer, 1:01:04 (11)
4. Robert Banfield, 1:04:05 (14)
5. Robert Annis, 1:02:22 (11)
6. George Wilson, 1:02:05 (10)
7. Ted Wassam, 59:04 (6)
8. Nick Miller, 1:03:04 (10)
9. Bruce Rich, 58:05 (5)
10. Jesse Van Zant, 54:05 (0) **2nd best time**

Team (by place) Mill Valley Athletic Club: Banfield, Wassam, Lynn Ludlow (16th), Rae Workman (20th) and Donald Chamberlin (37th)

Team (by actual time) Petaluma Spartans: Rich, Arner Gustafson (57:19), Robert Seaman (1:03:28), James Baggett (1:05:03) and Walter Bertram (1:03:38)

71 finishers; warm at the start, fog at the finish

39th Dipsea
September 11, 1949

The Dipsea entered a three year crisis in sponsorship. The Mill Valley Chamber of Commerce was losing interest in the event; they half-joked about getting the course direction reversed to bring the post-race spending to their city. An offshoot of the Chamber, Dipseans of Mill Valley, again under the chairmanship of Emil Pohli, was formed to stage the Race. Surviving Dipsea Indians were credited by Pohli with donating funds. In the more colorful language of the Olympic Club's *Olympian*, "When the smoke signal of distress floated in the air over Mt. Tamalpais, calling upon all 'Braves' to pungle up wampum to finance this year's race, 'Big Swede Chief' Turnblad called an emergency powwow of the Olympian tribe, at which sufficient money was donated to keep the historic race alive."

Marin's Hamilton Field Air Force base also served as a sponsor. Bonuses of their involvement were a performance by their "Negro drill team" and a jet bomber aerial show over the finish line. Also at the finish, the Dipsea handicapper, Attilio Maggiora, released a dozen homing pigeons.

Paul Juette became the fourth University of California runner to win the race, joining Donald Dunn, Clarence Hall and Allan Nelson. The 21-year-old sophomore, just out of the Army, was given a seemingly generous eight-minute handicap in his maiden Dipsea despite good collegiate credentials—he had captured the Cal-Stanford two-mile the previous spring.

Warren Fairbanks, a 15-year-old from Polytechnic High School in his first crossing ever of the Dipsea course, started one minute after the 15-minute maximum and took the lead at the top of the steps. Fairbanks held the lead for five more miles despite sustaining some bruises while trying to avoid a tree at the base of Suicide. But he could only watch helplessly when the long-striding Juette

finally flew by. "He [Juette] just looked like a big man, like a real runner," Fairbanks recalled 42 years later. Fairbanks would soon after win the City's high school cross country title and remains a competitive age group runner.

Joseph Kragel also passed Fairbanks, with less than a mile to go. Kragel was a Frenchman who had arrived in California six months earlier and was now a pressman for the *San Francisco Chronicle*. He claimed afterward, in French, that had he known there was another runner ahead (Juette), he would have run even faster. Kragel would win the best time award the following year.

Juette ended up with the day's second fastest time, 53:15. Best time honors again went, as in 1946, to William Steed. Steed came all the way from Washington, hitchhiking a good part of the distance because of a bus strike.

Bill Ranney, destined to become one of this country's top race walkers, debuted in 48th place. His long Dipsea career, which would include several top-10 finishes, would later be clouded by widespread allegations of cheating (he was once seen driving to Pantoll, then later crossing the finish line). Ultimately he would be banned from running.

The 1946 champion Charles Richesin was the lone scratch runner. He had set a record in the Arcata to Eureka 8-Mile Race the day before, then drove back to Marin for the Dipsea. Exhausted, he finished 26th.

Jim Shettler, Merle Knox and Fred Kline, who between them won eight Cross-City races, ended up 63rd, 68th and 70th, respectively, among the 85 finishers. For Shettler, 16, it was his first AAU race.

The team trophy was listed in several accounts as having gone to the Yancey Athletic Club but the San Francisco Athletic Club clearly had a lower point score.

There were a record eight past, present and future Dipsea champions in the Race. In finish order they were: Juette, Jack Kirk, Richesin, Jimmy McClymonds, Willie Dreyer, Shettler, William Mazzini and Ernie Marinoni.

□ The 85 finishers marked a high for the Dipsea between the years 1920 and 1963.

□ The program mentioned that the American Broadcasting Co. was covering the Race.

□ Newspaper accounts made much of the presence of William Oscar Johnson, running his 18th Dipsea (he was second in 1914) at the advanced age of 63. Johnson finished 80th, then announced his retirement from the Race.

□ The *Chronicle* reporter noted that Juette just beat his newspaper's Oldsmobile to the finish.

1. Paul Juette, 53:15 (8) **2nd best time**
2. Joseph Kragel, 53:39 (7)
3. Warren Fairbanks, 1:01:53 (14)
4. William Steed, 52:15 (4) **best time**
5. Art Thanash, 1:00:38 (12)
6. James Allen, 53:56 (5)
7. Robert Derrigan, 1:00:42 (11)
8. Calvin Mahlert, 53:46 (4)
9. Jim Kendall, 1:04:57 (15)
10. Jack Kirk, 55:06 (5)

Team San Francisco Athletic Club: Fairbanks, Thanash, Derrigan, Lowrie O'Donnell (11th) and Dominic Stratta (25th)
85 finishers; sunny, mild

40th Dipsea
September 10, 1950

Less than a month before the Race date, the organizers (the Dipseans, a small group of Mill Valley Chamber of Commerce members) decided to call off the event. This was despite rising interest; the 1949 turnout of 125 entries and 85 finishers was the largest since 1920. Runners petitioned the Pacific Association of the Amateur Athletic Union. Long distance chairman Art Articary promised to keep the event alive. Thus, for 1950 only, the Dipsea was sponsored by the sport's governing body, not by a private group.

The AAU magazine notes that $94 was raised to finance the Race—entry fees would not be charged until 1964. Twenty-five dollars came from the old Dipsea Indians Association, the group which founded the Dipsea. The rest was donated by individual AAU officials such as Articary himself, Frank Geis, who directed the Cross-City for decades, and Attilio Maggiora, who did the Dipsea handicapping. Three runners kicked in a total of $4. The $94 was spent as follows: $77.04 for trophies; $7.07 for "bread, mayonnaise and waxpaper"; $5.45 for certificates; and $4.44 for postage stamps. There were also donations by businesses. These included milk from the Marin Dell Dairy and meat for sandwiches from two meat companies. Past champions Ernie Marinoni and Willie Dreyer donated trophies. Some corners were cut—for example, no program was printed—but the Dipsea was saved.

The previous year, Balboa High's Jim Shettler, in his first AAU race, finished 63rd of 85 finishers in 65:51 (7hc). Obviously not impressing anyone, Shettler saw his 1950 handicap raised by two minutes, to nine. He went on to run the day's seventh fastest time and win by one minute, 47 seconds.

Shettler was already a standout prep miler, having taken second in the San Francisco championships. At 6'2" and 160 pounds, Shettler was described in newspaper accounts as "big Jim" and the "lanky 17-year-old blond." He would go on to become one of the greatest of all Northern California runners, twice winning the Cross-City Race among scores of other titles before dying of a heart attack at age 42.

The last runner Shettler passed was another San Francisco high schooler, Louis Butler of Polytechnic. Butler, the runner-up, flew to New Haven hours after the race to enter Yale on an academic scholarship.

Third in was Joe Kragel, the 23-year-old Frenchman who was dubbed the "pride of the *Chronicle* press room" by his fellow employees. He had been second the previous year. Kragel's 51:32 won the best time trophy by an extraordinary (and unmatched) five minutes, 21 seconds.

The Race was run in particularly thick fog, which might have had a bearing on the outcome. Defending champion Paul Juette and 1949 third-placer Warren Fairbanks both took wrong turns in Muir Woods and Ling Chen Wang, the fastest man in the field, followed them. The trio all ended up among the last finishers. Wang, of Hong Kong, had, three weeks earlier, won the Berkeley Marathon (a bit shorter than the standard 26.2 miles) in 2:28:29, a time below the then Olympic record. Juette and Wang, along with James Allen and Kragel, were the four scratch starters.

Most notable in terms of the future of the Dipsea was the appearance of the first woman. Women were barred from all AAU distance races and would be until 1971. Even the Olympic Games then offered nothing longer than 200 meters. But, running unofficially, Nancy Dreyer, wife of the 1941 champ Willie Dreyer, did cover the full course. Starting 25 minutes ahead of the first runner, the 44-year-old from Berkeley clocked a 1:36:36. Dreyer was the lone woman to run for five years, and there is no record of another female in the race until 1959. Dreyer was a nurse at Alta Bates Hospital in Berkeley and trained by running up the building's six stories.

❑ Bert Hooper, who won the high school trophy in 1920 and was third in 1921, returned and finished 55th.

❑ Only nine runners broke one hour, an all-time low.

❑ The park in which the Dipsea now finishes passed from County to State management. Today the popular beach is part of the Golden Gate National Seashore.

1. Jim Shettler, 58:27 (9) [1:47]
2. Louis Butler, 1:03:14 (12)
3. Joe Kragel, 51:32 (0) **best time**
4. Tony Stratta, 1:03:48 (12)
5. Bob Hillard, 59:54 (8)
6. Victor Gipson, 1:02:51 (10)
7. Bill Rodarte, 1:00:52 (8)
8. Alfred DeLormier, 56:53 (4) **2nd best time**
9. Thatcher Nance, 1:03:08 (10)
10. Robert Menzies, 1:02:32 (9)
Team Excelsior Marathon Club: Shettler, Hillard, Gipson, Nance and Aldo Pardini (22nd)
60 finishers; thick fog produced mud on course

41st Dipsea
August 26, 1951

Jack Kirk had raced every Dipsea since his first in 1930. (And through 1993 he still hasn't missed any). Twice he had won the best time award and twice he finished second. Finally, 21 years after his maiden Dipsea and on his 16th try (both were records, later surpassed), Kirk was first to Stinson Beach. But it was not without a splendid battle.

The initial fight was actually to stage the Race at all. Once again, a last-second effort was needed to "save" the Dipsea. No sponsor was found until August 13. Then, a San Francisco group, the South of Market Boys Club, stepped in. They quickly set an early date of August 26 (the Race had been held the second Sunday of September since 1940) and that was all the notice runners had.

The Dipsea's long-time handicapper, Attilio Maggiora, was on vacation so his duties passed to Ernie Marinoni (the 1940 winner) and others. Kirk thinks Marinoni was disposed to give him a break as he had been so long frustrated in trying to win; he was awarded two extra minutes from 1950. But Kirk's four minute handicap appears fair, particularly since it was the same given to Libero (Lee) Gentili, a Petaluma Spartan teammate who had finished second at Cross-City that May and who regularly beat Kirk at local road races.

Kirk had been most worried about the veteran Tom Loughran, now running with a 10 minute handicap. But Kirk caught Laughran on the Hogsback to take the lead. Gentili, however, remained close behind.

Kirk recalls, 42 years later, the ensuing events:

To get rid of Gentili, I sprinted down Steep Ravine. I didn't think anyone could go so fast down. But at the bottom, Gentili was still there. I said to myself, "How can I get rid of this guy?"

We were both tired and started walking up Insult. Then Gentili said, "I think you have a chance to win this year." That got me going.

When we began the downhill, I waited for the stile [at the first shortcut off Panoramic Highway], then darted over it right in front of him. I ran down to the finish as fast as I could and beat him by 10 seconds.

Paul Juette, the 1949 champ who had gotten lost in 1950, was only another 14 seconds behind. He easily had the day's fastest time, 53:40 from scratch. Kirk's 57:10 was second fastest.

Dipsea veteran Arner Gustafson, who had won the Berkeley Marathon the Sunday before, was 4th. Allan Nelson, the 1939 winner, finished 5th. Walter Deike, who would win the following year, got lost in his first Dipsea and came in 6th. Loughran ended up 10th. Marshall Clark, who would go on to become one of the nation's premier college track coaches, was 27th.

But perhaps the most notable name in the official results as printed by the AAU was that of the last place finisher, Nancy Dreyer (1:50:55, 15hc). Dreyer had run the previous year; now she was the first woman to appear in the results.

The Petaluma Spartans were dominant, taking four of the first five positions with Kirk their fifth different individual champion.

❑ A special one-mile women's race was staged "from the dairy on the hills behind Stinson Beach to the [Dipsea] finish line." Earlene Pecot (8:09), Mary Samuels (8:10) and Lois Dye (8:12), all from Willie Dreyer's Dreyer Athletic Club, were the tightly bunched three finishers.

❑ A then record seven of the finishers ran scratch.

❑ There was a 20-piece band on hand at the finish, financed, as it would be for the next several years, by a music industry trust fund.

❑ One newspaper account emphasized that, "Runners must report to the Mill Valley firehouse at 8:30 a.m. [the start was then at 10 a.m.] for a physical examination." This requirement, enforced at all AAU races, continued until the early 1970's.

1. Jack Kirk, 57:10 (4) [:10] **2nd best time**
2. Lee Gentili, 57:20 (4)
3. Paul Juette, 53:34 (0) **best time**
4. Arner Gustafson, 57:17 (3)
5. Allan Nelson, 59:54 (5)
6. Walter Deike, 58:10 (3)
7. Bill Ranney, 1:05:17 (10)
8. Anton Nelson, 58:40 (3)
9. Burrell Sullivan, 1:01:02 (5)
10. Price King, 1:00:13 (3)
Team Petaluma Spartans: Kirk, Gentili, Gustafson, Allan Nelson and Sullivan
45 finishers; heavy fog produced muddy sections

42nd Dipsea
September 7, 1952

Walter Deike, who won the NCAA 10,000 meter title that spring while a 31-year-old senior at the University of Wisconsin, was one of the best open runners to race the Dipsea in his prime. He certainly was one of the toughest; he finished the previous NCAA cross country championship after breaking his leg before the halfway mark on an iced-over course.

Deike was born in Germany and raised in Freeport, Illinois. He ran only one year while in high school there, then was called into military service during World War II. He served five years in the Army, in the infantry and as a bandsman, mostly in the Far East. After the War, he enrolled at the University of Wisconsin and joined the Badgers' strong track and cross country teams. Deike dropped out of college after his sophomore year and came to California (he would return to captain the Wisconsin cross country team, and earn his B.A. in 1952 in pre-medical studies).

Though Deike had run only 58:10 (3hc) in 1951 in his maiden Dipsea (he had gotten lost), his road race credentials since put him in with the 1952 scratch group. He quickly pulled away from his starting group of 10, two of them Dipsea champions (Jim Shettler and Charles Richesin). The *Chronicle* account noted: "Traditionally Dipsea racers stop at the fences [much of the course beyond Muir Woods was still used for cattle grazing]. But Deike had a full head of steam and he simply threw the front leg up and hurdled the three-and four-foot fences, track style. As evidence of his speed, he made up almost five minutes on [Kary] Fitzgerald over the [final] mile and one-half."

Deike's 51:45 was the day's fastest by over four minutes. The *Chronicle* headline read, "Dipsea Record Broken," referring to post-1938 course changes, but Bright's 1937 time was superior. Deike's winning margin of three minutes, 47 seconds, was the largest so far in Dipsea history. (Ralph Perry would win by even more the following year.) And Deike became the first scratch winner in 35 years; Mason Hartwell the only previous one in 1917. Deike raced in the red singlet of his alma mater, Wisconsin. He boarded a plane that evening for Chicago, where he was about to enroll at the University of Chicago Medical School.

Runner-up Kary Fitzgerald was an 18-year-old high schooler headed for the College of Marin. Jim Maddox, one of the scratch men, was 3rd. William Mazzini, who would win in 1955, was 6th. Lynn Ludlow, who lived on the course at the base of the Dipsea steps, was 8th.

Running unofficially, their entries denied but assigned handicaps and their times recorded, were 9-year-old Mike Dye (too young) and Nancy Dreyer. Ernie Marinoni, accompanying his young son Robert (17th), was unofficial as well.

The Race, emerging from its sponsorship woes, was credited as financed by the South of Market Boys, the California Jockey Club and by the Olympic Club's William P. Kyne.

❏ The *Chronicle's* account contains some surprising statements about the Dipsea course. "[Deike's] was one of the best performances ever turned in, since the course has grown rougher with the years. When Norman Bright . . . set the old course record of 47:22, the trail was cleared of fences and other obstacles and was smoothed by the constant traffic of hikers. Alas, hikers are a vanishing breed and the runners now plow over rough terrain."

1. Walter Deike, 51:45 (0) [3:27] **best time**
2. Kary Fitzgerald, 1:01:12 (6)
3. Jim Maddox, 55:49 (0) **2nd best time**
4. Price King, 57:06 (1)
5. Hal Grant, 1:01:22 (5)
6. William Mazzini, 1:03:30 (7)
7. John Kwartz, 1:02:35 (7)
8. Lynn Ludlow, 1:02:40 (6)
9. Walter Boehm, 57:49 (0)
10. Jim Shettler, 57:50 (0)
Team Mill Valley A.C.: Fitzgerald, Shettler, Jud Foreman (15th), M. Simpson (20th) and James Allen (25th)
40 finishers; sunny

43rd Dipsea
September 6, 1953

Ralph Perry scored the most lopsided win in the history of the Dipsea, finishing 6 minutes, 53 seconds ahead of runner-up Paul Juette. Indeed, he recalls being in the Stinson Beach showers when he heard the applause for the second finisher.

Perry, as a 17-year-old without any competitive open running background and in his first Dipsea, had been awarded an eight-minute handicap. He rather quickly overhauled the 10 men who started ahead of him, then had little trouble holding off 1949 champion Juette, who only ran 64 seconds faster from scratch. But, although he was comfortably in front, Perry didn't know it until he asked an official at Lone Tree how many runners were ahead. The response was a laugh, and "no one." "That was like a jolt from a cattle prod to really get me going," Perry recalled 38 years later.

Perry grew up within yards of the starting line, at 179 Tamalpais Avenue. Indeed, his boyhood newspaper delivery route included the starting area. Watching the Dipsea race, sometimes with close neighbors Phil Smith (who would win in 1961) and George Cagwin (who also became a Dipsea regular) was an annual tradition from around age 5.

Perry had gotten into running seriously only the year before, running varsity cross country and track as a junior at the Mt. Hermon School in Massachusetts. (Mt. Hermon, coincidentally, is home of one of the very few extant races in this country that predates the Dipsea. The prep school has staged an annual Pie Race since 1891; finishers below a cutoff time receive pies. Perry would win the race in his senior year and set a course record. That record was then broken by Frank Shorter, the future Olympic gold medal marathoner.) Perry jogged on the Dipsea course in preparation, but had never done a timed effort. He was the first Mill Valley resident to win the Dipsea.

One of Perry's threats, the scratch runner Dick Vierra, got lost in Muir Woods and never finished. But Vierra would have needed a course record to beat Perry. Vierra returned to Mill Valley and telephoned to report he was safe.

Third to finish—passed late by Juette—was Fresno State's Len Thornton. Thornton also had the day's third fastest actual running time. Fourth in was 56-year-old Victor Duran. Outstanding high school miler Duane Ludlow took 8th.

❏ Last to Stinson was Wilbur Taylor, who first competed in 1915 and then held the record, later broken by Jack Kirk, for most Dipsea finishes.

❏ This was the final Dipsea for Bruce Rich, part of this and five other Petaluma Spartan winning teams. Rich, who had finished as high as third in 1938, died of a heart attack at age 44, four months after the Race. His record for team trophies was broken by Darryl Beardall in 1964.

❏ Nancy Dreyer was again the only woman to run the course. She started 30 minutes before the scratch runners, 15 before the maximum handicap men. She was warmly welcomed by the finish line crowd, but her time was not recorded.

❏ San Francisco's South of Market Boys Club were now the chief organizers but sponsorship credit was also extended to Judge Timothy Fitzpatrick and other survivors of the original Dipsea Indians.

1. Ralph Perry, 55:03 (8) [6:56] **2nd best time**
2. Paul Juette, 53:59 (0) **best time**
3. Len Thornton, 56:07 (2)
4. Victor Duran, 1:05:09 (10)
5. Jud Foreman, 59:38 (4)
6. Medford Todd, 1:05:50 (10)
7. Frank Veloz, 1:02:53 (7)
8. Duane Ludlow, 57:22 (1)
9. Jack Kirk, 58:37 (2)
10. Anton Nelson, 59:59 (3)
Team Petaluma Spartans: Duran, Veloz, Kirk, William Mazzini (13th) and Bruce Rich (28th)
42 finishers; warm and clear

44th Dipsea
September 12, 1954

As a harbinger of future Dipseas, a woman was first to Stinson Beach. But Nancy Dreyer received no awards. For one, the 48-year-old mother of two and wife of 1941 champion Willie Dreyer had started herself with a 30-minute handicap; the maximum awarded was 15. And, of course, Dreyer was not officially entered; women would not be formally allowed into the Dipsea until 1971. Her time was not recorded, but was just below 1:20. This was the fifth and last time Nancy Dreyer ran. No other woman tried the Dipsea for five more years, no female would finish first for 19 years and no adult woman would win for 36 years.

Pre-Race attention was focused on Jesse Van Zant, one of the greatest runners ever to compete in the Dipsea. Van Zant won numerous national distance running titles, finished third in the 1948 U.S. Olympic marathon trials (but was passed over for a place on the team) and was in the midst of a three year (1953-55) win streak at Cross-City in which he was beating all of Northern California's best by huge margins. But, like many other brilliant runners before and since, he found the Dipsea educational, falling twice, finishing 6th from scratch and even missing the best time award.

Winning was Herb Stockman, a 22-year-old former Richmond High School track runner and football player who had just returned from a three-year stint in Korea with the Marines. Stockman had learned about the Dipsea purely by chance. He was doing some laps at City College of San Francisco, where he had temporarily enrolled, when a fellow student, Medford Todd, came alongside. Todd said he was preparing for the 1954 Dipsea (he had been sixth the year before) and invited Stockman to join him on the course. The pair took three or four training runs over the route and Todd was able to persuade Stockman, who had never done a non-track race before, to enter.

As an unknown, Stockman was given an eight-minute handicap, starting with the man who would win the following year, William Mazzini. Stockman quickly began overhauling the few men who had started ahead. He recalls, "I had counted off the runners who started ahead of me and then kept track of them as I passed them. Somehow I lost count and thought there were two more left. So I kept pushing extremely hard. My wife said I was white as a sheet when she saw me go over the last stile. I was surprised when they told me I won, I didn't know. It's a good thing I miscounted because I might have been tempted to give up pushing, though, as a Marine, I wasn't used to giving up."

Some low handicap men closed, but not enough, Stockman winning by exactly a minute. The triumph had immediate benefit for Stockman; famed running coach Bud Winter of San Jose State heard about it and recruited him to enroll at the college. Stockman's friend Todd finished 12th.

Ralph Love, a former standout at Piedmont High School and then running for Stanford, was 2nd. Love, who became a physician, remained active in the running world and temporarily resuscitated, in 1978, the Golden Gate Marathon.

Len Thornton finished 3rd for the second year in a row. He claimed the best time award, running six seconds faster than Van Zant.

Jack Marden, who would go on to become a national class miler and steeplechaser, finished 4th in his Dipsea debut. He would win the 1961 Cross-City. He still coaches track. Two of his sons, Jack and Jay, are currently among Northern California's best distance runners.

The high school trophy, one of the most important awards in the Dipsea's early days, was revived after a lapse of 33 years. It was donated by Tony and Manuel Brazil, who owned a dairy ranch that included the Hogsback section of the Dipsea. The award was won by Mel Dowdell, 8th overall, a miler at now gone Polytechnic High in San Francisco.

Among the few scratch starters was Hal Higdon. He ran 56:39 to finish 11th. Higdon, then at the University of Chicago with 1952 winner Walter Deike, has continued as one of the sport's best age-group runners. He has also written several books about running and is a columnist for *Runner's World* magazine.

Also debuting was Jim Imperiale, who would play a major role in the Dipsea over the next two decades and would win in 1959. As a Petaluma Spartan (he would later recruit many of his teammates for his new Marin Athletic Club), he finished sixth from last in 1:25:56.

The finish line was moved, for 1954 only, from the intersection of Shoreline Highway and Calle del Mar, where it had been since 1907, onto the driveway of the State Park maintenance yard. Reese measured this added 85 feet of distance.

The program proclaimed that the 1954 Race was the Dipsea's golden anniversary, as dated from the Boas-Coney match race of 1904. The '54 Race was also called the "Judge Edward P. Shortall Memorial Dipsea Cross Country Race" and all finishers received "Judge Shortall memorial medals." Shortall was one of the original Dipsea Indians. His daughter, San Francisco supervisor Clarissa Shortall McMahon, was the official starter. San Francisco's Mayor Elmer Robinson was the honorary chairman and Judge Timothy Fitzpatrick, founding father of the Dipsea, was again chairman.

1. Herb Stockman, 58:43 (8) [1:00]
2. Ralph Love, 55:43 (4)
3. Len Thornton, 54:30 (1) **best time**
4. Jack Marden, 59:31 (6)
5. Harold Kuha, 55:53 (2)
6. Jesse Van Zant, 54:36 (0) **2nd best time**
7. Jim Maddox, 56:04 (1)
8. Mel Dowdell, 59:22 (4) **1st HS**
9. Charles Richesin, 55:36 (0)
10. Arner Gustafson, 58:59 (3)
Team Flying "A" Athletic Club (Stockton): Thornton, Marden, Kuha, Richesin and Paul Hansen (20th)
54 finishers; clear, pleasant

45th Dipsea
September 18, 1955

Twenty-five years after running his first Dipsea—he was fourth in 1930—William Mazzini finally won. This quarter-century gap between debut and first victory was then a record for the Race, surpassing Jack Kirk's 21 years. It in turn would be surpassed by Norman Bright in 1970 (35 years), but Bright made fewer attempts than Mazzini. Mazzini was also, at 52, was the oldest Dipsea winner yet.

Mazzini was born in tiny Algoma, near Mt. Shasta. He worked most of his life on his family ranch in Cloverdale. He was an outstanding open runner in the 1930's, and was placed among the scratch men in 1934. He had a personal best Dipsea time of 52:55 from 1930.

Mazzini returned to Dipsea competition in 1949, still with the Petaluma Spartans. Though 46, he received only two handicap minutes and finished 74th of the 85 finishers. In 1952, he got seven minutes and finished 6th. In both 1953 and '54 he received eight minutes and was 13th, then 14th.

Suddenly, for 1955, Mazzini found himself with the maximum headstart of 15 minutes. He made the most of it. Starting with just six other runners, none of whom would finish in the top half, Mazzini soon had an enormous lead. He ran 1:47 faster than he had the year before and was able to hold off, by 66 seconds, the challenge of scratch man Wilford King. Mazzini was warmly greeted by what was described as "a small crowd."

Mazzini's first words upon finishing were, "I finally did it." He later told the *Independent Journal*, "I finally got a break this year and I knew if I couldn't win with 15 minutes handicap I'd never win. I got my second wind coming down the home stretch and then I knew I had it won. No, I'm not tired—I could run some more right now."

Mazzini's 1:05:02 was, by over four minutes, the slowest winning time yet. But that dubious record would last only one year.

Runner-up King's 51:08 was the fastest Dipsea time turned in between 1939 and 1959. King was a 25-year-old Stanford graduate who would go on to win the Cross-City Race in 1958 and '59.

Walter Van Zant, nephew of pre-Race favorite Jesse Van Zant (who ended up not competing), took 3rd. Walter had polio in his youth. Later, he became a prominent age-group competitor.

Robert Marinoni, a regular Dipsea entrant since he was 10 and son of 1940 champion Ernie Marinoni, finished 4th. Now 16 and at St. Ignatius in San Francisco, he won the high school trophy.

The second high schooler, 7th overall, was Wes Hildreth. Hildreth would be an inspiration for the lead character (Wes Holman) in the movie *On the Edge*, made two decades later by fellow Tamalpais High runner Rob Nilsson.

Also debuting, and also the inspiration for a character in *On the Edge*, was 18-year-old Darryl Beardall. Beardall would go on to win more road and cross country races in Northern California (approximately 300) than anyone, collect over 800 running trophies and log over 300,000 miles. He would finish in the Dipsea's top-10 more times (19) than any other runner, be a part of a record 22 winning teams and win outright twice. Given only two handicap minutes in his first year, he finished 9th.

❏ For apparently the first time, same day entrants were allowed to run, but they had to start from scratch. The other handicaps were not announced until Race morning.

1. William Mazzini, 1:05:02 (15) [1:06]
2. Wilford King, 51:08 (0) **best time**
3. Walter Van Zant, 59:46 (8)
4. Robert Marinoni, 1:04:11 (12) **1st HS**
5. Henry Stroughter, 59:59 (7)
6. Ralph Love, 53:07 (0) **2nd best time**
7. Wes Hildreth, 1:01:21 (8)
8. Harold Kuha, 53:22 (0)
9. Darryl Beardall, 56:11 (2)
10. Len Thornton, 55:33 (0)
Team Flying "A" Athletic Club of Stockton: Beardall, Charles Richesin (11th), Charles Curtis (15th), Paul Incardona (17th) and Jack Marden (28th)
40 finishers; mild

46th Dipsea
September 16, 1956

For the second year in a row, a runner with the maximum 15-minute handicap won. But unlike 1955, when a long-time veteran won, now it was Raymond Fuller, in his first and only Dipsea.

Just five of the 49 runners started with Fuller in the first group on a very hot morning. One was Wilbur Taylor, a veteran from the 1915 Race. Another was Jim Imperiale, who would win three years later. Only one other runner set off during the next four minutes.

Fuller went out quickly in the warm conditions. Imperiale made an attempt to keep up with him early, using a little known shortcut in Old Mill Park to pull even on the stairs. But Fuller, a bespectacled 28-year-old who had run track while at San Francisco State, soon was far ahead. Running strongly and seemingly unaffected by the heat, Fuller then had the trail to himself almost all the way to Stinson.

Two runners mounted serious charges from behind.

One was Jack Marden, developing into one of the region's best distance runners (he would win Cross-City in 1961). Marden started with the 2-minute group and actually caught Fuller coming onto the pavement at the end of the Race. Reaching Fuller's shoulder, Marden, a trackster with a potent kick, "felt sure I would win." But Fuller, fresher, accelerated and won by nine seconds. Marden did achieve the best time, upsetting Wilford King.

And Ralph Perry, the 1953 champion now at Harvard, ran brilliantly from scratch and, according to the *Independent Journal*, "was making a bid to overtake Fuller one-half mile from the finish." But Perry collapsed near the creekbed after the second Panoramic Highway shortcut. He was exhausted, unable to move, from his overambitious assault in the 85-degree heat. "It was like I was hit with a two by four," Perry recollects. "I got up, ran, and fell again. Then I remember seeing my good friend from college and training partner, Pete Reider, picking me up. But when another runner came along, Reider just dropped me to keep running!" Perry was brought to the finish line by stretcher, then recovered quickly. Reider ended up 3rd.

In the heat, Fuller was able to triumph with what remains the race's slowest winning effort ever, 1:07:52. His 52:52 clock time (actual time less handicap) is also the slowest ever for first place.

Fuller worked as an assembler for an Emeryville engineering firm at the time, had a 10-month-old daughter and raced for the San Francisco Athletic Club. He retains a special place of notoriety in Dipsea annals; he smoked before and after his training runs.

Finishing 4th, and winning the high school trophy, was Gordon Waldo, a 15-year-old sophomore at Calaveras High School.

In 8th place, in his maiden Dipsea, was Bill Morgan. He would win Cross-City in 1965. Walter Berger, who had won Cross-City that spring, was 13th (59:58; Scr).

Out of 50 starters, a record nine were past, present and future Dipsea champions. In finish order, they were: Fuller, Darryl Beardall, Charles Richesin, Mike Deasy, Jack Kirk, William Mazzini, Paul Chirone and Imperiale, plus Perry. Defending champion Mazzini saw his handicap cut by five minutes and his running time balloon by over 12. It was the debut for Deasy, who would win the following year.

Wilbur Taylor came in 33rd (1:25:39). Though he would enter again several years later, this was apparently his last finish.

The winning Flying "A" of Stockton team placed all their five scorers in the top nine.

❏ A staged picture of runners, taken on the Dipsea steps, had appeared in the popular national magazine *Saturday Evening Post* earlier in the year (January 4 issue).

1. Raymond Fuller, 1:07:52 (15) [:09]
2. Jack Marden, 55:01 (2) **best time**
3. Gordon Waldo, 1:01:54 (8) **1st HS**
4. Pete Reider, 57:34 (3)
5. Darryl Beardall, 55:38 (1)
6. Wilford King, 55:46 (0) **2nd best time**
7. Charles Curtis, 57:58 (2)
8. Bill Morgan, 1:05:09 (9)
9. Charles Richesin, 56:35 (0)
10. Al Reed, 1:02:47 (6)
Team Flying "A" Athletic Club of Stockton: Marden, Waldo, Beardall, Curtis and Richesin
49 finishers; extremely hot

(Above) 1958 winner Fernando Leon congratulated
by parents. (Jim Kean, Independent Journal)
(Right) Ralph Perry gets set to "rehydrate" with milk
following his 1953 victory. (Ken Molino)

47th Dipsea
September 16, 1957

Despite having finished second to the great Jesse Van Zant in the Cross-City Race four months earlier, 17-year-old Mike Deasy was given three additional handicap minutes from his Dipsea debut the year before. Deasy, just beginning his senior year at St. Ignatius High School (S.F.), then chopped seven minutes off his 1956 running time to win.

Starting in the same 5 minute handicap group with Deasy was Santa Rosa High's Alan Beardall, a future champion, in his first Dipsea. The two worked their way past the just 10 runners who had started ahead of them, Deasy leading and Beardall pursuing. But a half-mile from the finish Alan fainted and rolled into the same creekbed (after today's second Panoramic Highway shortcut) that had claimed Ralph Perry the year before.

Alan was finally aided by his brother Darryl, who had started four minutes later and was running strongly. Alan then told Darryl to "Go ahead, then come back later." Darryl, having lost considerable time, ended up 16th. Alan, finally revived by smelling salts, went on and placed 42nd in 1:10:46. He was then administered to, in the Stinson Beach firehouse, by Dr. Walter Deike, the 1952 champion who had come in 13th and was more than a little tired himself. All the skin on the back half of Alan's heel peeled off when he removed his sock.

Meanwhile, Deasy reached Stinson first, a broad grin on his face, a sizable 90 seconds ahead of Jim Maddox. Maddox was a former Cal trackster now competing for the Boston Athletic Association, organizers of the Boston Marathon. Two seconds behind Maddox was Gerald Joyner, an Air Force cross country champion stationed in Germany.

Next were two Marin County runners, John Reed and Wes Hildreth. Two other Marin runners in the top ten, George Cagwin and Bill Ranney, served as a harbinger of future Dipseas when locals would be increasingly prominent.

In 6th was Jack Marden, who would win Cross-City in 1961. Wilford King, who would win the next two Cross-City races, was 7th with the day's best time, 52:00. He was one of the two scratch men, with Deike. King had also won the best time award in 1955. Besides Alan Beardall, another future Dipsea champion made his debut, 44-year-old John Satti. He finished 33rd (1:04:47; 3hc). Also new to the Dipsea was Fred Baer (38th), a friend and track teammate of Deasy who would go on to a long career as a running writer and publicist. He helped Deasy by securing his father's car to drive Mike to Marin for a practice run the weekend before.

1. Mike Deasy, 55:00 (5) [1:30] **1st HS**
2. Jim Maddox, 52:30 (1) **2nd best time**
3. Gerald Joyner, 54:32 (3)
4. John Reed, 57:18 (5:30)
5. Wes Hildreth, 54:58 (3)
6. Jack Marden, 52:59 (1)
7. Wilford King, 52:00 (0) **best time**
8. George Cagwin, 1:04:27 (12)
9. Charles Curtis, 55:37 (3)
10. William Ranney, 1:00:14 (6:30)

Team San Francisco Athletic Club: Deasy, Reed, Ranney, William Ferlatte (15th) and Charles Lucas (22nd)

47 finishers; pleasant, some fog

48th Dipsea
September 14, 1958

In an exciting race, Fernando Leon became the third man ever to win the Dipsea from scratch.

As a high schooler in Tucson, Leon had run 4:25 for the mile and 9:32 for two miles, times near the Arizona state prep records although his school did not even have a track. During the summer of 1958, Leon, 20, lived in Marin while working for his uncle, Warren Mistron, superintendent of public works for the city of Larkspur. Preparing for his sophomore track season at the University of Southern California, Leon was doing quarter-mile intervals at the College of Marin track when a man, watching the workout, approached. It was Jim Imperiale, who would win the Dipsea in 1959, recruiting Leon to run the Dipsea for his Marin Athletic Club.

Leon didn't join the Marin A.C., but trained hard for the Dipsea. Indeed, his practice runs led him to believe he had a shot at Norman Bright's ancient course record. He had already finished second in the Cross-City Race earlier in the summer.

Leon set off last, with six other scratch runners. These included: the defending champion Mike Deasy; Wilford King, who had twice won the best time award and who had beaten Leon at the '58 Cross-City; and Laszlo Tabori. The Hungarian Tabori was the fastest runner, at least as measured by mile time, to attempt the Dipsea. He had been the third man, after Roger Bannister and John Landy, ever to run a sub-four minute mile and had taken fourth, 1.2 seconds from the gold, at the 1956 Olympic Games in the 1,500 meters. Tabori left Hungary after the abortive 1956 uprising there and settled in California.

It was a hot day, to Arizonan Leon's liking. The scratch group had less ground to make up than usual because, although the maximum handicap remained 15 minutes, it was awarded to only one man and just six runners received handicaps greater than five minutes. Taking advantage, five scratch men finished in the top 12, that group's strongest showing yet. One who missed was Deasy, who could only manage 1:06:30, 11 minutes off his '57 time. Another was Tabori. His miler's leg muscles aching, he dropped out altogether atop Cardiac, complaining vehemently in his thick accent, "This is not race for humans, this is race for animals."

Darryl Beardall, receiving a seemingly generous seven handicap minutes, took the lead. But he could only muster a 59:30; outside of the year he fainted (1962), this would prove his slowest Dipsea for the next 34 years. Bob Johnson, a 17-year-old track star at Polytechnic High (S.F), passed Beardall to go into first. He in turn was caught by Leon about a mile from the finish.

Johnson and Leon then "staged a nip and tuck duel for about a half mile" according to the *Independent Journal*. Leon finally pulled away, winning by 11 seconds.

King was 3rd, 61 seconds behind. His 52:16 was the day's second fastest time. Beardall was 4th. The winners of the next three Cross-City races were in the top 10; King (1959), Don Kelly (1960) and Jack Marden (1961).

Two future Dipsea champions finished 15th and 16th; respectively, Bob Hope, in his Dipsea debut, and John Satti. William Mazzini, who had won three years earlier, ended up next-to-last with the day's slowest time, 1:40:45.

The team award went to the Santa Clara Valley Youth Village, then carving a big name in Northern California running (they would produce eight of the ten Cross-City champions between 1957 and 1966; Tabori and history's first indoor 4-minute miler, Jim Beatty, were also members). The team was headed by Mike Ryan, whose name remains attached to one of the Bay Area's leading running stores, Ryan's Sports.

The Dipsea has had many serious injuries (none fatal) and 1958 produced a bizarre one. Rod Boucher, a 22-year-old Navy ensign attached to the

San Francisco-based carrier USS Oriskany and a former Providence College track runner, collapsed on the trail from the heat. A sheriff's deputy, Art Leal, and a park ranger, Eric Leffingwell, hiked down to pull Boucher out. When the trio reached Stinson Beach, Boucher, his blood sugars out of balance, went berserk, punching Leal and smashing through a car window with his fist. Boucher was finally subdued by a sizable group, handcuffed and taken to Marin General Hospital. There he was given "several servings of coffee with plenty of sugar" and intravenous fluids, and recovered. The incident was well-covered, particularly since *Independent Journal* photographer Jim Kean was slightly roughed up during the melee.

1. Fernando Leon, 51:15 (0) [:11] **best time**
2. Bob Johnson, 56:26 (5) **1st HS**
3. Wilford King, 52:16 (0) **2nd best time**
4. Darryl Beardall, 59:30 (7)
5. Don Kelly, 52:46 (0)
6. Charles Curtis, 56:16 (2)
7. Ned Benedict, 59:17 (5)
8. Bob Louden, 59:18 (5)
9. Tim Kelly, 59:19 (5)
10. Jack Marden, 54:33 (0)

Team Santa Clara Valley Youth Village: King, Beardall, Kelly, Rolf Gordon (14th) and Joe King (21st)
61 finishers; "sun-baked," 80 degrees

49th Dipsea
September 13, 1959

Jim Imperiale had a love affair with the Dipsea since he was eight, faithfully watching the Race that passed so close to his home (his father John was a Mill Valley police officer). But he did not begin racing the Dipsea until he was 33. In 1954, after training with Petaluma Spartan teammate William Mazzini, a boyhood running idol of Imperiale's, Imperiale finally entered. Describing his first five Dipseas, he says, "I bombed every time." Despite usually getting the maximum handicap, Imperiale never finished in the top half. His best time was 1:12:59; his worst, 1:40:33. But Imperiale vowed to give the Dipsea a last shot in 1959; to train hard, win and retire. He met his goals.

Few Dipsea runners prepared more diligently than Imperiale did in 1959. As he recalled 32 years later, "While the other runners were relaxing, I was working out, mornings and nights, rain or shine." He read all the literature on training techniques and adopted tips from many sources, particularly the fabled Australian coach Percy Cerutty. He ran repeatedly up the Dipsea steps, sometimes with weights on his hips, sometimes on his ankles, as '37 winner Paul Chirone advised him. He also ran up the steps backwards to further strengthen other leg muscles. He wore heavy sweat clothes to prepare for hot weather.

Imperiale made numerous training runs on all or parts of the course, each effort with a plan and time goal. Several were with the defending champion, Fernando Leon, who would spot Imperiale a handicap, then the two would race. He secured a pair of the new Adidas "Rapid" model cross country shoes Leon received from the University of Southern California. Other runs were with members of the Marin Athletic Club, the team he founded (by recruiting many of his Petaluma Spartan teammates), coached and financed. The Marin

A.C. would dominate the Dipsea until it disbanded in the mid-1970's.

Imperiale may also have made the greatest effort of anyone yet to find the shortest possible route to Stinson Beach. He was influenced by a remark that the Dipsea's first winner, John Hassard, had made to him about why he cut so much time in 1906 from 1905, "I found a faster route." He searched for the old markers placed by Norman Bright, another assiduous student of the trail, in the 1930's. He used a steel tape to ascertain distances. To find the fastest route down Steep Ravine, he floated helium balloons above the tree line, with communication by walkie-talkie. The direct line he uncovered, though, proved unrunnable.

As a 38-year-old with a poor Dipsea record (and, in Imperiale's opinion, receiving a break for his service to the running community), Imperiale was awarded the maximum 15 minute handicap. That was the just the opportunity he needed. He related to the *Independent Journal* afterward, "I told myself I'd drive myself to the finish line with everything I had or they'd have to carry me across the line."

Only four other runners—none of whom would break 1:10—started with Imperiale and only one more set off during the next six minutes. Darting over the course he knew so well, Imperiale built up a lead rarely seen before in the Dipsea. He managed to lop 10 minutes, 15 seconds off his best previous time. The closest any of the later starters got was 46 seconds, at the finish line.

Imperiale retired from competitive running immediately after his victory, although he continued coaching the Marin A.C. until 1963. He also directed the Dipsea in 1963, the year the Race was taken over by the Mill Valley Junior Chamber of Commerce.

Second in was Marin A.C. runner Tim Kelly of Berkeley. He just edged out, by three seconds, yet another teammate, Bob Hope. Hope was a Tamalpais High School student who would win the following year.

Defending champion Fernando Leon was 4th.

His 49:57 was the first sub-50 minute effort in the Dipsea since 1938. And he did it despite badly twisting an ankle a half-mile from the finish—"I heard it pop two or three times." Leon had prepared for the race by regularly running a rugged 8-mile course in the Santa Rita Mountains near his Tucson home while wearing a 25-pound hip belt of his own design.

Times were showing a quickening throughout. All the first 19 finishers, other than Imperiale, broke one hour.

Mike Tymn, who is now one of the country's leading writers about masters running, was 27th (59:42, 4hc). He was one place behind 62-year-old Victor Duran (1:10:34, 15hc).

Adrienne Rieger, 24, became the first woman to run since Nancy Dreyer in 1954, and second woman ever. Rieger operated Stinson Beach's Pelican's Nest restaurant (today the town library) with her husband Franz. Also completing the course unofficially was 14-year-old Steve Roulac. Following an AAU rules change, the minimum age for Dipsea entry had been raised back to 17.

The Marin A.C., beginning a 12-year victory streak (with one tie), handily won the team award.

1. James Imperiale, 1:02:44 (15) [:46]
2. Tim Kelly, 52:30 (4)
3. Bob Hope, 52:33 (3) **1st HS**
4. Fernando Leon, 49:57 (0) **best time**
5. Jesse Ochoa, 53:05 (3)
6. Joe King, 56:14 (6)
7. Tim Jordan, 54:40 (4)
8. Ned Sargent, 51:17 (0) **2nd best time**
9. Wes Hildreth, 52:36 (1)
10. Gerald Joyner, 54:45 (3)
Team Marin Athletic Club: Imperiale, Kelly, Hope, Ochoa and Hildreth
68 finishers; sunny, cool

50th Dipsea
September 11, 1960

Bob Hope, 18, turned in what was then the second fastest time in the history of the Dipsea, the fastest time ever by a winner and the second largest victory margin. His 47:41 remains the record for a high schooler. But a snafu involving the watches of the finish line crew, which delayed results for two hours, left lingering questions over the times.

The slightly built Hope—5'8" and 120 pounds—had raced the last two Dipseas. In 1958, he was 15th with a 1:02:54 and in '59, third in 52:33. For the 1960 Race, Hope, a standout cross country runner at Mill Valley's Tamalpais H.S., made a special effort to win. He trained diligently with Marin A.C. teammate Wes Hildreth. Typical workouts included 15 repeats up the second flight of steps, intervals up very steep Wildomar (a street near the steps) or repeat sessions on the Hogsback. Hope and Hildreth would take turns being Vladimir Kuts and Emil Zatopek, the two greatest distance runners of the era. On Saturdays, team coach Jim Imperiale would time training runs at various points along the course. Hope and Hildreth also looked into alternate, faster routes. They blazed one down Steep Ravine, only to have it ruled off-limits when all runners were restricted to a single path for the 1960 Race. He fondly recalls, 31 years later, "We had a lot of fun that summer."

Hope, with Imperiale lobbying handicapper Tommy Laughran on his behalf, was given the same three-minute handicap he had the previous year. "A lot of the handicapping then was based on politics," Hope now reflects. (Interestingly, a Tam classmate of Hope's, and a good friend, is today's handicapper Jim Weil.) Though the maximum handicap remained 15 minutes, only six runners, none of whom would finish better than 19th, started more than three minutes ahead of Hope.

Hope opened fast and took the lead going up out of Muir Woods. He maintained a killing pace to the top of Cardiac. "I was so tired by the top I wanted to quit," Hope remembers. "But I knew I had Steep Ravine not much ahead." He passed two unofficial runners, whose presence startled him. By White Barn he had an insurmountable lead. "I knew no one was behind me so I just coasted from then on. I didn't want to hurt myself."

Hope's bulge at the finish tape was five minutes, 27 seconds, surpassed in Dipsea annals only by Ralph Perry's 6:53 in 1953. Of his 47:41 clocking, Hope likes to believe a story he heard from one official who said his time was actually even faster but due to the uncertainty with the watches he could not be given the course record.

Second in was another prep, John Weinstein, who had just graduated from George Washington H.S. (S.F.) and was off to Harvard. Five seconds later came Darryl Beardall. Just four more seconds back was Fernando Leon, the lone scratch runner. Leon, winner of the best time award the two previous years, was considered a particular rival by Hope and Hildreth. When Leon passed Hildreth, he remarked, "I got you," to which Hildreth responded, "But you won't get Hope." Leon, a senior at USC with Olympic aspirations, also questioned the time, believing he had run faster than his posted 50:17. Hildreth finished 5th.

Hope's time was certainly remarkable enough to question (and some still do). It was just 19 seconds off Norman Bright's seemingly invincible record from 1937 and supplanted Mason Hartwell's 1912 mark of 47:56 as #2 on the Dipsea list. Both Bright and Hartwell were national class runners—and other national class runners had also tackled the Race—while Hope was just a very good high schooler. In Hope's behalf, he had recorded 48-minute training runs, and other high schoolers would run almost as fast in future Dipseas.

The Marin A.C., coached by defending champion Jim Imperiale and paced by Hope, placed five runners among the first seven (matching the record of the Humboldt Club in 1925.) No less impressive, 51 of the 106 pre-registered runners listed in the program were Marin A.C.-affiliated.

Five past, present or future Dipsea champions (Hope, Beardall, Leon, Jim Shettler and Perry) finished among the first 11. There actually were a record-tying nine in the race, but one, Charles Richesin, registered late and only ran unofficially.

❑ Thomas Laughran, a one-time Dipsea runner, was the AAU official now in charge of handicapping, replacing the long-serving Attilio Maggiora.

❑ Three teenaged girls—Silvia Duran, Bev Fontana and Louisa Zivnusla—started two hours early and completed the route, each in over two hours.

❑ There was the usual 25-piece concert band at the finish, still paid for by a grant, but few other golden anniversary touches.

❑ Judge Timothy Fitzpatrick was listed as the Race Chairman in the program, 55 years after he first held the title.

1. Bob Hope, 47:41 (3) [5:27] **best time, 1st HS**
2. John Weinstein, 55:08 (5)
3. Darryl Beardall, 52:13 (2)
4. Fernando Leon, 50:17 (0) **2nd best time**
5. Wes Hildreth, 54:30 (3)
6. James Jacobs, 55:43 (4)
7. Jesse Ochoa, 53:45 (1:30)
8. Jim Shettler, 53:21 (:30)
9. Stuart Sparling, 58:01 (5)
10. John Lacy, 56:04 (3)

Team Marin A.C.: Hope, Weinstein, Beardall, Hildreth, Ochoa

72 finishers; hot

51st Dipsea
September 17, 1961

Phillip Smith achieved a feat surely never to be repeated. He won in what was not only his first Dipsea, but his first race of any kind! (Jimmy McClymonds had apparently done the same in 1936.)

Smith grew up in Mill Valley and had watched the Dipsea for years. One of his friends from Tamalpais High School, Ralph Perry, won in 1953. Smith thought it was time to try the Race himself. Until then, the 23-year-old Smith was noted in sports for his tennis; he played for the Stanford varsity team.

Smith had an easy course load during a summer session between his junior and senior years at Stanford and began a rigorous, self-coached training program. He worked his way up to 100 mile weeks. And he joined the Mill Valley-based Marin A.C., which was dominating the Dipsea.

As a running novice, Smith was awarded the maximum 15 minute handicap. That first group had not placed a runner in the top 10 in the previous four Dipseas; this year they would account for four of the first five finishers. Smith quickly went to the lead with one runner, future champion John Satti, dogging him. Satti, who knew every shortcut, used his course knowledge to the maximum. He got ahead of Smith for a last time on a shortcut up out of Muir Woods. But Smith soon repassed him for good and then had a solo run to the finish line. The support of the Marin A.C. was evident (see photo of team coach Jim Imperiale splashing water on Smith by White Barn).

But Smith was not as alone as he thought; teammate Stuart Sparling closed to within 10 seconds at the tape. "I didn't know what to expect out there," Smith recalled 30 years later. "If I knew how close he [Sparling] was, I'm sure I could have gone . . . faster."

*Marin A.C. coach Jim Imperiale squeezes a wet sponge on winner Phil Smith,
1961. White Barn is in background. (Jim Kean, Independent Journal)*

Satti took 3rd, the only non-Marin A.C. runner among the top seven places. No team had ever achieved such dominance. Jack Kirk and John Adams, both also from Smith's maximum handicap group, followed. Next, with the day's best time—49:09, then the fourth fastest Dipsea ever run—was Darryl Beardall.

Jeff Fishback, who would break Norman Bright's 27-year-old course record in the Cross-City (Bay to Breakers) in 1964, made his only Dipsea run. Fishback, winner of a gold medal at the Pan Am Games in the steeplechase, was one of three scratch men. He finished 18th in 50:22. Jack Marden, current Cross-City champion, was another scratch runner; he ended up 43rd (58:26).

Marvin "Steve" Stephens, who would achieve many high finishes over the next 30+ years, debuted in 14th. Keith Conning, later to become a prominent writer on high school running and whose mother, Veda Young, had been in the 1919 Women's Dipsea Hike, finished his first Dipsea in 29th.

1. Phillip Smith, 58:29 (15) [:10]
2. Stuart Sparling, 51:39 (8)
3. John Satti, 59:39 (15)
4. Jack Kirk, 59:46 (15)
5. John Adams, 1:00:05 (15)
6. Darryl Beardall, 49:09 (3) **best time**
7. John Weidinger, 54:33 (8)
8. James Jacobs, 55:31 (8)
9. Wes Hildreth, 50:55 (3) **2nd best time**
10. Jack Snyder, 55:57 (8)
12. Walter Andrae, 55:24 (7) **1st HS**
Team Marin A.C.: Smith, Sparling, Kirk, Adams and Beardall
61 finishers; cool with some overcast

52nd Dipsea
September 16, 1962

Pre-Race speculation centered on whether Norman Bright's 25-year-old course record, which high schooler Bob Hope had missed by just 19 seconds two years earlier, would be broken, and by whom. There were two serious candidates. One was Darryl Beardall, who had run 49:09 the previous year and was in the midst of a six-year skein when he was all but undefeated in Northern California road races. He trained particularly hard for this Dipsea and clocked a couple of sub-47 minute practice runs, with a best of 46:30.

The other was Peter McArdle, perhaps the greatest runner to compete in the Dipsea in the post-World War II era. Then 33 (but appearing older because he was prematurely bald), McArdle was at the height of a career that brought him 17 United States championships at various distances, gold and bronze Pan American Games medals, a berth on the United States team at the 1964 Olympic Games in Tokyo (by virtue of winning the Olympic Trials Marathon) and election into the United States Track & Field Hall of Fame. Of McArdle's toughness, his wife Barbara said, "To watch him run was like watching a machine."

McArdle was a native of Ireland who came to the United States in 1956 and became an American citizen in 1962. ("I came here to run," he later said.) McArdle worked for the Manhattan and Bronx Surface Transit Operating Authority.

Earlier in September McArdle won the national 15 kilometer crown and, eight days before the Dipsea, the national 1-Hour title (he covered 11 miles, 1,236 feet). Later in the year, he would win the U.S. cross country championship.

Trying to insure a record, handicapper Tommy Laughran, who had invited McArdle to the Dipsea, blatantly altered the headstarts. Only one runner got more than a six-minute handicap

(Dipsea veteran Salvatore Lucia, who would struggle to a 1:47:25). Everyone else was bunched close to the three scratch men; McArdle, Beardall and, seemingly unfairly, the defending champion Phil Smith (it was only his second race of any kind). The theory was to have McArdle and Beardall pass the field quickly, then race head-to-head on a clear course. Local papers played up the McArdle-Beardall confrontation, one dubbing it "the race of the century."

McArdle and Beardall did go out strongly; in Darryl's words, "We raced neck and neck from the gun to Cardiac." Beardall's knowledge of shortcuts seemed to just offset McArdle's superior speed. Once the pair passed Jim Jacobs, they were alone in front.

But Beardall could not maintain the pace. Because a fellow worker had called in sick, Darryl had to cover the late shift the night before at his second job, which involved hauling 300-pound blocks of ice. He did not get to bed until 3 a.m.

Near the top of Cardiac, Darryl, completely drained, fainted. When he did revive, he went on running, finishing 53rd in the slowest Dipsea of his long career. Still, the day was not a total loss. His future wife Lynne, a friend of a friend and who had never met Darryl, had come along to watch. Though she was "not very impressed" when Darryl failed to show as early as expected (a reaction she was ashamed of when she learned what happened), the two ultimately hit it off and married a year later.

Meanwhile, McArdle went on alone against the clock, a daunting task in the Dipsea for someone new to the course. Reese notes an incident (earlier in the Race) when McArdle lost time at Redwood Creek in Muir Woods trying to get the attention of an official "locked in fond embrace" with his girlfriend. He then missed the racer's shortcut on Dynamite, instead following the regular trail (which later came to be known as "McArdle's Trail"). But somehow he found his way to Stinson, finishing in 47:30, eight seconds off Bright's record. Marin A.C. coach Jim Imperiale, a perceptive

student of the Dipsea, said that had the handicapping been "normal," with McArdle having more runners to pass later, he might have gotten the record.

Still, McArdle's run supplanted Hope's effort as the fastest time ever by a Dipsea winner, and remains so. Later McArdle was said to have called the Dipsea the craziest of races and fit only for mountain goats; he apparently couldn't run for a week and never even returned to the West Coast.

Jacobs came in 2nd, just over two minutes later. Stuart Sparling, the first Marin A.C. man, was next in the day's second swiftest time. His teammates Bill Ranney and Wes Hildreth followed.

San Carlos' Jim McNutt won the high school trophy, finishing 8th overall. Another prep, Redwood High's Randolph Keller, collapsed at the finish line from heat exhaustion and had to be rushed to Marin General Hospital, where he recovered. The incident frightened the South of Market Boys and played a major role in their decision to withdraw from sponsorship of the Dipsea.

Carl Jensen, a future Dipsea winner, debuted in 18th place (1:02:08, 3hc) as a 17-year-old.

Also debuting, at age 54, was Walt Stack (56th place; 1:24:56, with only 1 minute handicap!). Stack would go on to become one of the nation's best known and most inspirational figures in the running boom ahead. He founded the Dolphin South End (DSE) running club, which was at one time the largest such club in the nation and which introduced thousands of Bay Area runners to the sport. Stack and the DSE also started the Double Dipsea in 1970; it is now named for him. Stack, invariably shirtless, would continue to run the Dipsea and Double Dipsea until past his 80th birthday.
❑ Judge Timothy Fitzpatrick, 86, one of the Race's founders and long-time guiding figures, recalled earlier times in an address at the awards ceremony. It was to be his last Dipsea; he died the following summer.

1. Peter McArdle, 47:30 (0) [2:02] **best time**
2. James Jacobs, 53:32 (4)
3. Stuart Sparling, 51:15 (1) **2nd best time**
4. Bill Ranney, 56:02 (3)
5. Wes Hildreth, 54:20 (1)
6. Joe King, 57:47 (4)
7. Bill Ferlatte, 55:50 (2)
8. Jim McNutt, 55:53 (2) **1st HS**
9. Tom Tuite, 55:26 (1)
10. David Lower, 56:30 (2)
Team Marin A.C.: Sparling, Ranney, Hildreth, Ferlatte and Jay Pengra (13th)
61 finishers; hot

53rd Dipsea
August 25, 1963

For the first time in 43 years, the number of finishers rose above 100. The 120 who completed the 1963 Race were almost double the 61 of the previous year. The rising interest in physical fitness, which President Kennedy helped inspire, would push Dipsea entries sharply higher for the rest of the decade.

Also of major significance was a change (basically the last) in Race sponsorship. The South of Market Boys, which had staged the previous nine Dipseas, decided to withdraw. They were partly prompted by the frightening collapse of Randolph Keller at the finish line the previous year. Jim Imperiale, the 1959 winner and Marin A.C. coach, asked his friend Jim Gilmartin, sports editor of the *Independent Journal*, to assist in finding a new backer.

Responding to the rescue call was the Mill Valley Junior Chamber of Commerce (their name was later changed to "Jaycees"). They were a national service organization open to "any young man of good character between the ages of 21 and 35." The Mill Valley branch had been organized in 1958 (they secretly admitted women by using first initials only). Dick Sloan was credited as prime mover behind the takeover, and served as the 1963 Race chairman. Imperiale was retained as the meet director and set the handicaps. Jerry Hauke, destined to become the major force in the Dipsea to this day, assisted as a new Junior Chamber member.

The Jaycees name would remain associated with the Dipsea even after the chapter disbanded around 1980 ("There weren't enough people under 35 who could afford to live in Mill Valley," says Hauke). To keep the Race's insurance policy, Hauke continued to send chapter dues and an inflated membership roster (there was a 20 member minimum) to Jaycee headquarters. The ruse was finally discovered and the Race was incorporated as the Dipsea Race, Inc. The central directors, most still with roots in the Jaycees, now stage the Race under the name, "The Dipsea Committee."

The Committee also inherited the Jaycees' beer franchise at the annual Mill Valley Arts Festival. Sales at the big September event in Old Mill Park remain an important source of revenue for the Dipsea Race. Just before the festival closes each year, Dipsea veterans, many wearing their black shirts, gather at what has come to be known as "The Dipsea Beer Booth" to swap tales.

In the Race, Alan Beardall, who had such an unfortunate first Dipsea (in 1957, running second, he collapsed in a ditch), returned in triumph. Alan had been an exceptional runner at Santa Rosa High School, Santa Rosa Junior College (where he also pole vaulted, long jumped and played varsity basketball) and in road races. Still, he invariably ran in the shadow of his older brother, and constant training partner, Darryl.

But now, with a three-minute handicap, Alan felt he had a chance to win while Darryl, scratch, was aiming "only" for the best time award. (Their father, Raymond, was entered as well, with a 15 minute handicap.) Alan, a month shy of his 25th birthday, responded with a sensational 49:07, which would have been #3 on the all-time Dipsea list as recently as four years before, and won by 20 seconds. Darryl, in turn, met his goal by running 48:02 (5th place). The Beardall family had a particularly happy ride back to Santa Rosa that afternoon.

Alan had an unexpected companion for much of the way. A dog, Hobart, escaped from its Mill Valley owner and stayed with Beardall, save for one foray to chase a cow, to the finish line. Alan's closest human pursuer, 20 seconds behind at the tape, was Marin A.C. teammate William Ferlatte. Ferlatte's 48:27 was second to Darryl for the best time trophy. Never before had such a swift crossing failed to win the time prize. Third in was Bill Ranney, already under a cloud for suspected cheating in the Dipsea and in other races. Next was

Sigurd Hope, younger brother of 1960 winner Bob Hope (another brother, Barney, had been 23rd the year before). Sigurd was the first high schooler but did not get his trophy; the high school award was overlooked this one year only in the organizational transition.

There was anticipation over a battle for the team trophy when the Golden Gate Track Club fielded a strong team to challenge the dominant Marin A.C. But four of the Golden Gate aces were placed in the scratch group compared to just one Marin A.C. man, Darryl Beardall, and there was no contest. Marin A.C. scored an unprecedented sweep of the top six places.

1. Alan Beardall, 49:07 (3) [:20]
2. William Ferlatte, 48:27 (2) **2nd best time**
3. Bill Ranney, 52:35 (5)
4. Sigurd Hope, 51:39 (4) **1st HS**
5. Darryl Beardall, 48:02 (0) **best time**
6. Carl Jensen, 53:28 (5)
7. Joe King, 56:29 (8)
8. Ronald Davis, 48:31 (0)
9. Michael Patterson, 1:03:37 (15)
10. James Forsyth, 1:03:38 (15)
Team Marin A.C.: A. Beardall, Ferlatte, Ranney, Hope and D. Beardall
120 finishers; warm

(Above) Runner-up Tim Terriberry (left), winner
Gregg Sparks (center) and 3rd-placer Mark
Leonard, 1964. (Mayhew, Independent Journal)
(Right) Alan Beardall breaks the tape in 1963.
(Harold Mathias, Independent Journal)

54th Dipsea
August 30, 1964

The Mill Valley Junior Chamber of Commerce continued to instill new vigor into the Dipsea. The number of finishers rose to an all-time high of 169, including one woman. That record would then again be broken in each of the next seven Dipseas. A radio station, Marin-based KTIM, broadcast the entire Race live and results were reported on network television news. Coverage in the newspapers was expanded (although still a far cry from the earliest years when the Dipsea was a lead sports story in all San Francisco dailies). The *Independent Journal* ran an editorial headlined, "Dipsea is Like Breath of Fresh Air in Machine Age."

Scratch runners, though, were shabbily treated by the handicapping; it would have taken an all but impossible sub-41:19 for a scratch man to win. Gregg Sparks ran 52:19 with 11 handicap minutes to produce the fastest clock time (actual time less handicap, which matches the order of finish) outside of 1907. Indeed, the day's first nine clock times were all under Norman Bright's course record 47:22. Scratch man Bill Morgan ran the second fastest Mill Valley to Stinson Beach crossing ever, 47:29, and it only got him 10th place. Reaction to the 1964 handicapping paved the way for the momentous changes made the following year.

Sparks was a 17-year-old track and cross country runner at Tamalpais High School, the school that had already produced Dipsea champions in 1937, 1953, 1960 and 1961. He had gotten into running after his mother "grounded" him for poor grades but let him participate in sports—he chose running. Sparks become familiar with the course, and fit, through his passion for surfing. He would leave his surfboard in Stinson at a friend's house and run over on weekends, and sometimes after school, when he couldn't get a ride. Several times Sparks walked the full trail carrying his board. He got additional workouts through his job as a bicyclist for his father's delivery service.

Sparks was persuaded to enter the Dipsea by Sigurd Hope, younger brother of 1960 winner Bob Hope. Sigurd had seen Sparks on the Dipsea and persuaded him to be a "rabbit" on his own training runs. When he stopped being able to catch Sparks, he advised Gregg to enter for 1964.

Sparks, representing the Marin A.C., picked his way through the some 40 earlier starters. Last to be passed was Tim Terriberry, who had wondered off trail. Sparks shouted at Terriberry and got him back on course, then beat him to the tape by 80 seconds.

But Gregg didn't know he was first. When advised by an official of the number of runners ahead of him at Windy Gap, Sparks tried to count those he passed, then lost track. "So I kept pouring it on, thinking there might be someone ahead of me," he recalled.

Sparks mother Jeanne, who was on hand at the finish (the family rented a house in Stinson each summer), said afterward, "I can't understand it. At home he's so lazy; I can't get him to do any chores." The quote was widely printed. It was also her birthday, and she immediately had a gold charm, which she still treasures, made showing the figure of a runner.

Mark Leonard, a runner at Los Gatos High School, finished 3rd after leading at Windy Gap. Mark's father, George Leonard, then owned the ranchlands through which the Dipsea course passed beyond Steep Ravine.

Morgan was at the peak of his brilliant career; he had just won the national 30 kilometers title and would win Cross-City the following spring. But, as a first time Dipsea racer, he didn't take the quickest route. He also fell late in the Race, cutting his leg. And he later rued not beginning his final sprint earlier. Still, he gave Bright's ancient record its closest call yet, missing the mark by just seven seconds.

Morgan had started with, among others, the Beardall brothers, future winner Carl Jensen and

Wilcox High School's (Santa Clara) Mike Ryan, who had won the mile at the California State Meet that June. Ryan ran an outstanding 49:07 and won the high school trophy (then based on actual time). Still, that got him only 24th, one place ahead of Darryl Beardall.

Three high schoolers representing the Pleasant Hill Track Club (George Kennedy, Stanton Brodie and Jim Cagne) finished in the top seven. An even stronger challenge to Marin A.C. dominance of the team competition came from the Golden Gate Track Club. Indeed, team captain Karl Griepenburg and his runners went home thinking they had won the title. But again it was Marin A.C. taking the trophy. Griepenburg, to this day, insists his squad was somehow victimized; the unexplained absence from the results of the 11th, 12th, 21st and 29th finishers lends some credence to his argument.

Tom Dooley, 9th, went on to become one of the country's top racewalkers.

To keep the runners out of Stinson Beach summer traffic, the finish line was moved off Shoreline Highway. The runners were directed left off Shoreline down Arenal Avenue to finish in front of the Parkside Cafe at the junction of Calle del Mar. This finish was used for ten years; it became the terminus of the first Double Dipseas and is still a turnaround point in the Quadruple Dipsea. Reese calculates this change shortened the course 84 feet from earlier years.

Another course change involved a rerouting around the newly constructed house at 315 Panoramic Highway. The new owners claimed to have known nothing about the Dipsea "until one morning when [they] went out to get the paper and saw several people running by in track suits." They refused to grant an easement across their property, forcing runners to detour. Still, some racers, as they would for the next several years, followed the old direct line through the yard. In 1970, winner Norman Bright got through by befriending (with biscuits and other goodies) the owners' watchdog during training runs.

Donna Thurlby, a 26-year-old member of the all-women's Laurel Track Club in San Francisco, was duly listed among the entrants and finishers though women were still not considered "official." Thurlby, who took up running in her hometown Modesto after watching the big annual track meet there, started from scratch and covered the course in 1:23:42. She finished 169th and last, three-and-a-half minutes behind anyone else.

For the first time, an entry fee (50 cents) was charged. The fee went to $1 the following year, then rose slowly but steadily to $11 ($5 for children) in 1993. These fees would ultimately help provide the Dipsea with the sound financial footing it enjoys today.

❏ A rush of Race morning entries delayed the start by forty minutes, with the first runners setting off at 10:40. Late entrants were placed in the scratch group.

❏ There was an unfortunate incident at Lone Tree as young pranksters threw rocks down at the passing runners. At least one competitor was hit.

1. Gregg Sparks, 52:19 (11) [1:20]
2. Tim Terriberry, 56:39 (14)
3. Mark Leonard, 57:11 (14)
4. George Kennedy, 56:26 (13)
5. Richard McQueen, 57:39 (13)
6. Stanton Brodie, 58:04 (13)
7. Jim Cagno, 59:20 (14)
8. Mark Falcone, 52:38 (7)
9. Tom Dooley, 59:14 (12)
10. Bill Morgan, 47:29 (0) **best time**
24. Mike Ryan, 49:07 (0) **2nd best time, 1st HS**
Team Marin A.C.: Sparks, Falcone, Dooley, Darryl Beardall (25th) and Bill Ranney (31st)
169 finishers; foggy and cool

55th Dipsea
August 29, 1965

In 1965, the method for assigning handicaps was altered. This was perhaps the most significant change that had ever been made in the Dipsea; only the admission of women six years later would be comparable in impact.

Handicaps had always been individually assigned, based on the entrant's past record in the Dipsea and other races. From 1965, handicaps became based strictly on age (and, from 1969, on sex).

Several factors contributed to the change. One was the growth of the field; there were again new records for entrants (214) and finishers (190) and the task of evaluating each runner was daunting. Another was the rise of same day entries. In earlier Dipseas (and again in later ones), there had been a strict entry cutoff date, giving officials adequate time to set the handicaps. Also contributing was the rise in the general running population. The world of long distance had once been a small fraternity, mostly clustered around a handful of clubs. Now the sport's popularity was becoming widespread and no handicapper could know everyone's background. And there was discontent over two poorly handicapped Dipseas in recent years; the blatant attempt to aid Pete McArdle's course record bid in 1962 by lowering everyone's handicap and the seemingly too-generous handicaps of 1964 which produced clock times impossible for any scratch runner to beat.

So a new age-based handicap system was started. Compared to today, this first year's effort appears crude. There were only four start groups (all men); 15 minutes for those 45 years or older, 10 minutes for ages 40-44, 5 minutes for ages 35-39, and scratch for everyone 34 and younger. That made the scratch group enormous, over 85% of the field (only 23 runners of the 216 pre-registered had head-starts). In contrast, there had been several early years with no scratch runners at all.

But the most significant by-product of the change was that "average" runners no longer had a chance of winning. In prior years, the handicapping would theoretically give every runner (at least capable of breaking around 65 minutes) an equal opportunity; the one who ran best Dipsea day, compared to their past record, would win. At least two runners, Jimmy McClymonds and Phil Smith, had even won the Dipsea in their very first races. But from 1965 on, only runners clearly outstanding in their age group could entertain victory hopes.

Another, related result was that older and younger runners would come to dominate the Dipsea. In all but four of the prior 54 Dipseas, the winner had been aged 17 to 36. From 1965, only two winners would be in that age range. While part of this shift was due to an overall increase in racing by older runners, and in the opening of the Dipsea in 1966 to youngsters, most stemmed from the new handicapping.

One venerable Dipsea tradition did not change; complaining about handicaps. While individuals could no longer gripe about being singled out, whole age groups would now occcasionally unite in protest.

As the *Independent Journal* predicted, the new system "gave some of the old rascals just the break they needed"; the first three finishers were from the small 15-minute group. One of those "old rascals" was 51-year-old John Satti, who had perhaps complained loudest about his 1964 handicap.

Satti was from San Francisco's Italian North Beach section, one of six children whose father died before he was born. He left school after the eighth grade to join the Civilian Conservation Corps. After a stint in the Army, he worked as a security guard at Fort Mason, then as chief security officer at the Oakland Army Depot. He didn't take up running until 1955, at age 41.

A Dipsea regular since 1957, Satti was usually given the maximum 15 minute handicap, as in

1961 when he made his best finish, third place. Suddenly, in 1964, he was slashed to six minutes and noted sarcastically to the *Independent Journal*, "When I get a little older, they'll probably cut [my handicap] down to scratch."

Satti got his 15 minutes back and made the most of it. Nine runners set off with the first, maximum handicap group and the leaders among them had the trail to themselves. A duel immediately developed between Paul Reese, a 48-year-old just beginning his brilliant masters running career, and Satti. Reese, a Dipsea novice, followed the marked route. Several times after he took a lead, the Dipsea veteran Satti would take a shortcut and regain the fore.

Satti, renowned for rigorous training methods such as running over the course in hiking boots, prevailed. The short, stocky Satti, still spryly leaping over the last stiles, reached Stinson two minutes, one second ahead of Reese. Another 15-minute man, the San Rafael High School cross country and tennis coach Fred Hines, was 23 seconds farther back.

Reese and Satti met countless times in races over the next years and Reese notes this was the only time Satti ever beat him. Reese went on to found the NorCal Seniors running club and such important Northern California races as the Pepsi 20 Mile (now the Clarksburg 30K) and the 72-mile run around Lake Tahoe. In 1990, he became, at age 73, the oldest man ever to run across the United States, averaging a marathon a day for 124 days.

After Hines came 15 consecutive scratch runners. The tight battle for 4th thus proved the contest for best time as well. It was won by the barest of margins—even less than the one second shown in the results—as southern Californian star Roy Hughes just edged Bay Area ace Wayne Van Dellen.

Three of the great Dipsea figures of the era—Darryl Beardall, Wes Hildreth and Carl Jensen—came in 8, 9 and 10, respectively. Just the week before, Beardall had finished fourth in the Pikes Peak Marathon, which climbs and descends the 14,110' Colorado mountain.

Dave Barni of San Rafael High School was 12th and winner of the high school trophy. He remains an active competitor. The defending champion, Gregg Sparks, ran just 26 seconds slower than in 1964 but finished 13th. Jack Leydig, an outstanding runner who would go on to become one of the region's most important contributors to the sport (founder of the *NorCal Running Review*, president of the West Valley Track Club, an early seller of running shoes at races and now a leading t-shirt supplier), debuted at 17th. Jack Kirk, his Dipsea career suddenly revitalized by the handicap change, was 19th.

There were other notable debuts. Bob Bunnell, who would win two best time awards, ran 59:01 and came in 53rd. Don Pickett, who would win in 1968, ran 1:01:12 (5hc) and was 71st. Jim Myers, future president of the Tamalpa Runners, was 145th. And Mark Reese, a cross country and track runner at McLatchy High School in Sacramento and son of Paul Reese, began his lifelong passion with the Dipsea. Fifteen years later, he would publish the first history of the Race.

Again a woman, Mill Valley's Thea Hogan, ran. Her time was 2:36 from scratch and she was a distant last. Hogan, who had never practiced, told the *Independent Journal*, "I was totally winded before I got to Old Mill Park . . . [After] I borrowed a dollar from the Jaycee management and got four cans of beer and chug-a-lugged them. Then I hitch-hiked home."

❑ John Hassard, the winner of the first two Dipseas, appeared at the Race for the last time. He died in 1967.

❑ Twenty-five-year old Deanna Zane became the first Miss Dipsea. She recalls walking down a street in Mill Valley, where she lived, being approached by a Junior Chamber of Commerce official, invited to an interview, then selected. Her duties consisted of posing for photographs, firing the starting gun, riding to Stinson in a limousine, then handing trophies to (and kissing) winners.

1. John Satti, 1:01:50 (15) [2:01]
2. Paul Reese, 1:03:51 (15)
3. Fred Hines, 1:04:14 (15)
4. Ray Hughes, 50:05 (0) **best time**
5. Wayne Van Dellen, 50:06 (0) **2nd best time**
6. Thomas Beck, 50:51 (0)
7. Thomas Tuite, 51:44 (0)
8. Darryl Beardall, 51:46 (0)
9. Wes Hildreth, 51:53 (0)
10. Carl Jensen, 52:12 (0)
11. Steve Brown, 52:33 (0)
12. David Barni, 52:38 (0) **1st HS**
13. Gregg Sparks, 52:45 (0)
14. Phil Darnel, 53:05 (0)
15. Floyd Godwin, 53:08 (0)
16. Richard Dyer, 53:09 (0)
17. Jack Leydig, 53:24 (0)
18. Delfin Trujillo, 53:36 (0)
19. Jack Kirk, 1:08:46 (15)
20. Terry Record, 53:51 (0)
Team Marin A.C.: Satti, Hines, Beck, Beardall and Hildreth
190 finishers; hot

56th Dipsea
August 28, 1966

In reaction to the 1965 Dipsea, when the first three finishers all had 15 minute handicaps, the maximum headstart was cut to 11 minutes. It had been 15 for decades, and would be again in 1967. But this one-year change helped scratch runners take six of the top seven places, and produced the last scratch Dipsea winner.

There were now five starting groups: 45 years and over (11 minutes); 40-44 (8); 34-39 (5); 16 and under (4); and 17-34 (scratch). The 16 and under group was a new one as the AAU and the Race had just relaxed their prohibition against youths in longer races. Four runners 10 years and under would win during the next seven years. The scratch group comprised over 70% of the field.

Carl Jensen was a 21-year-old College of Marin student who had begun running the Dipsea in 1962 while at Novato High School. His best place was 6th in 1963; his best time, 50:45 in 1964. In '65 he ran 52:12 for 10th.

Jensen was at the peak of his running career. He had recently been sixth in the Culver City Marathon, earning a national ranking at the distance. He won the Ocean to Bay Marathon. He was second at the national 50K championships. He would be named the Pacific Association-AAU's 1966 Athlete of the Year and was Northern California's nominee for the nation's most prestigious honor for amateur athletes, the Sullivan Award.

But it was the Dipsea that was his passion. He trained rigorously for the Race, using the long summer nights to take many practice runs on the course with his Marin A.C. teammates and learn their secret shortcuts. His main training partner was Wes Hildreth, often a top 10 Dipsea finisher. Jensen acknowledges, "I remain beholden to Wes."

Jensen found himself in a battle throughout with fellow scratch runners Will Stephens of San

Mateo High School and southern California Ray Hughes, the previous year's best time winner. The trio worked their way through just about all the thin field of earlier starters. At White Barn, a band of Marin A.C. supporters cheered Jensen on, renewing his spirit. Four-minute handicap man Jack Lawson still led, Stephens was second, Hughes third, Jensen fourth.

But none of the front runners had Jensen's intimate course knowledge. With less than a mile to go, coming off Panoramic Highway for the second time, Jensen saw Hughes take the cut back across the creek used today and smiled. Carl stayed on the road some 75 more yards before darting into an obscure and treacherous shortcut "that required you to wave your arms like a paddlewheel to keep from falling." He then ran unseen on the creek's opposite bank. When he reemerged, Jensen was ahead of Hughes and Lawson. (Hughes would later protest in vain that Jensen's use of this shortcut in particular should have gotten him disqualified. Jack Kirk was one of those who came forward to say that shortcuts had always been part of the Dipsea.)

Jensen thought he was now in first but, upon hitting Highway 1, saw Stephens ahead. Jensen moaned. He was a marathoner and didn't like his sprint chances against the tall black high schooler. But Carl dug down for a supreme effort. Still trailing at the final turn—the left off Highway 1 at Arenal that was begun the year before—Jensen pulled away for a narrow win. (The results indicate a 10-second gap; it was likely less.) Jensen had cut 3:15 off his best previous time.

Though it was rare, there had been four previous winners from scratch (Mason Hartwell in 1917, Walter Deike in '52, Fernando Leon in '58 and Peter McArdle in '62) and Jensen's feat did not get particular media attention. But because it has not been repeated, Jensen's effort has now assumed almost legendary status.

Jensen's brilliant year would have a tragic ending. He was drafted into the Army in December and his request to be on the Army's racing team was denied. A week before the 1967 Dipsea, Jensen stepped on a mine while leading his platoon in Vietnam. Jensen suffered massive injuries—he required 9 1/2 pints of blood tranfusions and over 1,000 stitches—and spent 17 months in hospitals. Ultimately, 15 years later, he was able to return to the Dipsea.

Lawson held off Hughes for 3rd. Rich Delgado, who would break Norman Bright's course record in 1970, debuted in 5th place. Also debuting were two men who would be so profoundly moved by the Dipsea they would make films of it, Rob Nilsson and Pax Beale. Nilsson, who would write, produce and direct *On the Edge*, was 209th (1:10:46, scratch). Beale, who would make splendid 16mm movies of the 1969 and 1970 races, was 268th (1:27:59, 5hc).

Elaine Pedersen, a 29-year-old United Airlines stewardess supervisor and friend of Beale, was the lone woman finisher, albeit unofficial. Pedersen started with the five-minute group and ran 1:32:23 to finish 274th. One place behind her was the youngest entrant, 10-year-old Steve Ertman. Ertman had fallen and suffered the day's most serious injury, a fractured elbow. Peter Gamache of Lewiston, ME, father of future boxing champion Joey Gamache, finished 167th.

❑ There was a course walk, with the public invited, at 1 p.m. the day before the Race.

1. Carl Jensen, 48:57 (0) [:10] **best time**
2. Will Stephens, 49:07 (0) **2nd best time, 1st HS**
3. Jack Lawson, 53:22 (4)
4. Ray Hughes, 49:25 (0)
5. Rich Delgado, 49:58 (0)
6. William Mackey, 50:04 (0)
7. Wes Hildreth, 50:09 (0)
8. Laurence Rentschler, 54:25 (4)
9. Otis Miles, 1:02:06 (11)
10. Bob Bunnell, 51:22 (0)
11. Eugene Gillisan, 51:24 (0)
12. Thomas Bache, 51:31 (0)
13. Floyd Godwin, 51:32 (0)
14. Brian Rowbothan, 56:27 (4)
15. Jack Knutson, 56:29 (4)
16. Steve Brown, 52:51 (0)
17. William Bachrach, 53:07 (0)
18. Andrew Russell, 53:08 (0)
19. Delfin Trujillo, 53:10 (0)
20. John Stephens, 57:11 (4)
Team Marin A.C.: Jensen, Hildreth, Miles, Bunnell and Knutson
290 finishers; sunny, warm, some breeze

57th Dipsea
August 27, 1967

The 1967 Dipsea resembled an open, non-handicapped race; nine of the top 10 finishers (and 83 of the first 100) started scratch. But that one exception was the winner, Jack Kirk.

The maximum handicap was returned to the traditional 15 minutes after the 1966 experiment. But it was now reserved only for runners 58 and over and those 11 and younger. (This was the first year the very oldest and youngest runners started together; it's a tradition still maintained.)

Kirk, 60, quickly outpaced the rest of the first group. The veteran of every Dipsea from 1930, and winner in 1951, built up a huge lead and ran solo most of the way. Near the end, however, a few runners made it quite close.

In a thrilling and emotional finish, Kirk, already known for over three decades as "The Dipsea Demon," was first to the tape, by five seconds. He became the Dipsea's oldest champion (and remains so) and the first double winner since Oliver Millard in 1913.

Runner-up was Bob Bunnell of Terra Linda High School. He won, by another five seconds, a splendid Race-long duel from scratch with Rich Delgado, who three months earlier had finished second at Bay to Breakers. After several passes—Bunnell was swifter on the downhills, Delgado on the climbs—Bunnell finally got ahead for good when he used a little-known shortcut at the end of the second section on Panoramic Highway.

Bunnell then thought he had the Race won. When he saw a runner (Kirk) ahead on the final straightaway, "I thought maybe he was some jogger trying to get a good spot to watch the finish." Bunnell and Delgado recorded the then fourth and sixth fastest Dipsea times ever. In 1970, Delgado would break the Dipsea course record. In 1985, Bunnell would set the Quadruple Dipsea course record.

After Delgado, the next three men were also under 50 minutes. Bill Morgan, winner of the 1965 Bay to Breakers (in a course record), was 8th.

Making their debuts were two teenagers who would later set Dipsea course records, Don Makela and Ron Elijah. (With Delgado, there were thus three future record setters in the field). Makela was 9th in 50:38. Elijah ran 56:27 (3hc) at age 14 and finished 37th.

The father-son trophy was revived, courtesy of a gift by Stinson Beach sisters Harriett Greene and Ruth Miller. It was won by Robert Biancalana, a Dipsea veteran, and his 11-year-old son Joe. Another trophy was donated by William Hoffman for the first resident of Stinson Beach to finish. Ken Shockey won it in 1967. Armand Castro would then capture it six times before it was discontinued after 1974.

Elaine Pedersen was again the only female runner. While still "unofficial," she was credited with 159th (1:18:47; 15hc) in the results.

❑ Karl Griepenburg recalls the cursory nature of the required pre-Race physical examinations. The doctor at the Mill Valley Fire House was overwhelmed by the number of entrants and moved the runners along rapidly. Griepenburg recalls a stethoscope being placed absently on his shoulder and the doctor saying, "Go on, you're OK."

1. Jack Kirk, 1:02:56 (15) [:05]
2. Bob Bunnell, 48:01 (0) **best time, 1st HS**
3. Rich Delgado, 48:06 (0) **2nd best time**
4. Mike Dailey, 48:25 (0)
5. Stephen Brown, 49:10 (0)
6. Darryl Beardall, 49:54 (0)
7. Greg Chapman, 50:07 (0)
8. Bill Morgan, 50:22 (0)
9. Don Makela, 50:38 (0)
10. Joe Whytock, 50:44 (0)
11. Phil May, 56:01 (5)
12. John Satti, 1:02:17 (11)
13. John Noonan, 51:17 (0)
14. Edward Sias, 1:02:26 (11)
15. Darren Walton, 51:46 (0)
16. Will Stephens, 51:51 (0)
17. Ted Lydon, 51:53 (0)
18. Wendel Smith, 52:01 (0)
19. Steve Sofos, 52:05 (0)
20. Jack Leydig, 52:09 (0)
Team Marin A.C.: Bunnell, Beardall, Makela, Satti and Noonan
350 finishers; foggy, mild

(Left) Don Pickett, "Mr. Dipsea," winning in 1968.
(Above) Past winner William Mazzini goes through the
former stile at the start of the Hogsback, 1961. (Jim Kean,
Independent Journal)

(Above) Elaine Pedersen, lone woman in the 1967 Race, in tennis attire at start. (Travis Cart, Independent Journal)

(Right) Walter Andrae, assigned bib #1 because he was first alphabetically among the scratch runners, outsprints Larry Rentschler for 23rd place, 1965. (Courtesy Dipsea Committee)

58th Dipsea
August 25, 1968

Don Pickett, today known as "Mr. Dipsea," won a thrilling race. He passed two maximum handicap runners late; Jack Kirk at the end of the trail and 11-year-old Mike Wolford on the final straightaway.

Pickett had begun running three years earlier at age 37 after a long layoff; he had competed in high school and in his freshman year at the University of Oregon. Pickett was a member of the Olympic Club, but primarily as a chorister. "I had been drinking too many martinis and wanted to change," he recalls. "I was better known in the Club bar than in the athletic facilities." He gave up drinking and smoking on one day in 1965. An account of the Dipsea in the newspaper intrigued Pickett. He started doing laps around the club's track. One of the club's trainers, Eddie Haddad, worked with him, and he was soon doing repeat step workouts with weights.

Pickett ran the Dipsea in 1965 (71st), '66 (42nd) and '67 (25th), steadily improving. Now, turning 40, he picked up three additional handicap minutes. The import-exporter and father of three (one, 12-year-old Tom, also ran in 1965 then was immediately chauffered back to Tiburon for a swim meet; another, Toby, would team with Don years later to win three family trophies) made the most of it.

Mike Wolford, who turned 11 four days earlier, and defending champion Jack Kirk, 61, both had 15 minute headstarts. They battled one another throughout, building a huge lead over the rest of the field. Interestingly, the pair lived just a few miles apart in the Sierra foothills towns of Oakhurst (Wolford) and Mariposa (Kirk) and both were vegetarians. Wolford finally forged a lead in the last mile.

Pickett, meanwhile, had worked his way into third. "I knew I was doing well, but not how well," Pickett recalls. Then, at Insult, Carl Jensen, the '66 winner back after his serious injury in Vietnam, called out to him, "Old man Kirk is one-quarter mile ahead and then there's a kid. If you really get going you can catch them." That recharged Pickett.

He went by Kirk but still didn't see Wolford until making the then final left turn onto Arenal. Sprinting downhill, Pickett, wearing bib #721, caught and passed the young runner. He made a congratulatory gesture to Wolford (which "almost gave Haddad a heart attack, he thought I was going to help the kid in"). Wolford, who was already savoring the cheers of the finish line crowd, was crushed and began crying. Wolford's father and two brothers finished later.

Exactly a minute after Kirk came the first of a swarm of six talented scratch runners, all running 48:30 or better. They were led by San Jose State College's Byron Lowry in 47:51. This despite a wrong turn (it was Lowry's first Dipsea), which he estimated cost him 30 seconds, and having to work his way through the largest crush of runners yet. Lowry would earn a legendary status among local runners for his hill-running prowess and win two more best time awards. He also developed into a top open runner, finishing 5th in the 1971 Boston Marathon. In all, a record 11 scratch runners broke 50 minutes.

At least 11 women ran; only once before had there been more than one (three in 1960). Women were still unofficial, but listed in the results. First (441st overall) was a sensational five-year-old, Mary Etta Boitano. She ran with her father but was still knocked down several times along the trail. Mary Etta stole the show at the awards ceremony from trophy presenters George Rhoden, an Olympic gold medal runner, and Clyde Lee, the Warriors basketball player. Mary Etta would become perhaps the greatest female child distance running prodigy this country had ever known. She was one of three pre-teens debuting who would later win the Dipsea. The other two were her six-year-old brother Mike (322nd) and nine-year-old Vance Eberly (35th).

The Marin A.C. won its tenth consecutive team title but San Jose State's quintet, led by Lowry, made it close.

The Biancalanas again won the father-son trophy but this time it was Robert with a different son, Michael. That duo would also win in 1969.

□ In the results, 136 runners who took over one hour, 15 minutes, were simply listed alphabetically without place or time.

□ Among the finish line onlookers were Dipsea legend Mason Hartwell, winner of seven best time awards, and Dr. Robert Furlong of San Rafael, who was 47th in 1906 and claimed to have seen all 58 races.

□ Earlier in the summer, George Leonard, who owned the land through which the Dipsea Trail passed from Steep Ravine to Stinson Beach, donated a pair of 10-foot-wide permanent easements to the County. These sections (the two shortcuts off Panoramic Highway) insured a continuous public right-of-way the full length of the historic Dipsea Trail. Soon after, Leonard sold his 1,800-acre Mt. Tamalpais holdings to the new Golden Gate National Recreation Area.

□ The race netted $176 to the Jaycees on total expenditures of $1,200. The largest expense item, as usual, was survivors medals, which the record number of finishers depleted.

1. Don Pickett, 54:14 (8) [:07]
2. Mike Wolford, 1:01:21 (15)
3. Jack Kirk, 1:01:51 (15)
4. Byron Lowry, 47:51 (0) **best time**
5. David Cords, 47:56 (0) **2nd best time**
6. Darold Dent, 47:58 (0)
7. Jack Lawson, 48:15 (0) **1st HS**
8. William Ferlatte, 48:28 (0)
9. Michael Dailey, 48:30 (0)
10. William Mackey, 56:34 (8)
11. Edward Sias, 59:35 (11)
12. Darryl Beardall, 48:38 (0)
13. Bruce Johnson, 48:49 (0)
14. Lawrence Hoyt, 57:29 (8)
15. Darryl Berry, 49:32 (0)
16. Joe Whytock, 49:33 (0)
17. Pat Kelly, 57:42 (8)
18. Jerome Dirkes, 49:48 (0)
19. Ron Elijah, 50:14 (0)
20. Greg Patrick, 1:05:24 (15)
Team Marin A.C.: Ferlatte, Beardall, Hoyt, Elijah and Don Makela (21st)
601 finishers (465 timed); cool, some fog

59th Dipsea
August 24, 1969

A 10-year-old boy won, and his 14-year-old sister ran the fastest time ever by a woman.

The 17-year-age limit had again only been lifted in 1966, yet children were already flocking to the Dipsea and the issue of their safety had to be addressed in official mailings. Youngsters 10 and under would win four of the five Dipseas between 1969 and 1973.

Vance Eberly, a blond fourth grader, had run the Dipsea the year before. He clocked a 1:07:30 and finished 35th, although he said he took a few wrong turns. As a member of the new youth-oriented San Jose Yearlings, Eberly was becoming an exceptional age group runner. He set a national AAU under-10 mile record of 5:17. His coach, Gary Gallego, felt he had potential to win the Dipsea. Vance made one practice run over the course. (Which yielded a wonderful anecdote. After the practice, Vance wanted a second ice cream cone. His uncle refused, but said that if Vance won the Dipsea, he would buy him a "triple scooper." After Vance's victory, the uncle took Vance to a Baskin-Robbins, which said it didn't serve triple scoops. The uncle pulled out a newspaper article which quoted the promise and Vance was given his three scoops of chocolate-chocolate chip ice cream.)

There was confusion at the start line. Starter Bob DeCelle sent all the groups except one (men 40-44) off at the wrong times in relation to the scratch runners. So, although he was supposed to get 15 handicap minutes, Eberly enjoyed a 16 minute headstart over the scratch men. (Race results presented the "actual" handicaps but contained numerous errors regarding running times; some doubt whether the true times have ever been sorted out.)

Two of the dozens of youngsters from that first wave, Eberly and the previous Dipsea's runner-up,

Mike Wolford, ran shoulder to shoulder for much of the opening miles. Finally, on the Hogsback, Eberly pulled away, then was completely alone all the rest of the way to the finish. Eberly had been particularly determined to beat Wolford after Mike's father said his son was faster. Eberly's actual time (apparently accurate) was a brilliant 57:59, almost 10 minutes swifter than in 1968.

Next, in dogged pursuit but well behind and never seeing Eberly, was 46-year-old Flory Rodd. Rodd had predicted that he would win. NorCal Seniors teammate Peter Mattei countered that he would pass Rodd. Rodd responded, "If you [Mattei] pass me, I'll run right up your back." At the awards ceremony, Mattei, who ended up 4th, gave Rodd a shirt with footprints on the back. Rodd, Ed Sias (3rd) and Mattei are all erroneously listed in the results with 16 minute handicaps. They actually were in the 11-minute group, which itself was started a minute early in relation to scratch.

Wolford, who was the third runner to cross the finish line, was later denied his trophy and dropped all the way down to 118th in the results. Wolford had his 12th birthday three days before the Race so should have had only a 3-minute handicap, instead of the same 15 as Eberly. (This extreme 12-minute drop in assigned handicap for boys reaching their twelfth birthday was ended the following year.)

All things considered, the first scratch runner, Byron Lowry, had grounds for protest but was completely gracious. Lowry, despite having to work his way through the largest Dipsea field yet, turned in a sparkling 47:39, just 17 seconds off Norman Bright's ancient race record. Lowry also won a great personal duel, by 11 seconds and one place, over fellow scratch runner Ron Elijah. Elijah's 48:00 remains the second fastest high school time ever, behind only Bob Hope's occasionally questioned 47:41 in 1960. Elijah would set the all-time Dipsea record in 1971, then again in 1974.

Meanwhile women, although technically still "unoffical" according to AAU rules, for the first time competed for their own trophies (donated by the Heart Association) and were listed in the results. Several dozen ran. Thus the first recognized women's champion was Vance's 14-year-old sister, Vicki Eberly. She was assigned a 9 minute handicap, as were all women 13-39 (those younger and older got 15 minutes). Her group also set off a minute early. She ran an outstanding 1:02:02, which put her in 21st place, just nipped at the finish line by the determined last-second sprint of Jack Kirk. It was clearly the fastest recorded Dipsea crossing by a woman, superior to times made in earlier Races and in the old Women's Dipsea Hikes. Vicki and mom Myrrha (638th) also won the new Mother-Daughter trophy. (Vicki would break a leg in a training run on the course the following year.) Another sister, Valerie, 13, finished 60th.

While it was youth's day, Paul Spangler, 70, became the Race's oldest finisher yet. He ran 1:33:48 and was 529th. Now past 90, he still competes in road races.

❑ Norman Bright was located in Seattle and flown in by the Jaycees to hand out the awards. When veteran runner and writer Lynn Ludlow told him about the new handicapping system, "Bright's thoughts immediately began wandering." The seed for his 1970 comeback had been planted.

❑ For the first and only time, there was a tie for the team trophy, between the Olympic Club and the Marin A.C. The tie was considered a stunning upset in that Marin A.C. had won the ten previous years and the Olympic Club hadn't won since 1935. The Olympic Club, founders of the Dipsea, relied on a trio of talented San Jose State distance star recruits—Lowry, Andrew Volmer, and Darold Dent—to earn their share of the award. Another OC scorer was defending champion Don Pickett; badly affected by the day's heat, he was a "woozy" 10th. Apparently the traditional cross country tie breaking method—place of the sixth runner—was not employed; Marin A.C. would have then triumphed.

❑ Pax Beale and John Gorman made a splendid 16mm film of the race, with wonderful footage of Eberly, Rodd and others racing over the course. The film was transfered to videotape in 1993.

□ The 10th runner across the finish line, Jack Lawson, winner of the high school trophy the previous year, was unofficial and disqualified.

□ A crisis concerning use of the Dipsea steps was narrowly avoided. Mill Valley officials had barricaded the uppermost flight and part of the middle flight as unsafe after storms the previous winter. They suggested the runners use alternatives if repairs were not completed by Dipsea day. After much squabbling, funds were finally allocated for the job, today's third flight of steps was rebuilt, and the Race went off unaffected.

1. Vance Eberly, 57:59 (16) [3:06]
2. Flory Rodd, 57:05 (12)
3. Edward Sias, 57:49 (12)
4. Peter Mattei, 58:59 (12)
5. Larry Hoyt, 55:19 (8)
6. Byron Lowry, 47:39 (0) **best time**
7. Ron Elijah, 48:00 (0) **2nd best time, 1st HS**
8. Ralph Paffenbarger, 1:00:04 (12)
9. Andrew Volmer, 48:11 (0)
10. Don Pickett, 56:16 (8)
11. Darold Dent, 48:31 (0)
12. Pat Kelly, 56:33 (8)
13. William Mackey, 56:44 (8)
14. Robert Woodliff, 48:59 (0)
15. Don Makela, 49:15 (0)
16. A.R. Silva, 49:59 (0)
17. Darryl Beardall, 50:50 (0)
18. M.D. Suda, 1:07:08 (16)
19. William Ferlatte, 51:20 (0)
20. Jack Kirk, 1:08:01 (16)

Team (tie) Marin A.C.: Hoyt, Elijah, Makela, Beardall and Ferlatte; Olympic Club: Lowry, Volmer, Pickett, Dent and Jim O'Neil (27th).

722 timed finishers; sunny, hot, 85 degrees

60th Dipsea
August 30, 1970

Among many storied Dipseas, the 1970 Dipsea stands out. Reese calls it "one of the most sensational in Dipsea history." Indeed, for drama, it ranks among the greatest of all American distance runs.

Its story begins 35 years earlier. In 1935, Norman Bright, holder of several U.S. records and a world mark, made his Dipsea debut. Over a very muddy course, Bright ran the day's fastest time (52:53; scratch) but finished 2nd, 200 yards behind winner John Hansen. In 1936, expected to break the course record that Mason Hartwell set in 1912, Bright had an off day and was 19th. The next year, Bright, at his racing peak (in March, he set a course record in the Cross-City race that would stand for 27 years), left nothing to chance. He trained hard on the course, seeking out and secretly marking every shortcut (markers found by Jim Imperiale two decades later), cutting branches, opening fences and more. He did break Hartwell's standard, running 47:22, but again finished 2nd, ironically to a man with whom he shared many of his training tips, Paul Chirone.

Bright did not race the Dipsea again. He held various teaching jobs in different parts of the country. His marriage broke up and he was separated from his one child. He served in the military during World War II. But he never forgot his favorite race, and the tape he had never broken. And, despite many increasingly close calls, his Dipsea record still stood.

In the late 1960's, Bright faced his greatest challenge; failing eyesight that would ultimately leave him blind. He came to the 1969 Dipsea from Seattle as a guest of the Race, to hand out the awards and presumably congratulate the man who would break his course record. Instead, Byron Lowry missed his mark by 17 seconds. Bright heard, for the first time, about the new handicapping system which insured him the maximum headstart. He decided to make another bid for victory himself.

Bright's plan was based on what he dubbed his "60-60-60" formula; he felt he needed to break 60 minutes, at age 60, in the 60th Dipsea, to win. He made over 20 trips by bus from Seattle, where he was a counselor at West Seattle H.S, to Mill Valley to practice on and study the course. His preparations, partly necessitated by his failing vision, were even more meticulous than in 1937. Again he placed arrows to guide him, cleared rough patches, laid logs to ford streams, stashed water bottles and stationed friends and relatives along the way for assistance. He reopened the old direct route up Dynamite Hill, covering the entrance with a branch (and replacing the branch when he passed on Race day). His friend Chirone encouraged him throughout. Bright even fed bones to a dog that guarded the newly-built house on Panoramic Highway so that he alone could gain unimpeded access through the property. Prophetically, a picture of Bright was on the Dipsea Race program cover. Bright himself sensed the upcoming drama, telling *The Amateur Athlete*, "Wouldn't it be cool if I could win the race I hold the record for on a day when somebody else probably will break my record?"

His effort, fortunately captured on the film *33 Years to Victory* by John Gorman and Pax Beale (who helped in the effort by filing the soles of Bright's shoes for better traction), was remarkable. Again in the colors of the Olympic Club, as he had been decades earlier, Bright set off with the first group of men. But now he wore bib #1179. Waiting were a record 1,000 other entrants. One runner, a youngster named Daniel Martinez who did not know the course well, challenged him. Bright disposed of him by ducking into a shortcut at a key intersection; Martinez got lost and finished well back.

Bright leapt down Suicide; his years of high-level mountaineering undoubtedly helping. He hurdled barriers. He remembered every shortcut. Bright ran alone along the course he knew so well, aware that others were gaining. He twisted his ankle on a rock while crossing Redwood Creek, his grimace clearly caught on the film. Bright limped up Dynamite, but then ran through the injury.

Bright had stationed his nephew Ray Bright at White Barn. Norman asked Ray if anyone was in view. Ray saw no one but, to spur Norman on, said he spotted someone. Norman renewed his effort. Seconds later, Ray did see a pursuer through the thick fog. It was the swift Rich Delgado, who had been second overall at Bay to Breakers three years earlier.

But Bright, displaying flashes of his great innate speed, hung on. He was first into Stinson, meeting his time goal by running 59:46. He finally won the Dipsea, 35 years after his first attempt—a feat perhaps unmatched in American racing history.

The unbridled joy was short-lived. Streaking down the final straightaway was Delgado, finishing 16 seconds after Bright. Delgado's running time of 47:02 (2hc) broke Bright's legendary Race record. And then, 1:40 later, 19-year-old scratch man Don Makela crossed. His actual time was 46:42, a new best. Thus, a course record that had been altered only once in 58 years (another mark probably unparalleled in U.S. racing) was broken twice in 100 seconds! Bright later said, "I'm not unhappy about my record being broken, for it's good to see young runners improve and conquer new goals."

To add even more color, the 6th finisher was Jack Kirk, who had run with Bright in the '30's and who remains the Dipsea's only other 60-year-old winner. This was to be the 14th and last top-10 finish of Kirk's fabled Dipsea career.

More came out afterwards. Delgado, not completely familiar with the Dipsea course, had lost at least 15 seconds at the junction below Cardiac Hill until the next runner came along to direct him. Delgado had grown opposed to the idea of handicaps so skipped the two previous Dipseas. When he discovered that now, at age 30, he received two handicap minutes, Delgado phoned Dipsea director Jerry Hauke the night before the Race to enter. His course error might have cost Delgado the victory and record. Delgado's 47:02 remains the fastest ever by a runner with a handicap.

Makela, meanwhile, revealed two lucky breaks that helped him get through the largest Dipsea field to date. One was at Windy Gap; he went straight between the two new homes on Panoramic, on the old course, and was not stopped; others went longer to the right. And climbing out of Muir Woods, burly Pax Beale was clearing the way for Darryl Beardall, inadvertently aiding Makela as he came through. Makela had been the Marin County Athletic League cross country champion in 1968 while at Novato High School and was now a star at the College of Marin. This was his fourth Dipsea.

Actually, it was neither Delgado nor Makela that was expected to break the record but Ron Elijah or Bill Scobey. Elijah, who would indeed soon twice set Dipsea all-time marks, had been regularly beating Marin A.C. teammate Makela by 45 seconds or so in practice runs over the course. But at Windy Gap, Elijah took a longer route down than Makela. Elijah then made a supreme effort to re-catch Makela on the Muir Woods Road, and succeeded. But that downhill pounding exhausted him and Elijah "only" managed a 49:01. Scobey, unfamiliar with the course's shortcuts, had to settle for an impressive 48:21 in his first Dipsea.

A few weeks later, veteran Dipsea and AAU official Thomas Laughran announced he had measured the course and found it .2 miles shorter than that used in Bright's 1937 run. There was talk that Makela's mark should have an asterisk, like the one then in vogue for Roger Maris' 61 home runs. Reese, however, also measured the two routes some years after and concluded that they varied "by no more than 86 feet."

Scores of women ran. Leading them was Mary Cortez, part of a prominent family of Peninsula runners (brother Dave Cortez finished 4th). She finished 57th in 1:02:13 (9hc), just 11 seconds off the women's record.

❑ There were a high of 12 past, present and future Dipsea champions in the Race. Six (in order; Bright, Kirk, Darryl Beardall, Don Pickett, Alan Beardall and Mike Boitano) were among the first 23 finishers. Others included Homer Latimer in his debut, John Satti, Phil Smith, Vance Eberly (the defending champion who lost eight handicap minutes for turning 11 and finished 41st), Ernie Marinoni and Mary Etta Boitano.

❑ George Leonard, who had owned the land through which the Dipsea Trail passed from Steep Ravine to Stinson Beach, ran the Race for the only time. Joining him were his daughter Barbara Robben and nine-year-old grandson Michael. This was probably the first example of three generations of a family in the same Dipsea. Barbara has missed only two Dipsea Races since. George's son Mark had been third in the 1964 Dipsea. George and Wilma Leonard, who had donated a permanent Dipsea Trail easement to Marin County in 1968, were in the process of selling their Mt. Tamalpais holdings to the new Golden Gate Recreation Area. George Leonard died in 1991.

❑ Russ Kiernan, who would become one of the best, and best liked, of all Dipsea runners over the next quarter-century, debuted in 591st place.

❑ Dr. Paul Spangler, 71, covered the course in 1:31:07 and was 681st.

❑ Officials, not prepared for the record turnout, ran out of their supply of 900+ finish identification tags. Race chairman Bill Devlin said, "I'm sure we had more than 1,000 runners."

1. Norman Bright, 59:46 (15) [:16]
2. Rich Delgado, 47:02 (2) **2nd best time**
3. Don Makela, 46:42 (0) **best time**
4. Dave Cortez, 53:45 (7)
5. Bill Gray, 51:37 (4)
6. Jack Kirk, 1:02:50 (15)
7. Bill Scobey, 48:21 (0)
8. Ed Sias, 56:42 (8)
9. Howard Labrie, 48:50 (0)
10. Darryl Beardall, 50:54 (2)
11. Wes Hildreth, 50:57 (2)
12. Ron Elijah, 49:01 (0) **1st HS**
13. Don Pickett, 55:03 (6)
14. Pat Kelly, 55:07 (6)
15. Richard Burkhardt, 1:04:08 (15)
16. Ralph Paffenbarger, 56:15 (7)
17. George Derderian, 49:28 (0)
18. Alan Beardall, 51:36 (2)
19. S.L. Bartelate, 49:39 (0)
20. Peter Mattei, 56:43 (7)
Team Marin A.C.: Makela, Hildreth, D. Beardall, Bob Biancalana (28th) and Larry Hoyt (34th)
941 timed finishers, total probably over 1,000; foggy

111

61st Dipsea
August 29, 1971

Pressured by the growing women's rights movement, and after such highly publicized incidents as Jock Semple's failed attempt to physically remove Kathy Switzer during the Boston Marathon, the AAU opened long distance running to women. Dr. Frances Conley, the first woman to officially finish Bay to Breakers three months earlier, became the first official female Dipsea finisher. While she was the only woman in the top 20, the future impact of the change would be enormous.

The Race showed signs of being a repeat of 1970, with the wily veteran Norman Bright again battling a talented youngster, now Mike Boitano, 9. This time youth prevailed.

The Boitano family of San Francisco was already getting local media attention for their running exploits; soon they would be known nationally. The father, John, was a long-time smoker. The rest of the family, in their own words, "didn't do much of anything waiting for [him] to come home" from work. In late 1967, worried about his heart, John took up jogging and brought the family—wife Lucille, 5-year-old Mike and 4-year-old Mary Etta along. They started slowly but soon were doing marathons, and the Dipsea. They practiced diligently for the Dipsea, running the course many times. One workout was doing hard charges down Suicide, timed by John, then heading back uphill again for more.

Lucille, Mike and Mary Etta Boitano, plus Bright, Conley and over 100 others (the largest initial wave ever) started together with the maximum 15-minute handicap. Mike simply proved too swift for his fabled rival Bright. The youngster ran a splendid 58:53 and won by 75 seconds. Bright, his failing vision even more of a problem, slowed only 22 seconds from his winning 1970 effort. For the second year in a row he "ran under his age,"

meaning his time in minutes (60:08) was below his age in years (61). Only Ray Locke (1918) and Sal Vasquez (1993) have even done it once. But Bright had to settle for being runner-up for a record third time, as he had been in 1935 and 1937.

Owen Gorman, from southern California, took 3rd. Unfamiliar with the course, he followed Don Pickett much of the way.

Next was Ron Elijah in a new course record, 46:08. It remains the 2nd fastest time in Dipsea history, behind only his own 1974 effort. Don Makela's record 46:42 from 1970 stood only a year; Makela himself would finish 15th. Elijah, who had already carved a fine Dipsea record while at Novato High School, was a sophomore at Humboldt State.

Next came Conley, a neurosurgeon married to Olympic javelin thrower Phil Conley (who was 529th), in her historic run. Her 1:01:18 was a woman's record, superior to any recorded efforts in earlier years. Conley would reappear in the media in 1991 when she briefly resigned from the Stanford University medical faculty over charges of sexism.

Sixth was Jim O'Neil, who remains one of the world's premier age-group runners. Dave Cortez, who had won the first ever Double Dipsea the year before at age 12 (his brother Jose would win the 1971 Double), was 7th. Two seconds later came scratch runner Byron Lowry, a two-time winner of the best time award who now had to settle for 2nd fastest effort. Ninth, winning the high school trophy, was Mike Wolford; he had been second in 1968.

Fourteen-year-old Mitch Kingery, who would set still standing United States age records in the marathon the following two years, was 17th (52:35, 4hc).

Harry Cordellos, an outstanding blind runner, completed the Race in 1:21:04 (15hc). Cordellos ran touching and holding a friend, fellow DSE member Jack Bettencourt. A wonderful and inspirational film would later be made by Ray Gatchalian about Cordellos running the Dipsea.

Jimmy Nicholson, who would have a Dipsea

trophy named for him after his death in 1986, debuted in 48th (59:02, 7hc).

Also debuting was Len Wallach, later director of Bay to Breakers and author of a history of that race.

❑ The 12-year victory streak of the Marin A.C. was broken by the NorCal Seniors. The Olympic Club would have won the team title if Bright, who ran for them in the 1930's and again in 1970, had not competed unattached.

❑ The number of runners officially surpassed 1,000 for the first time; 1,170 entered and 1,117 (six more than Bay to Breakers) were recorded as finishers.

1. Mike Boitano, 58:53 (15) [1:15]
2. Norman Bright, 1:00:08 (15)
3. Owen Gorman, 53:00 (7)
4. Ron Elijah, 46:08 (0) **best time**
5. Fran Conley, 1:01:18 (15) **1st, fastest woman**
6. Jim O'Neil, 54:49 (8)
7. Dave Cortez, 52:53 (6)
8. Byron Lowry, 46:55 (0) **2nd best time**
9. Mike Wolford, 53:22 (6) **1st HS**
10. R. Martinez, 1:02:45 (15)
11. Mike Killeen, 51:52 (4)
12. G. Garbarino, 51:53 (4)
13. Don Pickett, 54:59 (7)
14. Peter Mattei, 56:14 (8)
15. Don Makela, 48:22 (0)
16. Pat Kelly, 55:23 (7)
17. Mitch Kingery, 52:35 (4)
18. Wes Hildreth, 49:39 (1)
19. Jack Bellah, 48:59 (0)
20. Ralph Paffenbarger, 57:07 (8)
Team NorCal Seniors: Mattei, Paffenbarger, Dennis Teeguarden (21st), Paul Reese (24th) and Bob Malain (25th)
1,117 finishers; fog, drizzle

62nd Dipsea
August 27, 1972

Mike Boitano, 10, became the first back-to-back winner since John Hassard in 1905-06. Ten-year-olds were now given 13 handicap minutes, two less than in 1970. But Boitano responded to this loss of headstart by running 2:16 faster than in '71 and winning by an even larger margin.

An 11-year-old from Westwood (Lassen County, CA), Debbie Rudolf, in her first trip over the Dipsea, was the early leader. She was caught by Mike, then the two youngsters ran together. Mike pulled away, his final margin enlarged by Rudolf's late fall. Boitano became the fourth double winner, joining Hassard, Oliver Millard and Jack Kirk. With dad John, he also won the father-son trophy. Rudolf achieved the all-time fastest crossing yet by a female, 1:00:56. Twenty years later, Megan McGowan would also win the women's best time award at age 11.

Third was Paul Reese, the 1967 runner-up, who had started with Mike Boitano. Fourth was Tom Hale, running a brilliant 46:47 from scratch. It was then the third fastest Dipsea ever, and remains #5. Hale, a University of Oregon sophomore, was the only scratch man among the first 19 finishers.

John Butterfield was 5th. With his wife Priscilla (513th), he captured the first husband-wife trophy.

Rich Delgado, who held the Dipsea course record for a scant 100 seconds in 1970, was 6th.

Several notable runners made debuts. Jim Weil, who would become a member of the Dipsea Committee and responsible for timing and handicapping, was 454th (1:09:35, 2hc). Dr. Joan Ullyot, who would set numerous records in her still-active career and become a leading writer and spokesperson on running (including author of the book, *Women's Running*, which helped fuel the nation's running boom), was 92nd (1:10:20, 15hc). Rich McCandless, who would run a 2:12 marathon 16 years later, was 99th (55:59, Scr).

Debbie Rudolf, 11, finishing 2nd in 1972, her father behind. (Independent Journal)

□ Though an increase had been forecast, the number of finishers actually fell for the first time since 1961.

□ This was the last appearance of the band at the finish line. It had been provided for decades through a grant by the American Federation of Musicians, Local #6. In some years there had been up to 25 peformers.

1. Mike Boitano, 56:37 (13) [2:19]
2. Debbie Rudolf, 1:00:56 (15) **1st, fastest woman**
3. Paul Reese, 59:12 (13)
4. Tom Hale, 46:47 (0) **best time**
5. John Butterfield, 51:53 (5)
6. Rich Delgado, 49:59 (3)
7. John Finch, 52:01 (5)
8. Peter Mattei, 55:02 (8)
9. Darryl Beardall, 52:14 (5)
10. Wes Hildreth, 51:17 (4)
11. Bob Malain, 55:19 (8)
12. Dennis Teeguarden, 54:26 (7)
13. Tim Killeen, 53:31 (6)
14. Daniel Martinez, 55:36 (8)
15. George Conlan, 54:50 (7)
16. Jim Nicholson, 55:06 (7)
17. Ken Napier, 55:18 (7)
18. Bill LaForge, 52:21 (4)
19. Don Pickett, 55:26 (7)
20. B.W. Edwards, 48:28 (0) **2nd best time**
34. Jack Bellah, 51:11 (0) **1st HS**

Team NorCal Seniors: Reese, Finch, Mattei, Malain and Teeguarden

1,023 finishers; thick fog produced wet, slippery conditions

63rd Dipsea
August 26, 1973

It was shocking enough that the Dipsea, its reputation built up over six decades as the ruggedest of races, was won by pre-teen boys in three of the four previous years. Now, in 1973, the winner was a 4'4", 60 pound, bespectacled 10-year-old girl in pigtails.

Mary Etta Boitano was the outstanding young American distance runner of her era, and perhaps of all time. She set a course record and won three Bay to Breakers titles (1974-76) before becoming a teenager. At the first ever women's national marathon championship, held in San Mateo, CA, on February 10, 1974, Boitano, 10, finished fourth in 3:01:15. The time was only 15 minutes off the women's world record. No woman under 19 had ever run faster. It remains the #1 United States girls' under-11 mark.

Mary Etta already had extensive Dipsea training. She first ran the Race in 1968, at age 5 (probably the youngest ever to complete it), then every year since. With her father John, mother Lucille, and year-older brother Mike, who won the 1971 and '72 Dipseas, she had been on countless practice runs. Prophetically, the Boitano family was featured on the cover of the 1973 Dipsea program, Mary Etta in front.

Mary Etta started with the first, 15-minute group. With her were Norman Bright, competing with a broken arm in a cast, and the 12-year-old runner-up from 1972, Debbie Rudolf. Five minutes later (10hc), Michael Boitano, the two-time defending champion, set off. Starting with an 8-minute handicap were men 45-49, a group that would produce five of the top nine finishers.

There was then a mixup at the starting line, delaying the 7-minute group (men 40-44) and all later starters by approximately a minute. This gave Mary Etta in effect a 16-minute head start over the scratch runners (but no edge against her nearest rivals; all the first ten finishers benefited equally).

Boitano led throughout, pulling steadily away from her only close pursuer, Rudolf. Knowing the trail so well, Mary Etta was never in danger of getting lost. But she had other fears, charmingly related to Reese in 1979:

"I was all alone, and I guess I was frightened because I was alone. Going through Muir Woods, I thought a bear might come and eat me up and I heard of incidents of sighted mountain lion and rattlers. So I guess being afraid at the Dipsea made me really excel to my fullest. I can't really pinpoint the most difficult part because it is all the Dipsea together which makes it difficult. The point at which I knew I was sure I had it won was when I crossed the finish line. I never knew, somebody could have caught up to me and passed me right at the finish line. I was expecting it to happen."

But no one was even close. At the tape, her margin of victory, ironically over Michael, was a sizable 2:39. Her actual running time of 58:53 broke Rudolf's women's course record by just over two minutes. Michael, 11, ran a fine 56:22 but his sister denied him a record setting third victory. The best previous family effort in Dipsea history was the first and third of brothers Allan and Andrew Baffico in 1947. Father John Boitano was 39th (1:03:30, 11hc) and mom Lucille 638th (1:30:56, 16hc). Mary Etta also won perhaps a record number of trophies, seven were handed to her by Congressman William Mailliard according to the *Chronicle* account.

Don Pickett, the 1968 champion, closed to within 20 seconds of Michael and got 3rd. Tommy Owen, Jr., a ten-year-old who won the Double Dipsea that year, was 4th. Rudolf finished 5th.

Darryl Beardall came in 11th, the first of the runners who had been inadvertently delayed a minute. The error certainly cost him a few places. Dave Cortez of St. Francis H.S. (Mountain View, CA), was 13th and won the high school trophy. Norman Bright finished 24th in his final Dipsea. Immediately behind was 59-year-old Albert Clark,

who continues to race the Dipsea (finishing in 1993 at age 79), and then Danny Martinez, who Bright had ourun and outfoxed during his 1970 win.

The first scratch runner, Ron Elijah, was only 15th. Elijah, too, was hurt by the lost minute and also had to battle his way past the record field of 1,135 finishers. His 49:11 was the slowest for a best time winner in a 13-year period (1966-78). He was the only runner to break 50 minutes.

Domingo Tibaduiza, who would be selected to five Colombian Olympic teams and is now one of the world's top over-40 competitors, was 40th (52:40, Scr) in his only Dipsea. Rich Kimball, one of the greatest prep milers California ever produced—he set an American H.S. indoor 1500m record of 3:50.0 the following February—was 48th (53:56, Scr).

Kees Tuinzing, a popular coach who would later found the Tamalpa Runners, the *Schedule* magazine of race listings and Total Race Systems, the region's leading finish line timers, was 670th (1:16:31, 1hc) in his debut.

❑ William Magner, the 1930 champion who first ran the Dipsea in 1921, returned and finished 1,058th (1:48:39, 16hc).

❑ For the first time, a computer was used to help with results. But technical problems (a recurring theme over the next years) kept the manual system alive.

❑ Also for the first time, Dipsea t-shirts were sold. Five hundred white cotton ones were ordered and priced at $2.50 each. Profits went to the Long Distance Running Committee of the Pacific Association-AAU. In future years, the Dipsea would disassociate itself from the AAU, saving a $1 per runner fee, and shirt sales would become a source of revenue for the Race itself.

❑ On July 19, the NorCal Seniors (who would win the 1973 Dipsea team title), had organized a match race over the course between their team and a visiting British masters contingent. Over 50 runners competed.

Handicaps adjusted to reflect starting line error
1. Mary Etta Boitano, 58:43 (16) [2:39]
   fastest woman
2. Michael Boitano, 56:22 (11) **1st man**
3. Don Pickett, 54:42 (9)
4. Tommy Owen, Jr., 59:44 (14)
5. Debi Rudolf, 1:02:25 (16)
6. Jim O'Neil, 55:42 (9)
7. Peter Mattei, 56:26 (9)
8. Bob Malain, 56:32 (9)
9. Pat Kelly, 56:35 (9)
10. Ralph Paffenbarger, 58:49 (11)
11. Darryl Beardall, 52:53 (5)
12. Owen Gorman, 55:34 (7)
13. Dave Cortez, 52:48 (4) **1st HS**
14. Gil Tarin, 55:52 (7)
15. Ron Elijah, 49:11 (0) **best time**
16. Paul Reese, 1:03:29 (14)
17. M.J. Nagel, 55:45 (6)*
18. Homer Latimer, 53:51 (4)
19. Mike Healy, 56:56 (7)
20. Ken Napier, 57:07 (7)
21. Gene Fitzgerald, 53:09 (3)
22. Chuck Stagliano, 54:20 (4)
23. M.A. Millward, 50:50 (0) **2nd best time**
24. Norman Bright, 1:07:00 (16)
25. Albert Clark, 1:07:08 (16)
*17th and 24th places were omitted in the results; subsequent finishers are moved up accordingly
Team NorCal Seniors: Pickett, Mattei, Malain, Paffenbarger and Reese
1,135 finishers; overcast and cool

64th Dipsea
August 25, 1974

This was an exceptionally competitive Dipsea, with several of the top finishers turning in performances that ordinarily would have won. Indeed, Ron Elijah's 44:49 not only remains the fastest Dipsea crossing ever, but is considered by many as the Race's single greatest achievement.

In reaction to the plight of the scratch men the previous year (the first of them, Elijah, was 15th overall), the maximum handicaps were cut slightly. Albert Clark, 60, who departed with the opening 14-minute group, was the early leader.

The battle was really joined when the era's two phenomenal young girls, defending champion Mary Etta Boitano, 11, and 1972 runner-up Debbie Rudolf, 13, set off with 12-minute handicaps. The two waged a splendid duel, which helped push Rudolf to shatter the women's course record. Rudolf's 56:11 would not be bettered by any woman until 1988, and still stands as #3 on the all-time list. Boitano's 56:55 was then the second fastest women's time ever, and still ranks #5.

The next of the major challengers, 12-year-old Michael Boitano, who won in '71 and '72 and was second in '73, had eight handicap minutes. He caught everyone who started ahead of him (including his sister Mary Etta right at the finish line) except Rudolf, and was in turn passed by just two men.

Darryl Beardall, who had missed only one Dipsea since his debut in 1955 (in 1959, when he was told he had a weak heart and only six months to live!), went off with a six-minute handicap. Now 37, he had already won more Northern California distance races than any other runner ever. He had also amassed ten top-10 Dipsea finishes (his record now stands at 19), with a high of 3rd, and had captured two best-time awards. But Darryl had never won, not as a Santa Rosa High School sensa-

After ten top-10 finishes, Darryl Beardall finally wins in 1974. Runner-up Debbie Rudolf visible behind. (Bob Hax, Independent Journal)

tion in the mid-50's, not when he dominated Bay Area road racing during the first half of the 1960's, not even when he was getting some handicap minutes in the early 1970's.

But now, in 1974, he ran brilliantly, becoming the oldest runner yet to break 50 minutes. He passed Michael Boitano, then Mary Etta late. He took the lead on the road in Stinson when he overhauled Rudolf. Beardall finally broke the Dipsea tape. No one had run more Dipsea races, 18, before winning. Beardall joined his younger brother Alan as a Dipsea champion; Michael and Mary Etta Boitano are the only other siblings with that honor.

Elijah, who Beardall most feared, had skipped the two previous Dipseas after his record 46:08 in 1971. Training for the Race was leaving him tired for cross country season at Humboldt State. Here is his account of his historic 1974 run, as related at the 1993 Dipsea Dinner.

It was my senior year at Humboldt and I decided I was really going to go for it. Don [Makela, his running partner] and I were doing some good training runs in practice, I got down to around 46:20-46:30. I felt that if I really rested up and took it easy the week before I could maybe go under 46.

People always ask me how I could get around 1,000 people. Everybody in the race was very helpful. They knew me, they would recognize me. I would run along and people would yell, "Here comes Elijah." And believe it or not, most people moved. I remember going up the stairs and a good friend of mine yelled, "Here comes Elijah, everybody move to the left" and everybody moved. So it was easy going up the stairs, I just went right up.

It was terrific. I got pumped up. Every time I would pass somebody they would pat me on the back or say something like "Go Ron, go Ron." It just kept that adrenalin going. I got to the top of Windy Gap. I would always be within 25 or 30 yards of my good friend Don but . . . now I couldn't even see Don. He wasn't in front of me, he was behind me. And I looked back and realized Don wasn't near me and I thought

I was off to a good race because I felt great and I wasn't even tired.

I went over the top and started running down. Parts were comical . . . coming down into Muir Woods there were five people standing there and I just went right into them. It was like a bowling ball hitting pins. They just went "Bam!" Some of them went into this barbed wire fence. After they got up they yelled some obscenities at me but I just kept going.

I would always catch my sister [Derry] at a certain point in the race. The last race, I caught her way up on Hogsback. This year she had two [handicap] minutes more and I caught her in Muir Woods. She couldn't believe it. So I knew when I caught her, she was like a marker, that I was off to a good race.

I ran all the way through Hogsback trying not to look back, trying not to make anybody behind me think I was in pain. I was pushing as hard as I could. I was in pain. All of us have little spots in the Race where we would back off, give ourselves a break. I would go hard through Hogsback, then I would hit the second Muir Woods [Rainforest] where nobody could see me and take it easy.

I remember getting to the top of Lone Pine where somebody would count your place. They said, "You're 45th." You look out and look down and there's maybe three people in front of you so I just said, "There's no way I'm going to catch 45 people when I could only see three." So I just ran as hard as I could. I would just let it go. When I went through the creek [Webb] I maybe passed five or six people. I went up Insult Hill and somebody said, "You're 12th." And so I said, "What happened to the other 20 people?" I saw like five people.

So at this point I was kind of feeling dejected because there was no way I was going to catch 12 people from here. So I kept running. I got over to the spot, I can't remember exactly, we used to, instead of crossing the creek [at the end of the second Panoramic shortcut], go up over a knoll and then cross the creek. I get to the top there and I look down and I see Mary Etta and Mike Boitano. They were down there near the bottom. My first feeling was then that I can't catch them, they're too far. But I forgot, they were good runners, but they were kids, so it was easy to catch up with them.

So the next feeling that I had as I was passing them was, "I'm winning. These are the winners of the last three years and I'm passing them."

So I run down through the street. I felt great crossing the finish line. They hand me a computer card. I look down at the computer card. It's got a number on it I can't make out. I turn to someone and ask, "What did I place?" "Third." "Who won?" "Some old guy." "Who was second?" "A little girl." It was Darryl Beardall and Debbie Rudolf. I had kind of forgotten about Darryl. I had thought I could catch him, but he had a great day and I couldn't get him.

The thrill I had in the Race was standing in the chute after and waiting to go through and I felt this tug on my shorts and I looked back and there was Mary Etta about this high [touching his hip] and she said, "Good race, Ron." It's one of the best memories of my whole running career.

Elijah's sensational 44:49 (listed as 44:42 in the Independent Journal the following day) smashed his own course record. No one since has run within two minutes of the time. Elijah's mark stands out even more in light of the smaller invitational fields now faced by the scratch runners. Helping him a bit was a shift in the finish line, from the intersection of Calle del Mar and Arenal to 150 yards down the maintenance yard driveway (used today) off Shoreline. Reese measured the change as a reduction of 104 yards, making it the shortest Dipsea course ever (6.75 miles).

Sixth in was future two-time champion Homer Latimer. He started a minute behind Beardall and ran one second faster. Were it not for Beardall's effort, Latimer would have become the oldest runner to break 50 minutes.

Danny Martinez, who had been bested in his battle with Norman Bright in 1970, was 7th. He also had a great run, 51:10 at age 14. So too did Peter Mattei, 8th. The long-time AAU official ran 55:22, probably a record (since broken) for runners over 50.

Don Makela, 12th, turned in the day's second fastest time, 46:43 (scratch). It is still the #4 Dipsea mark ever.

The Marin A.C. regrouped to upend the three-time defending champions NorCal Seniors and claim their 13th title.

Don Chaffee, who would win in 1979, was 102nd (1:00:44; 5hc) in his first Dipsea. Skip Swannack, who would be the women's winner at Bay to Breakers in 1978, debuted in 148th place (1:11:07; 13hc). Fifteen-year-old Brian Purcell, who would one day set the course record at the Western States 100 Mile Endurance Run, was 185th (1:03:35, 4hc) in his inaugural Dipsea.

❏ The actor Bruce Dern was 293rd (1:09:19, 6hc). He was in the North Bay filming a movie directed by Michael Ritchie, who lived by the Dipsea course and who encouraged him to enter. Dern later told Runner's World, "I'll never do it [the Dipsea] again; it's too dangerous. From the fourth to the sixth mile is definitely one of the more hair-raising experiences I've ever been through." Eight years later he would begin filming, as the lead, the Dipsea-inspired feature film On the Edge. Dern had been a 1:57 half-miler at the University of Pennsylvania, then an ultra-marathoner (in 1969 he ran a 50-miler in 7:06 the day before his marriage).

❏ Barbara Schwartz, a 21-year-old College of Marin student from Mill Valley, caused a sensation when she discarded her top in the Rainforest and ran in bare-chested. She told the Independent Journal afterward that she wanted "to be closer to nature . . . to feel those drops [of fog] on my body. No one hassled me. A few men made comments."

❏ In 1974 alone, a special handicap group was created based on weight. Men over 250 pounds got nine minutes.

❏ James Farren, whose son would be honored with the James Farren, Jr. Trophy, served as Dipsea chairman for the Jaycees.

1. Darryl Beardall, 49:57 (6) [:14]
2. Debbie Rudolf, 56:11 (12) **1st, fastest woman**
3. Ron Elijah, 44:49 (0) **best time**
4. Michael Boitano, 52:54 (8)
5. Mary Etta Boitano, 56:55 (12)
6. Homer Latimer, 49:56 (5)
7. Daniel Martinez, 51:10 (6)
8. Peter Mattei, 55:22 (10)
9. Jim Nicholson, 52:42 (7)
10. Tom Owen, 56:00 (10)
11. Don Pickett, 54:07 (8)
12. Don Makela, 46:43 (0) **2nd best time**
13. R. Vasquez, 53:10 (6)
14. Ralph Paffenbarger, 57:37 (10)
15. Ken Napier, 55:09 (7)
16. Bob Malain, 56:11 (8)
17. Gil Tarin, 55:23 (7)
18. T.J. O'Brien, 55:31 (7)
19. Bob Bunnell, 48:35 (0)
20. Dennis Teeguarden, 55:40 (7)
21. William Flodberg, 56:02 (7)
22. Byron Lowry, 50:06 (1)
23. Mike Healy, 56:15 (7)
24. Rod Berry, 55:18 (6)
25. Gene Fitzgerald, 52:26 (3)
34. R. Schupbach, 55:54 (8) **1st HS**
Team Marin A.C.: Beardall, Elijah, Pickett, Makela and Bunnell
1,063 finishers; foggy

65th Dipsea
August 24, 1975

For the only time in Dipsea history, a non-American citizen won. Joe Patterson was a 40-year-old milkman in Queensland, Australia, a job that left him, in his own words, "as fit as a Mallee Bull." He had taken up running just four years earlier and was now logging 80-100 miles a week.

He and several of his countrymen landed at San Francisco for a one day layover on their way home from the first official World Masters Track championships in Toronto. Patterson recalls, 18 years later:

Some of our members read in the newspaper that this race was on, just outside of San Francisco, so five of us decided to split the cab fare and head for Mill Valley.

The race officials were most friendly and could not do enough to make us welcome. My memories of the race are few, but battling my way up those lovely steps is quite clear. Then also later on in the event I can remember heading the wrong way and being put on the right track by the bloke coming second and lastly, I can remember running into Stinson and not knowing that I was the first one across the line.

After the race we Australians felt quite embarrassed as we had to rush straight back to San Francisco to catch a plane home, so the Jaycees put on the presentations as quickly as possible and also arranged us a lift back to town.

That also was a thrill for us from "Down Under" as we arrived back at our hotel in a big flashy Yankee convertible—for us "Crocodile Dundee" blokes that was really great as I don't think any of us had been in a convertible before and we had smiles on our faces like the cat that swallowed the canary.

That "bloke coming second" was Don Pickett, 47, who had started two minutes earlier (9hc). Pickett was the 1968 winner, and soon to be christened "Mr. Dipsea" for his devotion to the Race. Just past Cardiac, Pickett had worked his way into second behind 56-year-old George McGrath, another of the Australians and a multi-medalist at Toronto. Then, coming down the Swoop, Patterson flew past Pickett. But at the base of the Swoop, Patterson was unsure which of the two paths to follow. He stopped, blocked them both, waited briefly for Pickett's arrival, then asked, "Which way, matey?" Pickett instantly responded, "If you don't mind poison oak, follow me," and led Patterson down the then-legal Slash. Patterson grumbled "bloody goat path" but negotiated it successfully.

Patterson repassed Pickett. The battle continued on the Moors, the former ranch land opened for the first time to runners. (Runners flocked to this new route—a few had already been sneaking through the fences in recent years—abandoning the traditional Panoramic Highway shortcuts. But when the final downhill off the Moors was closed by Golden Gate National Recreation Area officials in 1977, the top racers returned to Panoramic.)

On the open grassland, both Patterson and Pickett passed McGrath, who had earlier missed the Slash shortcut. At the tape, the younger, speedier Patterson prevailed over Pickett by 11 seconds. Patterson's 51:58 set a record (since broken) for runners over 40. McGrath followed Pickett five seconds later. To this day, Pickett feels McGrath would have won had he known the shortcuts, a big "if" in the Dipsea.

Fourth was the defending champion Darryl Beardall, running almost a minute slower in the hot conditions and with one less handicap minute. Debbie Rudolf, the '72 and '74 runner-up, was 5th. Next came Byron Lowry. His 48:17 (2hc) earned him a third best time award, which tied him with Otto Boeddiker, William Churchill and Ron Elijah behind only Mason Hartwell.

In 49th place (1:03:45, 11hc) was nine-year-old Mike McManus. He would go on to become one of the greatest Dipsea runners ever, winning six best time awards. His father, Thomas, had already run several Dipseas.

Ron Elijah, who ran 44:49 the previous year, managed only a 56:33 (scratch) for 112th.

Lucille Boitano, mother of the 1971, '72 and '73 champions, took a misstep in Old Mill Park near the start and felt a sharp pain in her foot. But she kept going to finish 1,301st (1:50:49, 14hc). She later learned she had broken two bones. Son Michael finished 40th (57:37, 6hc), daughter Mary Etta 52nd (1:04:07, 11hc) and husband John 101st (1:07:09, 11hc).

❏ A little-noticed addition to the prize list, the awarding of numbered shirts to the first 25 finishers, would end up generating tremendous interest in future races. The shirts were actually a crude attempt to keep a record of the top finishers. Jerry Hauke relates: "The year before we had a terrible mess at the finish line. Someone dropped the numbered IBM cards we were using in the chutes and we ended up having to ask the runners who they finished behind and ahead of. So we thought we would just slap numbered T-shirts on the first ones to keep things clear!" The shirts were oversized to meet the task.

These shirts would give a whole group of runners, with little chance of winning, another still lofty goal. Indeed, the joy of some first-time shirt winners has often appeared comparable to that of the overall winners. The 1975 shirts were blue with a red number on the front and no other writing, not even a Dipsea logo. In 1976 and '77 they were yellow with blue numbers. The now-trademark black shirts were introduced in 1978, when the number awarded also rose to 35.

The shirts were originally handed out at the end of the finish chute, creating a lively scramble and occasional inequities. In 1975, noted runner and author Joan Ullyot was 26th across the line so did not get a shirt. When the official results appeared the original 12th place finisher was disqualified and Ullyot recognized as 25th. Today, shirts are handed out at the awards ceremony.

❏ There were 1,380 finishers, a new high. Over 600 of them, including the Australians, registered the morning of the Race.

□ Results were mailed so many months late that a 1976 entry application was attached. Late results would plague the Dipsea for several more years.
□ The high school trophy, which dates back to 1905, was discontinued a second time. It would be revived again in 1987.

1. Joe Patterson, 51:58 (7) [:11]
2. Don Pickett, 54:09 (9)
3. George McGrath, 58:14 (13)
4. Darryl Beardall, 50:51 (5)
5. Debbie Rudolf, 56:59 (11) **1st, fastest woman**
6. Byron Lowry, 48:17 (2) **best time**
7. Robert Biancalana, 56:18 (10)
8. Gil Tarin, 54:10 (7)
9. Bob Malain, 56:14 (9)
10. Bob Bunnell, 48:26 (1)
11. Dan Seamount, 58:41 (11)
12. Betsy White, 1:02:13 (14)
13. Don Makela, 48:22 (0) **2nd best time**
14. Bill Scobey, 51:23 (3)
15. T. Newhart, 52:32 (4)
16. Mike Healy, 55:35 (7)
17. Chuck Stagliano, 52:41 (4)
18. Karl Marschall, 58:05 (9)
19. Jimmy Nicholson, 56:20 (7)
20. Peter Mattei, 59:38 (10)
21. Wayne Zook, 1:03:42 (14)
22. W. Glad, 49:46 (0)
23. K. Rovtley, 59:59 (10)
24. J. Vreeland, 1:00:02 (10)
25. Joan Ullyot, 1:04:10 (14)
26. Dennis Teeguarden, 57:12 (7)
27. Larry Hoyt, 59:20 (9)
28. Hersh Jenkins, 50:26 (0)
29. Bruce Degen, 53:29 (3)
30. E.F. Fitzgerald, 53:30 (3)
31. T.C. Bertolino, 1:01:31 (11)
32. Greg Chapman, 51:42 (1)
33. C.W. Seekins, 1:04:50 (14)
34. John Finch, 57:56 (7)
35. Pat Kelly, 1:00:11 (9)
36. William Main, 1:03:18 (12)
Team Marin A.C.: Pickett, Beardall, Lowry, Biancalana, Bunnell
1,380 finishers; hot

66th Dipsea
August 29, 1976

In its way, this was the wildest and most dangerous of all Dipseas. Every attendance record was broken; there were 1,638 recorded finishers but by all estimates, including that of the Race organizers, well over 2,000 ran. This would remain the most runners ever in a single Dipsea; the Race would be split into sections, and entries limited, in all subsequent years.

The overcrowding produced an endless traffic jam on the course (a photo appeared on the front page of the next day's *Chronicle* showing a solid line of runners beyond Cardiac), three runners carried off the route in stretchers, traffic problems on Panoramic Highway (winner Homer Latimer swerved to avoid a car, fell, and finished with blood streaming from over his right eye), a 200 yard finish line backup which spilled onto Highway 1 (denying many the joy of running across the finish line, and hundreds of finishers were never timed or recorded) and bedlam afterwards as a near riot broke out when the supply of 1,500 survivor's medals ran out.

Up front, Paul Reese, the 1965 runner-up, paced the opening 14-minute handicap group. He led for much of the Race until he was passed by Don Pickett.

Meanwhile Latimer, 37, of Los Gatos, who had started with the 5-minute group, was literally tearing his way through the mobs. Though using physical contact to pass had been used before, and is now an unfortunate part of every Dipsea, Latimer's use of shoving was the first instance to receive widespread publicity. He told the *Independent Journal* about his initial attempts to get runners ahead to move aside. "At first I would tell them 'I think I have a chance to win—would you let me through?' All they'd do was hoot and holler. Thought it was real funny. Then I started yelling,

'Flyer's coming,' and they got out of the way." Speaking to the *Coastal Post* about his shoving, Latimer said, "I think I got some people angry, but it was the only thing I could do if I wanted to win."

Latimer flew past Pickett into third place on the Swoop, then asked Pickett which way to go. For the second year in a row, Pickett guided the winner through the Slash. Latimer then picked off Jimmy Nicholson, who had fallen in Steep Ravine, and, finally, on Insult, the leader John Finch. Finch told *Sports Illustrated*, which covered the Dipsea as a feature story, that Latimer ran that hill, "like he was shot from a gun."

Latimer then survived his own fall, quickly bounced up, and won by 21 seconds. *Sports Illustrated* reported, "[Latimer's] legs were torn and flecked with blood, and a bright crimson stream flowed from a gash on his forehead down his face and onto his chest." His 50:03 was the second fastest time of the day.

Latimer had run in previous Dipseas, with a high of 6th in 1974 (he missed 1975). Also in 1974, he had won the Double Dipsea in a sensational 1:43:37. (With his nine handicap minutes, Latimer's '74 time remains the fastest Double Dipsea finish ever.) Latimer had been coaching at San Jose's Leigh High School and was appointed, two days earlier, head track coach at Gavilan Junior College in Gilroy.

Finch, Nicholson, then Pickett followed. Fifth was Ted Cain, a brilliant hurdler and long-time Marin county track coach. But Cain's efforts in the Dipsea would come under the close scrutiny of skeptical fellow runners and he was later banned from the Race for life for cheating.

In 7th was Bob Bunnell in the day's best time by exactly two minutes, 48:03. Though he had one handicap minute (only men 16-24 were scratch), his effort in passing so many runners clearly stands out. Bunnell also lost considerable time at Windy Gap when he attempted to bypass the new homes by going left; he was blocked and had to return to the route on the right.

Debbie Rudolf, seemingly completing her bril-

liant Dipsea career at the young age of 15, was first woman and 15th overall.

Paul Thompson, now a doctor who reports on the physiological side of running for television broadcasts of the New York City Marathon and other races, was 20th.

❑ The finish line was moved an additional 45 yards down the park maintenance driveway, lengthening the course by that amount.

❑ As a measure of how many runners were in the Race, 77 father-son teams, 55 husband-wife teams and 11 mother-daughter teams competed for trophies.

❑ In 1976, the park at the finish line in Stinson Beach became part of the Golden Gate National Recreation Area (and therefore free of any admission fee); it had previously been a County, then a State park.

1. Homer Latimer, 50:03 (5) [:21] **2nd best time**
2. John Finch, 52:24 (7)
3. Jim Nicholson, 54:01 (8)
4. Don Pickett, 55:21 (9)
5. Ted Cain, 50:34 (4)
6. Gene Fitzgerald, 51:01 (4)
7. Bob Bunnell, 48:03 (1) **best time**
8. Gil Tarin, 55:04 (8)
9. Chuck Stagliano, 52:33 (5)
10. Darryl Beardall, 53:41 (6)
11. Robert Biancalana, 58:03 (10)
12. Don Chaffee, 53:07 (5)
13. Paul Reese, 1:02:47 (14)
14. Peter Mattei, 59:48 (11)
15. Debbie Rudolf, 59:57 (11) **1st, fastest woman**
16. Art Waggoner, 59:18 (10)
17. Ralph Paffenbarger, 1:00:22 (11)
18. Greg Chapman, 51:32 (2)
19. B.A. Love, 54:03 (4)
20. Paul Thompson, 52:18 (2)
21. A.M. Low, 1:01:18 (11)
22. Mike Healy, 57:26 (7)
23. R.G. Winkelman, 50:45 (0)
24. Bruce Degen, 55:06 (4)
25. Bob Lawrence, 56:11 (5)
26. T.C. Bertolino, 1:02:16 (11)
27. D.D. Sharp, 59:21 (8)
28. Boyd Tarin, 51:38 (0)
29. B. Armbruster, 55:56 (4)
30. Karl Marschall, 1:02:06 (10)
31. Petet Sweeney, 52:11 (0)
32. Larry Hoyt, 1:02:18 (10)
33. R.W. Emmons, 59:22 (7)
34. Michael Killeen, 52:28 (0)
35. Doug Basham, 59:33 (7)
36. Albert Clark, 1:06:38 (14)
Team Marin A.C.: Pickett, Cain, Bunnell, Beardall and Biancalana
1,638 finishers; warm

67th Dipsea
October 23, 1977

After the unruly 1976 race, more than a few people, including many residents of Stinson Beach, viewed the Dipsea as an event out of control. The subsequent assault on the 1977 Dipsea was the most serious challenge the Race ever faced. County Supervisor Gary Giacomini (who still represents west Marin) even stated, "There will never be another Dipsea if the numbers [of entries] are not worked out." The Stinson Beach Village Association, ironically headed by a godchild (Joan Reutinger) of 1912 Dipsea winner Donald Dunn, also pressured Race officials to limit entries so as to reduce related auto traffic.

Race organizers responded in several ways, including setting the first official route restrictions, ending 72 years of Dipsea history as a completely open course. To keep runners off Panoramic Highway near Stinson Beach (and therefore keep the main auto traffic artery open), everyone was diverted left in the final yards of the trail to the dangerous, and now infamous, leap over a stile onto Shoreline Highway. The downhill (known as "Moose Hill" or "MacDouche") at the base of the Moors was declared off limits. Also, conceding defeat to the Windy Gap homeowner who had waged a years-long campaign to bar access across her property, including putting up barbed wire barriers and hiring guards on Race day, the traditional direct route from the top of Bayview down to Muir Woods Road was officially declared off-limits. Runners were directed to the right onto the new State Park trail.

To insure that finish line backups would no longer reach Shoreline Highway, the finish was moved to its present location by the south Stinson Beach parking lot. (This alone added 173 yards to the distance; with the other changes, the course was now considered a new one for record purposes.)

Dipsea officials also kept publicity to a minimum and eliminated same day registration, practices still in effect. Race chairman Jerry Hauke noted, "We sent the entry notices as late as possible to make it difficult to get into the race . . . People practically had to come into Mill Valley to get an entry form." In addition, the first starting time was moved forward a half-hour, to 9:30 a.m., from the traditional 10 a.m. (Today, the first runners set off at 8:30 a.m.)

And to ease trail congestion, another historic change was made; the Race was split into separate sections—"Invitational," "Super-Jogger," and "Turtle"—to start one after another. The top 700 finishers in the five previous Dipseas were invited into the first Invitational group, from which all prizes would be awarded. The next 1,200 registrants were placed into the Super-Jogger section (renamed "Dipsea Runner" in the early 1980's), whose first runners set off at 10 a.m. This separate race was handicapped and timed the same as the Invitational but finishers received survivors medals only. (A trophy for first man and woman was initiated in 1985.) Any overflow would be placed in the Turtle group; it was to be non-handicapped, with all runners setting off together at 10:45 a.m.

The smaller Invitational field was immediately beneficial to the scratch and other low handicap starters, as there were fewer runners to pass. On the other side, the lead Super-Joggers now had to weave their way through the slowest Invitationals.

(Over the years, the process of "graduating" from the second group into the coveted Invitational section would be refined. Now it is based entirely on a runner's prior year finish; a designated number of top finishers from the second group displace a like number of later finishers from the Invitational. For 1993, the top 425 finishers from 1992 kept their Invitational status with the earliest Dipsea Runners moving up to replace the rest. Exceptions, upon appeal, are only rarely granted. Some runners now compete even when injured so as to try to retain their Invitational position.)

But these efforts were not enough to quiet

critics. Stinson officials, claiming they were not in on the planning process and that were no actual entry limitations, remained livid.

Adding to the tensions, another dry winter left Marin County in the most severe drought yet in its recorded history. The Dipsea had been held in September or the last Sunday of August (the set date since 1963), the heart of the dry fire season, for decades. The issue of emergency vehicle access to west Marin, over roads already regularly crowded by weekend beach-goers, was viewed with greater urgency.

Stinson Beach officials appealed to the County Board of Supervisors. (In happier days in the 1960's, the Board of Supervisors had regularly contributed $150 to the Dipsea to install the review platform by the finish line.) An emotional, two-hour hearing, packed with interested spectators, was held at the Marin Civic Center just five days before the Race. Marin County fire chief Richard Pedroli, responding to Supervisor Giacomini's question of whether it is dangerous to run the Race, said, "There's no question about it . . . We have the driest brush in the state of California." On a 3-2 vote (Barbara Boxer, then a supervisor, now a U.S. Senator, was among the two dissenters), the Board decided to force postponement of the Race, set for that weekend. They would reimburse the sponsoring Mill Valley Jaycees some $4,000 for the added expenses of sending cancellation notices, and refunds to those requesting them.

Still, nearly 150 runners, including Jack Kirk and one who had flown in from Boston, turned out on the scheduled date, an oppressively hot August 28. Some wore "Gypsy Dipsea" t-shirts. Race chairman Jerry Hauke handed out leaflets with a copy of the *Independent Journal* article announcing the cancellation and the appeal: "Please do not run the Dipsea trail today. Please do not add fuel to Stinson Beach's claim that we are an uncontrollable mob. The survival of the Dipsea Race comes first."

Most on hand still ran on their own in what has come to be known as the "Gypsy Dipsea." Don Pickett, among others, did succeed in getting the runners to leave in small groups and, although some in Stinson were upset, there were no major incidents. After continued talks, the Race was finally rescheduled for October 23, in the early part of the rainy season.

The change of date contributed to a decline in attendance after two years of meteoric rises. The proposed "Turtle" section was not needed, and was subsequently discontinued.

Defending champion Homer Latimer received the same five minute handicap he had the previous year. With the sharply reduced Invitational field, he now had only half the runners to pass as in '76, and it showed. Despite the longer course, he was able to knock over two minutes off his winning '76 time. Latimer also finished considerably less battered and bloody than in the 1976 "war."

Latimer was now a delivery driver for a florist. He ran without the beard he had in '76, but was again shirtless. He trained hard for the repeat win and it paid off with one of the greatest of all Dipsea performances. He won by 3:54, the fourth largest victory margin ever. His 47:56 was the day's fastest time (by 51 seconds) despite the presence of runners such as Bob Bunnell (3rd), Darryl Beardall (4th), Byron Lowry (5th) and Don Makela (12th), who, between them, had won eight best time trophies. The time is still among the 20 fastest Dipseas ever recorded. And Latimer's age of 38 stands out on that top-20 list; it is six years older than anyone else.

Paul Reese, 60, and Barbara Magid, 33, had set off with the first, 15-minute group and were the leaders over the opening half of the course. They ended up 15th and 18th (first woman), respectively.

Latimer worked his way through the pack, including Bob Biancalana, Bob Malain and Beardall, then was unpressed to the tape. Latimer became the third back-to-back winner (after John Hassard and Mike Boitano) and the tenth man to win with the fastest time.

Don Chaffee, who would win in 1979, started with Latimer and ended up 2nd. Bunnell, in the same 3-minute group with fellow Marin ace Lowry, won that battle and finished 3rd overall. Russ Kiernan began his unprecedented string of 12 consecutive top-ten finishes with a 7th. Biancalana, winner of many team and father-son trophies, got his highest place ever, 8th. One second behind was 1968 winner Don Pickett. Dick Houston, who, after his death, would have his name memorialized on the rugged, Dipsea-like Woodminster race in Oakland, was 14th.

The team title went to the new Tamalpa Runners, a broadly based, coed club founded in late 1976 by Kees Tuinzing, Jim McGowan, Al Kreuzberger, Don Pickett and others. It replaced the just defunct all-male Marin A.C. and its short-lived successor, the Marin Harriers, as the principal running club in Marin. Tamalpa would henceforth dominate Dipsea team scoring, winning the title every succeeding year.

❑ The Dipsea continued to be plagued by timing problems. Only the first 685 places were recorded (and perhaps not all accurately) and timing for the Super-Jogger section, including its unknown first finisher, completely broke down. Survivor medals were not handed out at the finish line, as was usual. The exact number of finishers is unknown. Complete, official results were never compiled—the only such year in Dipsea history—much less mailed. (The 1977 files are, however, still intact, and there is occasional talk among Dipsea aficionados of grinding out a results list.)

1. Homer Latimer, 47:56 (5) [3:54] **best time**
2. Don Chaffee, 51:50 (5)
3. Bob Bunnell, 50:06 (3)
4. Darryl Beardall, 54:27 (7)
5. Byron Lowry, 50:44 (3)
6. Bob Malain, 56:53 (9)
7. Russ Kiernan, 53:21 (5)
8. Robert Biancalana, 59:35 (11)
9. Don Pickett, 57:36 (9)
10. Jim Nicholson, 55:41 (7)
11. Paul Thompson, 51:45 (3)
12. Don Makela, 48:47 (0) **2nd best time**
13. Ted Cain, 54:20 (5)
14. Dick Houston, 1:02:36 (13)
15. Paul Reese, 1:04:49 (15)
16. William Flodberg, 57:11 (7)
17. Kees Tuinzing, 53:21 (3)
18. Michael Healy, 57:44 (7)
19. Barbara Magid, 1:05:46 (15) **1st, fastest woman**
20. Ralph Paffenbarger, 1:01:54 (11)
21. K.J. Shiflet, 53:55 (3)
22. R.A. Morris, 1:01:56 (11)
23. Orin Dahl, 58:33 (7)
24. Ragnar Thaning, 54:47 (3)
25. Lloyd Sampson, 56:56 (5)
26. Ed Jerome, 57:08 (5)
27. D.D. Sharp, 59:13 (7)
28. Peter DeMarais, 52:22 (0)
29. M.R. Shannon, 1:03:26 (11)
30. Steve Lyons, 57:29 (5)
31. Don Lucero, 1:01:32 (9)
32. Hans Roenau, 1:01:41 (9)
33. S.J. McCarron, 1:03:42 (11)
34. Dennis Gustafson, 57:44 (5)
35. Lane Mason, 55:47 (3)
36. Bill Dickerson, 1:02:13 (9)
Team Tamalpa: Bunnell, Beardall, Lowry, Kiernan and Biancalana
1,334 finishers; sunny near Mill Valley, foggy near ocean

68th Dipsea
June 4, 1978

Darryl Beardall denied heavily favored Homer Latimer's bid to become the first three-time champion, and became the Dipsea's sixth double winner himself. But staging the Race itself was the biggest hurdle.

Many of the Jaycees departed after the previous year's turbulence. One who stayed was Jerry Hauke. He was assisted by Jim Weil. Weil, who had run in the error-plagued 1977 Dipsea, had walked up to Hauke's door (they lived nearby in Mill Valley), knocked, introduced himself and offered to help. The pair then co-directed the Dipsea.

Fixing a date for 1978 and gaining the necessary approvals remained major problems. The Marin County Board of Supervisors fought for keeping the Race in October. Other jurisdictions offered their own suggestions. Hauke fixed on the first Sunday of June to be a "permanent" date (shifted to the second Sunday from 1983). Ultimately, the Board gave in, though they never gave the June date an official approval; they merely "acquiesced."

The full text announcing the historic change to June, as announced in the instructions, read: "The race this year is being held in early June. This is to avoid a repeat of last year's last minute change of date due to late summer fire danger. We have also been asked to avoid summer vacation season because of the weekend traffic crush at Stinson Beach. Early June was the best compromise we could come up with. We wanted to have it after the start of daylight savings time to allow for evening training runs. We wanted to avoid the rainy season, Bay-to-Breakers, and Memorial Day."

The change meant the end of the summer-long evening practice sessions that had been a part of the Dipsea since its inception. It also meant the Race would coincide with a show date for the

Mountain Play, another Mt. Tamalpais tradition (begun in 1913). Fidelity Savings and Loan (now Citicorp), which had a branch beside the course's opening yards, provided the Dipsea with seven buses to ease expected traffic congestion, a key concern of west Marin groups.

Also new were black shirts for the top finishers; they would quickly become one of the Race's most distinctive features. They had been blue when numbered shirts were first introduced in 1975, then yellow in 1976-77. The quantity awarded was also raised to 35 so as to include more women; no more than two had taken a shirt in each of the three previous Dipseas. (Within a decade, women would be winning nearly 40% of the shirts.) The 1978 black shirts had gold lettering; all subsequent ones had silver lettering. Some unnumbered black shirts were sold, a practice never repeated. In subsequent years, the black shirts, and those for sale—the color changes each year—have been of one trademark design (excepting the Diamond Jubilee year of 1985). They have never carried any sponsor names or other advertising.

On Race day, a major problem developed at the starting line when the scratch group was inadvertently delayed two minutes. This, in effect, raised everyone else's handicap by two minutes. Not a single scratch runner was then able to make the top 35, much less challenge for the top places. Pete Sweeney (who missed 35th by two seconds), Steve Ottaway (an Englishman who would become an important figure in Marin running, making his debut) and Rob Heierle were the lead scratch runners who would likely have won black shirts otherwise. Sweeney's 51:14 remains both the fastest actual and clock time that failed to win a black shirt.

Barbara Magid, a Bolinas schoolteacher who had started in the first group (with, in effect, a record 18 handicap minutes), led until the climb up Cardiac. There Beardall blasted by, not to be caught.

Beardall, 41, had already compiled a brilliant Dipsea record in his 23 Dipsea races since 1955,

winning in 1974, making the best time in 1961 and finishing in the top ten 14 times. (He has now extended that record to 19). Beardall told the *Independent Journal* afterwards, "I didn't get a chance to train for this year's race. I usually run the course a couple of times beforehand to see if the course has any new chuckholes or any other changes."

Despite three falls, Latimer, the runner-up, only slowed 64 seconds from his sensational winning run of the previous year. But Beardall, predicted by Latimer to win, improved by over four minutes.

Jim Nicholson was 3rd, as he had been in 1976. Russ Kiernan, today tied with Jack Kirk behind Beardall in number of top ten finishes (14), was 4th. Bruce Carradine, of the family of film actors, was 7th.

Magid ended up 8th and, for the second straight year, was lead woman. She also became the first woman ever to be part of the winning team.

Mike McManus, destined to become one of the greatest of all Dipsea runners, was 10th at age 12.

❑ The Invitational section was opened to the top 100 Super-Joggers from 1977. The Super-Jogger section itself was not filled. The first finisher listed from it was a woman, E.A. O'Neil. She was credited with a 1:05:43 (16hc), which was faster, by three seconds, than best time winner Magid. (Magid, on the other hand, claims her time was faster than shown.)

❑ Skip Swannack, who was first woman at Bay to Breakers two weeks earlier, finished 148th (1:11:07; 13hc).

The handicaps below are from the official results and reflect the two additional headstart minutes from the scratch group being sent off two minutes late. Why the one-minute handicap group (men 27-29) is shown as having only two minutes rather than three (e.g., Dane Larsen, 19th place) is unexplained.

1. Darryl Beardall, 50:03 (8) [:57] **2nd best time**
2. Homer Latimer, 49:00 (6) **best time**
3. Jim Nicholson, 55:13 (10)
4. Russ Kiernan, 53:35 (8)
5. Bob Malain, 57:51 (12)
6. Hans Roenau, 58:03 (12)
7. Bruce Carradine, 56:56 (10)
8. Dan Seamount, 1:01:00 (14)
9. Barbara Magid, 1:05:46 (18) **1st, fastest woman**
10. Mike McManus, 58:08 (10)
11. Paul Thompson, 52:24 (4)
12. Bob Bunnell, 50:39 (2)
13. Lane Mason, 52:41 (4)
14. Dick Houston, 1:02:45 (14)
15. Paul Reese, 1:05:05 (16)
16. Don Chaffee, 55:07 (6)
17. Ralph Paffenbarger, 1:03:30 (14)
18. Karl Marschall, 1:01:30 (12)
19. Dane Larsen, 51:36 (2)
20. Bill Kirchmeier, 59:43 (10)
21. J.C. Burton, 1:03:51 (14)
22. Pam Purcell, 1:06:05 (16)
23. Bill Brace, 1:02:10 (12)
24. Raoul Kennedy, 54:13 (4)
25. Orin Dahl, 58:20 (8)
26. T. Watkins, 56:28 (6)
27. P. Aagard, 54:31 (4)
28. R.A. Morris, 1:02:31 (12)
29. Tom Beck, 56:36 (6)
30. E.P. Lee, 56:58 (6)
31. Art Waggoner, 57:08 (6)
32. Bert Botta, 57:08 (6)
33. J. Miller, 59:09 (8)
34. Steve Lyons, 57:09 (6)
35. James Clever, 59:12 (8)
36. Peter Sweeney, 51:14 (0)

Team Tamalpa: Beardall, Kiernan, Roenau, Carradine and Magid
934 finishers; mostly foggy and cool, some sun at higher elevations

69th Dipsea
June 3, 1979

In a way, this was the closest Dipsea in history, with the eventual 1-2 finishers battling from the very start, passing one another at least five times, and finishing just three seconds apart.

As was becoming standard fare, women led much of the way. Mill Valley's 30-year-old Margaret Livingston, a recent arrival from Massachusetts via Colorado, started in the second wave of women (14hc) and went to the fore early. She then held the lead until halfway down Steep Ravine.

The decisive battle, however, began when Don Chaffee, 40, and Russ Kiernan, 41, departed with the six-minute group. The two were friends. Both lived in Mill Valley and both were teachers in San Francisco; Chaffee taught economics at Golden Gate University, Kiernan elementary schoolers at Francis Scott Key.

Chaffee, who would win, was a native of Detroit and graduate of Middlebury College (Vermont). He had begun jogging in his 20's, mainly to keep in shape for his first sport, handball. At 30, he and some friends decided to tackle a marathon and Chaffee began his racing career. He was quickly hooked, continuing even while on a teaching assignment in Africa—he treasures a photograph taken of Olympic immortal Kip Keino congratulating him after running a marathon in Kenya.

Chaffee and Kiernan were never more than a few yards apart as they moved through the field. Chaffee would gain on the uphills, Kiernan forge ahead on the downhills. Chaffee frequently had to wipe his glasses, fogged by the thick mist. When they went by Livingston ("Their feet weren't even touching the ground," Livingston, who moved aside, later noted), Chaffee was a stride ahead.

Near the end of the second shortcut on Panoramic, Kiernan, one of the Dipsea's great downhillers, advised Chaffee he was going to pass, confident he could negotiate the next very dangerous section of trail more quickly. Chaffee, in the intense but gentlemanly spirit of their competition, let Kiernan go by.

Then Kiernan made a fateful mistake. He had heard that an old route on the right bank of the creek was faster than the present trail, which crosses the creek (at a spot forever since known as "Kiernan's Crossing"). The first yards of that old route had just been cleared by some runners. Kiernan had seen their work when checking the area out himself the day before. What he didn't know was that the group stopped their work after only 20 yards when they discovered the path led to the fence line of a house. Kiernan was skeptical of the path, but took it anyhow as planned.

Chaffee hesitated a fraction of a second—did Kiernan know something?—then took the regular route. When Kiernan, after three stumbles through overgrown foliage, finally made the long leap back to the left bank, Chaffee was 20-30 yards ahead. With his somewhat superior leg speed (he was competing successfully in masters mile competitions), Chaffee was able to hold on to the tape, the intensity of the all-out effort evident in his face.

Nearly two minutes later, Don Pickett eked out a similar three-second margin over Livingston for third. Bob Malain, yet another three seconds behind, was 5th for the second year in a row. Next came San Rafael high schooler Trex Donovan, although some observers still insist that Trex inadvertently started in too early a handicap group. Donovan's parents became Dipsea regulars; his mother Judie would finish as high as seventh in 1984. Trex himself developed into one of the County's top prep distance runners.

Seventh, with the best time of the day, was 33-year-old Joe Ryan from Berkeley. A strong hill runner, Ryan was also a champion cyclo-cross racer. His 49:34 was the slowest to win the time award since 1965, a reflection of the longer course.

Early leader Pam Purcell was 9th. Pete Demarais, 16th, was the first scratch finisher, just edging, by one place and nine seconds, fellow Marin County ace Mike Arago.

Susan Mitchell, author, under the name Susan Trott, of many popular books that feature characters who run, was 30th. Louise Burns, soon to co-found (with another Dipsea runner, Mary Healy) the Women on the Run brand of sports clothing, was 34th.

Because an unofficial runner came in at the 14th position, and grabbed a black shirt at the end of the chute, the subsequent shirt awards were off. None were left for the true 35th finisher, Peter Eisenberg. One was especially made up for the Marin General physician saying "35 1/2" on the back.

The times of several early Super-Joggers as printed in the results were clearly in error; the first from that group remains unknown. Eve Pell, who would become a major force in the Dipsea over the coming years, debuted, running 1:18:09 (16hc) as a Super-Jogger.

❑ An abundant supply of Crystal Geyser mineral water was offered at the finish, as it would be every subsequent year. Kristin Gordon, wife of the company's president Peter Gordon, has been a high finisher for 20 years.

❑ To complete their filming of the blind Dipsea runner Harry Cordellos, Magus Films requested that he be allowed to wear the same bib number as in 1978. Their resulting short movie, *Survival Run*, has been an inspiration to many runners and non-runners alike.

❑ Total entries were limited to 1,400; 600 in the Invitational. The Super-Jogger field did not fill.

❑ Homer Latimer, who was injured, was the official starter.

❑ Leo Karlhofer, winner of the best time award in 1938, returned to watch.

❑ Claudia Shenefield (96th), in the first group of Invitational starters, was assigned bib #1. In future Dipseas, bib numbers 1-100 would be reserved for the corresponding finishers from the previous year.

❑ Finishers were offered a chance to buy a photo of themselves in the Race, taken by California

Marathon Photo. Later, Gene Cohn would become, and remain, the Dipsea's "official" action portrait photographer.

1. Don Chaffee, 51:40 (6) [:03]
2. Russ Kiernan, 51:43 (6)
3. Don Pickett, 57:22 (10)
4. Margaret Livingston, 1:01:25 (14) **1st, fastest woman**
5. Bob Malain, 57:28 (10)
6. Trex Donovan, 51:34 (4)
7. Joe Ryan, 49:34 (2) **best time**
8. Jim Nicholson, 55:36 (8)
9. Pam Purcell, 1:04:43 (16)
10. Bert Johnson, 52:58 (4)
11. Bruce Degen, 53:03 (4)
12. Betsy White, 1:05:51 (16)
13. Roger Daniels, 55:58 (6)
14. Barbara Magid, 1:06:09 (16)
15. Peter Demarais, 50:12 (0) **2nd best time**
16. Mike Arago, 50:21 (0)
17. Chuck Stagliano, 54:22 (4)
18. Bob Lawrence, 54:24 (4)
19. Ralph Paffenbarger, 1:02:36 (12)
20. Hans Roenau, 1:00:50 (10)
21. Bert Botta, 57:00 (6)
22. Bill Brace, 1:01:04 (10)
23. Steve Ottaway, 51:08 (0)
24. Herb Vanek, 1:01:15 (10)
25. Oren Dahl, 57:16 (6)
26. Bruce Carradine, 59:21 (8)
27. Dana Hooper, 1:03:26 (12)
28. Dane Larsen, 52:29 (1)
29. Susan Mitchell, 1:07:31 (16)
30. Darryl Beardall, 57:45 (6)
31. James Clever, 57:55 (6)
32. John Cobourn, 54:03 (2)
33. Louise Burns, 1:08:09 (16)
34. Lloyd Sampson, 54:17 (2)
35. Peter Eisenberg, 54:17 (2)
36. Bob Bunnell, 53:22 (1)
Team Tamalpa: Kiernan, Pickett, Ryan, Daniels and Magid
1,081 finishers; thick, misting fog

70th Dipsea
June 1, 1980

Speculation on who would win centered on the previous year's top four—Don Chaffee, Russ Kiernan, Don Pickett and Margaret Livingston. Virtually no one, herself included, thought much of the chances of a 39-year old mother of three new to the racing scene, Donna Andrews.

Andrews had taken up jogging late in her 30's. She had been in one previous Dipsea, with her husband, in 1977. In 1979, with her marriage breaking up, the Georgia-born Andrews focused her energies on competitive running. It wasn't easy. She would get up at 5:30 a.m., do 5-6 hilly miles in the open space above her Mill Valley home, make breakfast for her three sons, then be at work by 8:30 a.m.

Though growing fitter, Andrews remained concerned about her lack of Dipsea course knowledge. "None of the other women were very helpful," she recalled 12 years later. "Then Don Chaffee [the '79 winner] showed me all the shortcuts. He never thought I'd be such a competitor to him," she laughs.

Andrews would then make excuses to take breaks from her job as manager of the Marathon Fitness Center in Sausalito and sneak in practice runs on different sections of the course. She would commit every twist and turn on the route to memory, then later record them meticulously in a notebook and visualize them at night. "Though I actually only had one full practice run, I felt I had raced the course many, many times," she said. In a few road races before the Dipsea, her times greatly improved and she ran a debut 3:09 marathon in May.

Andrews had 15 handicap minutes, two less than the maximum. Always a strong uphiller, Andrews overhauled first starters Ruth Anderson and Marlys Hayden near the top of Flying Y. She then led

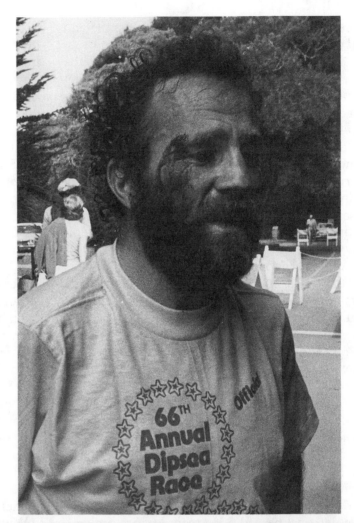

(Above left) Donna Andrews becomes the first adult woman to win the Dipsea, 1980. (David Mitchell)

(Above right) A bloodied Homer Latimer donned an official's shirt after winning the 1976 Dipsea. (David Mitchell)

(Right) Mary Etta Boitano, 10, wins the 1973 Dipsea. (Jim Kean, Independent Journal)

the rest of the way to the tape. "It was just me and God out there," she said immediately afterwards.

"I never once thought, before or during the race, that I would win. The most I ever thought about was maybe being first woman," Andrews reflected years later. "When I realized I was first, I kept expecting a man to come by." But, by running the downhills with unaccustomed bravado (her plunge down a steep slope is one of the outstanding running sequences in the movie *On the Edge*), Andrews kept all pursuers at bay. When one of the closest and most dangerous, Pickett, learned at Cardiac that he trailed by six minutes, he immediately reacted, "No way can I catch her."

Andrews' appearance, wearing bib #496, startled the finish line crowd. She was the first adult woman to win the Dipsea, with the first sub-60 minute effort by any woman other than the pre-teen phenoms Mary Etta Boitano and Debbie Rudolf. Andrews herself then burst into tears, the *Chronicle* account mistakenly saying it was water tossed on her that caused the wet cheeks.

Kiernan, meanwhile, was this time outdueling Chaffee. Having passed all the rivals he feared (Pickett the last, on Highway 1) and, being passed by no one, Kiernan thought he was winning. He had heard from several spectators that he was second, but assumed the leader was an unofficial interloper, never considering Andrews. Though he ran a personal best 51:23, a record (since broken) for runners over 40, Kiernan again had to settle for runner-up honors and the sobriquet of "Mr. Avis."

Bob Malain, who started with Pickett, took 4th. Chaffee was 5th.

In 6th, with the best time of the day for the second year in a row (48:37, 1hc) was Berkeley attorney Joe Ryan. Livingston, first woman in 1979, was 7th.

Little noticed in 8th (and only third from his five minute-handicap starting group) was Sal Vasquez in his maiden Dipsea. Though 40, he had only been running for less than seven months. Vasquez took two hairy spills, one down Suicide, a second when trying to pass in Steep Ravine. In the latter tumble he struck a branch, which penetrated his cheek. He finished with it noticeably protruding. The wound would later require stitches and leave a permanent scar. "I stopped for a while," the man who would go on to win a record five Dipseas told reporters, "but I thought I might as well finish." While down, Vasquez was passed by Ryan; no one would pass and stay ahead of him again until 1991.

Steve Ottaway was the first scratch runner, and the only one to get a black shirt, in 11th. Florianne Harp, who would win the following year, debuted in 16th (1:03:37; 13hc). Homer Latimer, returning for the first and only time since his back-to-back wins in 1976 and '77, was 20th. Two places behind was Toby Knepfer, at 14 the only black shirt winner under age 26.

❑ James Farren, Jr., in the late stages of cancer, again handed out the awards. He died a few months later. His ashes were then scattered on his beloved Dipsea Trail at Lone Tree. The James Farren, Jr. Memorial Trophy for "Sportsmanship, Leadership and Dedication to the Dipsea" was established in his honor.

❑ Andrews' first place trophy had the figure of a man on it; it would ultimately be redesigned. Another change her win brought was in the sizing of the black T-shirts. Andrews' shirt was so big she had a seamstress take it in. In all, a then record nine women won black shirts.

❑ Wilbur Taylor, who ran his first Dipsea in 1915, started but did not finish.

1. Donna Andrews, 59:51 (15) [1:32] **fastest woman**
2. Russ Kiernan, 51:23 (5) **1st man**
3. Don Pickett, 55:39 (9)
4. Bob Malain, 55:53 (9)
5. Don Chaffee, 52:33 (5)
6. Joe Ryan, 48:37 (1) **best time**
7. Margaret Livingston, 1:01:41 (13)
8. Sal Vasquez, 54:08 (5)
9. Darryl Beardall, 54:29 (5)
10. Jim Nicholson, 56:32 (7)
11. Steve Ottaway, 49:35 (0) **2nd best time**
12. W. Schafer, 54:36 (5)
13. Bonnie Storm, 1:05:08 (15)
14. Bruce Degen, 53:15 (3)
15. Dick Houston, 1:03:29 (13)
16. Florianne Harp, 1:03:37 (13)
17. Bert Johnson, 53:56 (3)
18. Peter Laskier, 54:01 (3)
19. Dave Houston, 54:04 (3)
20. Homer Latimer, 56:08 (5)
21. Roger Daniels, 56:11 (5)
22. Toby Knepfer, 54:14 (3)
23. James Clever, 56:17 (5)
24. Marilyn Moreton, 1:04:24 (13)
25. Bill Brace, 1:00:52 (9)
26. Joan Don, 1:06:55 (15)
27. Marlys Hayden, 1:09:07 (17)
28. Kees Tuinzing, 53:10 (1)
29. Keith Hastings, 55:21 (3)
30. Elaine Parliman, 1:07:29 (15)
31. Hans Roenau, 1:01:31 (9)
32. Bill Dickerson, 1:01:41 (9)
33. Lloyd Sampson, 55:49 (3)
34. Melinda Creel, 1:03:53 (11)
35. Dave Olson, 1:01:54 (9)
36. M. Crncich, 1:03:55 (11)
Team Tamalpa: Andrews, Kiernan, Pickett, Ryan and Ottaway
1,159 finishers; thick fog

71st Dipsea
June 7, 1981

Joe Ryan was the nearly unanimous choice to win. An *Independent Journal* feature the day before the Race had an oversized color picture of Ryan on the cover and predictions of his victory by all the insiders interviewed. Ryan had won the best time award the previous two Dipseas and now, turning 35, picked up two extra handicap minutes (from one to three).

The Berkeley attorney and cyclocross champion did make an all-out bid for victory. He even passed Sal Vasquez, the winner of the next four Dipseas who had started two minutes ahead of him. But then Ryan succumbed to the extreme heat. He slowed considerably beyond Cardiac and several runners went by him. Though his legs were now rubbery, somehow he got down Steep Ravine. Finally, Ryan collapsed near the creek just after the second section on Panoramic Highway. Brian Collins and Dane Larsen, two excellent runners, saw Ryan and came to his aid.

Ryan was immobile and incoherent, clearly in serious condition. Collins and Larsen soaked their shirts in the creek and applied the cool water to Ryan. Collins ran down for medical help. When he returned, he and Larsen, along with a running doctor who had stopped, Bill Dickerson (32nd in 1980), supported Ryan down to the emergency medical unit. Ryan saw his worried wife and began crying; the worst had passed. Ryan later told the *Independent Journal*, "I think they [Collins, Larsen and Dickerson] saved my life."

Meanwhile, far in front of everyone else, as she had been since passing Marlys Hayden going up Dynamite, was Mill Valley's 33-year-old Florianne Harp. Indeed, the petite (5'4", 100 pounds, 7% body fat) blonde with the trademark short, low-knee-lift stride had built so huge a lead that Ryan's valiant effort was already doomed. Though she slowed in

Steep Ravine—running down precipitous slopes was her lone weakness, and her lead was safe—Harp still won by a whopping 1:47.

Harp had attracted some pre-Race attention herself. Though she only started running five years before, and had been in just one Dipsea, an upgraded regimen during the past year of 100-plus mile weeks on Mount Tamalpais—despite a full-time job in marketing at a San Francisco hotel—had brought remarkable improvement. Harp's training included long early morning runs with a pair of friends, one of whom, Clyde Helms, would get the 35th and last black shirt. There were even longer runs on Saturdays with the Mt. Tamalpais Mountain Home group and Sunday self-described "death marches" with a small band from her Mill Valley house.

In March she was first woman at the Napa Valley Marathon in 2:52. In April, she ran the American River 50-Miler in 8:19. In May, she was first woman at the Pacific Sun Marathon. Then, at the DSE Practice Dipsea the week before the race, she seemed effortless in again leading all the women.

"It was only during that last week, after the Practice Dipsea, that I thought I might be able to do really well," Harp recalls. "I was really nervous race morning. I remember Margaret Livingston helping me braid my hair right before the start. I never knew my position during the race, I don't know where I actually took the lead. The heat didn't bother me. The only people I saw were at Cardiac and Insult. They said I was first woman. What I was really scared about was getting down Steep Ravine—I was so glad there was no one around to get me more nervous—then over the last fence, because I'm so terrible going downhill. I never knew I won until the finish. Then it was great. I just stayed at the beach all day, having fun being 'queen for a day'".

Vasquez, who would not again be beaten to the tape for years, took 2nd. Since Harp was given the first-place trophy, which bore the likeness of a male runner, he had to settle for the trophy intended for the first woman, with a female figurine.

Finishing 18 seconds behind Vasquez, in one of the greatest Dipsea runs ever, was 21-year-old scratch runner Rod Berry. His actual time of 46:48 was the fastest since the "modern" course was established in 1977. The route was even longer than in previous years because the Trench (Slash) at the base of Swoop Hollow, the direct route into Steep Ravine, was closed for the first time (and remains so). And Berry didn't even take the final Panoramic Highway shortcuts. He went over the Moors, as he had done when he last raced the Dipsea in the mid-1970's. He didn't know the direct final downhill to Stinson—the reason to take the longer Moors—was now off limits.

Berry's Dipsea career had begun inauspiciously in 1972; he got lost in his first Dipsea practice run and took over three hours to finish. But after it he rode back to Mill Valley in the same car with Norman Bright, who shared some Dipsea tips. Berry began "bugging" older Marin Athletic Club runners to let him tag along during practice runs. He developed into one of the greatest high school distance runners in Marin history, setting the still-standing County two-mile record of 8:53.4 while at Redwood High. In 1981, Berry was a standout steeplechaser on the Stanford track team.

Berry's 1981 time was listed as the modern Dipsea course record on entry forms for the '82 and '83 Races only. It was then replaced on Dipsea application and results mailings, seemingly erroneously, by his own slower 1983 time of 47:33. This remained the published standard until Mike McManus' 46:53 in 1991, now recognized as the modern course best. (A possible explanation is that the Trench was not officially recognized as permanently closed until after the 1982 Race.) Berry's 46:48, however, appears to be the true top mark.

Fourth was Tom Kirschner, 40. He had waged a Race-long battle with teammate Chuck Stagliano, who came in 10 seconds later in 5th. Both, with Vasquez, started in the 5-minute group.

Ron Elijah, holder of the all-time Dipsea course record, returned to the Race after a six-year hiatus and notched the day's second fastest time (48:47, Scr).

In 11th, with the second fastest women's time, was Sacramento's Sally Edwards. Edwards, a co-founder of the Fleet Feet chain of running stores, was beginning to promote a then completely new sport, triathlons.

Derry Bunnell (25th) would have have been part of the winning family team had she been permitted to pair with her brother Ron Elijah (8th). Instead, after the Race, officials teamed Derry with her husband Bob (40th) and the Bunnells narrowly missed top honors to Don (6th) and Toby (47th) Pickett.

❑ Carl Jensen, still the last Dipsea winner from scratch (1966), made an emotional return after a 15-year absence. Jensen had suffered massive injuries on a land mine in Vietnam a year after his win. When he was able to run again, he realized his old form was gone and he abandoned running for eight years. A friend, Bert Botta, helped encourage him "to come in from the cold." Now 36, Jensen ran a 1:01:03 (3hc), four minutes swifter than his target, and finished 110th. Following him was *Independent Journal* sports editor Ward Bushee, who had just written a story on Jensen.

❑ Ryan was not the only racer to require help in the heat. One passed out in Steep Ravine and fell into a tree. Another downed competitor was flown to Marin General by a Highway Patrol helicopter stationed at the finish, only then to be kept waiting for an ambulance (for which he was billed $93) to take him the final 300 feet to the emergency room door as required by a hospital rule.

❑ Jack Kirk was assigned bib number #1; defending champion Donna Andrews did not enter.

❑ For the first time since entry limits were applied in 1977, all 1,500 places were filled before Race day.

❑ Melinda Creel was awarded a black shirt for finishing 33rd, but was then disqualified for wandering onto an off-limits part of Shoreline Highway as she awaited her father's arrival. In all eight runners were disqualified, six for starting with the wrong group.

❑ Dipsea officials conducted a "trail seminar . . . a slow jog over the race course discussing the fine points of the Dipsea route selection" open to all runners on Saturday, May 16.

1. Florianne Harp, 57:43 (13) [1:47] **fastest woman**
2. Sal Vasquez, 51:30 (5) **1st man**
3. Rod Berry, 46:48 (0) **best time**
4. Tom Kirschner, 52:55 (5)
5. Chuck Stagliano, 53:05 (5)
6. Don Pickett, 57:12 (9)
7. Jim Nicholson, 57:18 (9)
8. Ron Elijah, 48:47 (0) **2nd best time**
9. Bob Malain, 57:52 (9)
10. Russ Kiernan, 53:58 (5)
11. Sally Edwards, 1:02:02 (13)
12. Andrea Eschen, 1:00:20 (11)
13. George O'Gara, 1:02:43 (13)
14. Steve Stephens, 53:47 (4)
15. Don Chaffee, 55:00 (5)
16. Bert Johnson, 53:28 (3)
17. Darryl Beardall, 55:34 (5)
18. Tony Hyun, 50:38 (0)
19. Steve Ottaway, 50:52 (0)
20. Patricia Whittinglsow, 1:05:55 (15)
21. James Clever, 58:02 (7)
22. Dan Seamount, 1:04:11 (13)
23. Hilary Naylor, 1:06:20 (15)
24. Bonnie Storm, 1:06:30 (15)
25. Derry Bunnell, 1:04:31 (13)
26. Keith Hastings, 54:34 (3)
27. B.R. Anderson, 52:35 (1)
28. John Cobourn, 52:39 (1)
29. Steve Lyons, 56:42 (5)
30. Barbara Levy, 1:07:07 (15)
31. Bill Kirchmeier, 1:01:10 (9)
32. Cheryl Flowers, 1:03:14 (11)
33. Marlys Hayden, 1:09:23 (17)
34. Elaine Parliman, 1:07:29 (15)
35. Clyde Helms, 55:39 (3)
36. Dave Roeber, 53:42 (1)

Team Tamalpa: Harp, Kirschner, Stagliano, Pickett and Elijah

1,257 finishers; extremely hot

72nd Dipsea
June 6, 1982

The stirring story of Sal Vasquez' rise from poverty in Mexico and alcoholism in Chicago to world-class runner befits his now-legendary status as perhaps the greatest of all Dipsea champions. (The account below borrows from George Frazier's insightful piece in the September 23, 1984, edition of *California Living Magazine*.)

Vasquez was born in rural Mexico and grew up, on the fringes of the law, in Mexico City. As a teenager, he worked long hours in a textile mill. At 19, he and the rest of the family followed his father to Chicago, arriving in winter with no knowledge of English.

Sal got a job at a printing plant (he would remain in the field for decades) at below-minimum wage. He also joined a semi-pro soccer team, the Chicago Mustangs of the American Soccer League. He started drinking after work, after soccer, and more frequently. He had several further brushes with the law, serving 54 days in a house of detention for drunk driving and public intoxication. He moved to San Francisco, where a sister lived.

Vasquez got a job at a printing plant, joined another soccer team, and met and married Mileny, a former Czech figure skater. The couple moved to Alameda. Sal resumed drinking. The problem got so severe that Mileny left him; reconciliations based on promises to stop drinking were soon broken.

In 1977, at Mileny's suggestion, Vasquez began jogging, mainly to work off his hangovers. He did so only sporadically. Then, ten weeks after the birth of their first daughter, Nicole, a "completely drunk" Vasquez hit a motorcyclist while driving through the Alameda tube (tunnel). Nicole lurched forward and hit the windshield. Sal ran away. He was stopped by a policeman.

Neither the motorcyclist nor Nicole was seri-ously hurt but the incident changed Vasquez's life. Severely shaken, Sal vowed to stop drinking, and this time he succeeded.

To help, he returned to running, starting with circuits of Oakland's Lake Merritt in late 1979. Another runner, Frank Smith, noticed him, recruited him for the Pamakid Runners club and guided his early training. Though Sal's first race was a fiasco (he missed a turn in the Oakland Half-Marathon, ran 17 miles of the marathon route, then had to drop out with bloody blisters), he was hooked. His ability was clearly evident. Within just months he was a major force on the national masters running scene and now holds numerous U.S. age records.

Vasquez first heard about the Dipsea, appropriately enough, from another legend, Norman Bright. Vasquez had been sent to Seattle by the Pamakids for a national masters 15K championship race. His host had the now-blind Bright over to visit. Bright asked Sal about Bay to Breakers and the Dipsea, two races where he had held the course record. Sal heard of the former, never of the Dipsea. He said he would "check it out."

When Smith told him he could win the Dipsea, Vasquez's interest perked. "I figured that if a blind man could do it, it couldn't be that tough," Vasquez laughs years later. Early trips to the course with Smith were less than auspicious; Sal couldn't believe the stairs and then later got lost several times, once for hours. But he kept coming back.

In 1980, Vasquez suffered two horrible falls, one resulting in a branch puncturing his cheek, but still finished 8th. In '81, he ran 51:30 at age 41 and finished 2nd. In '82, he began his unprecedented string of four consecutive (and now five total) Dipsea victories.

Vasquez was unsure whether to race the '82 Dipsea at all. He had a poor practice, then a relatively slow 10K the weekend before. But the Friday before the Race, he ran the Dipsea out and back—a rather grueling, unorthodox pre-race workout but one he would repeat in several future winning years—at a fast pace. He felt confident.

Race day, Eve Pell shook off Paul Reese, who started in her 17-minute, maximum handicap group, to take the early lead. The 45-year-old mother of three, and future winner (1989), held first until Vasquez passed her at the top of Insult. Characteristic of his efforts at all Dipseas, he was most gracious, lightly touching Pell, wishing her the best and all but apologizing for the pass.

In dogged but ultimately futile pursuit of Vasquez was Joe Ryan. The Harvard-trained lawyer and cyclo-cross champion had filled his cap with ice to avoid a repeat of the heat-induced collapse he suffered the previous year. Ryan ran 58 seconds faster than Vasquez but, starting two minutes behind him, ended as runner-up by 62 seconds. Ryan passed Pell near the end of the trail, saying "Excuse me."

Ex-San Ramon High School and Stanford star Roy Kissin ran the day's fastest time (49:09, Scr) and finished 11th. Kissin was co-producing the Dipsea-inspired movie *On the Edge*, which began filming in '82. Ron Elijah, the all-time Dipsea course record holder now running with a one minute handicap, had the second best time and came in two places ahead of Kissin.

Andrea Eschen (18th) was awarded the women's best time trophy over Barbara Magid. The Dipsea results, extended to tenths of a second for these two runners only, showed Eschen at 1:02:09.1 and Magid at 1:02:09.9. (Technically, non-track times are rounded up to the nearest second, which would have produced a tie for the award.) Magid got some consolation by winning the family trophy with daughter Jenny. Both Barbara and Jenny also had featured roles in *On the Edge*.

Hal Higdon, one of the nation's top masters runners and author of several popular books on the sport, came out from Indiana and finished 10th.

Bruce VonBorstel, who finished 32nd, ended up getting the last black shirt (#35). Three unofficial or disqualified runners had already made off with the others in the finishing chute. In future years, the shirts would be presented at the awards ceremony.

❑ Susan Mitchell, a prominent Mill Valley author under the name Susan Trott and a top masters competitor, suffered one of the Race's more serious injuries in a fall in the final woodland before Stinson Beach. Mitchell gashed her knee so severely that the bone showed.

❑ The previous winter had been one of the wettest and most destructive in Marin County history, leaving the Dipsea course in relatively poor condition.

❑ Defending champion Florianne Harp, who would have been a favorite, was running the Stockholm Marathon that day (she dropped out due to extreme heat). Harp had won the trip to Sweden by virtue of her first place at the Oakland Marathon the previous December.

❑ The *Independent Journal* did a front page story on Marin-native Reg Carolan, showing the ex-NFL footballer running up the Dipsea steps with his daughter Courtney as he trained for his 12th Dipsea. At 6'6" and 245 pounds, he was described as "perhaps the biggest competitor in the race." A few years later, Carolan collapsed and died while running around Phoenix Lake, at the base of Mt. Tamalpais.

❑ Four runners were disqualified for running in restricted areas and seven for having their entry fee checks returned for insufficient funds. They were all identified by bib number in the results.

❑ The '82 race, according to a profit-loss statement printed with the results, showed a net loss of $563.

❑ The James Farren, Jr. Memorial Trophy, for "Leadership, Sportsmanship and Dedication to the Dipsea Race," was presented for the first time and went to Jack Kirk.

1. Sal Vasquez, 50:53 (5) [1:02]
2. Joe Ryan, 49:55 (3)
3. Eve Pell, 1:04:28 (17) **1st woman**
4. Bob Malain, 58:32 (11)
5. Russ Kiernan, 53:03 (5)
6. John Cobourn, 51:27 (3)
7. Flory Rodd, 1:01:31 (13)
8. Roger Daniels, 55:40 (7)
9. Ron Elijah, 49:44 (1) **2nd best time**
10. Hal Higdon, 58:00 (9)
11. Roy Kissin, 49:09 (0) **best time**
12. Barbara Magid, 1:02:10 (13)
13. Darryl Beardall, 56:17 (7)
14. Steve Stephens, 52:33 (3)
15. Jim Nicholson, 59:17 (9)
16. Rob Heierle, 51:31 (1)
17. Tony Hyun, 51:01 (0)
18. Andrea Eschen, 1:02:10 (11) **fastest woman**
19. Bill Brace, 1:02:27 (11)
20. George O'Gara, 1:04:32 (13)
21. Dan Anderson, 52:34 (1)
22. Peter Laskier, 55:00 (3)
23. Keith Hastings, 55:03 (3)
24. Bob Bunnell, 53:15 (1)
25. James Clever, 59:16 (7)
26. Paul Reese, 1:09:22 (17)
27. Lou Otanez, 59:25 (7)
28. Christie Patterson, 1:03:29 (11)
29. Bert Johnson, 55:29 (3)
30. Dan Seamount, 1:05:34 (13)
31. Sal D'Acqusito, 53:40 (1)
32. Bruce VonBorstel, 55:48 (3)
33. Harrison Gunther, 52:50 (0)
34. Kees Tuinzing, 54:03 (1)
35. Martin Jones, 56:18 (3)
36. Dave Olson, 1:02:20 (9)

Team Tamalpa: Ryan, Pell, Kiernan, Cobourn and Daniels
1,286 finishers; sunny and warm

73rd Dipsea
June 12, 1983

Highlights of 1983 included the pioneering of a new route from Mill Valley to Stinson that was apparently faster than the Dipsea Trail and a splendid battle by two downhill demons in Steep Ravine.

Eve Pell and Patricia Whittingslow were the early leaders. Christie Patterson, who would win the Dipsea four years later, then took the lead on the Hogsback and held it beyond Cardiac. There she was passed by Russ Kiernan.

The popular Kiernan—he is highly regarded among Marin racers and there were several "Go Russ" signs placed on the course—is among the more fearless and talented of all downhillers in the modern Dipsea era. Prognosticators said that if he led entering the Race's late, steep, downhill stages he would win. But at the top of Steep Ravine, concentrating on the precipitous steps ahead, which he leaps four at a time, the usually sure-footed Kiernan fell face forward and skidded down. Bloodied and shaken, Kiernan was quickly up. But he may have momentarily lost a bit of his downhill bravado.

On Insult, Kiernan heard footsteps behind him and muttered, "Oh no, he's here." "He," of course, was Sal Vasquez, another of the race's premier downhillers ("But I am a little more careful than Kiernan going down," Vasquez notes). Vasquez, who also had fallen in Steep Ravine, passed Kiernan on this last uphill. But the drama was not over.

The two flew down the road, through the first shortcut and onto the road again. Then Vasquez took the wrong path into the second shortcut, one that that leads to an impassable deadend. Vasquez quickly realized his error and re-emerged on the road just ahead of Kiernan. The pair laughed, Russ saying he had hoped Sal would stay lost longer. Vasquez then beat Kiernan to the tape by 16 seconds, becoming the race's fourth repeat winner.

Kiernan, meanwhile, was runner-up for a record-tying third time.

Next was Rod Berry, running a brilliant 47:33 despite having sprained his ankle before Muir Woods. "I twisted it a couple of times [more] along the way. It's really sore. I had to stop a couple of times," Berry said while being attended afterward. Patterson, 4th, had the best time by a woman (1:01:32, 13hc). Fifth in 48:55 (Scr) was Berry's Stanford track teammate Roy Kissin, a brilliant runner who would qualify for the 1984 Olympic Trials at two distances.

It was the 13th finisher, Ron Rahmer, who would create the greatest sensation. Finding the quickest way from Mill Valley to Stinson has been a Dipsea tradition from 1904 and few, if any, have been more creative or successful than Rahmer. After much diligent research with maps and on the Mountain, Rahmer, a good but unspectacular 46-year-old Mill Valley runner, came up with a new route vastly different from that followed by all other runners and almost certainly faster.

Rahmer freely told about his find to his Tamalpa Runners Club friends but only two or three joined him. Instead of going up the Mill Valley steps, Rahmer veered right onto Cascade Drive. Near the end of the street, he went up the steep Zig-Zag Trail, joining Panoramic Highway by the Mountain Home Inn. He ran west on the Highway, then cut back onto trails (and shortcuts he cleared himself) to Pantoll. He next went down Steep Ravine Trail, ultimately recrossing Webb Creek back to Panoramic over a downed redwood. Rahmer then joined the traditional route on Panoramic Highway atop Insult Hill.

Rahmer's personal best time and record-high finish convinced several runners to try the route in the Double Dipsea two weeks later. There the results were conclusive; indeed, Rahmer finished second overall (behind Kiernan). The new route, though slightly longer but with only one major uphill (to Mountain Home) instead of two, was superior.

But use of the route was quickly banned.

Although Dipsea officials admired Rahmer's achievement—he would be awarded the Norman Bright Trophy in 1989—they realized the potential safety problems of hundreds of runners on Panoramic Highway. The route was effectively banned the following year by barring running "on or beside Panoramic Highway between the Mountain Home Inn and the water tank near the top of Insult Hill."

When the results were published, the family trophy was wrongly credited to Eve Pell and George Frazier. The pair never received the trophy and Pat and Keith Whittingslow were later recognized as its rightful winners.

Pell and Pat Whittingslow were involved in a second trophy incident. The traditional over-40 award was, this year only, earmarked for the first woman over 45 so went to Pell (18th) instead of true first master Whittingslow (12th). The 45+ designation arose to assuage older women over a plan to cut their maximum 17-minute handicap to 15. Though the 17 minutes were, after protests, ultmately reinstated (prompting a special notice to be mailed), the trophy ground rules were not changed back.

❑ Bib numbers were marked at the starting line, a practice still in effect, in an effort to combat cheating.

❑ Caroline Walker, who had held the women's world marathon record in 1970, was passing through Marin and offered massage therapy to Dipsea finishers.

1. Sal Vasquez, 50:42* (5) [:16]
2. Russ Kiernan, 52:58* (7)
3. Rod Berry, 47:33 (0) **best time**
4. Christie Patterson, 1:01:32 (13) **1st, fastest woman**
5. Roy Kissin, 48:55 (0) **2nd best time**
6. Bob Malain, 1:00:14 (11)
7. Roger Daniels, 56:41 (7)
8. Bert Johnson, 54:49 (5)
9. Keith Hastings, 55:00 (5)
10. Tom Kirschner, 55:08 (5)
11. Don Pickett, 1:01:27 (11)
12. Patricia Whittingslow, 1:05:34 (15)
13. Ron Rahmer, 57:35 (7)
14. Ted Cain, 56:30 (5)
15. Dan Anderson, 52:40 (1)
16. Martin Jones, 56:48 (5)
17. Jim Nicholson, 1:00:55 (9)
18. Eve Pell, 1:09:01 (17)
19. Bill Brace, 1:03:03 (11)
20. Steve Stephens, 55:07 (3)
21. Sal D'Acquisto, 53:12 (1)
22. Jim Miller, 59:13 (7)
23. Nick Epanchin, 57:30 (5)
24. Florianne Harp, 1:05:34 (13)
25. Robert Eichstaedt, 55:42 (3)
26. Bob Bunnell, 53:59 (1)
27. Everett Riggle, 1:02:00 (9)
28. Peter Laskier, 56:04 (3)
29. Mick Mitrovich, 56:05 (3)
30. Don Chaffee, 58:09 (5)
31. James Clever, 1:00:23 (7)
32. Harry Jones, 1:02:25 (9)
33. James Wilkins, 58:27 (5)
34. Lou Otanez, 1:00:34 (7)
35. Ronald Felzer, 58:37 (5)
36. Floy Dawson, 1:00:39 (7)

*The official results, as printed the following April and given above, differed from those recorded and reported at the time of the Race. Vasquez's official time was 44 seconds slower than the originally stated 49:58, Kiernan's 34 seconds slower (should be 44 seconds slower as well and his official time is raised 10 seconds here), and all others about 16 seconds faster.

Team Tamalpa: Kiernan, Patterson, Daniels, Hastings and Kirchner

1,270 finishers; sunny

74th Dipsea
June 10, 1984

In the 73 Dipseas prior to 1984, no runner had ever won more than twice. Sal Vasquez became the first triple champion—he now has won five times—with perhaps his greatest run.

Vasquez had felt his two previous Dipsea victories were less than all-out efforts, and was confident of another win. But an outstanding woman runner, Patricia English, forced him to dig deep. At age 44, Vasquez knocked 84 seconds off his previous Dipsea best. He would never again approach the 49:18 he ran this day.

In 1984, English, a 31-year-old dental hygienist out of San Anselmo in Marin County, was one of the nation's better distance runners. She had qualified for the first ever Women's Olympic Marathon Trials, held a month before the Dipsea, but chose not to compete so as to be fresher for other races. Training on Mt. Tam almost daily, she was particularly strong on uphills. When she entered the Dipsea for the first time, she immediately became the favorite to win.

English prepared diligently with coach (and boyfriend) Steve Ottaway, a sub-50 minute Dipsea runner himself who would finish 21st. The two figured that Vasquez might be able to lower his time to 50 minutes—his best was 50:42. So if English, starting seven minutes ahead of him, could come in below 57 minutes, she would win. English ran brilliantly, meeting that goal and then some. But Vasquez was up to the challenge.

English was unexpectedly shadowed much of the first half by Peggy Smyth, another outstanding hill runner who also lived in San Anselmo. English, later regretting that she didn't push the opening pace hard enough, finally pulled away from Smyth on Hogsback. At the base of Cardiac, English went into first overall by passing maximum handicap starter Judie Donovan. English then ran solo in front, noting afterward, "It's funny running in fear . . . hoping nobody will catch you. It's like trying to get away from a fire."

Vasquez, meanwhile, had already suffered a spill, which cut his left calf, in Hauke Hollow. But he bounced up to continue his relentless charge. It was coming down precipitous Steep Ravine, Vasquez' strength and English's weakest element, that Vasquez made up crucial ground. Still, at Insult, Sal remembers being told, "There is no way you can catch Pat." He pressed on, never seeing English. Then he caught the briefest glimpse of English's white shorts cutting into the second Panoramic Highway shortcut. Rejuvenated, Vasquez soon caught English. She said, "You dog!" He, ever the gentleman, replied, "Sorry, what am I going to do?" The incident helped perpetuate the now oft-repeated aphorism, "If he [Vasquez] can see you, he will catch you." Sal's time was just two seconds off that recorded by the winner of the best time trophy, Rod Berry, and almost two minutes faster than anyone else.

English's 56:38 was the second fastest ever by a woman, trailing only Debbie Rudolf's 56:11 from the shorter course year of 1974. English's time became the new modern course record, destroying by almost five minutes the mark set by Christie Patterson in 1983. Smyth, who would break this record in an even tighter duel with English four years later, finished 3rd.

Bob Malain was next, matching his highest finish in a brilliant Dipsea career. Russ Kiernan, the runner-up to Vasquez the year before, was 5th.

Berry took 6th despite badly spraining his ankle. While cutting in off the second Panoramic Highway shortcut (the steep few yards down to the creek are perhaps the most treacherous on the course), he misstepped. Kiernan, just ahead, recalls hearing "a blood-curdling cry." Berry somehow finished, even still winning the best time award, then was transported to Marin General Hospital. Berry had competed in a steeplechase the day before in a last, unsuccessful effort to qualify for the Olympic Trials. Had he qualified—he missed

by seconds—he would not have run the Dipsea. The year before, when Berry sprained his ankle on Dynamite, he had told the *Independent Journal,* "[1983] is the last time I'm going to run this race for a long time—that's for sure." Berry is now finally keeping that promise; he has never returned to the Dipsea.

Three other scratch runners, Doug Ehrenberg, Hal Schulz and Mike McManus, waged a Race-long battle. The trio finished one after another in places 22-24, just 11 seconds apart, Ehrenberg prevailing. Schulz, an older teammate of Berry's at Redwood High School (Larkspur) when both were among the County's top prep runners, had led the United States Olympic Trials Marathon two weeks earlier before dropping out. McManus would win six best time awards in the next eight years. Ehrenberg became an outstanding cyclist. Overall, a record nine scratch runners won black shirts.

Don Chaffee, the 1979 winner, fell and broke a bone in his shoulder.

❑ Vasquez inadvertently wore his Pamakids singlet inside-out. When race photographer Gene Cohn produced a picture of Sal crossing the tape, Vasquez initially insisted that the negative had been reversed. A blow-up of that picture now occupies a place of honor in Vasquez' home.

❑ Though English was a member of Tamalpa, she was under contract to race for the shoe company Saucony, so was not part of the winning team.

❑ Comedian and actor Robin Williams, who ran cross country while at Redwood High himself and still worked out in Marin, was admitted into the Dipsea on Race morning. He had last run the Dipsea nine years earlier. Williams finished 232nd, then quipped, "Besides the hills, the stairs and the downhill, it wasn't bad."

❑ Seventy-nine-year old William Magner, who won the Dipsea in 1931, finished in 2:18. Magner ran his first Dipsea in 1921. This 63-year spread between finishes was the all-time record for the Dipsea, tied by Jack Kirk in 1993. (Wilbur Taylor, who first competed in 1915, started the 1980 Race for a 65-year spread, but did not finish.)

□ For the first time since the modern handicapping began in 1965, there were starters every minute; the previous two or more minute intervals discarded.
□ The Race date was moved to the second Sunday in June, where it remains.
□ A Race morning pancake breakfast open to all debuted at the Stinson Beach Community Center; it was discontinued after a couple of years.

1. Sal Vasquez, 49:18 (4) [:20] **2nd best time**
2. Patricia English, 56:38 (11) **1st, fastest woman**
3. Peggy Smyth, 58:11 (11)
4. Bob Malain, 1:00:12 (12)
5. Russ Kiernan, 53:30 (5)
6. Rod Berry, 49:16 (0) **best time**
7. Judie Donovan, 1:09:59 (20)
8. Ted Cain, 53:59 (3)
9. George O'Gara, 1:06:00 (15)
10. Brett Freshwaters, 51:12 (0)
11. Darryl Beardall, 57:13 (6)
12. Wally Strauss, 1:03:19 (12)
13. Robert Alexander, 52:29 (1)
14. Butch Alexander, 52:33 (1)
15. Wink Luskin, 1:02:39 (11)
16. Bert Johnson, 54:50 (3)
17. Phillip Duncan, 52:08 (0)
18. Toby Knepfer, 52:29 (0)
19. Debby Hannaford, 1:03:33 (11)
20. Keith Hastings, 55:40 (3)
21. Steve Ottaway, 53:45 (1)
22. Doug Ehrenberg, 52:47 (0)
23. Hal Schulz, 52:56 (0)
24. Mike McManus, 52:58 (0)
25. Hazel Wood-Kuttin, 1:04:02 (11)
26. Ken Grace, 53:03 (0)
27. Ron Rahmer, 59:03 (6)
28. Don Pickett, 1:04:03 (11)
29. Sue Simons, 1:05:04 (12)
30. Kay Willoughby, 1:13:08 (20)
31. Toby Pickett, 53:09 (0)
32. Paul Reese, 1:13:14 (20)
33. James Clever, 59:28 (6)
34. Floy Dawson, 59:34 (6)
35. Barbara Magid, 1:07:41 (14)
36. Mick Mitrovich, 55:44 (2)
Team Tamalpa: Smyth, Kiernan, Donovan, Cain and Beardall
1,375 finishers; clear, cool, windy

75th Dipsea
June 9, 1985

In one of the great achievements in Dipsea history, Sal Vasquez not only won his 4th consecutive Dipsea, he captured, at age 45, the best time award as well.

Peggy Smyth, 33, was making a strong bid for the victory. She had first run the Dipsea in 1977, when she was somehow assigned a man's handicap. In 1984, she qualified for and ran in the first ever United States Women's Olympic Trials Marathon and finished third in the Dipsea. Now she was rigorously coached for the Race by her boyfriend Bill Ranney, who had several high finishes himself in a Dipsea career dating from 1949 (all later clouded by accusations of cheating).

With an 11-minute headstart, Smyth led for much of the Race. But, coming down Panoramic Highway beyond Insult, Smyth ran past the unofficially placed white mark that notes the faint path back into the brushy grassland. It had apparently been painted over by a vandal that morning.

Vasquez, relentlessly pursuing, went by the turn as well. But he realized the error first, then graciously called to Smyth. Vasquez was able to quickly join the shortcut route; Smyth lost more time bushwhacking back. When she finally regained the path, Vasquez was ahead and uncatchable. He then ran unpressed to his fourth consecutive win. Vasquez's final victory margin of 51 seconds made it clear the outcome would have been the same, missed turn or not.

Smyth held off Russ Kiernan, 3rd, by 11 seconds. Roger Daniels, with the highest place of his fine Dipsea career, was 4th. Christie Patterson, the winner two years later, followed with the second-best time by a female. Leslie McMullin, who also ran in the 1984 Olympic Trials Marathon, was a disappointed 6th. McMullin had inadvertently packed her racing shoes in a bag to be sent ahead to Stinson and ran in her heavier trainers.

Seventh was Don Pickett, just back from his honeymoon with the former Patti Jeffries. With his son Toby he won the Family Trophy. Eighth was cross country skiing champion Debbie Waldear of Kirkwood, in her Dipsea debut. She had missed the trail leading to Cardiac, losing time as she stayed on the longer fire road.

Jim Gibbons broke his ankle during the Race but still hobbled in 33rd. He was then transported to a hospital. Ranney crossed the line in 42nd place in his last Dipsea; he died of a heart attack in 1986.

George Frazier's winning of the 35th and last black shirt could not have been more dramatically scripted. Frazier, a popular Marin runner and journalist (he had written a weekly running column in the *Pacific Sun* and covered the Dipsea for the *Independent Journal*), had been trying for years to garner a shirt. His quixotic quest was becoming legendary in local circles. Frazier even held the job in the early 1980's of handing out black shirts to OTHERS at the awards ceremony.

It looked like another near-miss late in 1985 until misfortunes struck three runners ahead. Chris Thomas took a wrong turn. Next, on Shoreline Highway, Keith Hastings (a friend of Frazier's) succumbed to the heat and slowed, dizzy, to a near-walk. Then, on the final straightaway, Herb Vanek, also a victim of the heat, weaved to within yards of the line before dropping (taking some of the finish line fencing with him). Frazier leaped over him and was prematurely announced as finisher #35 although handed stick #37. But, later, two finishers ahead were disqualified; one for not registering and Ted Cain for apparently not starting in Mill Valley. (Cain had been suspected of cheating in earlier high Dipsea finishes; Race officials had begun marking bib numbers at the starting line in response.) Frazier thus got the final shirt, saying, "Now I can die happy." Hastings made it across in 38th, Vanek in 41st.

Another alleged cheating incident revolved around the recipient of the trophy as first Dipsea Runner, Ed Dux. Since Dux's times in other races weren't comparable to his recorded 52:39 (2hc), his performance was called into question by many runners and not generally accepted. Two weeks later Dux was caught cheating in the Double Dipsea and disqualified from that race. The trophy for first woman Dipsea Runner (2nd overall) went to a Swiss runner then living in Mill Valley, Heidi Quadri (1:03:02, 11hc).

❑ A special effort was made to locate past champions for the 75th anniversary Dipsea. Sixteen former champions lined up for an historic group photo at the starting line. A record-tying total of 12 past and future winners finished.

❑ The Friday night before the Race, a 75th anniversary dinner (this author's idea, then chaired by George Frazier) was held at another venerable Mill Valley institution, the Outdoor Art Club. The event sold out quickly. Talks were given by 1979 winner Don Chaffee (peeling one Dipsea shirt after another from his chest as he recounted his years in the Race), co-director Jerry Hauke, Thea Hogan, who was the only woman when she finished last in the 1965 Dipsea (Thea returned to run the '85 race, and was again the last Invitational finisher), "Mr. Dipsea" Don Pickett, Sal Vasquez and handicapper Jim Weil, who reviewed the greatest efforts by age then fantasized about the "all-time Dipsea race . . . the handicaps done by God . . . at the start would be every Dipsea runner, ever." Mark Reese presented a slide show. Then Pax Beale showed his film of the 1970 Dipsea, *Thirty-Three Years to Victory*. The gala concluded with the introduction of the guest of honor, Norman Bright, whom the Tamalpa Runners had flown down from Tacoma. He recited from Kipling.

❑ On Saturday, a group of runners guided Bright over the Dipsea Trail. Seventy-five and blind, he now needed over five hours to make the crossing that once took him 47 minutes. At Stinson Beach, Bright stripped off his clothing and frolicked in the surf. Bright was also on hand Race day to present the first Norman Bright Award, a trophy donated by his nephew Ray Bright, for "extraordinary effort in the Dipsea Race." Norman fittingly handed it to Jack Kirk.

□ Other special Diamond Jubilee touches included a specially designed T-shirt, diamonds on the bib numbers and a Dipsea Calendar with historic photos.

□ The James Farren, Jr. award went to Mike Restani, who had guided blind runner Harry Cordellos over the Dipsea several times, including in the '85 race (in 1:53:35) and in Ray Gatchalian's award winning film *Survival Run*.

1. Sal Vasquez, 49:56 (4) [:51] **best time**
2. Peggy Smyth, 57:47 (11) **1st, fastest woman**
3. Russ Kiernan, 52:58 (6)
4. Roger Daniels, 54:13 (7)
5. Christie Patterson, 59:14 (12)
6. Leslie McMullin, 59:51 (11)
7. Don Pickett, 1:01:23 (12)
8. Debbi Waldear, 1:01:30 (12)
9. Joe Ryan, 51:39 (2)
10. George O'Gara, 1:05:55 (16)
11. Patricia Whittingslow, 1:08:02 (18)
12. Bob Malain, 1:02:10 (12)
13. Darryl Beardall, 56:18 (6)
14. Wink Luskin, 1:01:27 (11)
15. Butch Alexander, 51:32 (1) **2nd best time**
16. Brian Maxwell, 51:40 (1)
17. Eve Pell, 1:10:51 (20)
18. Jim Moyles, 51:53 (1)
19. John Cobourn, 52:54 (2)
20. Steve Ottaway, 52:00 (1)
21. Barbara Magid, 1:06:22 (15)
22. Judie Donovan, 1:11:27 (20)
23. Mike McManus, 51:42 (0)
24. Brett Freshwaters, 51:51 (0)
25. Robert Alexander, 53:08 (1)
26. Dane Larsen, 53:15 (1)
27. Noel Lincicome, 54:16 (2)
28. Steve Stephens, 55:22 (3)
29. Morton Gray, 1:01:31 (9)
30. Joan Reiss, 1:11:40 (19)
31. Kate Harling, 1:07:41 (15)
32. James Goldsmith, 1:00:57 (8)
33. Jim Gibbons, 54:58 (2)
34. Jeanne Lavin, 1:04:00 (11)
35. George Frazier, 55:09 (2)
36. Chris Thomas, 55:16 (2)

Team Tamalpa: Kiernan, Daniels, Patterson, Pickett and Beardall
1,295 finishers; sunny and hot

76th Dipsea
June 8, 1986

Faced with the dilemma of either watching four-time champion Sal Vasquez continue winning, or even further penalizing men near his age with additional handicap reductions, Dipsea organizers came up with a change that was immediately dubbed "The Sal Vasquez Rule." Winners of any of the previous five Dipseas would now have one handicap minute deducted. The idea came from Dipsea handicapper Jim Weil, a track regular familiar with the system of adding extra weight to racehorses after victories. Vasquez therefore went off with four handicap minutes, one LESS than he had in his debut six years earlier.

Entries to the Dipsea closed just a few days after the April 1 mailing of the applications. There was therefore some grumbling when Gail Ladage-Scott, a locally unknown (but one-time San Francicso resident), 40-year-old runner from mountainous Durango, Colorado, was admitted days before the Race. Scott had been inspired to enter after seeing the movie *On the Edge*, just released a few weeks earlier, and by her own rapid improvements, which were soon to carry her to a U.S. masters marathon record. She said later, "I didn't think they'd let me in but I called them up and begged and they did." Scott flew in, was guided over the course Thursday by Jim Weil, then went on smash the women's all-time 40+ record and win by 42 seconds.

Eve Pell had been the heavy favorite on the strength of her already shining Dipsea career, her training on the course (she lives minutes from the steps), her 20-minute headstart and the 38:59 10K personal record she ran earlier in the spring. Pell did lead most all the way. But ever-closer cheers behind, starting at Cardiac, told her someone faster was gaining. The pass was on Insult, the same place Pell had lost her lead in 1982 to Sal Vasquez. Scott graciously said, "Great run, Eve. We'll both beat Sal."

They both did, Scott first, ending the Race's most extraordinary victory skein. Vasquez, never able to see the front runners, finished exactly two minutes behind Scott in 3rd. He still ran, at 47, an impressive 50:19, second swiftest of anyone.

It was an emotional win for Scott. She said later, "This area is close to my heart. My husband and I courted on the Dipsea Trail."

Winning the best time award was Mike McManus, starting a streak of his own. He would win the title six of the next seven years (he didn't race in 1989). The Oakland native, from a family of excellent runners, first ran the race as a ten-year old in 1976. He finished tenth in 1978 when he ran 58:08 (10hc) at age 12.

Brian Maxwell, a Canadian living in Berkeley who had once finished third in the Boston Marathon, was 27th. He was then experimenting with a new product, soon to be the phenomenally successful PowerBar energy food.

❑ Although women comprised only 17% (110) of the 647 Invitational finishers, they took five of the first six places, 11 of the top 20 and an all-time record 13 black shirts.

1. Gail Scott, 58:19 (14) [:42]
2. Eve Pell, 1:05:01 (20)
3. Sal Vasquez, 50:19 (4) **first man, 2nd best time**
4. Peggy Smyth, 57:25 (11) **fastest woman**
5. Debbi Waldear, 58:45 (12)
6. Christie Patterson, 1:00:43 (13)
7. Russ Kiernan, 54:13 (6)
8. Bob Malain, 1:02:01 (13)
9. Roger Daniels, 56:15 (7)
10. Mike McManus, 49:53 (0) **best time**
11. Kay Willoughby, 1:10:13 (20)
12. Joe Ryan, 52:25 (2)
13. John Cobourn, 52:37 (2)
14. Hazel Wood-Kuttin, 1:02:53 (12)
15. Wally Strauss, 1:04:05 (13)
16. Darryl Beardall, 58:13 (7)
17. Ann Hardham, 1:07:37 (16)
18. Heidi Quadri, 1:02:43 (11)
19. Wink Luskin, 1:02:48 (11)
20. Jeanne Lavin, 1:02:52 (11)
21. Jim Moyles, 52:56 (1)
22. Steve Ottaway, 53:13 (1)
23. Morton Gray, 1:02:16 (10)
24. Ken Grace, 53:30 (1)
25. Dane Larsen, 53:37 (1)
26. Don Pickett, 1:04:49 (12)
27. Brian Maxwell, 53:57 (1)
28. Mark Richtman, 54:00 (1)
29. Barbara Magid, 1:08:02 (15)
30. Toby Pickett, 53:25 (0)
31. Kate Harling, 1:09:36 (16)
32. Michael Lopez, 53:44 (0)
33. John Swyers, 58:46 (5)
34. Robert Eichstaedt, 55:47 (2)
35. Bert Johnson, 56:51 (3)
36. Debbie Hannaford, 1:04:59 (11)
Team Tamalpa: Pell, Patterson, Kiernan, Daniels and Willoughby
1,245 finishers; sunny and warm

(Above) Runner-up Gail Scott (left) and winner Christie Patterson discuss their seesaw 1987 duel. (Bob Hax, Independent Journal)

(Left) Dane Larsen presents his 1987 black shirt to his former Harvard track coach, and 1941 Dipsea best time winner, Bill McCurdy.

77th Dipsea
June 14, 1987

Christie Patterson, though a native of Marin County, had only discovered the Dipsea while in her 30's. In 1981, she had planned an outing to Stinson Beach with her daughter Kim when she found traffic blocked for the Dipsea Race. When Patterson finally got to Stinson, she was overwhelmed by what she saw. By the next year, at age 34, Patterson had begun running; her only previous athletics had been years of classical ballet study. She improved rapidly and was fifth (first woman) in the 1985 Dipsea with a 59:14 and sixth in 1986 with a 1:00:43.

Still, Patterson's main sport was Ride & Tie, where teams of two riders and one horse compete over long, cross country courses. The national championships were to be the week after the Dipsea. Despite being a full-time nurse and single mother, Patterson got herself fit for the Ride & Tie. The 1987 Dipsea was almost incidental.

Patterson was pulled to a fast early pace by Amy McConnell, an outstanding high school runner known for her uphill prowess (she would later set the women's record at the Mt. Tamalpais Hill Climb), who started in her 12-minute group. On the fire road beyond Cardiac, Patterson both passed Kay Willoughby (who would win in 1988) and caught sight of the last runner ahead, Gail Ladage-Scott, the defending champion who had started a minute ahead.

Patterson decided to go after Scott; her highest goal was to finish as first woman. When she didn't see Scott as expected on Swoop Hollow, she figured Scott was really flying. Actually, Scott, who lived in Colorado and had only been over the course once this year, had made a major course error. Scott veered right at the top of Swoop instead of plunging straight down, following the considerably longer "hiker's" Dipsea Trail. (This lovely but little known [to racers] section through alternating laurel, redwood and Douglas-fir forests is now dubbed the "Gail Scott Trail.")

Patterson was thus first down Steep Ravine. But her main worry, she recalls, was whether 11-year-old Kim, waiting for her without a chaperone at Stinson, was safe. At the base of Insult, Scott caught a surprised Patterson, said a few words, and passed back into first. Patterson tucked in behind. At the short climb back onto Panoramic after the first shortcut, Patterson glided past a now laboring Scott. Patterson was recharged but still expected a man to pass.

At the turn off Shoreline, Patterson saw Kim holding a sign that read, "Go, Mom" and blew a kiss. Kim was frenetic; Patterson wasn't immediately sure why. Then, when she made the final left turn, she realized why Kim had been so enthusiastic; she was winning. Christie saw her own mother watching in the crowd and almost stopped, but continued on to break the first tape of her life. "Next to the births of my two children [she would later marry fine Dipsea runner Tomas Pastalka and have a son], this was the greatest thrill of my life," Patterson recounts years later.

Patterson's 57:06 was the fifth fastest time ever recorded by a woman; it remains #8. Scott, running five seconds slower than her winning effort of the year before, followed 18 seconds later. Scott said emphatically afterward that Patterson, "Won [not] because I got lost . . . She outran me."

Russ Kiernan was 3rd, snapping the six-year streak as first man of Sal Vasquez. Vasquez did not start because of a sciatica problem, saying "If I don't think I can win, I won't run. If I want to enjoy the Dipsea Trail, I'll hike it and have a picnic."

Kiernan got some revenge of Patterson 13 days later at the Double Dipsea, passing her late to win and deny her bid to be the first same-year winner of both the Dipsea and the Double. (No one has done it yet.) Patterson did set the still-standing all-time women's Double Dipsea course record of 1:58:42. It remains that race's only sub-2 hour clocking by a woman.

Debbie Waldear was 4th. Her 57:35 was then the sixth fastest all-time women's mark.

Mike McManus (7th) repeated as winner of the

best time award; his 48:21 (Scr) was a sensational one minute, 53 seconds swifter than anyone else.

Fifteen-year-old McConnell finished 8th and won the newly-revived high school trophy. The trophy had originated in 1906 but lapsed twice (1922-1953 and 1975-1986). Now, qualified high schoolers were encouraged to enter and admitted directly into the Invitational section. McConnell became its first-ever female recipient. Erin Vali, winner of the trophy the next two years, was 14th. McConnell's University High School (S.F.) teammate Matt Metzger, who would win the trophy as a senior in 1990, was 17th.

Wally Strauss, 10th, had undergone triple by-pass heart surgery in 1977. Strauss, a Mill Valley doctor, performed Race morning Dipsea physical exams when they were still required by the AAU in the early 1970's.

Also remarkable was the 12th place finish of Nan Hall of Occidental. It was her first race of any kind.

Exceptionally cool weather—the fog was so thick that parts of the course were wet—produced fast times.

The family trophy went to Darryl Beardall (9th) and his nephew Tim (26th). Tim is the son of Darryl's brother Alan, winner of the 1963 Dipsea. Some runners questioned this extension of the definition of "family."

Darryl also won the first Jimmy Nicholson Award for the top runner over 50. Nicholson, who had seven top 10 Dipsea finishes in the eight races from 1974-1981, died the previous July while bicyling in Golden Gate Park.

Controversy swirled around the winner of the Dipsea Runner section, Joan Colman. Colman, despite her outstanding masters record (she would later be named the nation's best 45-49 female runner) and several appeals on her behalf, had not been admitted directly into the Invitational section, as Ladage-Scott had been the previous year. This perceived slight contributed to a major rift in the Tamalpa Runners Club and the formation of a new, short-lived racing team (Mach I). Colman's 1:02:21

(15hc) would have placed her 6th in the open Race and perhaps higher; Dipsea Runners have to pass the slowest Invitationals as well as earlier starters in their own race.

❑ The "Dipsea Doodles" attached to the results noted that "pressure to get into the race was unprecedented," that the 1,500-runner entry limit filled within a record six days, and that 41% of the runners were from Marin County.

1. Christie Patterson, 57:06 (12) [:18] **fastest woman**
2. Gail LaDage-Scott, 58:24 (13)
3. Russ Kiernan, 53:13 (7) **first man**
4. Debbi Waldear, 57:35 (11)
5. Bob Malain, 1:00:44 (14)
6. Kay Willoughby, 1:08:58 (21)
7. Mike McManus, 48:21 (0) **best time**
8. Amy McConnell, 1:00:41 (12) **first HS**
9. Darryl Beardall, 56:04 (7)
10. Wally Strauss, 1:03:10 (14)
11. Pete Sweeney, 50:32 (1)
12. Nan Hall, 1:00:34 (11)
13. Floy Dawson, 57:41 (8)
14. Erin Vali, 54:57 (5)
15. Judie Donovan, 1:11:03 (21)
16. Phil Bellan, 50:17 (0) **2nd best time**
17. Matt Metzger, 56:21 (6)
18. Hans Roenau, 1:03:24 (13)
19. John Cobourn, 52:28 (2)
20. Thomas Iredale, 53:35 (3)
21. Jim Moyles, 52:35 (2)
22. Patrick Kubley, 52:36 (2)
23. Caron Potts, 1:01:47 (11)
24. Eddie Balme, 51:54 (1)
25. Hazel Wood-Kuttin, 1:01:59 (11)
26. Tim Beardall, 54:01 (3)
27. Dane Larsen, 53:05 (2)
28. Ken Grace, 52:14 (1)
29. Morton Gray, 1:01:16 (10)
30. Milan Zeman, 55:17 (4)
31. Ann Hardham, 1:07:19 (16)
32. Noel Lincicome, 53:19 (2)
33. George O'Gara, 1:08:21 (17)
34. Don Pickett, 1:04:29 (13)
35. Ray Morris, 1:06:32 (15)
36. John Hodge, 51:34 (0)

Team Tamalpa: Patterson, Kiernan, Willoughby, D. Beardall and Strauss

1,293 finishers; cool and foggy, trail somewhat slippery

78th Dipsea
June 12, 1988

The 1988 Race was one of the tightest ever, the only time in Dipsea history that the top three crossed the finish line within 10 seconds of one another. And never have women so dominated, capturing all the top five places.

Kay Willoughby, a native of Allentown, Pennsylvania, and the mother of two grown sons, had not taken up competitive running until the age of 46, in 1982. She had been "jogging like other Ross housewives were," when Pat Patterson, a member of the Tamalpa Runners, introduced her to the club and Mt. Tamalpais. She made her Dipsea debut in 1983, finishing 120th (1:16:48, 17hc). Through running she met Milan Zeman (eventually to become her husband) and she joined him in the world of ultradistance races. Willoughby completed a few hilly 50-milers, which she credits for building her strength, but ultimately decided shorter races, "where the pain lasts less long," were more her forte.

Steve Ottaway, a top local runner and coach, recognized Willoughby's Dipsea potential after her sixth place in 1987 and told her she could win. She is a fearless downhiller, a critical asset in the Dipsea, and, at age 52, would receive the maximum 22-minute handicap. Ottaway developed a training plan which emphasized "hills, hills and hills" and Willoughby "followed it in every detail," though saying she never herself believed she could take first.

An amusing incident developed just before the Race. Zeman is well-known for uncovering obscure shortcuts, and keeping them secret. He wouldn't even tell Kay of one he knew in the area of Suicide. But a mutual friend, Ron Rahmer, shamed Zeman into revealing the secret route to Willoughby the night before. Willoughby checked it out Dipsea morning, and used it in the Race. Did this shortcut change the ultimate outcome? Years later, Willoughby laughs, "I did win by only seven seconds!"

Starting with the first group, Willoughby took the lead at once and never relinquished it, one of the few wire-to-wire leaders. One of her key concerns was not letting rival Eve Pell, who, at 51, started a minute behind her, pass on the uphills. Pell got to within 15 seconds of Willoughby at the top of Cardiac, but never closer.

Willoughby then recounts, "Milan had told me that the faster you go, the less chance of falling. I never ran so fast downhill in my life, and never will again." Indeed, she twisted an ankle going down Steep Ravine and thought all was lost. The ankle swelled considerably after the Race, but Willoughby didn't let it slow her.

But even more dangerous pursuers than Pell were gaining. Peggy Smyth and Patricia English (ironically, then Ottaway's girlfriend) were among the strongest trail runners in Northern California (both lived in San Anselmo). They started together (11hc) and waged a magnificent start-to-finish duel. Smyth actually thought it was Debbie Waldear, another top runner dressed in black singlet and shorts as English was, behind her. In the Rainforest, Smyth said, "Good running, Debbie" and heard English reply, "I'm not Debbie."

Smyth and English pushed one another throughout—never more than a few strides apart—at a pace faster than any woman had ever run in the Dipsea. Entering Steep Ravine, English got right up to Smyth, who offered her the trail. English declined and Smyth was able to hold her advantage to the tape.

The pair passed Pell just before the stile. But they did not see Willoughby until the final straightaway. They had cut almost all the 11 minutes from Willoughby's headstart, but it was not quite enough.

As Willoughby approached the tape, she introduced a final element of drama by inexplicably slowing—"I was so brain-dead that I tried to go UNDER the tape!," Willoughby recalls. But she won.

Just behind, Smyth prevailed in the duel with English for 2nd, by two ticks of the clock. That also meant that it was Smyth who collected the new (and still-standing) all-time women's Dipsea record of 55:47. And it was English's record, 56:38 from 1984, that she broke. Then onto the finishing lane came Pell, who would earn revenge the following year with an outright win.

Willoughby recalls, "Winning the Dipsea was the happiest day of my life. Because along with the victory I was drawn closer to Milan." The two were married in 1991. After the race, Willoughby, with Zeman, treated Ottaway to dinner (he came with English) at the pricey El Paseo Restaurant in Mill Valley as a thank you.

Willoughby's time (1:06:40) was the second slowest winning effort ever (excluding the long-course year of 1905), behind only Raymond Fuller's 1:07:52 in 1956. At the awards ceremony, she was presented with the first "Running Bear" sculpture, newly designed by Franco Vianello for the overall winner.

Two other important battles were also close. Scratch runner Mike McManus won the best-time award by just seven seconds over fellow East Bay runner Tom Borschel. It was McManus' third best time award, tying him with Otto Boeddiker, William Churchill, Byron Lowry and Ron Elijah behind Mason Hartwell's seven. Because McManus still placed only 14th, calls for aiding the scratch runners intensified. Borschel apparently holds the all-time Mt. Tamalpais ascent record; he went from the Dipsea starting line to the lookout tower atop Tam in 30 minutes, 32 seconds in a 1987 race.

Tight too were the first high schoolers. Irvine's Erin Vali won the trophy by finishing eight seconds, and one place, ahead of another 16-year-old, San Rafael's Paul Mankin.

Sal Vasquez, the four-time champion returning after a year's absence, was first man, 6th overall and more than two minutes out of first. Afterward he joked, "I never saw the women."

Joan Ullyot, one of the pioneering figures in women's running in this country, returned to the Dipsea after a 13 year absence and missed a black shirt by one place (1:09:35, 18hc). Ullyot also just missed in her last appearance in 1975, when only 25 shirts were awarded.

The family trophy went to Arnold Knepfer, a long-time local runner scoring his highest finish (20th), and his son Toby (46th).

Brian Purcell, who set the course record (16:24:00) at the nation's premier ultra, the Western States 100 Mile Endurance Run, just two weeks earlier, was 44th (53:36, 1hc).

❑ Bob Malain, tabbed a possible winner by some prognosticators, fell seriously ill the day before the Race and didn't run.

❑ Tomas Pastalka discovered and used a unique shortcut; dropping directly down to the beach from the Panoramic Highway-Highway 1 intersection and therefore avoiding much of the final half-mile. This shortcut brought Pastalka to the finish from the wrong direction (a practice ruled off-limits for subsequent Dipseas); he crossed the line then immediately turned around to finish the usual way.

1. Kay Willoughby, 1:06:40 (22) [:07]
2. Peggy Smyth, 55:47 (11) **fastest woman**
3. Patricia English, 55:49 (11)
4. Eve Pell, 1:06:08 (21)
5. Debbie Waldear, 57:04 (11)
6. Sal Vasquez, 51:48 (5) **1st man**
7. Russ Kiernan, 53:57 (7)
8. Nan Hall, 58:09 (11)
9. Darryl Beardall, 55:53 (8)
10. Joan Colman, 1:03:11 (15)
11. Tom Borschel, 49:21 (1) **2nd best time**
12. Erin Vali, 52:48 (4) **first HS**
13. Paul Mankin, 52:56 (4)
14. Mike McManus, 49:14 (0) **best time**
15. Wally Strauss, 1:04:59 (15)
16. Caron Potts, 1:01:06 (11)
17. Robin Davis, 1:01:32 (11)
18. Robert Alexander, 52:33 (2)
19. Judie Donovan, 1:12:34 (22)
20. Arnold Knepfer, 1:02:39 (12)
21. Ken Grace, 51:40 (1)
22. Pete Sweeney, 51:43 (1)
23. Phil Bellan, 50:53 (0)
24. Steve Ottaway, 53:00 (2)
25. Milan Zeman, 56:06 (5)
26. Butch Alexander, 52:09 (1)
27. Steve Lyons, 57:10 (6)
28. Floy Dawson, 59:12 (8)
29. Helmer Aslaksen, 52:13 (1)
30. Tom Iredale, 54:14 (3)
31. Robert Dickinson, 52:14 (1)
32. Don Pickett, 1:05:15 (14)
33. Michael Hoy, 56:18 (5)
34. Larry McKendall, 51:20 (0)
35. John Cobourn, 54:25 (3)
36. Joan Ullyot, 1:09:35 (18)

Team Tamalpa: Willoughby, Pell, Kiernan, Beardall and Strauss
1,278 finishers; warm, sunny

79th Dipsea
June 11, 1989

Eve Pell, a 52-year-old mother of three grown sons, was widely considered the favorite to win. Taking a break in her work as an award winning investigative journalist, she had gotten herself into nearly the best shape of her ten-year running career, cracking 40 minutes for 10 kilometers 13 days before the Dipsea. Pell had Dipsea experience, finishing 2nd in 1986, 3rd in '82, and 4th in '88. And she had 19 handicap minutes, That was two less than the year before—a legacy of the 1988 victory by her Mill Valley neighbor Kay Willoughby, who had also been 52—but still formidable for a sub-40 minute 10K runner.

Pell's biggest battle had been fought a couple of years earlier. A congenital back problem had left her virtually immobile for weeks in late 1986 and out of running for a year. One doctor had suggested a full body cast. All agreed that her Dipsea racing days, if not her running altogether, were over. But she showed remarkable tenacity. Pell eschewed surgery, instead following the training guidance of physical therapist Dennis Morgan. Soon she was taking long walks on Mt. Tam, then running again. Still, the pounding of the trail was a clear danger and she did only a handful of training efforts over the course prior to the 1989 Race.

Pell took the lead for good before the one-mile mark. Indeed, she got so far ahead that she recollects wondering, "Did a bomb wipe out everyone else." Still, she kept an alert ear behind; Pell had lead in both 1982 and 1986 before being overhauled a mile from the finish line. One of her sons, Peter McLaughlin, and friends Jonathan Dann and Keith Hastings stationed themselves at several places on the course to shout encouragment and advice. Pell got particular pleasure hearing Peter yell to her at White Barn, "Go, Mom, you're an animal!"

Eve Pell with winner's "The Bear" trophy, 1989. (Gene Cohn)

No one got close. By running a personal Dipsea best of 1:03:56—then the swiftest ever for a woman over 50 and 35 seconds below her previous PR from 1982—Pell won by a substantial one minute and 37 seconds. The 3rd place runner was an additional distant 2:06 behind.

Second place went to Joan Colman of Sausalito, the runner Pell most feared. She turned in a brilliant 59:33 at age 45, making her the oldest woman (by four years) yet to crack an hour. But, although just seven years younger than Pell, Colman had started six minutes later, and could only narrow, not erase, the gap. Already upset with the Dipsea Committee from 1987 (when she was not admitted into the Invitational section), Colman created a flap by criticizing the handicapping when she accepted her award.

There was a wonderful battle for 3rd, and best time, between scratch runners Phil Bellan and Tom Borschel. After passing one another a few times, Bellan, 27, of Mill Valley, pulled away going up Insult and prevailed by 14 seconds in 48:39.

Peggy Smyth was 5th in 57:19 (8hc). That brought Smyth her third woman's best time trophy.

Erin Vali from Irvine became the third runner ever to win the high school trophy twice. Once again, he did it by edging San Rafael's Paul Mankin.

Marvin "Steve" Stephens crossed the finish line 21st but was disqualified before the awards ceremony. His bib number had been linked to that of a runner taking an off-limits shortcut in Muir Woods and using abusive language, and Stephens, who had gone home, was unable to explain his side. When his name was cleared, Stephens was reinstated as the 21st runner in the results, but no subsequent finisher's place was altered. Chief beneficiary of the incident was Cynthia Chilton, who had won the Dipsea Runner section the year before. She got to keep the last numbered shirt, 35, though she was the 36th finisher.

In an emotional moment, the family trophy, renamed for 1963 winner Alan Beardall, who had died the previous December, was awarded to Alan's son Tim and brother (Tim's uncle) Darryl Beardall.

❏ Russ Kiernan, hobbled by internal health problems, had to watch from the sidelines, ending his extraordinary 12 year skein of top ten finishes.

❏ There was again course vandalism the night before the Race. One of the arrows on the Panoramic Highway shortcuts was painted over and replaced by another that led to a deadend. Some sharp branches were placed as unexpected hazards at leaps in Hauke Hollow and elsewhere.

❏ Largely because women had so dominated the top spots in 1988, there was an almost across-the-board three minute reduction in their handicaps. The minimum women's headstart was cut from 11 to 8, where it remains.

❏ Responding to complaints of unfairness, the Dipsea Committee substantially changed the procedure for entering the Race. In the preceding several years, applications were mailed on April 1 to all runners who had sent in self-addressed, stamped envelopes. The first 1,500 to return the applications were admitted; the Race usually filling within one to five days. This created a lively scramble at the Mill Valley post office (to secure an edge, some runners would use friends' Mill Valley mailing addresses) and meant that out-of-towners had little chance of gaining entry and that even long-time regulars could easily get knocked out.

Under the new system, still in use, there are four ways to secure entry. Those 500-600 runners automatically qualifying for Invitational status by finishing high enough in the Invitational section (currently the top 425) or Dipsea Runner section the previous year are exempted from the first come-first served rule. They are mailed applications and assured entry if they return them within a three week deadline. A like number of runners are admitted under the old first come-first served procedure, which now fills even quicker than before (in 1993, the first day after applications were mailed). Another 100 places are auctioned off to the highest bidders—the range of winning bids is, of course, kept a secret. Proceeds from this auction go the Dipsea Trail fund. A final 300 places are allotted by lottery; all applicants not admitted through the other three methods are put in a pool and names randomly drawn.

1. Eve Pell, 1:03:56 (19) [1:37]
2. Joan Colman, 59:33 (13)
3. Phil Bellan, 48:39 (0) **first man, best time**
4. Tom Borschel, 48:53 (0) **2nd best time**
5. Peggy Smyth, 57:19 (8) **fastest woman**
6. Darryl Beardall, 56:44 (7)
7. Debbi Waldear, 57:54 (8)
8. Erin Vali, 52:16 (2) **first HS**
9. Roger Daniels, 58:21 (8)
10. Pete Sweeney, 51:28 (1)
11. John Cobourn, 53:33 (3)
12. Paul Mankin, 52:37 (2)
13. Tad Beach, 50:39 (0)
14. Wally Strauss, 1:05:43 (15)
15. Robert Alexander, 51:45 (1)
16. Butch Alexander, 51:55 (1)
17. Thomas Iredale, 53:57 (3)
18. Richard Laine, 1:02:58 (12)
19. Lloyd Kahn, 58:59 (8)
20. Don Pickett, 1:05:03 (14)
*Steve Stephens, 55:10 (4)
21. George O'Gara, 1:10:28 (19)
22. Nan Hall, 59:50 (8)
23. Christie Patterson, 1:01:06 (9)
24. John Swyers, 57:08 (5)
25. Robert Dickinson, 52:19 (0)
26. Link Lindquist, 1:06:22 (14)
27. Steve Lyons, 57:23 (5)
28. George Frazier, 55:27 (3)
29. Tim Beardall, 52:29 (0)
30. John Hodge, 52:33 (0)
31. Kay Willoughby, 1:11:48 (19)
32. Everett Riggle, 1:02:51 (10)
33. Greg Nacco, 52:58 (0)
34. Amy McConnell, 1:01:59 (9)
35. Cynthia Chilton, 1:01:05 (8)
*Initially disqualified, then restored; see text
Team Tamalpa: Pell, D. Beardall, Daniels, Cobourn and Strauss
1,269 finishers; cool with coastal fog

80th Dipsea
June 10, 1990

The 1990 Dipsea was one of the most exciting in years. Eight year old Megan McGowan led for some 65 minutes until she was overhauled, on the last yards of the trail, by Sal Vasquez. McGowan was a 60-pound, second grader from Torrance in southern California. She had begun racing two weeks past her 4th birthday and had been recording remarkable times since.

McGowan started with the first (22 minute) handicap group. Joining her, with permission from the Dipsea Committee, was Bruce Phinney, running non-competitively. Phinney, a 30-year old, 33-minute 10K runner from San Rafael, was to insure that McGowan stayed on course. He was recruited a couple of days before when Megan's father Michael, who accompanied her the previous year in her debut in the Dipsea Runner section, injured his foot.

McGowan, with Phinney, had the lead by the steps, then stretched it to an astonishing almost six minutes at the top of Cardiac. Radio reports of McGowan's sizable lead kept the finish line crowd in high anticipation.

Second at the crest was 46-year old Sausalitan Joan Colman, who had started 13 minutes after McGowan. Colman was considered the pre-Race favorite on the strength of her 1989 record when she ran 59:33 for second place in the Dipsea, won two gold medals in the World Veterans Games and been named the nation's #1 45-49 year old road runner. But, unknown to most, she had missed several months of training over the winter with a stress fracture. Colman would end up running two minutes slower than in '89 and finish 4th.

So it was left to the peerless Vasquez to try to catch McGowan. When he passed Colman on Insult, he thought he had the Race won, and even began walking. But he was then informed that "a little girl was over two minutes ahead" and he bore down again. He finally caught his diminutive rival less than a half-mile from the finish line. It was Vasquez' all-time record fifth win. But his 52:05 actual time was his slowest since 1980, when he had a horrible fall, and well off his personal best of 49:18.

When, after the Race, word that McGowan had been "paced" began circulating, a storm erupted. Many runners were outraged. They argued that route-finding had always been an integral part of the race, that the history of the Dipsea is filled with stories of costly wrong turns, that other pre-teens did fine (including winning) on their own in the past, that Phinney may have provided greater assistance than simply pointing the way, and that the "pacing" precedent could lead to absurdity. Others countered that a child's safety overrides all these concerns, and that no rules were broken. (Dipsea organizers had addressed the issue as early as 1969, with Jerry Hauke writing in that year's "Dipsea Doodles": "It is our position that responsibility for the safety of small children lies with the parent. If the parent is unable to run along behind the child as protection, than the child should not be entered in the race.")

Third went to scratch runner Mike McManus. His 47:59, the best time since 1983 and a huge 2:24 swifter than anyone else, earned him his fourth fastest time award. That put McManus alone behind Mason Hartwell, with seven, on the all-time Dipsea list.

In 6th was first high schooler Matt Metzger of University High, San Francisco. The Tiburon resident was the current California State Division IV (small school) cross country champion.

At the awards ceremony, Jack Kirk, 83, presented McGowan's trophy. The Dipsea Demon had finished his 55th consecutive Dipsea, running 2:27:31 (22hc) after starting with McGowan. Next, Vasquez charmed the onlookers when he recounted his story of the Race, then called Megan forward and raised her in his arms. Vasquez has two daughters himself.

❑ Tim Minor, 31 (1hc), won the Dipsea Runner section by clocking 50:23, surpassed that day only by McManus' time. It remains the fastest time ever from the "second" race.

❑ Ken Wilson competed with a small cast on one foot. He was trying to preserve his place in the Invitational section and did so, finishing 93rd in 59:27 (1hc).

❑ Hans Roenau, a Dipsea veteran with many high finishes (6th in 1978), went the whole route on crutches in 3 hours, 36 seconds (15hc) and finished next to last. He was recovering from hip replacement surgery. Roenau would be awarded the James Farren, Jr. Memorial Trophy in 1993.

❑ Defending champion Eve Pell, likely to have been a favorite to win, announced early her intention to accept a journalism assignment that would put her in Czechoslovakia on Dipsea day.

(Above left) Peggy Smyth, on her way to setting the all-time women's Dipsea record in 1988, leads Pat English. (Gene Cohn)
(Above right) Jack Kirk, the "Dipsea Demon," at age 84 in 1991 Dipsea. (Gene Cohn)
(Opposite) Mike McManus, winner of six best time awards, 1991. (Vicki Chase)

1. Sal Vasquez, 52:05 (5) [:16]
2. Megan McGowan, 1:09:21 (22) **first woman**
3. Mike McManus, 47:59 (0) **best time**
4. Joan Colman, 1:01:32 (13)
5. Roger Daniels, 56:51 (8)
6. Matt Metzger, 51:11 (2) **first HS**
7. Tom Borschel, 50:29 (1) **2nd best time**
8. John Cobourn, 52:45 (3)
9. Debbie Waldear, 59:11 (9) **fastest woman**
10. George O'Gara, 1:10:14 (20)
11. Tim Beardall, 50:33 (0)
12. Bob Malain, 52:03 (1)
13. Paul Mankin, 52:03 (1)
14. Phil Bellan, 51:05 (0)
15. Robert Dickinson, 52:09 (1)
16. John Swyers, 57:14 (6)
17. Peggy Smyth, 59:29 (8)
18. Darryl Beardall, 59:35 (8)
19. George Frazier, 55:04 (3)
20. Link Lindquist, 1:07:08 (15)
21. Eric Allen, 52:11 (0)
22. Lloyd Kahn, 1:01:18 (9)
23. Wally Strauss, 1:08:20 (16)
24. Richard Laine, 1:05:20 (13)
25. Kay Willoughby, 1:11:36 (19)
26. Bruce Linscott, 53:39 (1)
27. Milan Zeman, 57:45 (5)
28. Butch Alexander, 53:45 (1)
29. Michael Hoy, 57:49 (5)
30. John Hodge, 52:55 (0)
31. Steve Lyons, 57:59 (5)
32. Michael Burton, 53:03 (0)
33. Toby Pickett, 54:03 (1)
34. Niamh Zwagerman, 1:02:06 (9)
35. Michael Lopez, 54:13 (1)
36. Ken Grace, 54:18 (1)
Team Tamalpa: Daniels, Metzger, Cobourn, Swyers, D. Beardall
1,238 finishers; sunny, warm

81st Dipsea
June 9, 1991

Megan McGowan, who, as an 8-year-old, led virtually the entire 1990 Dipsea before being overhauled by Sal Vasquez, was now not to be denied. And she won by overcoming several formidable obstacles. She lost two handicap minutes (22 to 20) by turning nine (on May 12). She could not have a pacer; her controversial use of one in 1990 provoked a rules change. And, living in southern California, some 400 miles from Mill Valley, McGowan had fewer opportunities to familiarize herself with the course than her leading competitors.

Still, under the tutelage of her father, Michael, a nutritionist, chiropractor and former competitive runner, she was well prepared. The pair came to Marin several times over the preceding months for runs over the course. The family had moved to Wrightwood, in the San Bernardino Mountains, which offered the training advantage of a 6,000' elevation. Megan did hard runs up a ski slope to 7,000' and long Sunday runs on the nearby Pacific Crest Trail at over 8,000'. She gained upper body strength and endurance by swimming and working out on her home Versa-Climber machine. Balance and flexibility were augmented through ballet. Her times came down, including a personal and national 5K record of 18:47 just before the Dipsea. No preparation was overlooked; Megan even wore red full-length pants so she could more efficiently slide down Suicide in case she fell.

McGowan, '89 champ Eve Pell, five-time winner Sal Vasquez, '89 runner-up Joan Colman and modern course record holder Rod Berry were considered the principal contenders. Colman and Berry never started and Vasquez had to abandon his usually irresistable charge when a calf injury flared during the Race. And Pell, starting a minute behind McGowan due to her "winner's penalty," could cut the margin by no more than a scant three seconds. McGowan won by 57 seconds.

McGowan set off with '88 champ Kay Willoughby; the pair, separated by 46 years in age, ran together until the stairs. There McGowan pulled away, gaining first place when she passed George O'Gara before the top of the third flight. She would never relinquish it. Building a two-minute lead at Cardiac, which she hit almost a minute under her target time of 46:00, she was basically unthreatened the rest of the way. With a wrong turn now the only way to lose, McGowan's memory of the route proved flawless.

"I was smiling and happy in Steep Ravine," Megan remembers when she finally thought victory was hers. By the tape, McGowan had knocked an impressive 3:49 off her time from last year. McGowan became the Dipsea's youngest champion ever, at 29 days beyond her ninth birthday, nine months younger than Mike Boitano was in 1971.

After Pell, Mike McManus stormed down the finishing straightaway, running an extraordinary 46:53 from scratch. And this on a course that was longer—Suicide Hill was closed (see below)—than in recent years. The effort brought McManus his fifth best time title.

Tim Minor, Dipsea Runner winner the year before, was 4th. Both he and McManus passed Vasquez and became the first men to finish ahead of him since Joe Ryan pulled the feat in Sal's maiden Dipsea of 1980.

Vasquez, refusing to go by Willoughby over the last yards, crossed the line holding her hand in 5th. At the awards ceremony, McGowan called Vasquez up to the platform. Just as in 1990, he lifted McGowan, to the crowd's warm applause.

A threat by State Park officials to deny the Dipsea a permit unless the open course was abandoned generated substantial pre-Race publicity. A cancellation, at first dismissed as unimaginable, became a distinct possibility as both sides dug in on their positions. State Park employees, backed by officials from Muir Woods, cited environmental damage from the Race, particularly from runners cutting their own shortcuts. The Dipsea Committee countered by saying they were willing to repair any damage, if such damage would be shown to them, and that the Dipsea route predated the parkland. Assemblyman Bill Filante was brought in at the Committee's request and a compromise was reached. The Committee agreed to finance several course "improvements" and to bar runners from a few shortcuts on Windy Gap, Suicide Hill and Swoop Hollow. Neither side considered the issue of an "open course" permanently settled and future disputes were expected (and did follow). Filante, who would die of cancer the following year, spoke at the awards ceremony.

Peter Carter, 12, became the first pre-teen male shirt winner in years, finishing 19th.

Don Kardong, who was fourth in the 1976 Olympic marathon, three seconds from the bronze medal, finished 31st. The former Stanford runner was covering the race for a *Runner's World* magazine feature (May 1992 issue). Kardong charmed the crowd at the awards ceremony by holding up his black shirt and saying, "I had just missed an Olympic medal by three seconds. I didn't want to miss one of these." In a rush, the 35th and last shirt had been claimed just eight seconds behind him.

❑ In a rare appearance of three generations of a family in the same Dipsea, matriarch Els Tuinzing was 551st (1:38:25, 22hc), her son Kees Tuinzing was 59th (57:39, 3hc) and his son, 12-year-old Andre, was 141st (1:06:00, 12hc). The popular Dutch-born Els extended her record as oldest female finisher (69). She would further extend the record to 71 in 1993.

❑ Jack Kirk, also setting a new age record at 84, struggled in at 2:33:28, almost 23 minutes behind the next-to-last Invitational runner. Afterward, as he got into his aged Volkswagen in Mill Valley for the ride back to Mariposa, Kirk told this writer, "I just couldn't get up the steps."

1. Megan McGowan, 1:05:32 (20) [:57]
2. Eve Pell, 1:05:29 (19)
3. Mike McManus, 46:53 (0) **first man, best time**
4. Tim Minor, 49:26 (1) **2nd best time**
5. Sal Vasquez, 53:48 (5)
6. Kay Willoughby, 1:08:48 (20)
7. Roger Daniels, 57:53 (9)
8. Bob Malain, 1:06:08 (17)
9. Link Lindquist, 1:05:37 (16)
10. Steve Lyons, 56:09 (6)
11. AnnaMarie Hagens, 58:41 (8) **fastest woman**
12. Darryl Beardall, 58:48 (8)
13. Erin Vali, 51:01 (0)
14. John Cobourn, 54:08 (3)
15. George O'Gara, 1:12:10 (21)
16. Richard Laine, 1:05:12 (14)
17. Greg Nacco, 52:14 (1)
18. Robert Dickinson, 52:23 (1)
19. Peter Carter, 58:42 (7)
20. Robert Alexander, 53:51 (2)
21. Lloyd Kahn, 1:01:55 (10)
22. Christie Patterson, 1:02:12 (10)
23. John Swyers, 58:15 (6)
24. Ken Grace, 53:18 (1)
25. Bradford Bryon, 53:18 (1)
26. Scott Strait, 53:22 (1)
27. Ken Wilson, 53:22 (1)
28. Jon Sargent, 56:23 (4) **1st HS**
29. Butch Alexander, 53:35 (1)
30. Robin Paine, 1:02:36 (10)
31. Don Kardong, 55:41 (3)
32. Kimberly Holmes, 1:00:41 (8)
33. John Hodge, 52:42 (0)
34. Alec Isabeau, 52:44 (0)
35. Don McCarthy, 56:49 (4)
36. Leslie McMullin, 1:01:51 (9)
Team Tamalpa: McGowan, Pell, Willoughby, Daniels and Lyons
1,188 finishers; foggy but windless, sunny on highest ridges

82nd Dipsea
June 14, 1992

Megan McGowan shocked just about everyone but herself and her father/coach Michael with a convincing, and seemingly effortless, repeat win.

McGowan had lost four handicap minutes from 1991; two for reaching her tenth birthday (in May), one for being a winner during the previous five years and another in a general reduction of the women's headstarts. It was the largest handicap loss that any runner had suffered in some 20 years.

Also considered fatal to McGowan's chances were the entries of three runners who were the best, or near the best, for their ages in the United States.

Shirley Matson, 51, had broken every major U.S. road record for women over 50 at distances from 5K (17:28) through the marathon (2:50:26). Several months earlier she had been one of the first two women ever admitted into the venerable Olympic Club, founders of the Dipsea. That honor, and a few visits to the course, convinced her to try the Dipsea for the first time.

Jim Bowers, 53, held the national high school mile record as a prep in Illinois. Years later, the airline pilot set the U.S. marathon record for masters. Though he raced infrequently in recent years, those marks indicate a talent rare in Dipsea annals. In March, Bowers won outright the rugged Lake Ilsanjo race in Santa Rosa, beating Alec Isabeau, who had run 52:44 from scratch at the '91 Dipsea. Bowers was immediately installed as co-favorite with Matson in what would also be a debut effort.

And Joan Ottaway (Colman until her marriage to Dipsea veteran Steve Ottaway earlier in the year) was returning. Ottaway, 48, had been 2nd in 1989, 4th in 1990. A serious knee problem slowed her during '91 but she underwent arthroscopic surgery and seemed fully recovered. Just two weeks before the Dipsea, Ottaway ran 36:48 at the Pacific Sun

10K, setting a national single-age record. McGowan's only good news seemed to be that five-time champion Sal Vasquez would miss the Race; he had injured a leg while skiing.

But right from the start, setting off in the same 16-minute group with Matson, McGowan showed her mettle and talent. She challenged the speedy Matson on Throckmorton, even setting the pace. Matson hung on through two flights of stairs, then lost contact with McGowan on the third set.

McGowan never eased up. Coming down the road after Hauke Hollow, McGowan passed 1989 champion Eve Pell, who had started three minutes ahead. Pell, considered a possible winner herself in '92 (she finished 6th), later reported that "Megan was flying." Down Suicide, Megan passed 1988 champion Kay Willoughby, a brilliant downhiller.

By Muir Woods Road, McGowan was in first for good. Matson kept up a dogged pursuit that would leave her a still substantial 1:13 behind at Stinson. No one else had a chance. Bowers (3rd), hesitating at a few of the course's trickier intersections, ran only 3:37 faster than McGowan; he had started eight minutes behind. Ottaway (4th), starting two minutes behind McGowan, ran three minutes slower. And Mike McManus (5th), scratch, never got within five minutes of McGowan.

Megan's actual time of 58:09 proved to be the fastest of any female in the race, and this from a third-grader. The time trophy added to the bounty she won, including "The Bear" for first overall, one as part of the winning team and the Norman Bright (presented by Bright himself) for the second successive year. She also became the Dipsea's first female two-time winner.

McGowan's clock time (actual less handicap) of 42:09—the all-but impossible time that it would have taken a scratch runner to beat her—was the fastest in 15 years. It immediately set off protests that women's handicaps needed to be reduced if scratch runners were ever again to have a chance of winning.

McManus won the best time award by an extraordinary 2:37 over runner-up Tim Minor and 4:01 over 3rd fastest Guy Palmer. This despite a nagging cramp, which slowed him. It was McManus' 6th best time award in six appearances as an adult, one short of the oldest record in Dipsea annals, the seven of Mason Hartwell. The previous fall, McManus had lost all his many Dipsea trophies; they were stored in his parents' house, which was destroyed in the Oakland hills conflagration.

Link Lindquist, 7th, pulled off the rare feat of matching his age in years (64) with his time in minutes (64:27).

There was a spirited battle for the later black shirts. The last 16 (places 20-35) were decided in a span of only 54 seconds. The final shirt, #35, went, for the second time, to George Frazier. Passed himself by Kurt Ryan on the final straightaway, Frazier then somewhat reluctantly went by his long-time mentor, 1968 champion Don Pickett, yards before the finish line. Frazier and Pickett had come in holding hands together the previous year.

Near the road at the foot of Suicide, a Muir Woods National Monument ranger recorded bib numbers and shouted, "You're disqualified" to some nine prominent Invitational section competitors (but missing the first to take the shortcut, Joan Ottaway). These runners had taken an obscure shortcut, an apparent violation of Dipsea rules which state that, "Runners must stay on trails while in Muir Woods." The ranger's words naturally unnerved the "disqualified" runners. One, perennial high finisher John Cobourn, actually stopped and argued, dashing his shirt chances. When three of the "disqualified" group—Steve Ottaway (Joan's husband), Kurt Ryan and George Frazier—finished in the top 35, the matter took on added urgency.

The Dipsea Committee, caught in a dilemma over holding to their open course principles and satisfying a key jurisdiction, opted, during a hasty discussion before the awards ceremony, for a compromise. No one was disqualified (Race rules state that only the Dipsea Committee can do so) but the names of each offender would be turned over to Muir Woods staff for a $25 trail violation fine (which was later raised to $100).

The issue became a *cause célèbre* within Marin's running community, some saying the group (which came to be known as "The Muir Woods Nine") should have been disqualified, others defending them, others saying the matter was being blown out of proportion. One of the Nine, Heidi Hugo, said she wasn't even in the Race. In an attempt to avoid further legal battles, a compromise fine of the original $25 was proposed. Cobourn and Steve Ottaway paid, the others, represented by attorney Mike Hoy (one of the Nine himself and a two-time black shirt winner) elected to defend themselves. On September 24, one day before the case was to be heard in Federal court in San Francisco, the defendants produced deed maps which showed that the shortcut area was apparently inside Mt. Tamalpais State Park (where not all shortcuts are proscribed) rather than Muir Woods. There was thus ambiguity over whether the issue was within Federal court jurisdiction and the case was dismissed. Ottaway and Cobourn eventually got refunds.

❑ The Sunday evening before the Race, there was a Dipsea Dinner at the Dipsea Cafe in Mill Valley. It was the first reunion since the lavish 75th anniversary affair in 1985. Nineteen champions attended, making it the largest gathering of former winners ever. They were, in order of year of victory: Alan Nelson, Ernie Marinoni, Charlie Richesin, Ralph Perry, Herb Stockman, Bob Hope, Phil Smith, Gregg Sparks, Carl Jensen, Don Pickett, Norman Bright, Mike Boitano, Mary Etta Boitano (who had become Mary Etta Blanchard two weeks earlier), Darryl Beardall, Florianne Harp, Sal Vasquez, Christie Patterson, Kay Willoughby and Eve Pell.

❑ Long-time Dipsea Committee member, and finish line timer, Jim "Birdman" Weil retired from the Committee earlier in the year. He still kept his role as handicapper. At the awards ceremony, he was honored with a black T-shirt numbered "0" and reading "BIRDMAN."

❑ Eyrle Aceves, 77, finished in just over 3 hours. It marked his first appearance in the Dipsea since being runner-up to Clarence Hall in the 1938 Race.

❑ High school star Brock Tessman, 16, won the trophy as first Dipsea Runner with his 55:37 (3hc). The official results wrongly show Invitational regular Albert Clark, 78, in the Dipsea Runner section and finishing ahead of Tessman.

1. Megan McGowan, 58:09 (16hc) [1:13]
   fastest woman
2. Shirley Matson, 59:22 (16)
3. Jim Bowers, 54:32 (8) **1st man**
4. Joan Ottaway, 1:01:09 (14)
5. Mike McManus, 47:18 (0) **best time**
6. Eve Pell, 1:06:22 (19)
7. Link Lindquist, 1:04:27 (17)
8. Russ Kiernan, 56:53 (8)
9. Tim Minor, 49:55 (1) **2nd best time**
10. Roger Daniels, 59:00 (10)
11. Robert Malain, 1:07:20 (18)
12. Guy Palmer, 51:19 (1)
13. AnnaMarie Hagans, 58:25 (8)
14. Leslie McMullin, 1:00:27 (10)
15. Robert Alexander, 52:57 (2)
16. Robert Dickinson, 52:23 (1)
17. Peter Carter, 57:30 (6)
18. Stephen Lyons, 57:37 (6)
19. Kelly Lawson, 59:43 (8)
20. Alec Isabeau, 52:06 (0)
21. Christie Patterson Pastalka, 1:02:06 (10)
22. Bruce Mace, 53:10 (1)
23. Ronald Brown, 54:11 (2)
24. Steve Ottaway, 54:13 (2)
25. Bradford Byron, 53:14 (1)
26. Jon Sargent, 55:17 (3) **1st HS**
27. Alan Reynolds, 52:21 (0)
28. Steve Stephens, 57:25 (5)
29. Lloyd Kahn, 1:02:30 (10)
30. Darryl Beardall, 1:01:38 (9)
31. Ken Grace, 53:46 (1)
32. Butch Alexander, 54:47 (2)
33. Don McCarthy, 57:53 (5)
34. Kurt Ryan, 53:55 (1)
35. George Frazier, 57:00 (4)
36. Don Pickett, 1:10:03 (17)

Team Tamalpa: McGowan, Lindquist, Kiernan, Daniels and Palmer
1,251 finishers; clear and mild

83rd Dipsea
June 13, 1993

Shirley Matson became the third different 52-year-old woman to win in six years and Dipsea newcomer Dave Dunham broke Mike McManus' six-Race undefeated streak as best time winner.

Matson, clearly the nation's top over-50 woman runner and holder of every major 50-plus U.S. record, was installed as the heavy favorite as soon as the 1993 handicaps were revealed April 1. Women in their 50's had been penalized only one minute, considered mild given their recent successes. So Matson, now a year older, had the same 16-minute headstart as in 1992 when she finished second to Megan McGowan. McGowan, meanwhile, was hit with a second successive four minute loss of handicap; two for turning 11, one in the general women's adjustment, and one more in a new interpretation of the rule that said winners lose a minute for EACH victory during the previous five years. When Matson blazed a sensational 36:46 at the local Pacific Sun 10K thirteen days before the Dipsea, her stock rose even higher.

But three strong runners, all basically new to the Dipsea, entered to keep Matson nervous. Most feared by Matson—even predicted by her to win—was Gabriele Andersen, 48. Andersen had gained worldwide fame during the 1984 Olympic marathon when she refused to be helped during the final quarter-mile despite obvious severe distress. She then went on to become the nation's top masters runner (she competed for Switzerland in the Olympics but holds dual U.S.-Swiss citizenship by virtue of her marriage to Dick Andersen, who also ran the '93 Dipsea). Gabriele even still held the U.S. masters 10K road record of 34:24 until the day before the Dipsea (when Francie Larrieu-Smith bettered it). She would start only two minutes behind Matson. Injuries, however, had forced Andersen to severely cut back her training and racing mileage during the previous two years.

Another was Joe Patterson, the Australian who won the 1975 Dipsea while on a one-day layover in San Francisco awaiting his flight home. Now 58, with a 12-minute handicap (five more than he had 19 years earlier), he was an unknown factor.

And third, although less likely a threat because he started scratch, was Dunham. Dunham had been voted New England's Runner of the Year in 1992 and once held the record at the prestigious, all-uphill Mt. Washington Road Race.

On a hot morning, Matson caught all who started ahead of her by Dynamite, the last being 8-year-old Rachel Pitts. (Pitts, one of four pre-teen Pitts siblings running with their parents, would hang on for the 35th and last black t-shirt.) By the time Matson hit Cardiac in 40:26, right on her target for a one-hour Dipsea, her lead was several minutes. Matson eased on the downhills—her finish time was 1:00:34, or 72 seconds slower than in '92—which opened the door slightly for Andersen.

Andersen did gain ground. But her pre-Race decision to take the clearer-to-follow but longer Moors route ended whatever slight chance she had to catch Matson. Andersen did notch the day's fastest women's time, by a single second over McGowan. She became the oldest runner, male or female, to win the best time award.

Meanwhile, Sal Vasquez, 53, was running one of the best Dipseas of his unparalleled career. Lightly regarded because he had to drop out of Pacific Sun with an injury, Vasquez scorched a 52:52 for 3rd place. He became only the third runner in Dipsea history, following Ray Locke (age 60) in 1918 and Norman Bright in 1970 (age 60) and '71 (age 61) to run a time in minutes below his age. McGowan surprisingly ran 64 seconds slower than in '92 and had to settle for 4th. A fall in Steep Ravine likely cost her the women's best time trophy.

Joe Patterson, who started with McGowan and ran with her much of the way, was next, 18 seconds behind.

Then came Dunham, winning a sensational

Race-long, back-and-forth duel with McManus. Dunham had arrived from his New Hampshire home only the previous afternoon, which gave him time only to take a practice jog over the second half of the course. So he made a point of tucking in behind McManus in the early going. Though they reached the top of the steps in a swift 5:34, the uphill specialist Dunham later said, "I would have preferred to go even faster."

Dunham twisted an ankle down Suicide and McManus surged ahead. Dunham caught back up on Dynamite. He finally opened daylight over McManus on the Hogsback, then stretched it to almost 40 seconds by the top of Cardiac (which Dunham reached in 32:25).

"I was running as hard as I could. He was just getting away," McManus reported afterward. "I concentrated on keeping him within reach for the downhills, and expected he wouldn't know all the shortcuts."

Dunham didn't make any route mistakes but McManus did recatch him on the downhill after Insult. Dunham, hearing McManus's steps on Panoramic, stepped aside for him at the second cut back onto the trail. McManus held a single stride lead going over the stile. But Dunham then unleashed a fearsome kick. He nipped Christie Patterson for 6th and finished eight seconds up on McManus.

Looking on was Thomas Hartwell, the 75-year-old son of Mason Hartwell. He had come out for the first time in decades to watch what appeared to be inevitable, McManus's tying of Mason's record of seven best time awards, which had stood since 1926. No one had beaten McManus in his previous six Dipseas. Instead, he saw his father's record survive. McManus also was denied a record fourth consecutive best time award; Hartwell and Otto Boeddiker, and McManus in 1986-88, also had streaks of three.

Next, 9th, was Russ Kiernan, his 14th top-10 finish, tying Jack Kirk and behind only Darryl Beardall (with 19). Kiernan joked at the awards ceremony how his 9th place finish gave him every top-10 black shirt, except #1.

Jon Sargent, a junior at Monte Vista H.S. (Alamo, CA), became the first three-time winner of the high school trophy, an award dating from 1906. But because he didn't finish in the top 50, which is as deep as Race day results were prepared, he was not acknowledged at the awards ceremony. In fact, his 75th was the worst place ever to capture the honor.

❑ Once again there were Race-threatening permit problems, this time with the Golden Gate National Recreation Area. Some GGNRA managers were insistent on keeping all runners on the Moors, eliminating the Panoramic Highway shortcuts. The Dipsea Committee was upset both with the late presentation of the demands and by what they felt was yet another in a series of restrictions. There was no permit within two weeks of the Race date; the Dipsea Committee was preparing to resurrect the old finish in Stinson Beach, avoiding the GGNRA parking lot, if necessary to keep the Race going. Finally, with the help of some intermediaries, the crisis was defused, at least temporarily. GGNRA officials issued the permit, but vowed to put new course restrictions in place for 1994. An exceptionally high number of rangers, many with note pads in hand, monitored the course.

❑ A Dipsea Dinner, organized by the author, was held at the Community Church of Mill Valley (on the course, opposite Old Mill Park) the Friday before the Race. A special attempt was made to round up best time winners and holders of 43 such titles were present. Speeches were made by Patricia English Fanelli, Joe Patterson, Rod Berry, Mike McManus, Byron Lowry and Ron Elijah.

❑ A Dipsea Race Hall of Fame was inaugurated in 1993. The first five inductees were announced at the dinner. They were: the late Judge Timothy Fitzpatrick and Emma Reiman, Jack Kirk, Norman Bright and Sal Vasquez. Fitzpatrick's plaque was accepted by Jim Stephenson in behalf of the Olympic Club, Reiman's by woman pioneer Elaine Pedersen. Bright and Vasquez were both present. Kirk received his, to a standing ovation, Race day after extending his record as the oldest finisher (age 86).

□ The hot weather, warmest since at least 1981, contributed to numerous medical problems. Three runners were transported to Marin hospitals but all were released soon after. One runner finished with his face and glasses completely covered in blood. April Powers, one of the fastest women ever to run the Race, suffered a bizarre spill in her maiden Dipsea. Having twisted her ankle earlier, she stumbled over the final stile and landed on her neck on the Shoreline Highway pavement. She still finished 21st.

But no story was more bizarre than Andre Tuinzing's. The 15-year-old collapsed some three times during the run. Someone put Andre in a car to revive him, removing his shoes. When Andre came to he set off running again, but forgot his shoes. He finished barefoot, in 425th place, the last position for automatic 1994 Invitational status. He then collapsed again. Huge blisters forced him to cancel a soccer trip planned for later in the month. He never found his shoes.

□ West Valley Track Club's expected challenge to Tamalpa's team title dominance fizzled when their top two stars, Joan Ottaway (injured) and Joe King did not run. Tamalpa easily won for the 17th straight year.

1. Shirley Matson, 1:00:34 (16) [:38]
2. Gabriele Andersen, 59:12 (14) **fastest woman**
3. Sal Vasquez, 52:52 (7) **1st man**
4. Megan McGowan, 59:13 (12)
5. Joe Patterson, 59:31 (12)
6. Dave Dunham, 48:24 (0) **best time**
7. Christie Patterson, 1:00:26 (12)
8. Mike McManus, 48:32 (0) **2nd best time**
9. Russ Kiernan, 57:58 (9)
10. Link Lindquist, 1:08:36 (18)
11. Bob Malain, 1:09:41 (19)
12. Leslie McMullin, 1:00:58 (10)
13. Greg Nacco, 52:05 (1)
14. Hank Lawson, 53:15 (2)
15. Mike Repp, 58:18 (7)
16. Gordon Abbott, 56:23 (5)
17. Butch Alexander, 53:25 (2)
18. Guy Palmer, 53:03 (1)
19. Robert Dickinson, 53:15 (1)
20. Steve Stephens, 57:19 (5)
21. April Powers, 1:00:21 (8)
22. John Swyers, 1:00:23 (8)
23. Scott Strait, 54:29 (2)
24. Debbi Waldear, 1:02:34 (10)
25. Erin Vali, 52:38 (0)
26. Bruce Linscott, 53:44 (1)
27. Kelly Lawson, 1:00:47 (8)
28. Don McCarthy, 57:49 (5)
29. Kim Rupert, 1:00:52 (8)
30. Kurt Ryan, 53:57 (1)
31. Jamie Wendel, 1:02:58 (10)
32. Mark Richtman, 55:02 (2)
33. Bruce Mace, 54:06 (1)
34. John Hodge, 54:10 (1)
35. Rachel Pitts, 1:15:19 (22)
36. Steve Lyons, 1:00:40 (7)
75. Jon Sargent, 58:25 (2) **1st HS**
Team Tamalpa: McGowan, C. Patterson, Kiernan, McMullin and Nacco
1,320 finishers; sunny and hot

Emma Reiman, the most successful of the Women's Dipsea Hikers, winning in 1920. (Courtesy Chuck Ford photos)

THE WOMEN'S DIPSEA HIKES

The five Women's Dipsea Hikes (1918-1922) stand out as pioneering events in women's sports. They may have been the first women's long-distance races in the United States. They were the only women's cross country races for decades. And they were certainly the nation's largest women's distance races until the 1970's.

The Hikes occurred even before women were first permitted into the Olympic Games, in 1928. During those 1928 Games, several women collapsed at the conclusion of the 800 meters, their longest race. That helped prompt an Olympic ban on all races beyond 200 meters that was not lifted until 1960. The women's marathon was only added to the Olympic schedule in 1984. But on the Dipsea course, more than 50 years before the AAU opened American distance racing to women, several hundred women did compete in as grueling a cross country race as any available to men.

Though called "hikes" to escape the AAU ban, they were bona fide races. The top entrants trained for the event, most all ran, winners were given trophies, times were recorded and posted.

The Hikes, completely separate from the Dipsea Race itself, were founded, sponsored and well promoted by the San Francisco newspaper, the *Call*. It was partly responding to the success its rival, the *Bulletin*, had with a race it started in 1912, Cross-City (today's Bay to Breakers).

1st Women's Hike
April 21, 1918

The inaugural Hike was Sunday, April 21, 1918; the "men's" Dipsea would be in September. The 307 entrants, some three-fourths from San Francisco, were advised to take the 8:15 a.m. ferry for Sausalito, which made a train connection to Mill Valley in ample time for the 10 a.m. start. Buses and stages also met the ferry to take spectators directly to the Willow Camp finish line. All had been sternly warned that, "Any person caught setting pace for a contestant will be detained by soldiers who will patrol the course, and the offending contestant will be disqualified." Other rules prohibited anyone under 17 and "professional hikers." The Dipsea Indians, organizers of the Dipsea, provided some of the timing staff, though Reese notes that two of the Indians, as a prank, dressed in women's clothes and ran toward the finish line moments before the first true finisher.

Here is the *Call's* account of that historic first Hike.

Edith Hickman of the Center Club won the Call's *Dipsea Hike from Mill Valley to Willow Camp, covering the distance in 1 hour 18 minutes 48 seconds. To Miss Hickman goes the honor of winning the first cross country hike ever held in the United States in which women were the exclusive participants.*

Miss Hickman took an early lead, as was expected by her coach, Eddie Stout [winner of the 1918 Cross-City], and was the first to reach the top of the stairs. She was never headed after that and finished about three minutes ahead of her nearest rival.

Miss Vivian Black, who won second place, made the trail in 1:20:20, and although she didn't arrive at the finish in as good a condition as did Miss Hickman, owing to an upset stomach caused by swallowing lemon juice, she announced after resting a few minutes on the beach that she felt fine and if necessary could walk home.

Miss E. Eahlman came in third, making the distance in 1:23:48. Miss Eahlman arrived at Willow Camp in fine shape and later went bathing in the surf.

Of the 177 girl hikers to toe the mark at Mill

Valley, 143 of them were listed as they arrived at Willow Camp. Oscar Turnblad, George James and Vincent Finigan, official scorers, after waiting for fifteen minutes decided that most likely the remainder of the girls had dropped out and closed up their books. Therefore the names of the 143 to finish are the only ones that are published. An hour before the hike started several hundred persons gathered around the starting point at Mill Valley to see the start of the first women's cross country hike ever held in the country.

Each train arriving at Mill Valley brought scores of persons anxious to see their girl friends who had entered the contest.

All Saturday evening the road leading to Willow Camp was crowded with touring cars filled to capacity with persons anxious to see the finish.

Frank Airey, proprietor of the Hotel Airey [Sea Beach Hotel] at Willow Camp, said that never in the history of the town had so many persons gathered to witness a race and never had so many machines gone over the trail.

More than 3,000 people were at Willow Camp, lined up along the road, waiting for the contestants to arrive.

Seven minutes after the shot was fired that sent the contestants over the trail the spectators at Willow Camp were advised of the start by the exploding of barrage bombs.

Within fifteen minutes after the hike had started the spectators at Willow Camp were being advised minutely of the status of the hikers at various points on the trail by soldiers from the Presidio, who wig-wagged the information from peak to peak.

At intervals of five minutes friends of the contestants at Willow Camp knew just where their favorites were on the trail and how they were placing on the trail.

This feature was the talk of the holiday crowds, who had gathered to see the hike.

One of the many features of the hike that evoked considerable comment was the fact that, with two exceptions, every girl who finished the hike arrived in good condition.

Judge T.I. Fitzpatrick [co-founder of the Dipsea Race], James Brennan and Edward Cunha were loud in their praises of the manner in which George James [the event's principal organizer, and the starter at the first Dipsea in 1905] and officials of the Call handled the hike. Luncheon was served the contestants within twenty minutes after they had negotiated the course. By 3 o'clock each contestant that had finished had had her lunch, and in most cases was found basking in the sun-kissed sands of the beach at Willow Camp.

Yesterday was a day that will long be remembered by the hikers and by the persons who witnessed the start and finish of the contest. It was truly a wonderful day.

1. Edith Hickman, 1:18:48
2. Vivian Black, 1:20:20
3. E. Eahlman, 1:23:48
4. Priscilla Mitchell, 1:26:37
5. Lucille Mahan, 1:27:14
6. May Gordon, 1:27:30
7. Helen Manning, 1:27:57
8. Edith Williams, 1:29:34
9. A. Eahlman, 1:31:14
10. Marion Mehl, 1:31:45

2nd Women's Hike
June 8, 1919

Clearly pleased with their first Hike, the *Call* announced that for 1919, "All plans have been made with the end in view of making this the biggest women's athletic event ever staged." Actually, entries fell to 142 and the number of finishers to 74 but the event was again judged a great success. Here is the account of the winner, Mrs. Marion Mehl of San Francisco (who had been assigned bib #1), as it appeared in the *Call*.

When I finished in tenth place in the Call race over the Dipsea trail last year I resolved firmly that I would not rest contented till I crossed that line a winner.

Last year I was very inexperienced. I jumped into the race on a dare; I had little or no preliminary training. In fact I did not even know the trail, and that cost me a position up among the first five, for on two occasions I got off on wrong roads, thereby losing several minutes. But I finished strong and, with every confidence that I could win and better last year's winners time.

This year I started my training nine weeks in advance. I went over the trail at least half a dozen times, once in the company of Edgar Stout [the 1918 Cross-City champion who had helped previous Hike winner Edith Hickman], who gave me some very valuable hints. I was thoroughly familiar with the course at least and that gave me great confidence.

When I stepped on the starting line it was with perfect assurance that I was going to beat my field to Dipsea [the finish]. I knew that the field was a much harder one to win from than that of a year ago.

When we got off I did not try to take the lead immediately. I took my time for the first half mile, sizing up my competitors as I jogged along. At the bottom of the big stairs I decided to let myself out and see what I could do. I was impatient and was feeling so fine that I could not restrain myself. It was here, too, that those who had started to make a hard pace began to show signs of exhaustion. As I passed contestant after contestant my confidence grew greater.

I passed the last group shortly after we reached the top of the stairs. Then I never looked around again. I kept on and on. I feel that if I had some one behind me spurring me on to greater efforts I would have cut down the time considerably more.

I took all the steep grades on a jogging run and alternated with a twenty or thirty yard walk when I was tired. On the down grades I generally walked at a fast clip until I rested again, then I broke into a run.

From the Lone Pine to Dipsea I never stopped running once. Several times during the race, especially after a long climb, I had slight pains in the side, but I did not let them worry me.

It was certainly fine to see the big crowd gathered waiting at Dipsea and to feel that I was first. I was not a bit exhausted after the race and the thrill of victory more than compensated for the pains spent in training and the hard work on the trail.

Emma Reiman, who would win two years later,

was runner-up. Anna Anderes, apparently the sister of 1916 Dipsea champion Henry Anderes, was third.

1. Marion Mehl, 1:15:56
2. Emma Reiman, 1:17:55
3. Anna Anderes, 1:18:42
4. Irene Manners, 1:19:02
5. Gladys Garcia, 1:20:23
6. Fanny Joy, 1:21:48
7. Olga Vallanes, 1:21:59
8. Frances Desmond, 1:26:18
9. Catherine Walther, 1:26:23
10. Nellie Holland, 1:27:02

3rd Women's Hike
May 8, 1920

This was the largest Women's Dipsea Hike, with 304 starters.

Several dozen prizes were donated. The *Call* contributed the first prize of a gold wrist watch, valued at a then sizable $75. The Olympic Club gave a sterling silver coffee set for second place. San Francisco Mayor James Rolph, Jr. donated a sterling silver loving cup. Other prizes included jewelry, hose, a bathing suit "to the heavyweight hiker," a "box of bonbons," and a "boudoir lamp." A trophy was offered to "the best looking girl." The Unione Sportiva Club, which had just won the first Dipsea team trophy the previous September, presented a trophy to the "first Italian girl." Also promised was a post-hike luncheon at the Sea Beach Inn. In the *Call's* words, "It will be a real luncheon, girls. No hash, beans, stale buns or the like." The Outdoor Art Club (still at the same site in central Mill Valley) was again used for check-in.

The winner was Mrs. Priscilla Mitchell Swearingen, who came "sprinting down the home stretch like a varsity trackster finishing a hundred yard dash." At the finish, "she turned a handspring ... her face wreathed in smiles." She had been fourth in 1918. Swearingen's time was a new record

1:14:44. Defending champion Marion Mehl was on hand to greet her. Runner-up for the second year in a row was Emma Reiman, 65 seconds behind.

The finish line crowd was "estimated at 5,000 by Sheriff A.H. Pape, lined up twenty deep . . . at Willow Camp." Local hotelier Frank Airey "remarked after the race that the crowd was the largest ever attracted to the sea beach at Willow Camp."

The Call correspondent made much of the women's outfits:

There was every color of the rainbow and then some. At the start it looked as if some Broadway musical show had suddenly disbanded and left its beauty chorus stranded. It seemed as if every hiker tried to outdo the other when it came to wearing something a bit different in the way of hiking togs.

Some wore khaki; others everything from what appeared to be the latest edict from Paree in the way of hiking costumes. But few wore skirts; the majority preferred khaki trousers and blue or black bloomers. Some wore pink and yellow waists; others wore white middies. All wore bandanas to keep their hair in shape.

Special note was made of the official race Kissel car going from Mill Valley to Willow Camp in forty-five minutes, and hitting 51 miles per hour on the return.

1. Priscilla Swearingen, 1:14:44
2. Emma Reiman, 1:15:09
3. Agnes Crwonka, 1:15:48
4. Dora Rhodes, 1:15:58
5. Anna Anderes, 1:16:40
6. Margaret Reis, 1:17:40
7. Angelina Ferrera, 1:17:49
8. Charlotte Lawrence, 1:19:28
9. Oppie Kosta, 1:21:31
10. Rosalie Emmott, 1:21:32

4th Women's Hike
May 15, 1921

San Francisco's *Bulletin* newspaper, founder of the Cross-City Race, took over sponsorship of the Hike. Entries fell but were still a very impressive 250. Of these, 125 started and 75 finished within the time limit of two-and-a-half hours for recording results. Over 100 volunteers, including a chaperone, Alma Reed, and a bonfire committee headed by Fire Commissioner William Mikulich, were acknowledged in the Hike program.

Emma Reiman, runner-up the previous two years, was now an easy winner. Though her time was slower than in 1920, Reiman finished more than five minutes ahead of the second woman.

The *Bulletin* correspondent, William Unmack, waxed rhapsodic about the blonde Reiman: "[Reiman] had a golden smile with her that typified the soul of contentment, health and happiness . . . If ever there was a natural-born girl athlete, that girl is Emma Reiman . . . Emma is the Mason Hartwell of the girls and that means champion of them all . . . She ran across that [finish] line in beautiful form— athletic form, I mean—and had every appearance of having just stepped out of a band-box . . . There was no dust, perspiration-streaked face, no drawn lines or signs of distress."

As first prize, Reiman was given a choice of the *Bulletin*'s silver cup or a $75 pearl necklace donated by the Oriental Pearl Company. She chose the cup, as did the next two finishers. After considerable debate about what to do with the necklace, it was awarded to Reiman as well.

Remarkably, three sisters who completed the 1921 Hike—Helen, Laura and Amelia Vezzani—are all alive in 1993.

1. Emma Reiman, 1:16:15
2. Emila Caldera, 1:22:10
3. Anna Anderes, 1:23:30
4. Elna Lane, 1:26:45
5. Peggy O'Mahoney, 1:27:55
6. Eleanor Jackson, 1:28:01
7. Frances Desmond, 1:28:32
8. Charlotte Lawrence, 1:28:45
9. Anna Ramos, 1:29:10
10. Margaret Wallace, 1:30:30

5th Women's Hike
June 11, 1922

Although they didn't know it, the 159 entrants, 52 starters and 45 finishers within the time limit were participating in the last major women's distance race in the United States for decades. Entries were down, although they were higher than the "men's" Dipsea for the fifth year in a row and sponsor support remained strong. The *Bulletin* continued to give the event feature coverage and the prizes donated exceeded those in the "regular" Dipsea. Special arrangements had even been made to transmit up-to-the-minute race progress reports to Willow Camp through a radio-telephone network linked to the City's Fairmont Hotel.

Emma Reiman won for the second successive year. Hike veterans Fanny Joy, Anna Anderes Furger and 1920 champion Priscilla Mitchell Swearingen followed. Here is Reiman's account of the race as it appeared in the *Bulletin*.

I realized when I entered the Bulletin's *annual Dipsea hike that I would have to be in the very best of condition if I expected to retain the laurel that I was fortunate enough to win. Spurred on by the ambition of being the only girl to win this great event on two occasions, I was able to get into the best of shape, and, believe me, it was that condition that told over the last part of the trail from Mill Valley to Willow Camp.*

I knew that if I were to make good my great hopes, I must establish an early lead over the other contest-

ants and I set out at a fast clip at the very start. As the finish drew near, however, I became possessed with another ambition—that of establishing a new record, and I am the happiest girl in the world to be able to say that I succeeded.

The credit of the victory, though, does not belong entirely to myself, but to Professor Ed. Sparks, who has assisted me in all of my training. The manner in which the Bulletin handled the event, too, is a credit to girls' athletics, and I sincerely hope that this hike will be continued for many years to come.

1. Emma Reiman, 1:12:06
2. Fanny Joy, 1:14:40
3. Anna Anderes Furger, 1:16:19
4. Priscilla Mitchell Swearingen, 1:17:09
5. Nellie Holland, 1:17:19
6. Josephine Urr, 1:18:10
7. Emilia Caldera, 1:19:03
8. Katy Jensen, 1:20:21
9. Violet Robin, 1:20:53
10. Eleanor Jackson, 1:21:43

It wasn't. Bowing to pressures from church groups that the Hikes were somehow immoral, and from some San Francisco physicians that they were dangerous, the event was permanently cancelled.

No women ran in the "regular" Dipsea until Nancy Dreyer in 1950, and no other woman until 1959. Reiman's time of 1:12:06 over the Dipsea would not be surpassed by a woman until 1969. Women were not officially allowed into the race until 1971. Since then, though, nine different women have won a total of ten Dipseas.

The rapid lowering of times during those five golden years of 1918 to 1922—Reiman's 1:12:06 was swifter than ten of the 71 men in the '22 Dipsea—invites speculation on "what might have been" for the Dipsea and women's sports in general had the Hikes been continued.

A celebration of the 75th anniversary of the first Dipsea Women's Hike was staged on April 21, 1993. Ninety women, including Elaine Pedersen, the only woman in the 1966 and '67 Dipseas, ran over the route. Some wore period costumes. Two

Hike survivors, Marie Krauter (93) and Laura Vez-zani Stratta (88), appeared at the start.

Emma Reiman
(1899-1990)

Emma Reiman was clearly the greatest of the Women's Dipsea Hikers. She was twice a winner and twice second in her four races. And she set a women's course record that would not be broken for 57 years.

But Reiman had no further opportunities to race after 1922. She went on to become one of the leading figures in San Francisco Bay Area hiking circles, serving as president of both the California Alpine Club and the Mt. Tamalpais Conservation Club. She lived independently for years in her own lovely home near the Dipsea steps. She married, for the first time, while in her 40's.

Reiman's later years, however, were tragic. Alone after her husband died (she had no children or close relatives) and in failing health, she was forced to live first in a mobile home, then in a nursing facility. Finally, she was strapped into a wheelchair for her own safety. The "happiest girl in the world" with "a golden smile . . . that typified the soul of contentment, health and happiness" died alone in 1990 at age 91. The one friend she asked to be notified was not told for two years.

In 1993, Emma Reiman was selected as one of five initial inductees into the Dipsea Race Hall of Fame.

(Above) Women's Dipsea Hikers and their beaus, circa 1920. (Courtesy Stinson Beach Historical Society)

(Right) Start of the Women's Dipsea Hike, in front of the old Mill Valley train depot, circa 1920. (Ted Wurm collection)

1912 winner Donald Dunn. Killed in World War I, he was the first champion to die (Courtesy Joan Reutinger)

Below are biographical sketches, for their post-victory years, of the 72 Dipsea Race winners. As of September 1993, 33 of these champions were alive (presented as "Still Running"). Jimmy McClymonds, born March 29, 1905, the year of the first Dipsea, is the oldest, two months senior to Ernie Marinoni.

Deaths have been confirmed for 30 others (listed in the "672nd Step" below). Of the 28 of these with known birth and death dates, ten died while they were in their 80's, nine in their 70's, three in their 60's, three in their 50's, two in their 40's and one, Donald Dunn, at age 23.

Neither Reese nor I have been able to learn much about the remaining nine winners. Two, George Berhmann and Albert Gorse, were born more than 100 years ago so are listed in the "672nd Step" although I have not found them in the California death record files. The remaining seven, all but one of whom would now be at least 85 years of age, are listed as "Unknown."

Unconfirmed dates are presented with question marks.

> "Old Dipsea runners never die.
> They just reach the 672nd step."
> —Jack Kirk, the Dipsea Demon

THE 672ND STEP

John Geoffery Hassard, 1905, '06
(January 28, 1887-January 17, 1967)

Hassard moved to Fallon, in Nevada, where he both farmed and worked for the Truckee-Carson Irrigation District as a superintendent. He retired to Yuba City, CA, in 1957. He never married.

Hassard was a regular visitor to Dipsea Races over the decades—his last appearance was in 1965—and he inspired many younger runners. Hassard died, 11 days short of his 80th birthday, of an aortic aneuryism. He is buried in Yuba City's Sutter Cemetery.

William Joyner, 1907
(January 22, 1890-November 12, 1958)

On January 31, 1909, Joyner won the first marathon held on the West Coast. Sponsored by the Examiner, it was run over a muddy course from the town of Belmont north to Van Ness and Geary in San Francisco. Joyner took the lead at mile 15 and clocked a 2:55:18. *Examiner* columnist Sidney Peixotto wrote: "I look upon the Marathon race of yesterday as the greatest athletic event in the history of San Francisco ... William Joyner, one of our own city boys, born and reared in our dear old town, coming through the streets accompanied by a thousand men and boys, cheered by 20,000 of his fellow townspeople, as he ran with steady stride to the finish line, awakened in the hearts of thousands of youths a new desire ... Thousands of boys would give their whole soul to be William Joyner."

Later in the year, Joyner won also won a major indoor marathon in 3:04.

Joyner was soon after recruited by the Olympic Club and remained an active member for decades. He was also an avid hiker, heading off from his San Francisco home to Mt. Tamalpais on weekends and to the Sierra on vacations. His weight never went above 135 pounds.

Joyner married in 1911 and remained wed to Helen the rest of his 47 years. They had one daughter, Marion (Weissgerber), and two grandsons. He worked all his life for a single company, the Clinton Construction Co. of San Francisco, beginning as an office clerk and ending up one of the owners.

Joyner returned to many Dipseas as an observer and an official.

George Behrmann, 1908
(circa 1890-deceased)

Behrmann is presumed deceased based on his 1890 birth date.

Basil Lamar Spurr, 1909
(1891-October 11, 1947)

Spurr ran for the Olympic Club in future Dipseas after his Siaplamat Indians team broke up. He served in World War I, then worked for years as an electrician.

Upon his death in Fairfield, CA, he was survived by his wife (Thelma), three children (Basil, Jr., Patricia Austin and Adrienne Spurr) and two grandchildren.

Oliver J. Millard, 1910, '13
(1884-April 7, 1963)

By the time he retired from competition in 1918, Millard was recognized as one of the greatest runners ever in Northern California. His Cross-City Race course record from 1914 stood for 23 years. Millard joined the Olympic Club in 1912 and was later bestowed honorary life membership.

He was married (Marie) but apparently had no children. His remains are inurned in Olivet Memorial Park, Colma, CA.

Albert Gorse, 1911
(circa 1890-deceased)

Gorse finished in the top ten in the next four Dipseas following his victory, including second in 1912. Mary Schwartz, widow of 1925 Dipsea runner-up William Schwartz, mentioned that Gorse

had inspired and guided her husband's running career. Gorse is presumed deceased based on his 1890 birth date.

Joseph Donald Dunn, 1912
(1893-June 3, 1916)

Donald Dunn died three months before the 1916 Dipsea, the first champion to pass away. Here is his obituary, as reprinted from the Olympic Club's *Olympian*:

On the date of the annual [1916] Dipsea race some of us heard for the first time of the death of Donald Dunn, popularly known as Jimmy Dunn, winner of the 1912 race. He was killed in France. This popular athlete was a sophomore at the University of California when the war broke out. He joined a Canadian regiment and eight months ago was sent across the channel to 'somewhere on the western front.' He won a lieutenant's commission for bravery and was in command of a mine laying squad when he was killed.

The entire contingent was wiped out in a counter charge by the Germans. When killed, Dunn was acting as captain, the superior officer having been killed during the first five minutes of action.

Dunn was born in Melbourne, lived in South Africa, went to school in England, and came to Berkeley six years ago. He took to the Marin hills early and was a great favorite among the enthusiastic hikers who applauded him for his achievement in 1912.

Dunn's family last saw him at the christening of his niece, and godchild, Joan Reutinger, in England in 1915. More than 75 years later, Reutinger still writes about the Dipsea for Marin publications. She is also the author of a history of Willow Camp (Stinson Beach). Reutinger says that Dunn's first place trophy has always occupied a place of prominence on the mantle of her family home and helped influence her own sons to run the Dipsea many times.

(Top left) Oliver Millard (#2), one of the greatest of all Dipsea champions, in 1916. The Race winner, Henry Anderes (#77), is in background. (Courtesy Mark Reese). (Top right) Mason Hartwell, winner of seven best-time awards, while a star runner at Oakland High School, 1907. (Courtesy Thomas Hartwell). (Bottom left) 1920 winner William O'Callaghan in World War I. (Courtesy Patricia Sturges). (Bottom right) Torrey Lyons, the 1934 winner, in the Air Corps during World War II. (Courtesy Dorothy Lyons)

Andrew D. Ahern, 1914
(?-June 16, 1980)

Ahern remained in the sport after his 1914 win, both as a competitor—he finished third in Cross-City in 1922—and as a trainer (coach) for the Olympic Club. He came to many later Dipseas.

Lee H. Blackwell, 1915
(1887-December 23, 1969)

Blackwell was married (Mamie) for 59 years. He had a son, Lewis, two grandchildren and five great grandchildren. He died in Sacramento, where he had moved in 1940. His twin brother Winton died October 5, 1981, also in Sacramento County.

Henry A. Anderes, 1916
(March 12, 1893-January 24, 1977)

Anderes continued racing in the Dipsea, and was part of the winning Humboldt Club Team (8th overall) as late as 1924. He died in San Mateo County and was survived at least by his wife.

John Mason Hartwell, 1917
(September 6, 1889-September 2, 1971)

Hartwell raced his last Dipsea in 1926, when he won his seventh best time award. He then continued to come to Dipseas for decades, first as an official, later as an observer.

Hartwell worked for Wells Fargo Bank in San Francisco until 1932, then started his own rug cleaning and laying business.

Hartwell remained a runner into his 70's. He particularly enjoyed unmarked paths through Tilden Park near his home in the Berkeley-Oakland hills.

After bouts with cancer and Alzheimer's disease, Hartwell was moved into a nursing home. He died four days short of his 82nd birthday. His longtime wife, Clara, passed away at age 94. They were survived by two children (Thomas Hartwell and Margaret Rocca) and six grandchildren. Thomas still

has Mason's 1910 best time and 1917 winner's trophies, both kept in pristine condition. He brought them to the 1993 Dipsea Dinner. Mason's younger brother, Ben, now over 100, still lives in Mill Valley; a younger sister, Florence, also survives.

Percy Harold Gilbert, 1918
(August 21, 1898-September 27, 1985)

Gilbert was a factor in the Dipsea for several more years after his win. By 1922, he had moved up to the elite one-minute handicap group, starting ahead only of his friend, U.S. Olympian Bill Churchill.

Gilbert worked as a health inspector for the City of Los Angeles for 27 years before retiring in 1964. He then moved to Santa Paula in Ventura County, CA, where he lived the remainder of his years. He died, after a long illness, in his home at age 87. He was survived by his wife, Wanda, and step-daughter, Dorothy Dillinger.

Victor R. Hay Chapman, 1919
(January 23, 1896-May 30, 1964)

Chapman and his wife Clara had two children, Barbara (Wessenger) and Robert, and seven grandchildren. He died in San Diego and was buried in Fort Rosecrans.

William Patrick O'Callaghan, 1920
(May 29, 1896-May 14, 1976)

Soon after winning the Dipsea, O'Callaghan gave up running on the insistence of his fiance and later wife Alice. She believed, as perhaps most people did then, that running was harmful to the heart. Ironically, it would be Alice dying, of a heart attack, two decades before William.

The couple had two children, William F. and Patricia (Sturges) and five grandchildren. When one of those grandchildren, Pamela, took up running, he gave her his Dipsea trophy; she still has it. Another grandchild, Kathy, started running in 1993 and only then learned her beloved "Papa Gray" was a Dipsea champion; he had spoken little of his running accomplishments.

O'Callaghan worked for years as office manager for Davey Tree Service in San Francisco. His favorite hobby was playing the piano.

Illtred William Letcher, 1923
(February 24, 1880-July 31, 1966)

Letcher entered no other Dipseas. He continued practicing as a dentist on Fillmore Street in San Francisco into the early 1960's. He died in Contra Costa County, CA.

William K. Westergard, 1924
(December 12, 1899-July 25, 1985)

Westergard became a popular figure in his 27th Avenue, Sunset District (San Francisco) neighborhood, where he lived in the first house built on the block. He worked as a salesman for Russell Creamery in the Mission District. Westergard maintained his Danish roots as a member of the Danish Lodge, off Market Street. When his first wife died, Westergard remarried at age 80. He was later afflicted with Alzheimer's disease. He had no children. All his running trophies were stolen.

Angelo Frediani, 1929
(1903-deceased)

Frediani continued to live in North Beach the rest of his life, working as a stonemason. He married, but had no children. Ernest Cereghino, a surviving San Francisco Athletic Club teammate, says Frediani died "a long, long time ago."

William Winnie Magner, 1930
(October 5, 1904-July 25, 1990)

Magner returned to finish the 1984 Dipsea, achieving a 63-year span between his first (1921) and last Dipsea that was finally matched by Jack Kirk in 1993.

After his Dipsea victory, Magner coached women's athletics. He also taught in San Francisco public schools, spending many years as head of the industrial arts department at George Washington High School. In the mid-1950's Magner was Bill Russell's high jump coach at the University of San Francisco when the basketball star was attempting to become the first to clear 7 feet.

Magner moved to Marin in 1974. After his wife Georgette died in 1982, Magner began showing up at Terra Linda High School track practices. Head coach Veronica DeMartini remembers:

First he started with advice for the coaches, telling us a lot about the techniques used in his era. Then he started working directly with the kids. They called him "Pops." He made a great impression on them. When we honored him at one of the team's annual awards ceremonies, the kids gave him gifts. One girl gave him a Terra Linda blanket, so he would be comfortable when sitting in the stands. He addressed the dinner, and I was crying.

Bill could fix anything. Whenever we gave up on a part to repair, a broken hurdle or the like, he would go into his machine shop in San Francisco and make the part. He worked on spikes, on starting blocks, on takeoff marks for the jumpers. He fixed our hurdles so they would be less dangerous for the inexperienced youngsters. He really cared.

In 1983, Magner was diagnosed with cancer. Though doctors didn't expect him to survive a year, he fulfilled his last great wish—to go the 1984 Olympic Games in Los Angeles. He then lived six more years, his final months with his daughter, remaining alert to the end. Magner last appeared at the 1989 Dipsea Race awards ceremony.

Francis O'Donnell, 1931
(1904-December 20, 1989)

O'Donnell remained an Olympic Club member for the rest of his life, 59 years, after his Dipsea win. He became a familiar figure at the Club track and swimming pool, in his later years coming over with help of a cane from his apartment on nearby Leavenworth Street. He also faithfully came to watch the Dipsea. His last visit was in 1989, when he was alert and cheerful.

Torrey Lyons, 1934
(March 7, 1915-May 15, 1991)

Lyons never returned to the Dipsea; his win being his only trip over the course. He soon after gave up competitive running to devote more time to his other many interests.

He graduated from the University of California, Berkeley, with degrees in forestry and plant pathology, then earned a doctorate in vegetable crops from Cornell University.

He worked all his life in agriculture. One job was developing a hydroponic garden on Wake Island for Pan Am Airlines to feed passengers who stopped there on early trans-Pacific flights. Most of his years was spent performing farm advisory work for the University of California, Davis. After retiring, he worked another ten years for an organization dedicated to improving grain yields in developing countries and lived in Argentina, Tunisia and Nepal.

In 1942 he married Dorothy Morris, who survives him. The couple had four children. Also in 1942, Lyons joined the Air Corps and, based in Guadalcanal, flew B-17's during World War II.

Lyons remained an avid skier, backpacker and fisherman all his life. In his late years, he became debilitated with Alzheimer's disease. His condition finally forced him out of his long-time Davis home, two blocks from the U.C. campus. He died soon afterwards.

John Hansen, 1935
(March 25, 1903-January 31, 1991)

Hansen lived his entire life in Sonoma County, CA, spending his final years in the small town of Glen Ellen.

Paul Chirone, 1937
(July 16, 1913-January 30, 1990)

After his Dipsea victory, Chirone joined the Merchant Marines, later seeing active service during World War II. Then he worked as a stonemason. His most ambitious project was the stone work at the Jesuit home, El Retiro, in Los Altos. Chirone also built the fireplace in the American Legion Log Cabin in San Anselmo, of which he was a long-time and well-loved member.

Chirone also continued to play a part in the Dipsea, though he ran it again only infrequently. He was listed as a course worker in numerous race programs into the 1960's and helped Norman Bright in his stirring 1970 victory.

In his late years, Chirone lived as a caretaker in a large house in San Anselmo and became somewhat of a town legend. He was a favorite of area children; one of his tricks was playing the harmonica with his nose. He loved to tend his garden and care for animals. He was also active in the Catholic Church.

Chirone's end came suddenly; active one day, dead from a massive stroke the next.

San Anselmo paid Chirone a high tribute. A stone planter in front of Town Hall was dedicated to him. The flowers in it are always kept fresh. A plaque bears the inscription: "Paul Chirone, 1937 Dipsea Champion, If You Can't Bring Happiness To Yourself, Bring It To Others."

He never married and had no children of his own.

Clarence Hall, 1938
(1916?-July 4, 1991)

The only post-Dipsea information on Hall comes from Eyrle Aceves, a teammate at California and second to him in 1938. Aceves says that Hall returned to the Sacramento Valley to teach, that he died in 1991 (in San Diego County), and that he was survived by at least a daughter, Jean (Gunther).

In 1965, winner John Satti admires medal won by the first champion, John Hassard. This was Hassard's last appearance at the Race. (Richard Smith, Independent Journal)

William Ludwig Dreyer, 1941
(February 23, 1904-April 6, 1992)

Dreyer married his sweetheart Nancy two months after his 1941 victory.

Dreyer maintained a vigorous lifestyle throughout his 88 years. In 1943, he ran 30-50 miles per day (which included a roundtrip from his home in Berkeley to his job in Richmond) for a period of seven months without missing a day. The feat was noted in the "Ripley's Believe It or Not" syndicated feature in newspapers throughout the country. In 1944, Dreyer and Jack Kirk were the only two entrants in the Petaluma Marathon, Dreyer winning in 2:56:55. In his entire running career, Dreyer estimated he received over 1,000 trophies and medals.

He founded the Dreyer Athletic Club and, in subsequent decades, coached some 3,500 runners, many of them youngsters. He was particularly an expert in race walking, and served on the sport's national committee for several years. The Amateur Athletic Union honored him with their prestigious 50-Year Pin in 1978, noting he was still active.

Dreyer also was prominent in helping women participate in the sport. In 1947, he organized a women's cross country race in Berkeley and the United States' first sanctioned women's race walk in Petaluma. He also brought Nancy into the Dipsea, the first woman to run it. They both ran from 1950 through 1954, after which Nancy was no longer allowed on the course.

In 1959, the Dreyers moved from Berkeley to the small northern Sacramento Valley community of Paradise. He worked as a landscaper and tree surgeon for his own Dreyer's Woodland Flora. He died in a Paradise nursing home in 1992, seven years after Nancy. The couple was survived by a son, William, and daughter, Nancy (Taylor), four grandchildren and three great grandchildren.

Leslie Joseph French McGregor, Jr., 1948
(May 4, 1918-October 15, 1977)

McGregor married eight weeks after his Dipsea triumph. His wife, Evelyn, who survives him, had been present Dipsea day. The couple lived for years in South San Francisco. They had four children; Leslie, Donald, Paul and Patricia. McGregor worked as a butcher in the City's Lakeshore District.

The Parkinson's disease that had afflicted McGregor as a young man ultimately returned. He had three delicate brain surgeries (performed by Dr. Bertram Feinstein, first husband of U.S. Senator Dianne Feinstein) but his condition deteriorated. After many difficult years, he died in the Veteran's Hospital in Palo Alto.

McGregor never raced again after his Dipsea win.

Paul David Juette, 1949
(April 4, 1928-November 27, 1980)

Juette ran the Dipsea again in 1950 (getting lost), then won the best time award in both 1951 and 1953.

He married (Elinor) while at the University of California, from which he received a degree in geology. The couple had three children; Christine, Marlene and Michael. Juette worked in water resources management in Sacramento. In later years, after separating from his wife and family, he tried a variety of jobs in Northern California (such as in a candle factory in Redwood City). For years he had no fixed address, living in his camper; he loved to travel throughout the wilderness areas of California, hiking and fishing.

Juette never lost his passion for running, jogging throughout his life. At the age of 52 he decided to resume training, after a long layoff, and bought a new pair of shoes. The strain—his first run was eight miles—likely contributed to the fatal heart attack he suffered a few days later. He was found in his car three days after his death, along with the new shoes and a log of those last runs.

James M. Shettler, 1950
(August 9, 1933-July 2, 1976)

Shettler went on to become one of the best runners in Northern California history. Among scores of local victories were the Cross-City Races of 1952 (by 41 seconds at age 18) and 1962. Also in '62, he set a PR of 9:12 in his track specialty, the steeplechase.

After graduating from San Francisco State College, Shettler served in the Coast Guard. He then became a biology instructor at Diablo Valley Community College, rising to head of the department. Running remained his passion, and he diligently trained 50 miles a week or more for years in an era when that was considered unusually high.

When Shettler turned 40, he became one of this country's top masters runners, capturing several national titles. Shortly after winning the U.S. 25K crown, Shettler suffered a cardiac arrest while running and died instantly.

The event stunned the local running community. The "running boom" was at its peak and many were claiming that distance running provided immunity to heart problems. An autopsy by the noted runner and physician Joan Ullyot revealed that cholesterol deposits had blocked a small blood vessel, disturbing the heart's rhythm and leading to the fatal stoppage. Len Wallach notes, in his book, *The Human Race,* that Shettler had inadvertently been on the longest training run of his life the day before his death; he and a friend had gotten lost in the Oakland hills.

Walter Earnest Deike, 1952
(August 27, 1921-April 15, 1963)

Deike earned his medical degree in 1957. He then moved to southern California to set up his practice.

At age 41, Deike drowned while swimming in Mendocino Bay. The headline story in the *Mendocino Beacon* began: "A Los Angeles resident lost his life late Monday afternoon because no one with the knowledge of the seriousness of what he was attempting was at hand to dissuade him from attempting it. His foolhardy action was to attempt to swim from the easterly end of Main Street . . . to the mouth of the river. He had gone some 200 yards . . . when he cried for help." Rescue units were summoned but to no avail. Although a "large delegation of town residents . . . kept watch for hours patrolling the beach and shoreline," his body was never recovered.

William S. Mazzini, 1955
(October 26, 1902-July 31, 1978)

After his victory, Mazzini continued to race in the Dipsea; in several 1960's races, he was among the last finishers.

When Mazzini's parents died, the family ranch in Cloverdale was sold. Mazzini's many running trophies disappeared as well. Mazzini moved to Weed in northern California, where his brother John lived. He coached running there. His last years were spent in a convalescent home.

Peter J. McArdle, 1962
(1929-June 24, 1985)

In 1963, McArdle won both the national AAU and the Pan American Games 10,000 meters titles. In 1964, McArdle won the Olympic Trials marathon, then represented the United States in the Olympic Games marathon in Tokyo (23rd place). Soon after, back problems forced him to retire from running. In 1972, he was inducted into the United States Track & Field Hall of Fame.

After a 19-year absence, McArdle returned to the sport in 1984. He had seen a group of runners on the Columbia University track near his job (with the transit authority) and promptly started jogging in his work clothes and shoes. Within months, he set a world best for runners 55 and over at 10,000 meters of 34:08.

In 1985, at age 56, he collapsed and died from a massive heart attack at the finish line after a training run over the Van Cortlandt Park cross country course. Van Cortlandt, in the Bronx, New York City, is the most hallowed cross country site in the United States and was the scene of many of his greatest victories. A major race in the park is now named for him and a plaque there honors him as well. His wife, Barbara, who still lives in the couples' long-time Teaneck, New Jersey, home, said, "He died doing what he loves best."

Veteran New York running writer Eddie Coyle's obituary for him began, "Pete McArdle's death aroused a greater sense of personal loss among more people than that of any other athlete I can remember."

McArdle had three daughters and a son.

Alan Gary Beardall, 1963
(September 21, 1938-December 1, 1988)

After graduating from Los Angeles Chiropractic College, Alan went on to become a world-reknown chiropractor, the author of 12 technical books on clinical kinesiology.

Beardall lived in Lake Oswego, Oregon. There he raised five sons; in age order, Christopher, Tim, Michael, Thomas and Matthew. Tim became a standout prep runner and turned in several outstanding Dipsea times (50:33 in 1990). Michael also runs; Thomas died at 16. Alan continued to run and remained a factor in age group competition both on the track and roads.

He returned for the Dipsea several times as well. He described his last visit in a letter to Reese: "I was purposely elbowed by a Marin County runner and knocked unconscious as I was trying to pass him on a stairway. I finished the race but certainly did not do as well as I had anticipated."

In 1988, while in England conducting a chiropractic seminar, a 50-foot truck plowed head-on into his car and Alan and his wife were killed instantly. His brother Darryl and father Ray established running trophies in Alan's name at his alma mater, Santa Rosa High School, and at the Dipsea (the family trophy). Appropriately, the Dip-

sea's first Alan Beardall Family Trophy was won by Darryl and Tim.

John Satti, 1965
(January 29, 1914-July 20, 1991)

Except for a three-year stint with the Army, John Satti lived all his life in San Francisco; the last 40 years on 37th Avenue in the Richmond district.

Four years after his Dipsea win, Satti retired from his Federal government position as chief security officer at the Oakland Army Depot. He then worked, also in security, for the Bank of California until he was 72.

In his last years, Satti's running interests shifted to shorter distances, with great success. He set numerous U.S. age records at distances through 200 meters, and even held the world 65+ high jump record. But he also continued to faithfully return to the Dipsea, competing into his 70's. John's other passions included betting on horses, handball and swimming.

Satti and his wife of 52 years, Margaret, had one daughter, Janice, two grandsons, and, at John's death, one great grandson. He died after a long bout with asbestosis. Satti's deathbed request was to have his ashes scattered over the Dipsea Trail.

Alfons Coney and Charles Boas, whose match race in 1904 spawned the Dipsea, also deserve mention here.

Coney, recognized by the Dipsea Indians as the key founder of the Dipsea, remained an important Race official. The first winner's trophy was named for him. He died in San Francisco on February 6, 1949, at age 81.

Boas died in August, 1924, also in San Francisco. A nephew, Roger Boas, who served as chief administrative officer for San Francisco, donated the Boas Brothers trophy to the Dipsea in 1965 in memory of Charles and his own father Ben. It was presented to the first over-40 runner.

James Dale McClymonds, 1936
(March 29, 1905-

McClymonds ran a couple more Dipseas after his win but few other races. He now regrets not starting his running career sooner.

He married (Hazel) in 1939; they remain wed. They had one son (Alfred) and four grandchildren.

McClymonds moved to Corte Madera in Marin County when he worked at the Mare Island shipyard during World War II. He then bought and operated a 15-acre chicken farm in Petaluma. The couple retired to the small community of Fish Camp, near Yosemite, where they loved to hike, in 1962.

McClymonds remains active at age 88. He draws, paints and sculpts and still enjoys hiking although saying "Yosemite is just too crowded now."

Allan Nelson, 1939
(November 22, 1916-

Nelson had a long career with the United States Foreign Service. His first posting was in Finland, where he came to be known as the "running diplomat." He next was Chief of Finnish Language broadcasts for Voice of America in New York. That got him assignments to cover the Boston Marathon, which he ran in 1953.

Nelson was then off to South Africa as press officer for the American Consulate. While there he completed that nation's famous 54-mile Comrades Marathon. Other assignments were in Sweden, Athens (he ran the Athens Marathon), Washington, Cyprus and Vietnam. After retiring from the Foreign Service in the early 1970's, he worked part-time for Korbell Champagnes.

Nelson ran a total of 11 Dipseas, the last in 1973. Knee problems forced him to give up running; his last road race, with his grandson, was in 1980. He spoke at the 1992 Dipsea Dinner.

Allan, and his wife of 53 years, Vergie, the woman who greeted him at the finish line in 1939 with a kiss, live in Monte Rio.

Ernest Paul Marinoni, 1940
(June 5, 1905-

Following his Dipsea triumph, Marinoni continued a 32-year stint as physical fitness director for the Berkeley YMCA. One of his prize pupils, who developed a similar zeal for exercise, was Jack LaLanne. Marinoni also started, during summers, one of the first gymnastics schools on the west coast, in Gualala, CA.

He continued to run the Dipsea, as did his son Robert, starting at age 10. In 1971, Ernie also won a trophy at the Double Dipsea.

In the early 1970's, Marinoni and his wife Hazel (who died in 1990) moved to a house on a 10-acre parcel just outside Placerville in the Sierra foothills.

Marinoni remains remarkably active. He teaches physical fitness classes at local high schools. He started a distance run, called Mountain Misery. He delivers meals to senior citizens. He still runs, practices karate (he's a 4th degree black belt), bowls, and works out in the large gym he constructed beside the house. Marinoni weighs 135 pounds now; he was 132 when he won the Dipsea.

But his main sport, largely due to knee problems from running, has become bicycling. He's ridden over 50 "centuries" (100-milers). When he was 80, he covered 240 miles in 16 hours of riding time. In 1991, at age 86, he picked up several gold medals in his age category at the world bicycling championships in Italy. In 1992, he competed in Russia.

Besides Robert, Ernie has two daughters, Barbara and Helen. He also has five grandchildren and an oldest great grandchild of 20.

Sal Vasquez en route to a record fifth Dipsea win, 1990. (Gene Cohn)

Charles Richesin, 1946
(1929-

Following his Dipsea win, Richesin attended Fresno State College, which he chose to train with pole vault immortal Cornelius Warmerdam, and the University of the Pacific in Stockton, from which he graduated. While in Stockton, he helped put together and coached several winning Dipsea teams.

Richesin continued to improve as a runner, winning the best time award in the 1948 Dipsea and placing second in the 1954 Cross-City. He also competed in the Olympic Trials in modern pentathlon.

From Stockton, Richesin moved to Hawaii, where he lived and coached for 25 years. One of his star pupils was Duncan MacDonald, who ran a state prep mile record and later held the American record at 5,000 meters.

Richesin returned to California in 1980. He then moved back to Marin County, where he owned a memorabilia shop and helped coach football at his alma mater, San Rafael High. Richesin, divorced with four children, retired to Hawaii in 1992.

He is hopeful of getting corrective surgery on a bothersome knee and racing the Dipsea again. In 1993, Richesin received a 36th annual (1946) Dipsea Race black shirt with the number "1" on the back.

Allan Baffico, 1947
(1931-

In 1948, Allan finished fourth, one place behind older brother Andrew, in the Cross-City Race. After graduating from Balboa—his mile best down to 4:59—Allan entered the Army. He ran for the Fort Ord (CA) team while in basic training. Upon his discharge in 1952, he raced briefly again, then gave up running. In recent decades, his only sport has been water skiing.

Allan has worked in landscaping for 32 years. He has five children and 11 grandchildren and lives in Redwood City.

Jack Gardner Kirk, 1951, '67
(October 3, 1906-

Jack Kirk is the most fabled of all Dipsea racers. And his legend continues to grow even though he has not been a factor in the Race since finishing sixth in 1970. In 1993, running in his now trademark long pants and shirt, Kirk completed his 58th consecutive Dipsea. Virtually every earlier finisher and spectator came over to watch as he picked up his pace over the last yards to hold off another runner. The finish extended Kirk's record as the oldest runner, 86, ever to complete the Dipsea.

Kirk's record of consecutive Dipsea finishes now stands alone in the nation, if not the world; John Kelley's comparable streak at the Boston Marathon having ended after 1992. (Kelley had started his streak in 1932, two years after Kirk. But because the Dipsea then missed a total of six years, Kelley's streak grew longer, to 61 consecutive finishes.)

The greatest threats to Kirk's streak have come from balky cars. He owns several models, but all are decades old. Kirk did stop running Bay to Breakers in 1990, citing the dangers of overcrowding.

Kirk continues to live rustically and isolated on his 400-acre creekside property south of Mariposa. (In 1993, he was awakened in a close encounter with a bear going after his just picked apricot harvest.) He never married. After a dispute with a PG&E repairman, Kirk has been without electricity or telephone for years. He usually sleeps in one of the several aging Volkswagen "bugs" scattered about. He carved a jogging path around his own lake and now does all his running on it.

Kirk retains a keen interest in wildflowers and hosts botanists wishing to study the two plant species (a pussy-paws and a lupine) that grow only on his property (and a neighbor's) and nowhere else in the world. Several Dipsea veterans also visit.

Ralph Barton Perry III, 1953
(March 17, 1936-

Perry went on to run track at Harvard under the college's famed coach, and Dipsea veteran (best time award in 1941), Bill McCurdy. Ralph raced the Dipsea just once more, in 1956. Poised to take the lead late in the race, he collapsed from exhaustion and was brought to a hospital on a stretcher. To this day, he says a victory from scratch (as he attempted in '56) "would have been 100 times better" than his 1953 win.

Perry attended Stanford Law School. He married (Betsy) in 1961. They have two children, Daniel and Catherine, and one grandchild. In 1963, soon after graduating, Perry moved to southern California to practice. He is now a partner at Graven, Perry, Locke, Brody and Qualls, specializing in business litigation, and lives in Pasadena.

Perry continued to run, but not competitively. Arthroscopic surgery on both knees effectively ended his running career. His sports passion is now tournament level handball.

Herbert Egar Stockman, 1954
(October 13, 1931-

Stockman graduated from San Jose State with a major in education. His first job was teaching and coaching at Hanford High School in the San Joaquin Valley. He took the cross country team from 12 to 90 students and the track team from 30 to 170.

Then he and wife Marliss and their growing family (they have four daughters, Diana, Marla, Paula and Sandra, now ranging in ages from 25 to 39) moved to Wickliffe, Ohio. Again Stockman coached. He formed the successful Blue Ribbon track club, whose members set several American junior records. He also started a thriving Tupperware sales company.

The family moved back to California in 1978. The following year he began coaching at Irvine H.S. He was an assistant for seven years, head coach for three. One of his motivational tools was showing the film, *Survival Run*, of the blind Harry Cordellos in the Dipsea.

Stockman had continued to run after college, but not competitively. In the 1960's he hurt his knee playing football. It bothered him for years. He finally had surgery in 1977 and, with too much cartilage removed, was told not to run again.

He returned to the Dipsea for the first time in 1992 for that year's reunion dinner.

Michael John Deasy, 1957
(January 31, 1940-

Deasy ran in several more Dipseas before ending his competitive career. He has long worked for CalTrans in the Bay Area. He and his family live in San Ramon.

Ernest Fernando Leon, 1958
(December 16, 1937-

Leon earned varsity letters on USC's powerful track teams in 1959, 1960 and 1961 and was twice named the school's top cross country runner. He then returned to his native Tucson, where he began a wood carving business. Leon then moved back to California. Now divorced, he lives on a farm outside Gonzales in the Salinas Valley.

Wood carving remains his passion and he has been chosen for several prestigious projects, such as the restoration of the Gallatin Building in Monterey. He also teaches woodworking classes at Soledad Prison.

Leon has recently begun running again and is collecting age division awards. In 1992, he ran a 36:13 for 10K at age 54. He ponders returning to the Dipsea.

Jim Imperiale, 1959
(April 9, 1921-

Imperiale kept his vow and retired from Dipsea competition, and all racing, after his victory. He continued, though, to have a major impact on the Dipsea. He still coached the team he founded, the Marin A.C., which dominated Dipsea team competition. He would be out almost every summer evening timing his runners on workouts over the course. Finally, in 1963, tired of the fundraising side of the club (many of the expenses ended up coming out of his own pocket), Imperiale stepped down "to turn the club over the runners."

Also in 1963, after the South of Market Boys decided to discontinue their sponsorship, Imperiale rallied to help save the Race. He approached Jim Gilmartin, sports editor at the *Independent Journal*, to run an appeal for a sponsor. Soon after, the Mill Valley Junior Chamber of Commerce responded, and they have basically been at it ever since. Imperiale served as the 1963 Meet Director, which included marking the course and setting the handicaps.

Imperiale earned his living as a mechanic. In 1959, he worked for the Navy on Treasure Island. Later he switched to the Army Reserve in the Presidio. He retired in 1977. In 1981 he moved to Santa Rosa, where he still lives. He is divorced and has two children and two grandchildren.

Reese said of him, "Few people in the entire history of the Dipsea have made the contribution to the betterment of the race as has Jim Imperiale."

Robert S. Hope, 1960
(March 9, 1942-

After his sensational win, Hope never again raced the Dipsea. He joined the Army and did some running there. He returned to Marin to work in the lumber business. In 1975 he married (Roberta). In 1977, the couple moved to Petaluma. They have two children, Miriam and Jordan.

Religion—he is a born again Christian—plays a large role in his life. Hope stays fit, and runs regularly, but does not compete in races.

Phillip M. Smith, 1961
(September 30, 1937-

For Smith, 1961 was his only year of intense running. He races the Dipsea faithfully, not missing a single year since his win, but has never again been a factor up front. He enters no other races. His main sport is squash, where he is nationally ranked. He also golfs and continues to play tennis.

He works for Montgomery Securities in the City. The firm is known for its hectic pace and Smith says every work day "is a Dipsea." He lives with his family, which now includes grandchildren, in Sausalito in Marin County.

Gregg Edward Sparks, 1964
(July 12, 1947-

Sparks went to the California State meet in the mile for Tamalpais High in 1965. That was also the year he ran his last Dipsea.

He attended College of Marin, then enlisted in the Navy. Sparks served two tours in Vietnam. The war experience affected him and, when he returned, he stopped running, became a smoker and battled a drinking problem. He drifted through a variety of jobs, such as logging, fishing and detective work. He also began writing poems (some published) and painting.

He now lives in San Francisco with his third wife. He has three children. He still surfs.

Carl James Jensen, 1966
(November 23, 1944-

On August 17, 1967, a year after his Dipsea triumph, Jensen stepped on a land mine in Vietman while serving as point man for his Army platoon. He suffered massive injuries throughout his body; both legs and a hand mangled, part of his intestines blown out, jaw broken, loss of hearing.

He spent 17 months in five hospitals, finally achieving a remarkable recovery. Ironically, Jensen had only just missed being assigned to safer duty on the Army's running team.

Upon returning to his native Marin, Carl attended San Francisco State to complete his studies. He coached cross country and the distance runners in track at his alma mater, Novato High School. Among his runners there was Ron Elijah, who would set the all-time Dipsea course record. Jensen tried running again but, frustrated about not being able to return to his old form, gave up the sport completely for eight years. He was also embittered about the injury and the futility of his Vietnam experience.

Jensen continued to work with young people and, to be in better condition for the wilderness hikes he led for the YMCA, finally started running again. An old high school running rival, Pat Johnson, who also had been wounded in Vietnam, helped in the comeback, as did Bert Botta.

Jensen was finally ready to return to his beloved Dipsea in 1981. He has run six more times since.

Jensen lives in Kentfield with his wife, Susan, in a home with a lovely view of Mt. Tamalpais. He has a daughter in college. He owns a landscaping company.

Donald Stewart Pickett, 1968
(January 11, 1928-

Don Pickett has affectionately earned the sobriquet of "Mr. Dipsea" for his exploits in the Race and for his unselfish help to other runners. In both 1975 and 1976, he directed the ultimate winners, competing against him, onto the proper path. He also hosted post-Dipsea parties for years and his Tiburon house was long a runners haven. He was a co-founder of the Tamalpa Runners, who have played a major role in the Dipsea. In 1985, at the 75th Dipsea banquet, a friend, George Conlan, presented Pickett with the customized license plate, "DIPSEA." It has been Pickett's plate ever since. (Race director Jerry Hauke possesses "DIPSEA1.")

Pickett has remained competitive in masters

competition locally and beyond, winning scores of track, road and cross country titles. His greatest strength remains the Dipsea, finishing 2nd in 1975, 4th in 1976, 3rd in 1979 and 1980 and collecting a total of 12 shirts. He's been on 10 winning teams and with son Toby garnered four family trophies. He was honored with the James Farren, Jr. Memorial Award in 1986.

Don has another son Tom (who has also run the Dipsea), a daughter Rebecca and three grandchildren. His first wife Pat died of cancer; he has been married to the former Patti Jeffries, also a runner, since 1985. The couple operate an import-export business.

Vance Charles Eberly, 1969
(January 7, 1959-

Eberly continued running competitively. At Los Gatos High School he was a star, winning his league cross country title as a sophomore. He then went on to West Valley Junior College and San Diego State, where he was captain of the cross country team. His personal records were 9:07 in the steeplechase and 3:51 for 1,500 meters. But injuries dogged his career.

Eberly obtained masters degrees in athletic training, then chemistry, at San Jose State. In 1993, Vance received an M.D. degree from the University of Southern California. His specialty is orthopedic surgery.

In recent years, Vance has been running only recreationally, to relieve the stress of his medical studies.

Norman Bright, 1970
(January 29, 1910-

Bright's vision continued to deteriorate following his Dipsea win and he was completely blind within the decade. While he still had partial vision (and even after, with assistance), Bright continued to run brilliantly, setting numerous track and road distance records.

In the World Masters Championships in Toronto in 1975, he became the first runner in the world over 65 to break five minutes for 1,500 meters, clocking 4:59.8. Ironically, he partially credits his poor vision for the record; he led by some 80 yards but didn't know it, continually pressing though victory was assured. He has held the national age 65-69 road record for 20 kilometers (1:20:53) since 1976; no one has come within three minutes.

In 1985, Bright was flown, through the generosity of the Tamalpa Runners, to the Bay Area from Tacoma to be guest of honor at the 75th anniversary Dipsea banquet. Pax Beale's film of Bright's 1970 win, *Thirty Years to Victory* was shown, then Bright addressed the audience, reciting Kipling. The next day, Bright was escorted over the Dipsea Trail, almost certainly for the last time. He came to the Race's awards ceremony to present the new Norman Bright Trophy. Donated by his nephew Ray, it is now annually awarded for "Extraordinary Effort in the Dipsea Race." Bright also returned for the 1992 and 1993 Dipseas.

Bright now lives in a nursing home in Seattle. During the move there, his remaining running trophies and ribbons were stolen (though his Dipsea victory trophy remains safe at the home of his only daughter in Cleveland, and he donated his 1937 shoes to the Race). In recent years, he has battled cancer and a degenenerative hip. But his mind remains sharp, able to recall details of his many dangerous mountain climbs and of his great races.

Bright is still active. Indeed, in a conversation in 1992, he excitedly informed me he had "just set a world record"; on a course of his own design near his home.

Michael Boitano, 1971, '72
(October 24, 1961-

Mike now works at his father's business, the Atlas Screw Machine Company in San Francisco. He lives in Richmond. Boitano still runs, but now only "for fun." He did complete the 1993 Double Dipsea.

Mary Etta Boitano, 1973
(March 4, 1963-

Mary Etta was first female at the next three Bay to Breakers (1974, in a record 43:22, through 1976). She attended Mercy High School in San Francisco, where she stopped running to play softball. She took up the sport again at San Francisco State, where she set a school record at 5,000 meters. After graduating, Mary Etta worked as a registered nurse in Sonoma. She continued to run, although non-competitively.

In 1992, Mary Etta married Rich Blanchard (and is now Mary Etta Blanchard). Twelve months later, the couple had their first child, a son John. Mary Etta was running again within weeks.

Darryl Beardall, 1974, '78
(October 22, 1936-

Beardall continues to run the Dipsea every year; through 1993, he's finished 37 times, a total surpassed only by Jack Kirk's 58. His Dipsea trophy collection is now clearly the largest of any runner ever. Since his second win in 1978, he has extended his record to 19 top-ten finishes and has been part of a record 22 winning teams. With his nephew Tim, son of his late brother Alan, he has won three family trophies. Darryl also won the Jimmy Nicholson Award, for lead runner over 50, in 1987 and '89. He won the Double Dipseas of 1977 and 1989.

Outside the Dipsea, Beardall remains a prolific racer; his well-worn Tiger Jayhawk model racing shoes a familiar sight. By his count, he has logged over 300,000 miles, won 300 races outright and collected 800 trophies and 4,000 medals, all saved and filling several rooms of his and his father's homes. Injuries, however, have seriously slowed him—but not stopped him (probably no one better deserves the appellation "Iron Man")—in recent years.

Darryl still works for his lifelong employer, the Northwestern Pacific Railroad. He continues to live in Santa Rosa, where he grew up. He and wife Lynne (they met at the 1962 Dipsea) have three sons and two daughters. They are, in descending age order: Scott, DeeLynn, Kelly, Clayson and Wendy. All have run, at least three competitively.

Joe Patterson, 1975
(September 10, 1934-

Patterson has remained a competitive age-group runner, traveling to various masters competitions worldwide. In 1993, he returned to the Dipsea for the first time, finishing fifth.

Patterson has sold his long-time milk delivery business. He lives with his wife Terri in Southport, on Australia's Gold Coast.

Homer Latimer, 1976, '77
(1939-

Latimer has lived largely outside the United States since his two Dipsea wins, teaching and coaching in several South American countries. He has not returned to the Dipsea in nearly 15 years and no longer races competitively.

Donald Morris Chaffee, Jr., 1979
(January 2, 1939-

Chaffee came back to finish fifth in the 1980 Dipsea, then began a cutback in his racing intensity. In the mid-1980's, he moved with his wife, former Dipsea runner Linda Miller, and three young children (Donald, Douglas and a daughter Meryl) to Grand Rapids, Michigan, where he teaches. Both Don and Linda are Michigan natives.

In 1985, Chaffee charmed the 75th Anniversary dinner audience by peeling off his eight numbered Dipsea t-shirts, one by one, during his talk.

Chaffee now also competes in triathlons.

Donna Andrews, 1980
(August 20, 1940-

Two weeks after winning the Dipsea, Andrews set a women's record of 2:12:02 at the Double Dipsea. But that may prove to be the last highlight of her racing career.

A sciatica problem, likely the result of her rigorous schedule, surfaced. She visited numerous doctors, chiropractors, even faith healers, each eager to "cure" a Dipsea champion, but all were unsuccessful. The pain continued when she ran hard or raced. When Andrews had to drop out of a race in Golden Gate Park, "and I am not a person who drops out of anything," she says, she realized her racing days were over.

But Andrews has remained fit through occasional running and other sports such as windsurfing, swimming, yoga, fast walking and, most recently, mountain biking. Now in her 50's, she says she feels as healthy as ever, "But nothing has brought the same thrill as running."

She has become a successful health products distributor. She has three grown sons—Brett, Chad and Todd—and lives in Mill Valley.

Florianne Harp, 1981
(March 2, 1948-

Two weeks after her Dipsea win, Harp's strong bid to become the first female Double Dipsea champion ended one-quarter mile from the finish. Tim Johnston, visiting the area from England, came up to her shoulder, asked her the way, then went past. Later that summer Harp achieved personal bests of 35:51 for 10K and 2:46:57 at the Oakland Marathon.

Harp had another good year in 1982, mostly in ultramarathoning, including a win at the 37.5-mile, 10,000-foot climb up Haleakala on Maui. But in 1983, years of 100-120 mile weeks caught up with her. She suffered a series of injuries; two stress fractures, a long-undiagnosed hamstring problem and had an operation on her foot. When finally recovered, she resumed running but at lower mileage and non-competitively.

In 1989, she married Stuart Gordon (and is now Florianne Harp Gordon), whom she had met while both were at the 1981 New York City Marathon. She moved to San Francisco. With additional free time, she has increased her mileage and intensity a notch, places well as a master in smaller races and talks of again running the Dipsea.

Sal Vasquez, 1982, '83, '84, '85, '90
(December 15, 1939-

Vasquez continues to compete at the highest levels. He is virtually never beaten by anyone his age in regional races.

Given that no one else won more than twice since the Race began in 1905, and that victors are now penalized with handicap cuts (the "Sal Vasquez Rule"), his record of five victories may stand forever. And gaining a handicap minute virtually every year, Vasquez appears capable of adding to his total. In 1993, at age 53, he ran a sensational 52:57.

Sal and his wife Mileny live in Green Valley in Solano County, CA, with their teen-aged daughters Nicole and Courtney. He now owns a successful industrial cleaning business.

Gail Scott, 1986
(May 18, 1946-

Scott returned to the Dipsea only once more, in 1987, when she finished second after taking a wrong turn. In October, 1987, Scott set an American masters record of 2:37:13 for the marathon that stood for four years.

Christie Bellingall Patterson, 1987
(April 15, 1948-

Two weeks after her Dipsea win, Patterson set a still-standing women's record of 1:58:42 in the Double Dipsea. In 1990, she married consistent high Dipsea finisher Tomas Pastalka (and is now Christie Pastalka). They live in Belvedere.

Christie put her competitive running on hold to give birth, at age 42, to a son, Tomas. Though still working as a full-time nurse, she has managed to return to peak form. In 1993, she finished seventh

in the Dipsea and was first woman, for a record third time, in the Double Dipsea.

Kay Stewart Willoughby, 1988
(January 20, 1936-

Willoughby continues to run competitively, although not at the same level of intensity as in 1988. In recent years, she has been plagued by injuries and has turned to biking to stay fit.

Willoughby married Dipsea black shirt winner Milan Zeman in 1991 (and is now Kay Willoughby-Zeman). The couple live in Ross. She works in real estate.

Eve Pell, 1989
(April 9, 1937-

Pell has become increasingly successful in her career as an investigative reporter. Several of her documentaries have aired on national television and she has received a number of journalism awards.

Although her work schedule has cut into her training time, Pell continues to race. The Dipsea clearly remains a focus.

Megan McGowan, 1991, '92
(May 12, 1982-

Megan continues to set national age records. She won the U.S. Junior Olympic cross country title in 1992.

After her 4th place in 1993, Megan reiterated her plan to "retire" from the Dipsea, at age 11, to concentrate on her track career. Her ultimate goal remains the Olympic Games.

Shirley Matson, 1993
(November 7, 1940-

One of the first statements from the newly-crowned 1993 champion Matson was, "I will be back."

UNKNOWN

Information on these champions is particularly meager, and I was unable to determine if they remain alive.

Dan Quinlan, 1921
(1903?-)

There is some evidence that Quinlan died in Santa Clara in 1985.

Earl A. Fuller, 1922
(1904-)

Fuller ran in a few subsequent Dipseas, but his later whereabouts are not known.

John Cassidy, 1925
(1905-)

Cassidy continued to compete in the Dipsea for several years and won the best time award in 1928.

The only later information on Cassidy comes from Mary Schwartz, widow of William Schwartz who finished second to him in 1925. She and William met Cassidy in the mid-1950's when he was a contractor during construction of the Cala Foods supermarket at Leland and Rutland streets in their Visitacion Valley (San Francisco) neighborhood. Mary was then surprised to learn that Cassidy had married her Mission High School friend Naomi Reed. Mrs. Schwartz says the Cassidys had no children. A neighbor later reported Cassidy had died.

Lloyd J. Newman, 1926
(circa 1900-)

Neither Reese nor I uncovered any information on Newman.

William Fraser, 1927
(1909?-)

Fraser quickly developed into one of Northern California's best runners. In the next four Dipseas, he achieved the best actual time twice and the second best time twice. He also was second in the Cross-City in 1929 and third in 1930 and 1932. Jim Imperiale recalls meeting Fraser in the late 1950's and says he was active in horseshoe competitions.

Wayne Morefield, 1928
(circa 1905-)

Morefield finished third in the 1930 Dipsea. There is a photograph of Morefield attending the 1963 Dipsea with his neck in a brace.

Raymond Fuller, 1956
(1933?-)

Fuller apparently lived in Walnut Creek in the 1970's but his present whereabouts are not known.

(Opposite top) A record 19 winners at the 1992 Reunion Dinner, Dipsea Cafe, Mill Valley. From left, standing: Ralph Perry, Phil Smith, Darryl Beardall, Gregg Sparks, Carl Jensen, Charles Richesin, Herb Stockman, Bob Hope, Don Pickett, Mike Boitano, Mary Etta Boitano, Kay Willoughby and Sal Vasquez; seated: Florianne Harp, Christie Patterson, Eve Pell, Norman Bright, Ernie Marinoni and Allan Nelson. (Kennard Wilson)
(Opposite bottom) Rod Berry, modern course record holder, admires Hall of Fame plaques presented to Norman Bright at the 1993 Dipsea Dinner. (Kennard Wilson)

WINNERS OF THE DIPSEA
(with age, team, actual time, handicap, margin of victory)

1905	John Hassard, 18, Oakland HS, 1:12:45 (10hc) [1:37]
1906	John Hassard, 19, Century AC, 49:55 (5hc) [:03]
1907	William Joyner, 17, Siaplamat Indians, 55:35 (15hc) [:25]
1908	George Behrmann, ?, Siaplamat Indians, 54:20 (9hc) [1:20]
1909	Basil Spurr, 18, Siaplamat Indians, 55:00 (8hc) [:30]
1910	Oliver Millard, 26, Un, 55:00 (6hc) [:13]
1911	Albert Gorse, ?, Visitacion AC, 57:00 (6hc) [:30]
1912	Donald Dunn, 19, Berkeley HS, 52:36 (6hc) [1:10]
1913	Oliver Millard, 29, Olympic Club, 51:18 (1:30hc) [2:20]
1914	Andrew Ahern, ?, Un, 1:01:00 (15hc) [2:00]
1915	Lee Blackwell, 27, Un, 56:00 (7:30hc) [1:42]
1916	Henry Anderes, 23, Un, 58:50 (12hc) [:12]
1917	Mason Hartwell, 28, Olympic Club, 51:39 (Scr) [2:48]
1918	Percy Gilbert, 20, Oakland YMCA, 55:56 (8:30hc) [:31]
1919	Victor Chapman, 23, Un, 52:46 (6:30hc) [1:09]
1920	William O'Callaghan, 24, USI, 51:30 (5hc) [1:14]
1921	Dan Quinlan, 18?, Un, 57:25?, (9hc) [1:05?]
1922	Earl Fuller, 18, Un, 58:10 (8hc) [:18]
1923	William Letcher, 43, Un, 56:32 (10hc) [1:54]
1924	William Westergard, 23, Olympic Club, 51:39 (4hc) [:36]
1925	John Cassidy, 20, Humboldt Club, 55:26 (9hc) [:20]
1926	Lloyd J. Newman, ?, Un, 53:01 (8hc) [:06?]
1927	William Fraser, 18?, Humboldt Club, 58:48 (10hc) [:15]
1928	Wayne Morefield, ?, Un, 52:00 (8:30hc) [:20]
1929	Angelo Frediani, 26, USI, 56:32 (10hc) [1:38]
1930	William Magner, 25, Olympic Club, 54:13 (9hc) [1:55]
1931	Francis O'Donnell, 27, Olympic Club, 52:00 (6hc) [:30]
1934	Torrey Lyons, 19, UC Berkeley, 53:02 (5hc) [1:02]
1935	John Hansen, 32, Petaluma Spartans, 57:22 (5hc) [:31]
1936	Jimmy McClymonds, 31, Un, 55:47 (8hc) [:41]
1937	Paul Chirone, 24, Petaluma Spartans, 53:06 (6hc) [:16]
1938	Clarence Hall, 22?, S.F. YMCA, 50:41? (2:30hc) [:13]
1939	Allan Nelson, 23, Petaluma Spartans, 55:21 (10hc) [:20]
1940	Ernie Marinoni, 35, Petaluma Spar., 1:00:04 (10hc) [:16]
1941	Willie Dreyer, 37, Victory AC, 56:26 (8hc) [:36]
1946	Charles Richesin, 17, Mill Valley AC, 1:00:22 (10hc) [:25]
1947	Allan Baffico, 15, Excelsior, 59:27 (14hc) [1:00]
1948	Leslie McGregor, 30, Un, 57:04 (8hc) [:02]
1949	Paul Juette, 21, Un, 53:15 (8hc) [1:24]
1950	James Shettler, 17, Excelsior, 58:27 (9hc) [1:47]
1951	Jack Kirk, 44, Petaluma Spartans, 57:10 (4hc) [:10]
1952	Walter Deike, 31, Un, 51:45 (Scr) [3:27]
1953	Ralph Perry, 17, Mt. Hermon School, 55:03 (8hc) [6:56]
1954	Herb Stockman, 22, Thorbs AC, 58:43 (8hc) [1:00]
1955	William Mazzini, 52, Petaluma Spar., 1:05:02 (15hc) [1:08]
1956	Raymond Fuller, 23, SFAC, 1:07:52 (15hc) [:09]
1957	Michael Deasy, 17, SFAC, 55:00 (5hc) [1:30]
1958	Fernando Leon, 20, Un, 51:15 (Scr) [:11]
1959	James Imperiale, 38, Marin AC, 1:02:44 (15hc) [:46]
1960	Bob Hope, 18, Marin AC, 47:41 (3hc) [5:27]
1961	Phil Smith, 23, Marin AC, 58:29 (15hc) [:10]
1962	Peter McArdle, 33, NYAC, 47:30 (Scr) [2:02]
1963	Alan Beardall, 24, Marin AC, 49:07 (3hc) [:20]
1964	Gregg Sparks, 17, Marin AC, 52:19 (11hc) [1:20]
1965	John Satti, 51, Marin AC, 1:01:50 (15hc) [2:01]
1966	Carl Jensen, 21, Marin AC, 48:57 (Scr) [:10]
1967	Jack Kirk, 60, Un, 1:02:56 (15hc) [:05]
1968	Don Pickett, 40, Olympic Club, 54:14 (8hc) [:07]
1969	Vance Eberly, 10, San Jose Yearlings, 57:59 (16hc) [3:06?]
1970	Norman Bright, 60, Olympic Club, 59:46 (15hc) [:16]
1971	Michael Boitano, 9, DSE, 58:53 (15hc) [1:15]
1972	Michael Boitano, 10, DSE, 56:37 (13hc) [2:19]
1973	Mary Etta Boitano, 10, DSE, 58:43 (16hc) [2:39]
1974	Darryl Beardall, 37, Marin AC, 49:57 (6hc) [:14]
1975	Joe Patterson, 40, Australia, 51:58 (7hc) [:11]
1976	Homer Latimer, 38, Un, 50:03 (5hc) [:21]
1977	Homer Latimer, 39, Un, 47:56 (5hc) [3:54]
1978	Darryl Beardall, 41, Tamalpa, 50:03 (8hc) [:57]
1979	Donald Chaffee, 40, Excelsior, 51:40 (6hc) [:03]
1980	Donna Andrews, 39, Tamalpa, 59:51 (15hc) [1:32]
1981	Florianne Harp, 33, Tamalpa, 57:43 (13hc) [1:47]
1982	Sal Vasquez, 42, Pamakids, 50:53 (5hc) [1:02]
1983	Sal Vasquez, 43, Pamakids, 49:58 (5hc) [:16]
1984	Sal Vasquez, 44, Pamakids, 49:18 (4hc) [:20]
1985	Sal Vasquez, 45, Pamakids, 49:56 (4hc) [:51]
1986	Gail LaDage-Scott, 40, Un, 58:19 (14hc) [:42]
1987	Christie Patterson, 39, Tamalpa, 57:06 (12hc) [:18]
1988	Kay Willoughby, 52, Tamalpa, 1:06:40 (22hc) [:07]
1989	Eve Pell, 52, Tamalpa, 1:03:56 (19hc) [1:37]
1990	Sal Vasquez, 50, Un, 52:05 (5hc) [:16]
1991	Megan McGowan, 9, Tamalpa, 1:05:32 (20hc) [:57]
1992	Megan McGowan, 10, Tamalpa, 58:09 (16hc) [1:13]
1993	Shirley Matson, 52, Olympic Club, 1:00:34 (16hc) [:38]

WINNERS OF THE BEST TIME AWARD

MEN

1905	Cornelius Connelly, 1:04:22* (Scr); 2nd	1952	Walter Deike, 51:45 (Scr); 1st
1906	John Hassard, 49:44* (5); 1st	1953	Paul Juette, 53:59 (Scr); 2nd
1907	Otto Boedikker, 53:35 (4:30); 12th	1954	Len Thornton, 54:30 (1); 3rd
1908	Otto Boedikker, 51:45 (2); 8th	1955	Wilford King, 51:08 (1); 2nd
1909	Otto Boedikker, 51:46 (Scr); 21st	1956	Jack Marden, 55:01 (2); 2nd
1910	Mason Hartwell, 52:43 (3:30); 2nd	1957	Wilford King, 52:00 (Scr); 7th
1911	Mason Hartwell, 52:01 (Scr); 3rd	1958	Fernando Leon, 51:15 (Scr); 1st
1912	Mason Hartwell, 47:46* (Scr); 3rd	1959	Fernando Leon, 49:57 (Scr); 4th
1913	Oilver Millard, 51:18 (1:30); 1st	1960	Bob Hope, 47:41 (3); 1st
1914	Oliver Millard, 49:30 (Scr); 7th	1961	Darryl Beardall, 49:09 (3); 6th
1915	Mason Hartwell, 50:40 (Scr); 3rd	1962	Peter McArdle, 47:30 (Scr); 1st
1916	Walter Jones, 51:18 (:30); 12th	1963	Darryl Beardall, 48:02 (Scr); 5th
1917	Mason Hartwell, 51:39 (Scr); 1st	1964	Bill Morgan, 47:29 (Scr); 10th
1918	Wiliam Howden, 54:38 (2:30); 14th	1965	Roy Hughes, 50:05 (Scr); 4th
1919	William Churchill, 50:14 (Scr); 11th	1966	Carl Jensen, 48:57 (Scr); 1st
1920	Mason Hartwell, 49:57 (Scr); 8th	1967	Bob Bunnell, 48:01 (Scr); 2nd
1921	William Churchill, 50:40 (Scr); 6th	1968	Byron Lowry, 47:51 (Scr); 4th
1922	William Churchill, 53:55 (Scr); 18th	1969	Byron Lowry, 47:39 (Scr); 6th
1923	Paul Nieman, 51:01 (Scr); 9th	1970	Don Makela, 46:42* (Scr); 3rd
1924	William Westergaard, 51:39 (4); 1st	1971	Ron Elijah, 46:08* (Scr); 4th
1925	William Westergaard, 52:00 (Scr); 12th	1972	Tom Hale, 46:47 (Scr); 4th
1926	Mason Hartwell, 52:53 (4:30); 6th	1973	Ron Elijah, 49:11 (Scr); 15th
1927	Andy Myrra, 53:03 (4); 2nd	1974	Ron Elijah, 44:49* (Scr); 3rd
1928	John Cassidy, 50:54 (4); 9th	1975	Byron Lowry, 48:17 (2); 6th
1929	William Fraser, 52:29 (Scr); 27th	1976	Bob Bunnell, 48:03 (1); 7th
1930	William Fraser, 51:43 (Scr); 24th	1977	Homer Latimer, 47:56 (5); 1st
1931	Jack Kirk, 50:54 (Scr); 17th	1978	Homer Latimer, 49:00 (6); 2nd
1934	Leo Karlhofer, 51:39 (1); 7th	1979	Joe Ryan, 49:34 (2); 7th
1935	Norman Bright, 52:53 (Scr); 2nd	1980	Joe Ryan, 48:37 (1); 6th
1936	George Wilson, 53:09 (4); 5th	1981	Rod Berry, 46:48* (Scr); 3rd
1937	Norman Bright, 47:22* (Scr); 2nd	1982	Roy Kissin, 49:09 (Scr); 11th
1938	Leo Karlhofer, 49:15 (Scr); 7th	1983	Rod Berry, 47:33* (Scr); 3rd
1939	Clarence Hall, 50:35 (1); 10th	1984	Rod Berry, 49:16 (Scr); 6th
1940	Jack Kirk, 55:20 (5); 2nd	1985	Sal Vasquez, 49:56 (4); 1st
1941	William McCurdy, 54:18 (5); 3rd	1986	Mike McManus, 49:53 (Scr); 10th
1946	William Steed, 52:55 (1); 4th	1987	Mike McManus, 48:21 (Scr); 7th
1947	George Cole, 55:06 (3); 6th	1988	Mike McManus, 49:14 (Scr); 14th
1948	Charles Richesin, 52:04 (3); 2nd	1989	Phil Bellan, 48:39 (Scr); 3rd
1949	William Steed, 52:15 (4); 4th	1990	Mike McManus, 47:59 (Scr); 3rd
1950	Joe Kragel, 51:32 (Scr); 3rd	1991	Mike McManus, 46:53* (Scr); 3rd
1951	Paul Juette, 53:34 (Scr); 3rd	1992	Mike McManus, 47:18 (Scr); 5th
		1993	Dave Dunham, 48:24 (Scr); 6th

WINNERS OF THE BEST TIME AWARD (cont.)

WOMEN

1971	Francis Conley, 1:01:18* (15); 5th
1972	Debbie Rudolf, 1:00:56* (15); 2nd
1973	Mary Etta Boitano, 58:43* (16); 1st
1974	Debbie Rudolf, 56:11* (12); 2nd
1975	Debbie Rudolf, 56:59 (11); 5th
1976	Debbie Rudolf, 59:57 (11); 15th
1977	Barbara Magid, 1:05:46 (15); 19th
1978	Barbara Magid, 1:05:46 (18); 9th
1979	Margaret Livingston, 1:01:25 (14); 4th
1980	Donna Andrews, 59:51 (15); 1st
1981	Florianne Harp, 57:43 (13); 1st
1982	Andrea Eschen, 1:02:10 (11); 18th
1983	Christie Patterson, 1:01:32 (13); 4th
1984	Patricia English, 56:38* (11); 2nd
1985	Peggy Smyth, 57:47 (11); 2nd
1986	Peggy Smyth, 57:25 (11); 4th
1987	Christie Patterson, 57:06 (12); 1st
1988	Peggy Smyth, 55:47* (11); 2nd
1989	Peggy Smyth, 57:19 (8); 5th
1990	Debbie Waldear, 59:11 (9); 9th
1991	AnnaMarie Hagans, 58:41 (8); 11th
1992	Megan McGowan, 58:09 (16); 1st
1993	Gabriele Andersen, 59:12 (14); 2nd

*Recognized as a course record

COURSE RECORDS

MEN

1905	Cornelius Connelly, 1:04:22*
1906	John Hassard, 49:44
1912	Mason Hartwell, 47:46
1937	Norman Bright, 47:22
1970	Rich Delgado, 47:02**
	Don Makela, 46:42
1971	Ron Elijah, 46:08
1974	Ron Elijah, 44:49
1977	Homer Latimer, 47:56***
1981	Rod Berry, 46:48
1983	Rod Berry, 47:33****
1991	Mike McManus, 46:53****

*Significantly longer course than future Dipseas
**Held the record for 100 seconds, until Makela finished
***A new course for record purposes began in 1977; subsequent marks are not necessarily superior to Elijah's 1974 time
****Listed as records in Dipsea Race materials although slower than Berry's 1981 time

WOMEN

1918	Edith Hickman, 1:18:48*
1919	Marion Mehl, 1:15:56*
1920	Priscilla Swearingen, 1:14:44*
1922	Emma Reiman, 1:12:06*
1969	Vicki Eberly, 1:02:02**
1971	Fran Conley, 1:01:18
1972	Debbie Rudolf, 1:00:56
1973	Mary Etta Boitano, 58:43
1974	Debbie Rudolf, 56:11
1980	Donna Andrews, 59:31***
1984	Patricia English, 56:38
1988	Peggy Smyth, 55:47

*From Women's Dipsea Hikes
**Listed in results but technically unofficial entrant
***Though a new course for record purposes began in 1977, Andrews' 1980 mark is the first recognized in Dipsea materials

Ron Elijah completes the fastest crossing of the Dipsea ever, 44:49, in 1974. (Independent Journal)

FASTEST ACTUAL TIMES

MEN

(scratch unless noted)

1. Ron Elijah, 44:49* (1974); 3rd
2. Ron Elijah, 46:08 (1971); 4th
3. Don Makela, 46:42* (1970); 3rd
4. Don Makela, 46:43 (1974); 12th
5. Tom Hale, 46:47 (1972); 4th
6. Rod Berry, 46:48 (1981); 3rd
7. Mike McManus, 46:53 (1991); 3rd
8. Byron Lowry, 46:55 (1971); 8th
9. Rich Delgado, 47:02* (2hc) (1970); 2nd
10. Mike McManus, 47:18 (1992); 5th
11. Norman Bright, 47:22* (1937); 2nd
12. William Morgan, 47:29 (1964); 10th
13. Peter McArdle, 47:30 (1962); 1st
14. Rod Berry, 47:33 (1983); 3rd
15. Byron Lowry, 47:39 (1969); 6th
16. Bob Hope, 47:41 (3hc) (1960); 1st
17. Byron Lowry, 47:51 (1968); 4th
18. Mason Hartwell, 47:56* (1912); 3rd
    Homer Latimer, 47:56 (5hc) (1977); 1st
20. Mike McManus, 47:59 (1990); 3rd
21. Ron Elijah, 48:00 (1969); 7th
22. Bob Bunnell, 48:01 (1967); 2nd
23. Darryl Beardall, 48:02 (1963); 5th
24. Bob Bunnell, 48:03 (1hc) (1976); 7th
24. Rich Delgado, 48:06 (1967); 3rd
25. Andrew Volmer, 48:11 (1969); 9th
26. Jack Lawson, 48:15 (1968); 7th
27. Byron Lowry, 48:17 (2hc) (1975); 6th
28. Bill Scobey, 48:21 (1970); 7th
    Mike McManus, 48:21 (1987); 7th
30. Don Makela, 48:22 (1971); 15th
    Don Makela, 48:22 (1975); 14th
32. Dave Dunham, 48:24 (1993); 6th
33. Mike Dailey, 48:25 (1967); 4th
34. Bob Bunnell, 48:26 (1hc) (1975); 10th
35. William Ferlatte, 48:27 (2hc) (1963); 2nd
36. William Ferlatte, 48:28 (1968); 8th
    B.W. Edwards, 48:28 (1972); 20th
38. Mike Dailey, 48:30 (1968); 9th
39. Ronald Davis, 48:31 (1963); 8th
40. Mike McManus, 48:32 (1993); 8th

WOMEN

1. Peggy Smyth, 55:47* (11hc) (1988); 2nd
2. Patricia English, 55:49 (11hc) (1988); 3rd
3. Debbie Rudolf, 56:11* (12hc) (1974); 2nd
4. Patricia English, 56:38* (11hc) (1984); 2nd
5. Mary Etta Boitano, 56:55 (12hc) (1974); 5th
6. Debbie Rudolf, 56:59 (11hc) (1975); 5th
7. Debbie Waldear, 57:04 (11hc) (1988); 5th
8. Christie Patterson, 57:06 (12hc) (1987); 1st
9. Peggy Smyth, 57:19 (8hc) (1989); 5th
10. Peggy Smyth, 57:25 (11hc) (1986); 4th
11. Debbie Waldear, 57:35 (11hc) (1987); 4th
12. Florianne Harp, 57:43 (13hc) (1981); 1st
13. Peggy Smyth, 57:47 (11hc) (1985); 2nd
14. Debbie Waldear, 57:54 (8hc) (1989); 7th
15. Nan Hall, 58:09 (11hc) (1988); 8th
16. Megan McGowan, 58:09 (16hc) (1992); 1st
17. Peggy Smyth, 58:11 (11hc) (1984); 3rd
18. Gail Scott, 58:19 (14hc) (1986); 1st
19. Gail Scott, 58:24 (13hc) (1987); 2nd
20. AnnaMarie Hagans, 58:25 (8hc) (1992); 13th

*Race record when set

FASTEST CLOCK TIMES

1. William Joyner, 40:35 (15hc), 1907; 1st
2. Frank Bartosh, 41:00 (14), 1907; 2nd
3. Gregg Sparks, 41:19 (11), 1964; 1st
4. Robert Howden, 41:20 (15), 1907; 3rd
5. Vance Eberly, 41:59 (16), 1969; 1st
6. Darryl Beardall, 42:03 (8), 1978; 1st
7. Megan McGowan, 42:09 (16), 1992; 1st
8. Frank Kispert, 42:10 (15), 1907; 4th
9. Ed Hartley, 42:35 (15), 1907; 5th
10. Tim Terriberry, 42:36 (14), 1964; 2nd
11. Homer Latimer, 42:56 (5), 1977; 1st
12. Homer Latimer, 43:00 (6), 1978; 2nd
13. Mark Leonard, 43:11 (14), 1964; 3rd
14. Jim Nicholson, 43:13 (10), 1978; 3rd
15. Shirley Matson, 43:22 (16), 1992; 2nd
16. George Kennedy, 43:26 (13), 1964; 4th
17. Phil Smith, 43:29 (15), 1961; 1st
18. Wayne Morefield, 43:30 (8:30), 1928; 1st
19. Mike Boitano, 43:37 (13), 1972; 1st
20. Stuart Sparling, 43:39 (8), 1961; 2nd

Well over a thousand trophies have been awarded through the decades at the Dipsea. Listed below are the trophies currently presented annually (or only recently discontinued), that are not already cited in the yearly results, e.g. overall winner, men's and women's best time winner and team. Examples of lapsed trophies include ones for the first Stinson Beach, Mill Valley and Marin County resident finishers, one for "novice" (first-time Dipsea entrant) and ones for the second- and third-fastest actual times. (The men's second best time winner is already noted in all the yearly accounts.)

OVER-40 (Boas Brothers Trophy)
(with finish place, actual time; women from 1979)
1967   Robert Biancalana (24th, 1:00:31)
1968   Don Pickett (1st, 54:14)
1969   Larry Hoyt (5th, 55:19)
1970   Don Pickett (13th, 55:03)
1971   Owen Gorman (3rd, 53:00)
1972   Dennis Teeguarden (12th, 54:26)
1973   Don Pickett (3rd, 54:42)
1974   Jim Nicholson (9th, 52:42)
1975   Joe Patterson (1st, 51:58)
1976   John Finch (2nd, 52:24)
1977   Darryl Beardall (4th, 54:27)
1978   Darryl Beardall (1st, 50:03)
1979   Don Chaffee (1st, 51:40); Betsy White (12th, 1:01:25)
1980   Russ Kiernan (2nd, 51:23); Joan Don (26th, 1:06:55)
1981   Sal Vasquez (2nd, 51:31); Pat Whittingslow (20th, 1:05:56)
1982   Sal Vasquez (1st, 50:53); Eve Pell (3rd, 1:04:28)
1983*   Russ Kiernan (2nd, 52:48); Eve Pell (18th, 1:09:01)
1984   Sal Vasquez (1st, 49:18); Judie Donovan (7th, 1:09:59)
1985   Sal Vasquez (1st, 49:56); Pat Whittingslow (11th, 1:08:02)
1986   Sal Vasquez (4th, 50:19); Gail Scott (1st, 58:19)
*Awarded to first over-45

OVER-50 (Jimmy Nicholson Trophy)
(with finish place, actual time)
1987   Darryl Beardall (9th, 56:04)
1988   Russ Kiernan (7th, 53:57)
1989   Darryl Beardall (6th, 56:44)
1990   Sal Vasquez (1st, 52:05)
1991   Sal Vasquez (5th, 53:48)
1992   Shirley Matson (2nd, 59:22)*
*Should have gone to Jim Bowers (3rd, 54:32)

FATHER-SON
(with finish place, father first)
1947   Dominic (36th) & Tony (33rd) Stratta
1948   Dominic (15th) & Tony (17th) Stratta
1949   Dominic (25th) & Tony (56th) Stratta
1950   Dominic (15th) & Tony (4th) Stratta
1951 to 1966 - not awarded
1967   Robert (24th) & Joe (49th) Biancalana
1968   Robert (26th) & Mike (36th) Biancalana
1969   Robert (24th) & Mike (22nd) Biancalana
1970   Frank (33rd) & George (61st) Harrison
1971   Jim (120th) & Mike (11th) Killeen
1972   John (68th) & Mike (1st) Boitano
1973   John (39th) & Mike (2nd) Boitano
1974   tie; Gil (17th) & Boyd (56th) Tarin, John (69th) & Mike (4th) Boitano
1975   Gil (8th) & Boyd (51st) Tarin
1976   Gil (8th) & Boyd (28th) Tarin

MOTHER-DAUGHTER
(with finish place, mother first)
1969   Myrrha (579th) & Vicki (21st) Eberly
1970   Lucille (606th) & Mary Etta (280th) Boitano
1971   Lucille (886th) & Mary Etta (154th) Boitano
1972   Lucille (738th) & Mary Etta (57th) Boitano
1973   Carroll (156th) & Kathleen (337th) O'Conner
1974   Carroll (280th) & Elizabeth (430th) O'Conner
1975   Carroll (149th) & Kathleen (822nd) O'Conner
1976   Barbara (247th) & Anna (181st) Carlson

(Left) Byron Lowry in 1969 with the second of his three best time trophies. (Courtesy Jim Stephenson) (Below) The silver trophy, with three stag horns as handles, awarded to 1905 best time winner Cornelius Connelly, 1993. (Kennard Wilson, courtesy Frank Silva)

HUSBAND-WIFE
(with finish place, husband first)
1972 John (5th) & Priscilla (513th) Butterfield
1973 Owen (12th) & M. (282nd) Gorman
1974 not listed
1975 Gene (67th) & Betsy (13th) White
1976 Mike (22nd) & Mary (119th) Healy

FAMILY (Alan Beardall Trophy from 1989)
(with finish place, relationship)
1977 Paul (15th) & Mark (52nd) Reese; father-son
1978 Pat (48th) & Keith (72nd) Whittingslow; wife-husband
1979 Barbara Magid (15th) & Jennifer Biddulph (56th); mother-daughter
1980 Russ (2nd) & Don (102nd) Kiernan; brothers
1981 Don (6th) and Toby (47th) Pickett; father-son
1982 Barbara Magid (12th) & Jennifer Biddulph; mother-daughter
1983 Pat (12th) and Keith (77nd) Whittingslow; wife-husband
1984 Don (28th) & Toby Pickett (31st); father-son
1985 Don (7th) & Toby Pickett (39th); father-son
1986 Don (26th) & Toby Pickett (30th); father-son
1987 Darryl (9th) & Tim Beardall (26th); uncle-nephew
1988 Arnold (20th) & Toby Knepfer (46th); father-son
1989 Darryl (6th) & Tim Beardall (29th); uncle-nephew
1990 Tim (11th) & Darryl Beardall (18th); nephew-uncle
1991 Christie Patterson (22nd) & Tomas Pastalka (73rd); wife-husband
1992 Joan (4th) & Steve (24th) Ottaway; wife-husband
1993 Leslie McMullin (12th) & Jim Hampton (47th); wife-husband

JAMES FARREN, JR. MEMORIAL
"Sportsmanship, Leadership and
Dedication to the Dipsea"
1982 Jack Kirk
1983 Jerry Hauke
1984 Russ Kiernan
1985 Mike Restani
1986 Don Pickett
1987 Bob Knez
1988 Ralph and Barbara Brabo
1989 Dick and Carolyn Wilson
1990 Merv Regan
1991 Sandra Robbins
1992 Barry Spitz
1993 Hans Roenau

NORMAN BRIGHT
"Extraordinary Effort in the Dipsea Race"
1985 Jack Kirk
1986 Don Chaffee
1987 Barbara Magid
1988 Jim McGowan
1989 Ron Rahmer
1990 Mike McManus
1991 Megan McGowan
1992 Megan McGowan
1993 Dave Dunham

HIGH SCHOOL* (Van Vliet, 1906-21; Brazil Brothers, 1954-74)
(with school, actual time, handicap, finish place)
1906 John Little (Lick, S.F), 56:58 (12hc), 2nd
1907 A. Codington (Cogswell, S.F.), 1:02:17 (15hc), 6th
1908 William Maghetti (San Rafael), 1:00:45 (10hc), 12th
1909 William Henderson (Humboldt Evening, S.F.), 1:00:30 (10hc), 13th
1910 Harold Young (Fremont, Oakland), 58:30 (7hc), 5th
1911 H. Morton (Mountain View), 1:03:36 (5hc), 23rd
1912 E. Lloyd (Fremont, Oakland), 56:22 (7hc), 5th
1913 Clarence Fugua (Cogswell, S.F.), 59:05 (6hc), 6th
1914 Ray Glennon (Cogswell, S.F.), 1:00:50 (12hc), 4th
1915 E. Schwarz (Oakland Tech), 1:05:43 (10hc), 16th
1916 E. Schwarz (Oakland Tech), 58:46 (10hc), 5th
1917 Victor Chapman (Commercial Evening, S.F.), 56:27 (7hc), 3rd
1918 William Crockett (Alameda Evening), 1:00:45 (7hc), 23rd
1919 Clifford Vis (Alameda), 1:03:03 (10hc), 4th
1920 Bert Hooper (Humboldt Evening, S.F.), 1:01:59 (7hc), 37th
1921 C. Green, 1:00:26 (7:30hc), 20th
1922 to 1953—not awarded
1954 Mel Dowdell (Polytechnic, S.F.), 59:22 (4hc), 8th
1955 Robert Marinoni (St. Ignatius, S.F.), 1:04:11 (12hc), 4th
1956 Gordon Waldo (Calaveras), 1:01:54 (8hc), 4th
1957 Mike Deasy (St. Ignatius, S.F.), 55:00 (5hc), 1st
1958 Bob Johnson (Polytechnic, S.F.), 56:25 (5hc), 2nd
1959 Bob Hope (Tamalpais, Mill Valley), 52:33 (3hc), 3rd
1960 Bob Hope (Tamalpais, Mill Valley), 47:41 (3hc), 1st
1961 Walter Andrae, 55:24 (7hc), 12th
1962 Jim McNutt (San Carlos), 53:53 (2hc), 8th
1963 not awarded
1964 Mike Ryan (Wilcox, San Jose), 49:07 (Scr), 24th

1965   Dave Barni (San Rafael), 52:38 (Scr), 12th
1966   Will Stephens (San Mateo), 49:07 (Scr), 2nd
1967   Bob Bunnell (Terra Linda, San Rafael), 48:01 (Scr), 2nd
1968   Jack Lawson (Modesto), 48:15 (Scr), 7th
1969   Ron Elijah (Novato), 48:00 (Scr), 7th
1970   Ron Elijah (Novato), 49:01 (Scr), 12th
1971   Mike Wolford, 53:22 (Scr), 9th
1972   Jack Bellah (Leigh, San Jose), 51:11 (Scr), 34th
1973   Dave Cortez (St. Francis, Mountain View), 52:48 (4hc), 13th
1974   R. Schupbach, 55:54 (8hc), 35th
1975 to 1986—not awarded
1987   Amy McConnell (University, S.F.), 1:00:41 (12hc), 8th
1988   Erin Vali (Irvine), 52:48 (4hc), 12th
1989   Erin Vali (Irvine), 52:16 (2hc), 8th
1990   Matt Metzger (University, S.F.), 51:11 (2hc), 6th
1991   Jon Sargent (Monte Vista, Alamo), 56:23 (4hc), 15th
1992   Jon Sargent (Monte Vista), 55:17 (3hc), 26th
1993   Jon Sargent (Monte Vista), 58:25 (2hc), 75th

*In some years, this trophy was awarded to the high schooler with the fastest actual time, in others (as at present) to the first to finish. Also complicating the award list was the AAU rule, enforced in the first decades of the Dipsea, that no runner could win more than one individual trophy. If the first high school runner earned a place prize, the high school trophy went to a later finisher. This happened at least in 1912, 1915 and 1916.

DIPSEA RUNNER*
(with actual time, handicap)
1985   Ed Dux (52:39, 2hc)**; Heidi Quadri (1:03:02, 11hc)
1986   John Hodge (53:22, Scr); Twyla Willis (1:09:57, 11hc)
1987   Joan Colman (1:02:21, 15hc); Craig Roland (1:00:49, 8hc)
1988   Cynthia Chilton (1:05:14, 11hc)
1989   Michael Burton (52:55, Scr)
1990   Tim Minor (50:23, Scr)
1991   Mark Richtman (53:08, 1hc)
1992   Brock Tessman, (55:37, 3hc)
1993   Mitchell Shandley (52:47, 1hc)

*Although the second, Dipsea Runner section began in 1977, a trophy for first man and woman was not awarded until 1985. From 1988, the trophy went to first place overall only.
**This mark is questioned because of Dux' subsequent disqualification for cheating in the Double Dipsea. Thomas Iredale (54:20, 2hc) was the next man to finish.

MISCELLANEOUS DIPSEA RECORDS

Most victories 5, Sal Vasquez (1982-85, 1990)

Oldest winner Jack Kirk, 60 years, 10 months, 24 days (1967)

Youngest winner Megan McGowan, 1991 (9 years, 28 days)

Largest victory margin 6:56, Ralph Perry (1953)

Smallest victory margin :02, Leslie McGregor (1948)

Longest span, first Dipsea to victory 35 years, Norman Bright (1935-1970)

Most Races before victory 18, Darryl Beardall

Most years between victories 16, Jack Kirk (1951-1967)

Most best time awards 7, Mason Hartwell

Most best time awards (woman) 4, Debbie Rudolf and Peggy Smyth

Largest best time margin 5:21, Joseph Kragel (1950)

Oldest best time winner (man) Sal Vasquez, 45 (1985)

Oldest best time winner (woman) Gabriele Anderson, 48 (1993)

Most second place finishes 3, Jack Kirk, Norman Bright and Russ Kiernan

Most top-five finishes 8, Jack Kirk, Darryl Beardall and Russ Kiernan

Most top-ten finishes 19, Darryl Beardall

Most consecutive top-ten finishes 12, Russ Kiernan (1977-1988)

Most team awards 22, Darryl Beardall

Highest average place (minimum 5 Dipseas) 2.9, Sal Vasquez

Most Dipsea finishes 58, Jack Kirk (consecutive from 1930)

Most years, first Dipsea to last 63, Bill Magner (1921-1984) and Jack Kirk (1930-

HANDICAPS

The Dipsea has always been a handicapped race. Runners are given headstarts over the zero-handicap men, known as the "scratch" group. The first one to the finish line wins. A runner's actual time less his or her handicap is called "clock time"—it matches what the official clocks started with the scratch group read. For scratch runners, actual and clock times are always identical.

From 1905 until 1965, handicaps were individually assigned, based on perceived ability. An official or committee of officials would assess each entrant's past performances and assign the headstart. Unknown runners would be lumped into a middle ground "safe" group. The maximum ("limit") handicap was generally 10 or 15 minutes, occasionally less (with a low of six in 1913). Scratch, or "the place of honor," was reserved for only the very greatest runners; there were several years with no scratch starters. Most handicaps were whole minutes, although 30 second intervals (and even 15 second intervals) were commonly used in earlier years.

In 1965 a momentous change was made; handicaps became based entirely on age. No longer would every entrant, however "ordinary" (provided they were capable of running approximately 65 minutes, which was usually near the sum of the best scratch time plus the maximum handicap), have a theoretical equal chance of winning. Only those who clearly excelled in their own age groups could win. Also, the scratch group became much the largest in the Race.

In 1969, when women began running the Dipsea in significant numbers, the handicaps became based on both age and sex. The first "woman," 10-year-old Mary Etta Boitano, won in 1973. Nine different women (and only one man) have won from 1980 through 1993.

Jim "Birdman" Weil, an expert on computers and oddsmaking (he's a regular at local horserace tracks), has been the Dipsea's handicapper for the past 15 years. His famous trademark response to criticisms of the handicaps is, "Run faster." Weil prepared the following statement of modern Dipsea handicapping policy for this book.

The head start assignments derived from historical record times are based in part on judgment, but year-to-year adjustments since 1982 have been based on five guidelines:

1. Handicaps are assigned to promote competition to win. They are not based on average performances by many winners in each age group.

2. Handicaps are based on actual performances in Dipsea races, not measures of human potential taken form other distances or other races. This is the only way to include the effects of the Dipsea's unique terrain and time lost passing other runners.

3. Handicaps are adjusted to reflect superior performances each year. This does not mean that every new single-age record forces a change in the handicaps.

4. Handicaps should change over time, as better record times are achieved each year. Men's times are now relatively stable, but as of 1993 women's times continue to improve, sometimes dramatically.

5. Some judgment is still needed to set handicaps when individual runners—such as Ron Elijah, Sal Vasquez, Megan McGowan and Shirley Matson—set records that are several minutes faster than prior records or records by runners of nearby ages. These superior efforts are adjusted by one or two minutes to smooth the handicapping "line" (the graph of head start minutes vs. age).

In recent years there have been 23 separate starting groups in each of the Invitational and Runner sections—one every minute from a 22 minute headstart down through scratch. (There is talk of lowering the maximum headstart to 20 minutes.) The only group that hasn't had their handicap changed since the age formula began in 1965 is men 21-24; they have always been scratch.

Beginning in 1986, anyone having won the Dipsea within the previous five years lost one handicap minute (the so-called "Sal Vasquez Rule"). From 1993, these runners lost a minute for each such win (the "Megan McGowan Rule").

In 1974 only, men over 250 pounds received a special handicap.

Below, in a condensed format, are the handicaps in minutes ("m") for each Dipsea since 1965.

1965
15m\over 44; 10m\40-44; 5m\35-39; Scr\under 35.

1966
11m\over 44; 8m\40-44; 5m\34-39; 4m\under 17; Scr\17-33.

1967, 1968
15m\over 57, under 12; 11m\45-57; 8m\40-44; 5m\35-39; 3m\12-14; Scr\15-34.

1969*
Men: 15m\over 57, under 12; 11m\45-47; 8m\40-44; 5m\35-39; 3m\12-14; Scr\15-34.
Women: 15m\over 39, under 13; 9m\13-39.
*Due to errors at the start line, actual handicaps differed from the assigned ones given above. To get actual headstarts over the scratch group, deduct 2m from men ages 12-14 and add 1m to all other groups.

1970
Men: 15m\over56, under 11; 12m\55-56; 8m\51-54; 7m\45-50, 11-12; 6m\40-44; 5m\35-39; 4m\13-15; 2m\30-34; 1m\27-29; Scr\16-26.
Women: 15m\over 39, under 13; 11m\26-39; 9m\13-25.

1971
Men: 15m\over 56, under 11; 13m\55-56; 10m\50-54; 8m\45-49, 11; 7m\40-44, 12; 6m\13-14; 4m\35-39, 15; 1m\33-34; Scr\16-32.
Women: 15m\over 25, under 14; 10m\14-25.

1972, 1973*
Men: 15m\over 56, under 9; 13m\55-56, 9-10; 10m\50-54, 11; 8m\45-49, 12; 7m\40-44; 6m\13-14; 5m\35-39; 4m\33-34, 15; 3m\30-32; 2m\28-29; 1m\25-27; Scr\16-24.
Women: 15m\over 25, under 14; 10m\14-25.
*In 1973, all groups with 7 or fewer handicap minutes were inadvertently delayed one minute beyond the assigned handicaps given here.

1974
Men: 14m\over 56; 13m\55-56, under 11; 11m\53-54; 10m\50-52; 9m\over 250 pounds; 8m\45-49, 12; 7m\40-44; 6m\36-39, 13-14; 5m\35; 4m\33-34, 15; 3m\30-32; 2m\28-29; 1m\25-27; Scr\16-24.
Women: 13m\over 25, under 11; 12m\11-14; 11m\15-25.

1975, 1976
Men: 14m\over 56; 13m\55-56; 12m\54; 11m\52-53, under 12; 10m\50-51; 9m\47-49; 8m\45-46, 12; 7m\40-44; 6m\39, 13-14; 5m\36-38; 4m\33-35, 15; 3m\30-32; 2m\28-29; 1m\25-27; Scr\16-24.
Women: 14m\over 33; 13m\26-33, under 11; 11m\11-25.

1977
Men: 15m\over 56; 13m\55-56, under 10; 11m\52-54; 9m\47-51, 10-11; 7m\40-46, 12; 5m\33-39, 13-14; 3m\27-32, 15; Scr\16-26.
Women: 15m\over 33, under 11; 13m\26-33; 11m\11-25.

1978, 1979*
Men: 14m\over 57, under 10; 12m\55-57; 10m\50-54, 10-11; 8m\45-49; 6m\40-44; 4m\35-39, 13-14; 2m\30-34, 15; 1m\27-29; Scr\16-24.
Women: 16m\over 33, under 11; 14m\26-33; 12m\11-25.
*In 1979, the scratch group was inadvertently started two minutes late; add two minutes to all other assigned handicaps above to get the actual headstarts over scratch.

1980, 1981*
Men: 13m\over 57, under 10; 11m\55-57; 9m\50-54, 10-11; 7m\45-49, 12; 5m\40-44; 3m\35-39, 13-14; 1m\29-34, 15; Scr\16-28.
Women: 17m\over 44; 15m\34-44, under 11; 13m\26-33; 11m\11-25.
*Same as 1980 except women ages 11-12 got 13m.

1982, 1983

Men: 17m\over 64; 15m\62-64; 13m\58-61, under 10; 11m\55-57, 10; 9m\50-54, 11; 7m\45-49, 12; 5m\40-44, 13; 3m\35-39, 14-15; 1m\29-34, 16-17; Scr\18-28.

Women: 17m\over 44, under 10; 15m\40-44, 10; 13m\35-39, 11; 11m\12-34.

1984-1986*

Men: 20m\over 66, under 6; 19m\66, 6; 18m\65; 17m\63-64, 7; 16m\62; 15m\61, 8; 14m\60; 13m\59, 9; 12m\57-58; 11m\56, 10; 10m\54-55; 9m\53, 11; 8m\51-52, 12; 7m\49-50; 6m\47-48, 13; 5m\46, 14; 3m\41-43, 15; 2m\36-40, 16; 1m\29-35, 17; Scr\18-28.

Women: 20m\over 47, under 9; 19m\47; 18m\45-46; 17m\44; 16m\43; 15m\41-42, 9; 14m\40; 13m\38-39, 10; 12m\35-37, 11; 11m\12-34.

*Same as 1984 except, in 1985 and '86, women age 9 got 16m and women age 10 got 14m.

1987

Men: 22m\over 68, under 7; 21m\68; 20m\67; 19m\66, 7; 18m\65; 17m\63-64; 16m\62, 8; 15m\61; 14m\60; 13m\59, 9; 12m\57-58; 11m\56, 10; 10m\54-55; 9m\53, 11; 8m\51-52, 12; 7m\49-50, 13; 6m\47-48, 14; 5m\46, 15; 4m\44-45, 16; 3m\41-43, 17; 2m\35-40, 18; 1m\28-34, 19-20; Scr\21-27.

Women: 22m\over 51, under 9; 21m\51, 9; 20m\50; 19m\48-49, 10; 18m\47; 17m\45-46, 11; 16m\44; 15m\43, 12; 14m\41-43, 13; 13m\40, 14; 12m\38-39, 15; 11m\16-37.

1988

Men: Same as 1987 except age 27 got 1m.

Women: 22m\over 51, under 9; 21m\51, 9; 20m\50; 19m\48-49, 10; 18m\47; 17m\46, 11; 16m\45; 15m\44, 12; 14m\43, 13; 13m\41, 14; 12m\40, 15-16; 11m\17-39.

1989

Men: 22m\over 68, under 7; 21m\68; 20m\67; 19m\66; 18m\65, 7; 17m\64; 16m\63; 15m\62, 8; 14m\61; 13m\60; 12m\59, 9; 11m\58; 10m\56-57, 10; 9m\55; 8m\53-54, 11; 7m\52, 12; 6m\50-51, 13; 5m\48-49, 14; 4m\45-47, 15; 3m\42-44, 16; 2m\38-41, 17; 1m\33-37, 18; Scr\19-32.

Women: 22m\over 54, under 9; 21m\54; 20m\53, 9; 19m\52; 18m\51, 10; 17m\50; 16m\48-49, 11; 15m\47; 14m\46, 12; 13m\45; 12m\44, 13; 11m\43, 14; 10m\41-42, 15; 9m\40, 16-18; 8m\19-39.

1990, 1991

Men: Same as 1989 except add 1m to age 32 in 1990 and to age 31 in 1991.

Women: 22m\over 55, under 9; 21m\55; 20m\54, 9; 19m\53; 18m\52, 10; 17m\51; 16m\49-50, 11; 15m\48; 14m\47, 12; 13m\46; 12m\44-45, 13; 11m\43, 14; 10m\41-42, 15; 9m\40, 16-18; 8m\19-39.

1992

Men: Same as 1991.

Women: 22m\over 56, under 9; 21m\56; 20m\55; 19m\54, 9; 18m\53; 17m\52, 10; 16m\51; 15m\49-50, 11; 14m\48; 13m\47, 12; 12m\46, 13; 11m\44-45, 14; 10m\41-43, 15; 9m\40, 16-18; 8m\19-39.

1993

Men: 22m\over 68, under 7; 21m\68; 20m\67; 19m\66; 18m\65, 7; 17m\64; 16m\63; 15m\62, 8; 14m\61; 13m\60; 12m\58-59, 9; 11m\57; 10m\56, 10; 9m\55; 8m\53-54, 11; 7m\52, 12; 6m\50-51, 13; 5m\48-49, 14; 4m\45-47, 15; 3m\42-44, 16; 2m\38-41, 17; 1m\31-37, 18; Scr\19-30.

Women: 22m\over 57, under 9; 21m\57; 20m\56; 19m\55, 9; 18m\54; 17m\53; 16m\52, 10; 15m\51, 11; 14m\49-50; 13m\48, 12; 12m\45-47, 13; 11m\44-45, 14; 10m\41-43, 15; 9m\40, 16-18; 8m\19-39.

Timothy Fitzpatrick leading the Dipsea Indians on the traditional day-before brisk walk over to Willow Camp, circa 1920. In some years this was done at night, lit by torches. (Courtesy Frank Maher)

ORGANIZERS OF THE DIPSEA RACE

One of the enduring Dipsea traditions—true in 1905, in 1993 and for most every year in between—is that the Race is organized by a committee of volunteers. This is unlike many of today's major races, where a paid director has primary responsibility. Even more unusual, the Dipsea has not had (or sought) "sponsors." Most goods and services have traditionally been donated. From 1964, when the first entry charge (50 cents) was levied, runners fees have financed the Race. To many, this all-volunteer, strictly non-commercial approach is part of the Dipsea's appeal.

The Dipsea has also managed to survive despite several major organizational changes; such changes have often proved fatal to other old-time races. Below is a chronology of the organizers of the Dipsea Race.

1905-1924, Dipsea Indians

The Race was founded by, and guided through its crucial formative years, by the Dipsea Indians. These were members of San Francisco's influential Olympic Club who had formed a sub-group specifically to stage the Dipsea. The "Dipsea Indian," a facial portrait of a native American chief in full head dress, became (and long remained) the Race's symbol.

Mike Buckley, one of the Indians, provided an introduction to Reese's book and cited key long-time workers. Buckley singled out: "Leon Pinkson, who never failed year after year to supply the trucks, autos and buses for the transportation of men and fodder. Harry Smith, who always hustled the news items and publicity sources; likewise Douglas Erskine who also doubled in handicaps. The medicos, silent men who sidetracked the glamor, and patched and mended countless emergency cases, without a serious fatality. And the

Treasurer/Secretary panel, Vince Finigan and Oscar Turnblad, who met the bills, usually head on, and occasionally in desperation whispered an apologetic, 'Gimme a few bucks. The heat's on and even the tide's run out on us!'"

But clearly the towering figure in the founding and nurturing of the Dipsea was Timothy I. Fitzpatrick (1876-1963). His was the first name listed on the first Dipsea Race program.

Fitzpatrick was born in San Francisco. His early sports passion was baseball; in his later years it would be golf. He graduated from St. Ignatius College, today's University of San Francisco, in 1893. In 1897, he received his law degree from Hastings. The following year he began a private law practice.

In 1900, Fitzpatrick joined the Olympic Club; he remained a member for 63 years and was a director for 22. As an original Dipsea Indian, he was appointed their first, and would remain their only, "Big Chief" (Race director). Fitzpatrick's vision, integrity, contacts, organizational skills and force of personality helped the Dipsea survive and grow.

When the Dipsea Indians handed over the Race to the Olympic Club itself in 1925, Fitzpatrick remained the principal official. After the Club withdrew its sponsorship in 1931, Fitzpatrick stepped back but continued to keep a close watch. In the early 1950's, when the Dipsea was in financial danger, Fitzpatrick was a leader in rallying the surviving Indians to help. For 1954, the golden anniversary of the Coney-Boas match race, he stepped in again as chairman to insure the Dipsea was up to old standards. He continued as the Dipsea Race Chairman until the year of his death.

Meanwhile, Fitzpatrick became one of the most respected of San Francisco's judges. In 1915, he was named police magistrate. In 1920, he was elevated to the Superior Court. He also lectured on probate law, his specialty, at the University of San Francisco Law School. He never married; his closest survivor is today another Superior Court judge, nephew Roy Williamson.

One of Fitzpatrick's obituaries read, "Friends in every walk of life sorrowed at the death of a man of strength and service without peer in San Francisco memory." Fitzpatrick was one of the five initial inductees into the Dipsea Race Hall of Fame.

The Dipsea Indians proved a hearty lot. Almost three dozen attended the group's 50th reunion dinner in the City in 1954. Here are excerpts from an account of that reunion, written by Frank Herman for the October, 1954, *Olympian*.

The fiftieth anniversary of the Dipsea Indian Marathon last month was celebrated in typical tribal style with a big Powwow in the "wigwam" of the Family Club. These annual get-togethers find many of the old warriors who were among the braves who did a war dance on the shores of the Pacific Ocean at Stinson Beach at the end of the first race still full of vim and enthusiasm about the historic race. That seven-mile, dusty trail leading from Mill Valley over the hills to the quaint little seaside village where the surf lashes the sandy shore, is something which can never be erased from the memory of these pioneer Dipsea Indians . . .

It was a happy reunion of valiant hikers who derive keen enjoyment reminiscing about ye olden days, when walking over dusty trails was a regular outing. Landmarks of the original trail were touched upon with due reverence by septuagenarians, whose eyes gleamed with all the brilliance of youth as they recalled happy incidents along the trail and during the never-to-be-forgotten days and nights at Stinson Beach.

The last annual Dipsea Indian reunion was held in 1963. A few survivors, particularly Lloyd Roach (who recorded an oral history for the Anne

Kent California History Room at the Marin County Civic Center Library), assisted Reese in the 1970's. All the Dipsea Indians are now gone.

1925-1931, Olympic Club

Organization of the Race was assumed directly by the Olympic Club. The change was relatively minor—the "Winged O" logo replaced the Indian chief figure on the program cover—as many Dipsea Indians, including Fitzpatrick, remained in their usual roles. Charles Hunter, who served as the Olympic Club's "trainer" (coach) for running, became a key figure in the Race.

1934-1938, Sunrise Breakfast Club

After the 1931 Race, with the nation in the Depression, the Olympic Club withdrew its sponsorship. The Dipsea was in danger of disappearing. After a two-year hiatus, the Sunrise Breakfast Club, another influential San Francisco group, stepped in. The Club, which was headed by Peter Maloney, formed a separate Dipsea Committee. Many Olympic Clubbers continued working the Race and Fitzpatrick remained the Referee. Several former champions (such as Oliver Millard, Mason Hartwell and William Joyner) served as Race officials.

1939-1953, Mill Valley Chamber of Commerce

Marvelous Marin, Inc., a group seeking to further development of Marin County in the heady days after the Golden Gate Bridge opened (1937), came forward to stage the Dipsea for three years. A co-organizer was the Mill Valley Chamber of Commerce, which would remain involved, although some years only marginally, through 1953. The Stinson Beach Progressive Club joined in for the 1940 Dipsea and continued for several Races.

Also in 1939, the front of the Dipsea program stated, for the first time, that the Race was "under supervision [of the] Pacific Association Amateur Athletic Union." AAU officials such as Art Articary, Frank Geis, Tommy Laughran and Bob DeCelle would play major roles in the Dipsea over the next years.

Jerry Hauke, guiding figure of the Dipsea Race for over 30 years; 1991. (Court Mast, Independent Journal)

The late 1940's and early 1950's, after four Dipseas had already been cancelled (1941-1945), were troubled ones sponsor-wise. A sub-group of the Mill Valley Chamber, with Emil Pohli and "Dipsea Committee" chairman Irving Links as key workers, staged the Race in 1949 as "The Dipseans." Articary and the AAU itself kept the Race alive in 1950.

1954-1962, South of Market Boys

The South of Market Boys, a San Francisco social club, took on the Race in 1954 and restored stability. Judge Fitzpatrick continued to be listed, right below the honorary chairmen (the mayors of San Francisco), as chairman on the programs. Art Articary had primary responsibility for the Race itself. The handicapping, which had earlier been by committee, was now done by individuals, first Attilio Maggiora, then Tommy Laughran.

1963-1977, Mill Valley
Junior Chamber of Commerce

The Mill Valley Junior Chamber of Commerce stepped in for the 1963 Race. The Junior Chamber, which later shortened its name to Jaycees, was a national service organization for men aged 21 to 35. (The Mill Valley chapter surreptitiously admitted a few women by only using first initials.) The Race chairmanship rotated annually; Dick Sloan, a prime mover in the sponsorship switch, was the first. Jerry Hauke, who had been a director of the Mill Valley Parks & Recreation Commission (a Mill Valley park is named for him), also began his work on the Race in 1963. He remains the Race's hardest working organizer. An important financial contributor was Mill Valley's Fidelity Savings.

1978-, The Dipsea Committee

After the turbulent 1977 Dipsea season, when more than a few Marin groups would not have minded seeing the Race ended, the Jaycees basically ended their involvement. Membership had been falling anyhow; "There weren't enough people under 35 who could afford to live in Mill Valley,"

laughs Hauke. Hauke stayed on, assisted in 1978 by Jim Weil, a runner who had offered to help. In later years they were joined by Bob Knez, then Merv Regan, to form what came to be known as the Dipsea Committee. These four remained the directing quartet through 1991, when Susan Hoagland was added and Weil became a director emeritus.

To maintain event insurance, the Committee had continued sending chapter dues and an artificial, inflated membership roster (to meet the 20 member minimum) to Jaycee headquarters. The ruse was finally uncovered. (Although many people still associate the Race with the Jaycees.) In 1989-90, the Committee incorporated and obtained trademark protection for the Race name and logos.

Today, over 200 volunteers and more than a dozen captains, most multi-year repeaters, assist with the Race. Crystal Geyser, which provides thousands of bottles of water to the Race, is now the most important business donor.

DIPSEANA

DIPSEA INN

The Dipsea Inn, original destination of the Coney-Boas bet that spawned the Dipsea Race, opened in 1904. It was built, isolated on the sand, some 1.3 miles north of today's central Stinson Beach by William Neumann amidst William Kent property. The stretch of beach where the Inn sat came to be called "Dipsea," and the phrase "racing to Dipsea" (or "going to Dipsea") was used for years afterward.

The Inn struggled; the proposed extension of the Mt. Tamalpais rail line, which was to bring tourists to the Inn, was never built. The Inn was finally torn down in 1918 and some of its wood used in construction of the new Dipsea Lodge.

The site of the original Dipsea Inn is today's 198 Seadrift Road in the posh Seadrift enclave developed by the Kent family in 1950. The other of Seadrift's two streets is called Dipsea Road.

DIPSEA LODGE

The Dipsea Lodge was built in 1920 directly on the sand near the center of today's Stinson Beach. It was owned by Newman Fitzhenry (husband of Eve Stinson of the community's founding family) who hauled lumber from the old Dipsea Inn to help build it. The Lodge had a restaurant, dressing rooms, cottages and tents.

The Dipsea Lodge was torn down in 1939 after several lean years. In turn, some of its lumber then went into a beach seawall.

DIPSEA HIGHWAY

In the early 1920's, a private group led by Newman Fitzhenry, owner of the Dipsea Lodge, spearheaded efforts to improve the narrow, winding road between Manzanita Junction and Stinson Beach. The group, which came to call itself the Dipsea Highway Association, helped raise some $100,000 for the project. The completed 12-mile route was named the Dipsea Highway, as it went "from the Valley to the Sea" like its famous trail counterpart. It would be marked with signs in the shape of a Dipsea Indian.

The Highway was dedicated on November 15 and 16, 1924. Ceremonies were organized by the San Francisco Chamber of Commerce which, according to a report in the San Francisco Business newspaper, "considers this [new road] one of the most important projects now under way in the entire San Francisco Bay district."

The paper also reported that "all bad curves have been eliminated," a claim many of today's travelers will dispute. "A caravan of automobiles and stage buses" left Manzanita for Stinson, where a luncheon was held at the Dipsea Lodge.

While the Dipsea Highway name was shortlived—it is today more prosaically called Highway 1 or Shoreline Highway—a few Dipsea Indian road signs survive in private collections.

MISS DIPSEA

During the years of 1965 through 1970, the sponsoring Mill Valley Junior Chamber of Commerce selected a Dipsea Queen, or Miss Dipsea, to hand out awards and pose for publicity photographs. In 1968-1970, a "court" of other young women was chosen as well.

The 1965 queen was 25-year-old Deanna Zane. She recalls simply being approached by a Jaycee official while walking through downtown Mill Valley, then being interviewed before her "election." Through the Race, she would later meet her husband, San Rafael Jaycee Al Vickers. The couple still live in Mill Valley. In the early 1980's, her 14-year-old son Michael walked down to watch the start of the Race. He got so caught up he decided to run, though his broken arm was in a cast. He did not return to his worried parents until late in the afternoon.

Dipsea Inn

(Opposite page, top) Dipsea Inn, terminus of the Boas-Coney bet and of the first Dipsea, circa 1905.

(Bottom) 1986 promotional poster for the Dipsea-inspired motion picture, "On The Edge." Left to right; Chris Johnson, unknown, lead Bruce Dern, Bill Sevald, Garry Bjorklund. (Courtesy Fred Sandrock)

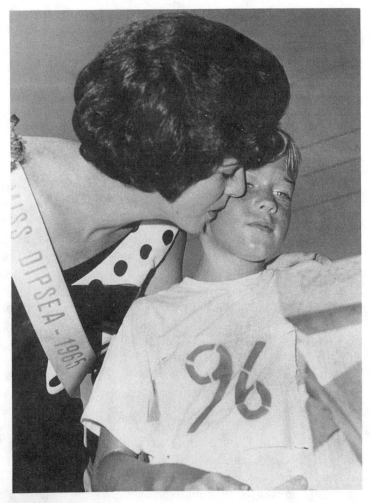

(Top) The 1965 Miss Dipsea, Deanna Zane, congratulates 11-year-old David Nelson, who finished 149th. (Independent Journal)

(Left) The Boitano family, winners of dozens of Dipsea trophies including three first places, 1973. From left; Mary Etta, Lucille, Michael and John. (Courtesy Mark Reese)

Subsequent queens included Dolores White of Marin City (1968), Anita Northwood (1969) and Arlinda Sebring (1970).

Miss Dipsea was discontinued in 1971, the first year women were recognized as official entrants by the AAU.

DIPSEA RACE HALL OF FAME

In 1993, a Dipsea Race Hall of Fame was begun. It will honor "those runners and officials whose performance in, or service to, the Race has been of the highest possible level over a period of years." Plans are under way to secure a permanent site for the Hall, which ultimately will include other Dipsea memorabilia and records. The five initial inductees were Norman Bright, Jack Kirk and Sal Vasquez and, posthumously, Judge Timothy Fitzpatrick and Emma Reiman.

DIPSEA MOVIES

In May, 1986, the feature film *On the Edge,* based on the Dipsea Race, was released in theaters nationwide. It was written, directed and co-produced by Rob Nilsson.

Nilsson, as Robert Nelson, had become fascinated with the Dipsea while at Tamalpais High School decades earlier, and had run it several times. He had also already won a directorial debut prize at Cannes for his film, *Northern Lights.*

Nilsson drew on Dipsea runners from the 1950's and 1960's—Wes Hildreth (model for the lead Wes Holman), Darryl Beardall (who became Beard), Don Pickett and others for his original script. He recruited Bruce Dern, an excellent runner who had competed in the Dipsea, to star. Roy Kissin, who won the Dipsea best time award in 1982, assisted with the story.

The movie tells of a once-top runner (Holman, played by Dern) who had been rather unfairly barred from racing by the AAU after accepting under-the-table payments. Years later, at 44, he decides to abandon his career and family to return to Marin and to train to win the Dipsea (called "Cielo To Sea" in the movie, and contested on a longer course over Mt. Tamalpais). He ultimately reconciles with his father (played by Bill Bailey) and his old coach (played by John Marley). He also has a torrid romance with an aerobics instructor (played by Pam Grier); her character would be completely omitted from the theater version and then later partially restored in the video release.

Holman is harassed before and during the race by his old nemesis, Owen Reilly (Jim Haynie), the man who turned him in to the AAU and now the Cielo To Sea director. An attempt is made to physically remove Holman during the race but several of the top runners (one played by leading marathoner Garry Bjorklund) come to his aid. Holman takes the lead near the end but then stops to wait for the next runners, to finish in a symbolic tie.

Many local runners participated as extras in scenes filmed on Mt. Tamalpais. This author, playing himself as the race announcer, spoke the last words in the movie.

The *New York Times* review, written by Nina Darnton, says, "Wes Holman ... is a thinking man's Rocky Balboa. He learns lessons that go well beyond the notions that an individual with grit is invincible and that heroism means winning alone. *On the Edge* is an upbeat, beautifully photographed film ... The film is paced like a race—gaining steadily in excitement and finally sprinting forward to a dramatic conclusion ... The director and the cinematographer (Stefan Czapsky) have composed exquisite shots of some of the most beautiful scenery in the United States ... As in 'Chariots of Fire,' the film conveys the excitement of running."

Several other professional films have been made of the Dipsea. Tim Amyx, a Mill Valley runner, assembled his footage from several mid-1980's Races and produced a stirring, 40-minute video, *The Dipsea Race.* Ray Gatchalian, a runner and Oakland fireman, was the prime mover behind the inspirational and award-winning film, *Survival Run,* about blind runner Harry Cordellos racing the Dipsea. Pax Beale, a veteran Dipsea runner, produced 16mm films (now on videotape) of the 1969 and 1970 races.

THE "ALTERNATE" DIPSEAS

DOUBLE DIPSEA

The Double Dipsea is a handicapped, out-and-back race over the Dipsea Trail staged by the Dolphin South End (DSE) Runners. It was organized in 1970 by Walt Stack after several earlier fun runs. Marsha Manit has been the race director since 1977. The National Trophy Company has always been a key sponsor. The Double is held on the Saturday two weeks (13 days) after the Dipsea. It generally draws 200 to 400 runners, with a high of 433 in 1988.

The Double starts in Stinson Beach, at the west edge of the same maintenance yard driveway used near the end of the Dipsea. It finishes there as well. (The start and finish were originally by the Parkside Cafe.) Some 10 years ago, permit problems with Mill Valley forced the halfway turnaround from the Depot to Old Mill Park, shortening the route by around .4 miles.

The Double also employs its own handicap format, which has remained unchanged since 1970. All women receive 30 minute headstarts. For the men, the handicaps are: 30 minutes—age over 57 and under 11; 25 minutes—50 to 57; 20 minutes—45 to 49; 15 minutes—40 to 44; 9 minutes—30 to 39 and 11 to 15; Scratch—16 to 29.

At the Double, as at the Dipsea in its early decades, no runner can win more than one trophy per year. There are special categories for heavyweight men (over 200 pounds) and women (over 140 pounds). Every finisher receives a patch.

Russ Kiernan, three times a runner-up in the Dipsea without winning, has won the Double Dipsea eight times. Homer Latimer, Darryl Beardall and Don Chaffee are the only runners to have won both the Dipsea and the Double; none did it in the same year. Hilary Naylor is the lone woman to win the Double. Jose Cortez is the only runner to have won from scratch.

The course records (actual running time) are 1:38:26 for men, shared by Butch Alexander and Larry McKendall, and 1:58:42 for women, by Christie Patterson. In 1980, Ivor Welch completed the Double (in 4:49:54) at age 85.

The race is now officially called the Walt Stack Double Dipsea in honor of the DSE's legendary founder.

Overall Winners with (Age), Actual Time

Year	Winner
1970	David Cortez (12), 2:09:45
1971	Jose Cortez (19), 1:47:57
1972	Ralph Paffenbarger (49), 1:54:51
1973	Tommy Owen (10), 2:05:08
1974	Homer Latimer (35), 1:43:37
1975	Bob Biancalana (50), 1:59:59
1976	Jim Nicholson (45), 1:53:40
1977	Darryl Beardall (40), 1:49:45
1978	Bob Malain (51), 1:57:50
1979	Russ Kiernan (41), 1:51:02
1980	Don Chaffee (41), 1:49:04
1981	Tim Johnston (40), 1:52:44
1982	Michael Duncan (32), 1:45:46
1983	Russ Kiernan (45), 1:51:00
1984	Russ Kiernan (46), 1:48:32
1985	Roger Daniels (49), 1:48:57
1986	Hilary Naylor (39), 2:04:50
1987	Russ Kiernan (49), 1:48:02
1988	Russ Kiernan (50), 1:51:58
1989	Darryl Beardall (52), 1:58:21
1990	John Cobourn (43), 1:50:46
1991	Russ Kiernan (53), 1:54:35
1992	Russ Kiernan (54), 1:57:22
1993	Russ Kiernan (55), 1:56:43

Russ Kiernan in Steep Ravine, 1987. He has won 8 Double Dipseas. (Frankie Frost, Independent Journal)

Fastest Actual Times, Male and Female, with (Age)

1970 Jose Cortez (18), 1:45:43; Mary Cortez (16), 2:23:07

1971 Jose Cortez (19), 1:47:57; Elaine Pedersen (34), 2:43:44

1972 Greg Chapman (24), 1:46:41; Chris Sakelarios (12), 2:30:56

1973 Bob Bunnell (23), 1:43:16; Mary Etta Boitano (10), 2:17:17

1974 Homer Latimer (35), 1:43:47; Debbie Rudolf (13), 2:13:52

1975 Byron Lowry (28), 1:42:37; Betsy White (37), 2:15:26

1976 Paul Thompson (29), 1:42:49; Mary Etta Boitano (13), 2:23:50

1977 Don Chaffee (38), 1:47:52; Louise Burns (37), 2:19:20

1978 Kim Schaurer (28), 1:47:58; Barbara Magid (35), 2:13:40

1979 Pete Demarais (21), 1:44:32; Marilyn Moreton (32), 2:20:26

1980 Miguel Tibaduiza (22), 1:42:08; Donna Andrews (39), 2:12:02

1981 Michael Duncan (31), 1:50:37; Florianne Harp (34), 2:07:51

1982 Michael Duncan (32), 1:45:46; Florianne Harp (35), 2:07:17

1983 Edward Geer (27), 1:52:35; Cynthia Chilton (29), 2:15:06

1984 Butch Alexander (31), 1:38:26; Peggy Smyth (32), 2:01:34

1985 Butch Alexander (32), 1:41:54; Christie Patterson (37), 2:03:57

1986 Mike Wheeler (37), 1:52:17; Hilary Naylor (39), 2:04:50

1987 Larry McKendall (26), 1:38:26; Christie Patterson (39), 1:58:42

1988 John Hodge (26), 1:43:00; Janet Mumford (30), 2:13:25

1989 Greg Nacco (29), 1:47:11; Kim Rupert (34), 2:08:54

1990 Mark Richtman (35), 1:45:59; Trish Arbogast-Kluge (30), 2:06:43

1991 Greg Nacco (31), 1:45:14; Jamie Wendel (40), 2:07:32

1992 Guy Palmer (33), 1:46:42; Christie Patterson Pastalka (44), 2:13:07

1993 Mike McManus (27), 1:39:48; Elizabeth Vitalis (28), 2:03:56

QUADRUPLE DIPSEA

The Quadruple Dipsea—four crossings of the Dipsea Trail—was organized as a race in 1985 after a group of friends had run it informally the two years before. Jack Cover was the first race director; John Medinger has been in charge ever since. The Bay Area Ultrarunners are organizers.

The Quadruple, which has some 9,000 feet of both uphills and downhills over its 28 miles, begins and ends in Old Mill Park, Mill Valley. The Stinson Beach turnaround is by the Parkside Cafe. As at the Double, runners must stay on the Dipsea Trail, with few shortcuts permitted. The race is not handicapped.

The Quadruple is held on the Saturday after Thanksgiving. There have been several years when the seasonal bridge over Redwood Creek in Muir Woods had already been removed, creating a wet crossing for the runners. The date is also exposed to storms; a particularly strong one wreaked havoc in 1989. Still, the Quadruple has been growing in popularity, hitting highs of 149 starters and 122 finishers in 1991.

The men's record of 3:52:29 was set by Carl Andersen in 1992 on a course actually longer than those of earlier years; Swoop Hollow was off-limits. The women's record of 4:32:16 by Kathy D'Onofrio has stood since 1987.

Mill Valley runners Mike McKenzie and Hans Roenau might have been the first to ever complete a "quadruple," performing the feat on July 30, 1978. After Roenau, famished, stopped to pick some blackberries, McKenzie came in a few minutes ahead.

Winners, Male and Female, with (Age) and Time

1985 Bob Bunnell (35), 4:05:25; Melinda Creel (28), 5:06:23

1986 David Roth (33), 4:13:26; Judy Milgram (44), 5:27:01

1987 Dan Williams (38), 4:00:02; Kathy D'Onofrio (23), 4:32:16

1988 Doug Schrock (37), 4:12:31; Darlene Wallach (37), 5:02:46

1989 Tim Ball (31), 4:07:39; Melinda Creel (32), 5:02:00

1990 Bill Brown (35), 4:10:04; Kate Bricker-Kent (28), 4:49:16

1991 Dan Williams (42), 4:18:42; Karyn Kroljic (32), 5:29:35

1992 Carl Andersen (32), 3:52:29; tie, Melinda Creel (35) and Karyn Kroljic (33), 5:10:47

PRACTICE DIPSEA

Like the Double, the Practice Dipsea is staged by the Dolphin South End (DSE) Runners. It was first contested on August 10, 1969; Frank Evans led 25 finishers with Elaine Pedersen, the only woman, 5th overall.

Until 1977, two Practices were held the Sundays prior to the Dipsea. Now the DSE stages one "official" Practice the Sunday before the Dipsea with occasionally another run over the course in the fall.

The Practice starts at Old Mill Park in Mill Valley and finishes by the Parkside Cafe in Stinson Beach. The number of finishers has varied from 25 (1969) to 331 (1983). The race records are 48:39 by Mike McManus in 1986 and 58:47 by Debbie Rudolf in 1975. (Some results, which may bear on the records, are missing.)

The non-handicapped Practice is the least formal of the three "alternate" Dipseas. The entry fee has long been just $1 (now $2), there are no shirts, the only awards are five men's and women's place ribbons and the course is not marked. There are also no provisions for return rides; many runners hitch a ride back to Mill Valley.

Mary Etta Boitano (1973), Homer Latimer (1977) and Florianne Harp (1981) presaged Dipsea victories with wins at the Practice.

Winners, Male and Female, with Time

1969   Frank Evans, 1:09:15; Elaine Pedersen, 1:13:30
         John Sheehan, 1:06:00; Mary Etta Boitano, 1:26:39
1970   Gerry Haslam, 59:35; no women
1971   Jim Howell, 54:57; Grace Ruth, 1:38:03
         Jim O'Neil, 56:46; Vicki Paulsen, 1:11:57
1972   Butch Alexander, 54:01; Chris Zumwalt, 1:27:36
         Dave Dunbar, 53:45; Judy Karan, 1:14:07
1973   Male winner unknown; Mary Etta Boitano, 1:01:14
         Bill Long, 50:44; Lucy Bunz, 1:11:40
1974   no results printed
1975   Bob Bunnell, 50:37; Debbie Rudolf, 58:47
         Dave Muela, 52:07; Mary Etta Boitano, 1:01:34
1976   Mike Timmerman, 52:29; Mary Etta Boitano, 1:11:18
         Carlson, 54:22; Mary Etta Boitano, 1:03:36

1977   Homer Latimer, 49:38; Louise Burns, 1:10:16
1978   Mike Timmerman, 53:04; Colleen Fox, 1:09:48
1979   Jim Myers, 55:28; Sue Gladney, 1:02:09
1980   Raoul Kennedy, 53:40; Valerie Doyle, 1:08:46
1981   Butch Alexander, 51:58; Florianne Harp, 1:00:55
1982   Roy Kissin, 49:32; Peggy Smyth, 1:00:01
1983   Butch Alexander, 49:50; Florianne Harp, 1:06:55
1984   no results printed
1985   Wyborn Mercer, 53:24; Barbara Levy, 1:06:26
1986   Mike McManus, 48:39; Anne Capers, 1:04:50
1987   Bud Napolio, 50:07; Amy McConnell, 1:00:03
1988   Fred Haber, 52:50; Amy McConnell, 59:45
1989   Robert Meckfessel, 55:27; Deirdre Reidy, 1:07:41
1990   Steve Stephens, 54:21; Patricia Story, 59:52
1991   Vince Fausone, 52:00; Libby Hill, 1:04:10
1992   Eric Ellisen, 54:16; Peggy Lavelle, 1:03:12
1993   Eric Ellisen, 52:32; Jamie Wendel, 1:01:52

Award-winning photograph of Leslie Acoca falling after the Stile, 1991. She required oral surgery, but raced again in 1993. (Marian Little Utley, Independent Journal)

INDEX

Below is an index of names that appear at least once in the 83 Dipsea Race accounts. To keep this list of manageable size, only the FIRST year the name appears is cited. In a few cases, this year may be earlier than the runner's main period of achievement. Also note that names found in other sections of the book may not necessarily appear below.

Cohn, Gene (1979)
Cole, George (1947)
Collins, Brian (1981)
Colman, Joan (1987)
Coney, Alfons (1905)
Conlan, George (1972)
Conley, Francis (1971)
Conley, Phil (1971)
Connelly, Cornelius (1905)
Conning, Keith (1961)
Connolly, S.V. (1907)
Cordellos, Harry (1971)
Cornell, Bob (1905)
Cords, David (1968)
Cortez, Dave (1970)
Cortez, Jose (1971)
Cortez, Mary (1970)
Coughlin, Bob (1946)
Craig, C.H. (1913)
Craig, Elliot (1908)
Cramer, Stewart (1948)
Creel, Melinda (1980)
Crncich, M. (1980)
Crockett, William (1918)
Cunningham, John (1926)
Cunningham, Glenn (1937)
Curtis, Charles (1955)
Cushing, D.A. (1905)

D'Acquisto, Sal (1982)
Dahl, Orin (1977)
Dailey, Mike (1967)
Daniels, Roger (1979)
Dann, Jonathan (1989)
Darnell, Phil (1965)
Davis, Richard (1928)
Davis, Robin (1988)
Davis, Ronald (1963)
Dawson, Floy (1983)
Day, Isaac (1909)
Deasy, Mike (1956)
DeCelle, Bob (1969)
Decker, Neal (1930)
Degen, Bruce (1975)
Deike, Walter (1917)
Delgado, Rich (1966)
DeLisle, Ernest (1928)
DeLormier, Alfred 91950)

DeMar, Clarence (1931)
DeMarais, Peter (1977)
DeMartini, T. (1926)
Dent, Darold (1968)
Denton, Richard (1917)
Derderian, George (1970)
Dern, Bruce (1974)
Derrigan, Robert (1949)
Devlin, Bill (1970)
Dewey, Ray (1940)
Dickerson, Bill (1977)
Dickinson, Robert (1990)
Dirkes, Jerome (1968)
Dixon, George (1934)
Dixon, Warren (1930)
Don, Joan (1980)
Donovan, Judie (1979)
Donovan, Trex (1979)
Dooley, Tom (1964)
Dowdell, Mel (1954)
Dreyer, Nancy (1941)
Dreyer, Willie (1941)
Duncan, Phillip (1984)
Dundas, N.E. (1915)
Dunham, Dave (1993)
Dunn, Donald (1912)
Duran, Silvia (1960)
Duran, Victor (1953)
Dux, Ed (1985)
Dye, Lois (1951)
Dye, Mike (1952)
Dyer, Richard (1965)

Eames, Frank (1924)
Eberly, Myrrha (1969)
Eberly, Vance (1968)
Eberly, Valerie (1969)
Eberly, Vicki (1969)
Ebner, Ralph (1918)
Edmonds, Granville (1920)
Edwards, B.W. (1972)
Edwards, Sally (1981)
Ehrenberg, Doug (1984)
Ehret, Steve (1927)
Eichstaedt, Robert (1983)
Eisenberg, Peter (1979)
Eisman, Roland (1927)
Elijah, Derry (1974)

Elijah, Ron (1967)
Ellison, William (1937)
Emenegildo, N. (1919)
Emmons, R.W. (1976)
English, Patricia (1984)
Epanchin, Nick (1983)
Erskine, Douglas (1905)
Ertman, Steve (1966)
Eschen, Andrea (1981)
Estep, Joe (1930)
Estep, Richard (1930)
Estrella, S. (1906)
Evans, G. (1905)

Falcone, Mark (1964)
Fairbanks, Warren (1949)
Farren, James (1974)
Farren, James Jr. (1974)
Felzer, Ronald (1983)
Ferlatte, William (1957)
Ferrari, Louis (1946)
Finch, John (1975)
Finigan, Vincent (1946)
Fiora, Natale (1919)
Fishback, Jeff (1961)
Fisk, C. (1907)
Fitzgerald, Gene (1973)
Fitzgerald, Kary (1952)
Fitzpatrick, Timothy (1923)
Flodberg, William (1974)
Flowers, Cheryl (1981)
Foley, Hugh (1914)
Fontana, Bev (1960)
Foran, Frank (1946)
Foreman, Jud (1952)
Forsyth, James (1963)
Fozzi, Ettore (1930)
Fraser, William (1927)
Fratini, Ed (1927)
Frazier, George (1982)
Fredericks, J. (1916)
Frederickson, R. (1906)
Frediani, Angelo (1929)
Freshwaters, Brett (1984)
Frost, C.C. (1920)
Fugua, Clarence (1913)
Fuller, Earl (1922)
Fuller, Raymond (1956)

Furlong, Robert (1906)

Gallego, Gary (1969)
Gamache, Joey (1966)
Gamache, Peter (1966)
Garbarino, G. (1971)
Gatchalian, Ray (1971)
Geis, Frank (1950)
Gelding, R.B. (1915)
Gentili, Libero (1951)
Gerhardt, Peter (1918)
Giacomini, Gary (1977)
Gibbons, Jim (1985)
Gilbert, Percy (1918)
Gillisan, Eugene (1966)
Gilmartin, Jim (1958)
Giordanengo, Pietro (1922)
Gipson, Victor (1950)
Glad, W. (1975)
Glarner, Andrew (1905)
Glennon, Ray (1914)
Godwin, Floyd (1965)
Goldsmith, James (1985)
Gordon, Kristin (1979)
Gordon, Peter (1979)
Gordon, Rolf (1958)
Gorman, John (1969)
Gorman, Owen (1971)
Gorse, Albert (1909)
Goso, Vincenzo (1924)
Grace, Ken (1984)
Grant, Hal (1952)
Gray, Bill (1970)
Gray, Morton (1985)
Greene, Harriet (1967)
Griepenburg, Karl (1964)
Grundisch, Frank (1948)
Gunther, Harrison (1982)
Gustafson, A. (1910)
Gustafson, Arner (1947)
Gustafson, Dennis (1977)

Haaviland, W. (1916)
Haddad, Eddie (1968)
Hagans, AnnaMarie (1991)
Hale, Tom (1972)
Hall, Clarence (1936)
Hall, Nan (1987)

Handley, Albert (1939)
Hannaford, Debbie (1984)
Hansen, John (1935)
Hansen, Paul (1954)
Haran, Gene (1941)
Hardham, Ann (1986)
Harling, Kate (1985)
Harp, Florianne (1980)
Harrison, William (1905)
Hartley, Ed (1907)
Hartman, M. (1907)
Hartwell, Ben (1908)
Hartwell, Florence (1908)
Hartwell, George (1908)
Hartwell, Mason (1908)
Hartwell, Thomas (1910)
Hartwell, William (1910)
Hassard, John (1905)
Hastings, Keith (1980)
Hauke, Jerry (1963)
Hayden, Marlys (1980)
Hazeleur, Clarence (1924)
Healy, Mary (1979)
Healy, Mike (1973)
Heierle, Rob (1978)
Heino, Emil (1923)
Helganz, Charles (1926)
Helms, Clyde (1981)
Henderson, Will (1909)
Henry, James (9136)
Higdon, Hal (1954)
Higgen, R.W. (1951)
Higgins, William (1913)
Hillard, Bob (1950)
Hildreth, Wes (1955)
Hines, Fred (1965)
Hodge, John (1987)
Hogan, Thea (1965)
Hoffman, William (1967)
Holden, John (1947)
Holmes, Kimberly (1991)
Hood, F. (1916)
Hooper, Bert (1920)
Hooper, Dana (1979)
Hooper, H.S. (1922)
Hope, Barney (1963)
Hope, Bob (1958)
Hope, Sigurd (1963)

Houston, Dick (1977)
Howden, Robert (1907)
Howden, Watson (1911)
Howden, William (1908)
Hoy, Michael (1988)
Hoyt, Lawrence (1968)
Hughes, Ray (1965)
Hugo, Heidi (1992)
Hunter, Charles (1913)
Hyun, Tony (1981)

Imperiale, Jim (1954)
Incardona, Paul (1955)
Iredale, Thomas (1987)
Isabeau, Alec (1991)
Isle, Ray (1940)

Jacobs, James (1960)
Jacobson, Edgar (1917)
Jeffries, Patti (1985)
Jenkins, Hersh (1975)
Jensen, Carl (1917)
Jerome, Ed (1977)
Johnson, Bert (1979)
Johnson, Bob (1958)
Johnson, Bruce (1968)
Johnson, John (1909)
Johnston, William (1911)
Jones, Harry (1983)
Jones, Martin (1982)
Jones, Oliver (1914)
Jones, Walter (1916)
Jordan, Tim (1959)
Joyner, Gerald (1957)
Joyner, William (1907)
Juette, Paul (1949)
Juhl, Eric (1936)
Jung, Al (1910)

Kahn, Lloyd (1989)
Kappelmann, F. (1916)
Kardong, Don (1991)
Karlhofer, Leo (1934)
Kean, Jim (1958)
Keegan, Jack (1930)
Keller, Randolph (1962)
Kelley, Johnny (1930)
Kelly, Don (1958)

Kelly, Pat (1968)
Kelly, Tim (1958)
Kemmerle, Martin (1917)
Kendall, Jim (1949)
Kennedy, George (1964)
Kennedy, Raoul (1978)
Kent, William (1908)
Kienzle, Fred (1921)
Kiernan, Russ (1970)
Killeen, Mike (1971)
Killeen, Tim (1972)
Kimball, Rich (1973)
King, J.B. (1908)
King, Joe (1947)
King, Price (1951)
King, Wilford (1955)
Kingery, Mitch (1971)
Kirchmeier, Bill (1978)
Kirschner, Tom (1981)
Kirk, Jack (1905)
Kispert, Frank (1907)
Kissin, Roy (1982)
Kline, Fred (1947)
Knepfer, Arnold (1988)
Knepfer, Toby (1980)
Knox, Merle (1947)
Knutson, Jack (1966)
Kragel, Joe (1913)
Kreling, Tiv (1946)
Kreuzberger, Al (1977)
Kubley, Patrick (1987)
Kuha, Harold (1954)
Kuts, Vladimir (1960)
Kwartz, John (1941)
Kyne, William (1952)

Labrie, Howard (1970)
Lacy, John (1960)
LaForge, W.A. (1972)
Laine, Richard (1989)
Landy, John (1958)
Lara, Frank (1938)
Larrieu-Smith, Francie (1993)
Larsen, Dane (1941)
Larson, Louis (1930)
Laskier, Peter (1980)
Latimer, Homer (1924)
Laughran, Thomas (1934)

Lavin, Jeanne (1985)
Lawrence, Bob (1976)
Lawson, Hank (1993)
Lawson, Jack (1966)
Lawson, Kelly (1992)
Leal, Art (1958)
Lee, Clyde (1968)
Lee, E.P. (1978)
Lee, Welton (1951)
Leffingwell, Eric (1958)
Leon, Fernando (1917)
Leonard, George (1964)
Leonard, Irving (1929)
Leonard, Mark (1964)
Leonard, Wilma (1970)
Letcher, William (1923)
Levy, Barbara (1981)
Leydig, Jack (1965)
Lincicome, Noel (1985)
Lindner, Jules (1924)
Lindquist, Link (1989)
Linn, Vernon (1934)
Linscott, Bruce (1993)
Little, John (1906)
Livingston, Margaret (1979)
Lloyd, E.C. (1912)
Lobig, John (1921)
Locke, Carroll (1924)
Locke, Ray (1914)
Lockhart, Earl (1935)
Logan, Loyed (1908)
Lopez, Michael (1986)
Lopez, Philip (1917)
Louden, Bob (1958)
Love, B.A. (1976)
Love, Ralph (1954)
Low, A.M. (1976)
Lower, David (1962)
Lucas, Charles (1957)
Lucero, Don (1977)
Lucia, Peter (1930)
Lucia, Salvatore (1962)
Ludekins, Charles (1920)
Ludlow, Duane (1953)
Ludlow, Lynn (1948)
Ludlum, Al (1937)
Ludwig, Harry (1913)
Ludwig, Vergie (1939)

Luskin, Wink (1984)
Lydon, Ted (1967)
Lyons, Steve (1977)
Lyons, Torrey (1934)

Maata, Milton (1926)
MacCono, Andrew (1938)
Mace, Bruce (1992)
Mackey, William (1966)
Mackoto, Otto (1926)
Maddox, Jim (1952)
Maggiora, Attilio (1929)
Maghetti, William (1908)
Magid, Barbara (1977)
Magner, Georgette (1930)
Magner, William (1921)
Mahlert, Calvin (1949)
Mailliard, William (1973)
Makela, Don (1967)
Malain, Bob (1971)
Maloney, Peter (1934)
Mancuso, Joseph (1921)
Mankin, Paul (1988)
Marden, Jack (1954)
Marden, Jay (1954)
Marinoni, Ernie (1939)
Marinoni, Robert (1948)
Maris, Roger (1970)
Marisch, Frank (1918)
Marschall, Karl (1976)
Martinez, Daniel (1970)
Martinez, R. (1971)
Mason, Lane (1977)
Matson, Shirley (1992)
Mattei, Peter (1969)
Mauerhan, A. (1908)
Maundrell, George (1906)
Mauras, John (1917)
Maxwell, Brian (1985)
May, Phil (1967)
Mazzini, William (1930)
McArdle, Peter (1917)
McCandless, Rich (1972)
McCarron, S.J. (1977)
McCarthy, Don (1991)
McClymonds, Jimmy (1935)
McConnell, Amy (1987)
McCourtney, M. (1905)

McCurdy, William (1906)
McGee, James (1910)
McGeehan, William (1908)
McGowan, Jim (1977)
McGowan, Megan (1990)
McGowan, Michael (1990)
McGrath, George (1975)
McGregor, Leslie (1948)
McIntyre, Loren (1939)
McKendall, Larry (1988)
McLaughlin, Peter (1989)
McMahon, Clarissa (1954)
McManus, Mike (1917)
McManus, Thomas (1975)
McMillan, Angus (1908)
McMillan, Lane (1918)
McMullin, Leslie (1985)
McNabb, John (1938)
McNamara, Tom (1922)
McNutt, Jim (1962)
McQueen, Richard (1964)
McShane, J.J. (1908)
McWilliams, Fred (1922)
Menzies, Robert (1950)
Mericone, Amerigo (1931)
Merrick, Owen (1937)
Metzger, Matt (1987)
Mielenz, Harvey (1929)
Miles, C.W. (1922)
Miles, Otis (1966)
Millard, Oliver (1910)
Miller, George (1947)
Miller, Jim (1978)
Miller, Nick (1948)
Miller, Ruth (1967)
Mills, Al (1917)
Millward, M.A. (1973)
Minor, Tim (1990)
Mitchell, Susan (1979)
Mitrovich, Mick (1983)
Moir, William (1906)
Molinari, Charles (1912)
Montenrose, J. (1940)
Moore, M. (1906)
Morefield, Wayne (1928)
Moreton, Marilyn (1980)
Morgan, Bill (1956)
Morgan, Dennis (1989)

Morris, Ray (1977)
Morrison, J. (1916)
Morton, H.L. (1911)
Motioni, Ariadono (1931)
Moyles, Jim (1985)
Mulas, Michele (1920)
Munro, Randolph (1911)
Murillo, Carlos (1928)
Murphy, Fred (1918)
Myers, Jim (1965)
Myrra, Andy (1926)
Myrra, Jonni (1926)

Nacco, Greg (1989)
Nagel, M.J. (1973)
Nance, Thatcher (1950)
Napier, Ken (1972)
Nathan, Jacob (1924)
Naylor, Hilary (1981)
Nehar, James (1913)
Nelson, Allan (1939)
Nelson, Anton (1951)
Nelson, William (1946)
Newhart, T. (1975)
Newkirk, Carl (1922)
Newman, Lloyd (1926)
Nicholson, Jimmy (1971)
Nieman, Paul (1920)
Nilsson, Rob (1966)
Noonan, John (1967)

O'Brien, T.J. (1974)
O'Callaghan, William (1916)
O'Connor, William (1935)
Ochoa, Jesse (1959)
O'Donnell, Frances (1931)
O'Donnell, Lowrie (1949)
O'Gara, George (1981)
Olson, Dave (1980)
O'Neil, E.A. (1978)
O'Neil, Jim (1969)
O'Neill, Hugh (1918)
Ortega, Joe (1934)
Otanez, Lou (1981)
Ottaway, Steve (1978)
Owen, Tommy (1973)

Paffenbarger, Ralph (1969)

Paine, Robin (1991)
Palmer, Guy (1993)
Pampa, Angelo (1926)
Pappas, Joe (1928)
Pappas, William (1930)
Pardini, Aldo (1950)
Parliman, Elaine (1980)
Pastalka, Tomas (1987)
Patrick, Greg (1968)
Patterson, Christie (1982)
Patterson, Joe (1975)
Patterson, Kim (1987)
Patterson, Michael (1963)
Patterson, Pat (1988)
Pecot, Earlene (1951)
Pedersen, Elaine (1966)
Pedroli, Richard (1977)
Pell, Eve (1937)
Pelleretti, Armando (1941)
Pengra, Jay (1962)
Perfoss, Al (1918)
Perkins, L.H. (1915)
Perry, Ralph (1953)
Peters, Bill (1939)
Phelan, James (1919)
Phinney, Bruce (1990)
Pickett, Don (1965)
Pickett, Toby (1968)
Pickett, Tom (1968)
Pietri, Dorando (1940)
Pinkson, Leon (1946)
Pinther, Alfred (1916)
Pitts, Rachel (1993)
Pohli, Emil (1939)
Portost, A.M. (1915)
Potts, Caron (1987)
Powers, April (1993)
Purcell, Brian (1974)
Purcell, Pam (1978)

Quadri, Heidi (1985)
Quinlan, Dan (1921)

Raber, J.E. (1906)
Rahmer, Ron (1983)
Ranney, William (1949)
Ransom, Guy (1905)
Reading, J. (1912)

Record, Terry (1965)
Reed, Al (1956)
Reed, John (1956)
Reese, Mark (1905)
Reese, Paul (1965)
Refford, F. (1910)
Rehberg, William (1909)
Reider, Pete (1956)
Reiss, Joan (1985)
Rentschler, Larry (1966)
Repp, Mike (1993)
Restani, Mike (1985)
Reutinger, Joan (1977)
Reynolds, Alan (1992)
Rhoden, George (1968)
Rich, Bruce (1936)
Richards, Edwin (1922)
Richards, J.S. (1911)
Richesin, Carlo (1948)
Richesin, Charles (1946)
Richesin, Jimmy (1948)
Richtman, Mark (1986)
Rieger, Adrienne (1959)
Rieger, Franz (1959)
Riggle, Everett (1983)
Riley, Stanislaus (1946)
Roach, Maurice (1916)
Robben, Barbara (1970)
Robbins, Fred (1913)
Robinson, Elmer (1954)
Robinson, William (1934)
Rodarte, Bill (1950)
Rodd, Flory (1969)
Roeber, Dave (1981)
Roenau, Hans (1977)
Rossi, Angelo (1934)
Roulac, Steve (1959)
Rovtley, K. (1975)
Rowbothan, Brian (1966)
Rudolf, Debbie (1972)
Rupert, Kim (1993)
Russell, Andrew (1966)
Russell, Floyd (1946)
Russell, Wayne (1909)
Rutherford, Robert (1919)
Ryan, Joe (1979)
Ryan, Kurt (1992)
Ryan, Mike (1958)

Salmi, John (1909)
Samuels, Mary (1951)
Sampson, Lloyd (1977)
Saredio, Bruno (1918)
Sargent, Ned (1959)
Sargent, Jon (1991)
Sarlin, Walter (1931)
Satti, John (1957)
Savedra, Albert (1937)
Schafer, W. (1980)
Schulz, Hal (1984)
Seamount, Dan (1975)
Sharp, D.D. (1976)
Shenfield, Claudia (1979)
Shortall, Edward (1954)
Schou, N.G. (1908)
Schupbach, R. (1974)
Schwartz, Barbara (1974)
Schwartz, William (1925)
Schwarz, E. (1915)
Scobey, Bill (1970)
Scott, Arnold (1935)
Scott, Gail (1986)
Scribante, Ottorino (1919)
Seaman, Robert (1940)
Seekins, C.W. (1975)
Semple, Jock (1971)
Sequeria, Jose (1919)
Shannon, M.R. (1977)
Shearn, John (1922)
Shettler, Jim (1912)
Shiflet, K.J. (1977)
Shockey, Ken (1967)
Shorter, Frank (1953)
Sias, Ed (1967)
Siemens, Ed (1946)
Silva, A.R. (1969)
Silva, Frank (1905)
Simons, Sue (1984)
Simpson, M. (1952)
Sloan, Dick (1963)
Smith, Frank (1982)
Smith, Harry (1946)
Smith, Phil (1953)
Smith, Wendel (1967)
Smyth, Peggy (1984)
Snyder, Jack (1961)

Sofos, Steve (1967)
Spangler, Paul (1970)
Spanton, Will (1913)
Sparks, Gregg (1964)
Sparks, Jeanne (1964)
Sparling, Stuart (1960)
Spurr, Basil (1909)
Stack, Walter (1962)
Stagliano, Chick (1973)
Stanford, Leland (1923)
Steed, William (1946)
Stephens, John (1966)
Stephens, Steve (1961)
Stephens, Will (1966)
Stephenson, Jim (1993)
Stockman, Herb (1954)
Storm, Bonnie (1980)
Stout, Edgar (1918)
Strait, Scott (1991)
Stratta, Dominic (1924)
Stratta, Laura (1947)
Stratta, Tony (1924)
Strauss, Wally (1984)
Stroughter, Henry (1955)
Suda, M.D. (1969)
Sullivan, Burrell (1951)
Sutcliffe, Frank (1922)
Swannack, Skip (1974)
Sweeney, Peter (1976)
Switzer, Kathy (1971)
Swyers, John (1986)

Tabori, Laszlo (1958)
Takushi, Takeo (1946)
Tamlander, E. (1927)
Tarin, Gil (1973)
Taylor, Wilbur (1939)
Teeguarden, Dennis (1971)
Terriberry, Tom (1964)
Tessman, Brock (1992)
Thall, Ed (1937)
Thanash, Art (1949)
Thaning, Ragnar (1977)
Thomas, Chris (1985)
Thomas, William (1939)
Thompson, Lester (1905)
Thompson, Paul (1976)
Thornton, Len (1953)

Thurlby, Donna (1964)
Tibaduiza, Domingo (1973)
Tiensu, Albert (1924)
Tiensu, Uno (1925)
Todd, Medford (1953)
Tomasini, Amadeo (1919)
Torrengo, D. (1939)
Trujillo, Delfin (1965)
Tuite, Tom (1962)
Tuinzing, Andre (1991)
Tuinzing, Els (1991)
Tuinzing, Kees (1973)
Turnblad, Oscar (1946)
Tymn, Mike (1958)

Ullyot, Joan (1972)

Valentine, Joseph (1905)
Vali, Erin (1987)
Valin, Frank (1936)
Van Dellen, Wayne (1965)
Van Tassell, Floyd (1909)
Van Zant, Jesse (1947)
Van Zant, John (1941)
Van Zant, Walter (1955)
Vanek, Herb (1979)
Vasquez, Mileny (1982)
Vasquez, Nicole (1982)
Vasquez, R. (1974)
Vasquez, Sal (1916)
Veloz, Frank (1953)
Vierra, Dick (1953)
Vis, Clifford (1919)
Vlught, Robert (1912)
Vollmer, Ted (1939)
Volmer, Andrew (1969)
Vreeland, J. (1975)

Waggenet, Julian (1906)
Waggoner, Art (1976)
Waldear, Debbie (1985)
Waldo, Gordon (1956)
Walfisch, Otto (1946)
Walker, Caroline (1983)
Wallace, Robert (1946)
Wallach, Len (1971)
Wallbridge, Charles (1909)
Walters, Charles (1909)

(Above) Left to right; Darryl Beardall, Don Pickett, Bob Biancalana and Bob Bunnell after the 1975 Dipsea. Biancalana and Bunnell are wearing the first t-shirts ever awarded. Behind is James Farren, Jr. (Courtesy Bob Bunnell)

(Right) The "seasonal" bridge over Redwood Creek. (Brad Rippe)

Kennard Wilson

Barry Spitz (44) is the official Dipsea Race historian and announcer. In 1992 he received the James Farren, Jr. Memorial Trophy for "Sportsmanship, Leadership and Dedication to the Dipsea."

Barry is presently "At the Races" editor for *Running Times* magazine and writes running columns for the *Marin Independent Journal* and *City Sports* magazine. He has been an editor at *Runner's World*. He is the author of *Best Running Trails of the San Francisco Bay Area* and the hiking guide, *Tamalpais Trails*.

Barry resides in San Anselmo, six miles from the Dipsea Trail, with his wife Pamela and daughters Sally (3) and Lily (1).

ORDERING ADDITIONAL BOOKS

To order additional copies of *Dipsea, The Greatest Race*, send a check for $27.95 (hardcover)/$18.95 (paper), plus applicable sales tax and $2 per order shipping, made payable to: Potrero Meadow Publishing Co., P.O. Box 3007, San Anselmo, CA 94979.

The author will be happy to honor requests to autograph or otherwise personally inscribe the book.

THE DIPSEA FOUNDATION

The author encourages those who love the Dipsea to support the Dipsea Foundation. It was established in 1993 as a charitable organization for funding improvements and maintaining the historic Dipsea Trail, other hiking and running trails on and around Mt. Tamalpais, and for sponsoring amateur athletics. Those interested in receiving more information about the Dipsea Foundation, or wishing to make a donation, should write to: The Dipsea Foundation, P.O. Box 30, Mill Valley, CA 94942.

DIPSEA RACE APPLICATION PROCEDURE

To apply for entry into the Dipsea Race, send a request for an application and a self-addressed, stamped envelope to Dipsea Race, Box 30, Mill Valley, CA 94942, before mid-March. (Applications are automatically sent to finishers from the previous year.) All applications are mailed April 1.

Complete and return the form immediately. Race openings are filled by the order completed applications are received. Some additional places are reserved for the highest bidders in the Dipsea "Auction." Also, all applicants have a final chance for entry through the Dipsea "Lottery." See the application form for details.

New entrants, with few exceptions, are initially placed in the Dipsea Runner section; they can "run" their way into the Invitational section in subsequent years.

The Race is held on the second Sunday in June.

Good luck!